John Sherman

GREAT DEBATES IN AMERICAN HISTORY

From the Debates in the British Parliament on the Colonial Stamp Act (1764–1765) to the Debates in Congress at the Close of the Taft Administration (1912–1913)

EDITED BY

MARION MILLS MILLER, LITT.D. (PRINCETON)

Editor of "The Life and Works of Abraham Lincoln," etc.

IN FOURTEEN VOLUMES

EACH DEALING WITH A SPECIFIC SUBJECT, AND CONTAINING A SPECIAL INTRODUCTION BY A DISTINGUISHED AMERICAN STATESMAN OR PUBLICIST

VOLUME ELEVEN

ECONOMIC AND SOCIAL QUESTIONS: PART TWO

With an Introduction by CHARLES R. VAN HISE
President of the University of Wisconsin

CURRENT LITERATURE PUBLISHING COMPANY
NEW YORK

CONTENTS OF VOLUME ELEVEN

iii

ILLUSTRATIONS IN VOLUME ELEVEN

INTRODUCTION

CONTROL OF TRUSTS BY COMMISSION[1]

MONOPOLY has never been recognized in this country by common law or by statute law, neither has it ever been so recognized in England. However, coöperation in industry, both by combination and by contracts, has been recognized by the laws of both countries. The distinction is fundamental. In England in the Middle Ages both common and statute laws were very stringent against combinations and contracts in restraint of trade. But Parliament, more than sixty years ago, wiped out all these statutes against such combinations and contracts, provided they were not monopolies, contrary to public policy, or immoral.

In this country in colonial days the laws were very strict against combinations and contracts in restraint of trade. But here also there was a gradual amelioration of the laws, until coöperation was permitted along many lines, including division of territory, limitation of output, and even fixing of prices; provided always that as a result of the coöperation the combinations or contracts did not result in monopoly, were not general, were not immoral, or were not contrary to public policy.

Thus we see that the law in regard to combinations and contracts in restraint of trade went through a similar revolution both in this country and in England, and that the laws finally became very liberal. In other countries also the laws in regard to coöperation are liberal. By gradual development the principle has been reached,

[1] Adapted from an address delivered before the Economic Club of New York, November 1, 1912.

XI—1

1

for most civilized nations, that freedom in trade means freedom to combine as well as freedom to compete. This was the situation in this country when, in 1890, the Sherman law was enacted, and immediately the wheels of industry, so far as combination was concerned, were turned back to the condition of the Middle Ages. All combinations and contracts in restraint of trade were prohibited, and this applied to the latter even if limited in extent or confined in time. This national legislation led to an influenza of similar legislation in the States, and within a few years more than thirty of them had passed statutes against combinations and contracts in restraint of trade, many even more drastic than the Sherman law.

The question now arises, What were the results of these statutes? The Sherman act contained two separate provisions, one prohibiting every contract and combination in the form of trust or otherwise in restraint of trade as illegal; another declaring that monopoly or attempt to monopolize is also illegal.

By the public it was supposed that "every contract and combination in restraint of trade" meant what the words said, and that Congress in using these words meant to pass a new and drastic law replacing the common law; indeed, the earlier decisions of the Supreme Court took this point of view, and held that the reasonableness or unreasonableness of a contract or combination was immaterial. However, in the Standard Oil and Tobacco cases the court took an entirely new attitude, and stated that only restraint of trade which was undue was meant to be covered by the law (although the word "undue" is nowhere in the act), that the restraint meant was that which was not permitted under the common law, and therefore that only those contracts or combinations were prohibited by the law which were unreasonably in restraint of trade.[1]

[1] The Standard Oil Company of New Jersey, et al., *vs.* The United States, Appeal from the Circuit Court of the United States for the Eastern District of Missouri, May 15, 1911. U. S. Reports, Vol. 221, p. 1.

American Tobacco Company *vs.* The United States. Appeal from the Circuit Court of the United States for the Southern District of New York, May 29, 1911. U. S. Reports, Vol. 221, p. 106.

Why was this change in front made? It is a fair conclusion that the investigations of the Supreme Court led them to the view that, if the Sherman act were enforced in accordance with its terms, prohibiting all contracts and combinations in restraint of trade, this would create an impossible situation. Therefore they inserted the words "undue" or "unreasonable" into the law, so as to make it, as nearly as possible, accord with the common law, which existed before the act was passed; and thus they started a second cycle of development by common law. One cycle of evolution in regard to this matter had been sufficient in Germany, England, and other countries. America is the only civilized nation which must go through this development twice.

While these recent decisions of the Court do not go far enough, they clearly point the way to a ground intermediate between the alternatives commonly supposed to be before us: "regulation of monopoly or regulation of competition," and this is: freedom of competition, prohibition of monopoly, permission to coöperate, and regulation of coöperation. If it can be assumed that the alternatives as stated contain all of the possible solutions it is easy to reach a conclusion. We must not have monopoly, and therefore we are driven to the other conclusion: regulation of competition; but since the assumption is fallacious the conclusion has no foundation.

Now what is the situation with which we are confronted? The Sherman law and the State anti-trust laws are upon the statute books. We have gone through one stage of development and have made the first step in the second stage, and now it is proposed to neutralize the decision of the Court by defining "reasonable" so that it shall mean prohibition of all contracts and combinations in restraint of trade, and thus succeed in getting statute law back to where Senator Sherman and the people thought they had got it thirty years ago through the enactment by Congress of the Sherman act. This would be the beginning of a third cycle of development.

This solution of the problem of combination makes me think of the philosopher, Harold Udgardin, by name, an Eskimo, who lives up on Hudson Bay. Harold has one trap now set in the same place where it has been for twenty years, and he continues to trim it; he has not yet caught a fox in it, but he will not consider changing its location, as it is a good place, he reasons, and ought to catch a fox.

Notwithstanding that the trap of the Sherman act has never caught a fox for twenty years, and only smells in one or two places of a tail or a leg, it is proposed to strengthen its "springs" and sharpen its "teeth" with the expectation that it will then catch a sufficient number of foxes to become the solution of the great fundamental problem of concentration of industry.

In regard to the Sherman act, it has been assumed that its only violators are the great combinations. This assumption is made in practically all discussions of the question. The Steel Trust, the Tobacco Trust, and a few other large combinations are mentioned; and it is supposed that the small business men and the small producers are not acting in violation of the law. But the principle of coöperation which the Sherman act tries to suppress extends from the great industrial centers like New York to the country crossroads. Does it make any difference here in New York whether you buy coal or ice or any standard article of one company or another? Of course not. It doesn't make any difference in the country crossroads either. The principle is the same for the large and small men: one is violating the law just as certainly as the other. I am willing to stand for enforcement of law when the law is enforced alike for all; but when one man is picked out because he is in the front seat, or because it is good politics to attack him, and ninety-nine or nine hundred and ninety-nine others are allowed to escape, I say that it is a profoundly immoral situation. And that is exactly the existing situation in this country. The politician who cries "Break up these trusts; destroy them," says with the very same breath, "We must have coöperation among the farmers."

The cranberry growers of Cape Cod, New Jersey, and Wisconsin sell about 90 per cent. of their products through an agency down here in Hudson street. Have we heard of the Attorney-General prosecuting these farmers? There would be a great and shrill cry if that were done, and there would be many votes lacking to the Administration when it came to election.

In this country we have not a special situation which concerns a few men, but a general, irresistible impulse. It is all very well to ask, "Has the time come when a few rich men shall defy the law?" but Edmund Burke said more than a century ago, "I do not know the method of drawing up an indictment against a whole people." And that is the situation which we have in this nation as regards combination. There is just as copper-riveted an arrangement between the three icemen in the village, or the cranberry growers, as there is in steel or tobacco; and any just solution of the problem of combination must be applied not only to the steel and tobacco magnates but also to the small tradesmen and the farmer.

The Attorney-General of the United States[1] says that if we can only break up each of the great combinations into six, or eight, or ten parts, these different parts will compete; that the tendency to competition under such circumstances is irresistible. But the tendency for co-operation in this twentieth century is so much stronger than the tendency for competition that we shall never restore the latter in the old sense. There will be competition between different classes of goods; there will be competition between the great mail order houses and the village grocer; there will be competition in service. I am just as anxious as anyone to have trade regulated by competition as far as possible; but, as a matter of fact, competition has failed hopelessly in this country adequately to control prices or to control quality, and we all know it.

We have recognized the failure of competition to secure quality, by the establishment of the pure food laws. Why should we have pure food laws if competition will give us good quality? If articles are fraudulently sold so important to the general welfare as foods, there is a remedy in the courts. If a thing is sold me as pure strained honey, which is wholly innocent of having any

[1] George W. Wickersham in the *Century Magazine*, Vol. LXXXIII, No. 4, p. 619.

relation whatever with a bee, I have been fraudulently
dealt with and I have a remedy in law. Why don't I take
my case to the courts? Because the loss is so small that
it is impracticable for the individual thus to obtain redress. Finally recognizing the fact that competition is
wholly inadequate to secure pure food, national and State
laws have been enacted, and special officers have been
designated upon whom is imposed the duty of protecting
the public. When we confessed that competition did not
regulate quality, and imposed the duty of protecting the
public upon administrative officers, we succeeded in getting pure food, or a reasonable proportion of pure food
at least, and never until then.

Now, why is it that competition to regulate prices has
broken down? Because of the simply enormous advantages which come with coöperation. We agree that the
nation will not return to the country grist mill. But this
does not settle the question regarding the magnitude that
is permissible. It is asserted that a great many of
the large industrial organizations have exceeded the
magnitude which gives the highest efficiency. I may
assert upon the other hand that very few of them have
gone beyond the stage which gives increased efficiency.
Neither party can prove his case. He hasn't the facts
necessary to do so.

While for iron and steel it has been proved that a
hundred million-dollar combination is economically more
efficient than a ten million-dollar combination, it has not
been proved that a thousand million-dollar combination
is more efficient than a hundred million-dollar combination, since no investigation has been made to determine
this point. The question is one for scientific investigation, and it is to be hoped that the National Bureau of
Corporations will do the work. Similar investigations
should be made for other lines of industry, so that we
may have a scientific foundation upon which to decide
how far we shall permit magnitude.

That magnitude alone, or even a control of fifty per
cent. of the business done in an industry, is not proof of
inefficiency is shown by conditions in foreign countries.
The German steel combine has control of a larger per-

centage of the iron product of Germany than the United States Steel Corporation has for the United States. The German steel combine gives greater freedom to the individual plant than do the combinations in this country: it is a federation rather than a consolidation. The same thing would have been true here had it not been for the Sherman act. Men who build up a business dislike to surrender its management to someone else. Affiliation of the different companies in the same business was developing in this country in the same way as in England and Germany, on the principle of coöperation. Then the trust was declared to be unlawful, and so arose the holding corporation: and now, again driven by law, the holding corporation is passing to the complete merger. Each step was to escape the last decision of the court, because of the irresistible tendency for coöperation. Germany and England are vastly more fortunate than we are in this respect.

One other force which has led to general coöperation in industry is the waste of competition in its relation to our natural resources. We have some five thousand bituminous coal operators who, from the mines, could produce perhaps 200,000,000 tons of coal per annum more than the present market demands. In consequence these men, unable to coöperate except in violation of law, are competing, with the inevitable result of very wasteful mining. Indeed, more wasteful mining of coal is going on in this country than in any other civilized nation. It is appalling, the amount of the coal that is left underground through existing methods of exploitation. If these five thousand operators were allowed to agree upon limitation of output and division of market, it would be possible to reduce these frightful wastes, which will be disastrous to our industry a few centuries hence.

It has been proposed that the concentrations in industry should be so divided that no one corporation shall have more than fifty per cent. of any business. It makes little difference, from the point of view of coöperation, whether the great combinations are dissolved so that no one combination has more than fifty per cent. or thirty per cent. of a line of business; or so that there are

ten with ten per cent., or twenty with five per cent.
The demonstration of this lies in the fact already
cited, that thousands of farmers may coöperate in mar-
keting their products just as perfectly as do the five
great manufacturers of steel. This they do in various
parts of the country for fruit, for cotton, and for other
products. Some of the State legislatures were bright
enough to appreciate this situation, and in order to prevent the farmers from being hit by their anti-trust bills
they exempted agricultural products so long as these
were in the hands of the producers. This was true for
Texas, Louisiana, Illinois, and South Dakota. But naturally the United States courts declared these features
unconstitutional as being special legislation and not giving equal protection under the laws. Therefore I believe
we shall ultimately permit coöperation. If, however, we
retain freedom of competition, permit concentration sufficient to give efficiency, allow reasonable coöperation,
and prevent monopoly, this will require regulation just
as it has been necessary to regulate the railroads. This
done, the Sherman law will be forgotten. It is now on
the way toward oblivion. Has there been any prosecution of the railroads for violations of the Sherman act
because of collusion in fixing rates? And yet these companies are just as flagrant violators of the Sherman act
as any other class of corporations. Why is it that nobody proposes to indict the railroads for collusion? Simply for the reason that the rates which they can charge
are controlled by commissions, national and State. Nobody has any longer any wish to make them any further
trouble, because the public is protected by its commissions. That is the sum of the whole matter. However,
it is a wrong condition when we have on the statute
books a law of a kind which requires Justice to close one
eye and pass by the men in control of one great group of
industry and at the same moment, with the other eye, see
other men not one whit more guilty. We ought to remedy the condition so that honorable business men shall
not be in the unfortunate position of being technical
violators of statutes which it is not advantageous, from
the public point of view, to enforce.

The substance of my proposed remedy is that there be an interstate trade commission and State trade commissions, which shall have substantially the same powers to regulate coöperation in industry that the Interstate Commerce Commission and the State commerce commissions have in regard to the public utilities. It seems to me that the appointment of these commerce commissions and the administrative bodies for the pure food laws points the way for the next constructive step in the development of the laws regulating industry. It would perhaps be chimerical, with public opinion as at present, to propose the repeal of the Sherman act, but by amendments to this act the situation may be met. The Sherman act, by the Supreme Court, can be left to apply, as defined, to monopoly. Unreasonable restraint of trade may be defined as monopolistic restraint of trade, and it is rather generally agreed that monopoly should be prohibited. To make the matter perfectly clear another amendment should allow reasonable coöperation, but such coöperation should be under the watchful eyes of administrative commissions in order to protect the public. They should exercise powers under broad, simple rules of law, and detailed regulations should be formulated by the commissions. Unfair practices should be prohibited—and by unfair practices we mean what was meant by immoral practices in the common law. But the most vital point of the law would be this: that when the individual is wronged through unreasonable prices or rebates or other discrimination it becomes the duty of a public commission to handle his case. The aggrieved individual should not be obliged to carry his case through the machinery of the courts; he should make complaint to an administrative commission, and it should become the duty of that commission, representing the public, and him as a part of the public, to secure redress. This, while the greatest, is but one of the many advantages which may be gained through the establishment of trade commissions, national and State.

CHAPTER I

THE SHERMAN ANTI-TRUST LAW

John Sherman [O.] Introduces in Senate Bill against Trusts—Debate: In Favor, Sen. Sherman, Zebulon B. Vance [N. C.]; Opposed, James Z. George [Miss.], George G. Vest [Mo.], William M. Stewart [Nev.], John T. Morgan [Ala.]; Amendments by John H. Reagan [Tex.], Sen. George, George F. Hoar [Mass.], John J. Ingalls [Kan.], Are Adopted, and Amendment Offered by Richard Coke [Tex.] Is Tabled; Bill Is Committed; New Bill Is Reported; It Is Adopted by Both Houses, and Approved by President Harrison.

ON December 4, 1889, John Sherman [O.] introduced in the Senate a bill to declare unlawful trusts and combinations in restraint of trade and production. It was referred to the Committee on Finance, of which Senator Sherman was chairman. The committee reported the bill on January 14, 1890. It came up for discussion in the Committee of the Whole on February 27.

SHERMAN ANTI-TRUST BILL

SENATE, FEBRUARY 27, 1890

The bill was read. It was as follows:

Be it enacted, etc., That all arrangements, contracts, agreements, trusts, or combinations between persons or corporations made with a view or which tend to prevent full and free competition in the importation, transportation, or sale of articles imported into the United States, or in the production, manufacture, or sale of articles of domestic growth or production, or domestic raw material that competes with any similar article upon which a duty is levied by the United States, or which shall be transported from one State or Territory to another, and all arrangements, contracts, agreements, trusts, or com-

10

binations between persons or corporations designed or which tend to advance the cost to the consumer of any such articles are hereby declared to be against public policy, unlawful, and void.

Sec. 2. That any person or corporation injured or damnified by such arrangement, contract, agreement, trust, or combination may sue for and recover, in any court of the United States of competent jurisdiction, of any person or corporation a party to a combination described in the first section of this act, the full consideration or sum paid by him for any goods, wares, and merchandise included or advanced in price by said combination.

Sec. 3. That all persons entering into any such arrangement, contract, agreement, trust, or combination described in section 1 of this act, either on his own account or as agent or attorney for another, or as an officer, agent, or stockholder of any corporation, or as a trustee, committee, or in any capacity whatever, shall be guilty of a high misdemeanor, and on conviction thereof in any district or circuit court of the United States shall be subject to a fine of not more than $10,000 or to imprisonment in the penitentiary for a term of not more than five years, or to both such fine and imprisonment, in the discretion of the court. And it shall be the duty of the district attorney of the United States of the district in which such persons reside to institute the proper proceedings to enforce the provisions of this act.

James Z. George [Miss.] spoke in opposition to the bill.

He questioned the constitutionality of the bill and its efficiency if it were constitutional. He discussed first the inefficiency of the bill.

It is somewhat obscure; in some parts ambiguous. It is a criminal and penal statute. Its second section provides for the recovery of a penalty. Its third and last section provides for an indictment and punishment of offenders for crimes defined in the first.

In considering such a bill Congress must necessarily determine with care what will be its meaning and effect in the courts. This is essential to prevent a result which would be both absurd and highly prejudicial, to wit, that Congress means one thing in passing the bill and the courts in enforcing it shall give it another and different meaning.

Being a penal statute, and nothing else, it will be construed strictly in favor of alleged violators. Nothing will be brought within it which is outside of its plain words. Enlargement by construction will not be allowed.

I proceed now to the analysis of the bill to see what it provides for, what it prohibits, what it punishes, and what it permits as lawful.

In the first place, it must be noted that the bill deals only with agreements, arrangements, and combinations. It denounces and punishes these when made with a certain intent, but it neither punishes nor affects in the least any act done in pursuance of these combinations. It punishes a conspiracy with intent to do certain things, but treats these things when done as perfectly lawful, as harmless, even meritorious.

The making of the combination with the prohibited intent is the *corpus delicti*,[1] the criminal act denounced by the statute. The crime, in the main, is complete and perfect when this agreement is made. The bill makes no difference, except in one case, whether acts are afterward done in pursuance of the agreement or not. If no such act be done, still the making or entering into the agreement is criminal and punishable. If such act be done, it is neither punishable in itself, nor does it aggravate in any way the criminality of the combination. It is not a case (and this must be borne in mind) where the original agreement is one of a series of acts, all of which are necessary to be done in order to constitute the crime. But the entering into the agreement or combination (for these words cover the whole of the words descriptive of the crime as used in the bill) is *per se* the crime and the whole of it.

The first thing which attracts our attention, therefore, is that if the agreement or combination, which is the crime, be made outside of the jurisdiction of the United States it is also without the terms of the law and cannot be punished in the United States. Mark that. Then if these conspirators are foreigners and remain at home, or, being citizens, shall cross our borders and enter into any foreign territory and there make the combination or agreement, they escape the criminal part of this law; and proceedings carrying out the combination may be carried on with impunity in the United States. The raising of prices and the prevention of free and full competition may all take place in the United States, and yet no crime has been committed.

That this is a serious and not a mere fanciful and hypo-

[1] "The body of the crime."

thetical objection is manifest. For it is certain, if the bill become a law, all combinations and agreements involving large amounts and therefore seriously affecting the welfare of the people of the United States will be made outside of the jurisdiction of the United States. Canada and Mexico are near neighbors, and the former will certainly become the locality in which these agreements will be made, as it has become the refuge of embezzlers at this day. The law will therefore operate only on little sinners, little men, combining with reference to interests so small as not to justify the expense and trouble of a visit to Canada or Mexico in order to make the agreement or combination. So that the bill is a sham so far as the real criminals are concerned, the men whose wealth enables them to fleece and rob the people.

But suppose, what I think, however, is highly improbable, some of these great combinations should be made in the United States. Will the case be any better for the people in whose interests we profess to legislate? The combination must, under the bill, be made "with the intention to prevent full and free competition in the importation, transportation, or sale of articles imported into the United States."

Here we have serious ambiguity and doubt, and it is impossible to say with certainty what the bill means. The word "imported," which describes the article about which the agreement is to be made, is in the past tense, and means, grammatically, articles already imported, and shows that the agreement must be in reference to articles which have then at the time of making the agreement been imported; yet in the same sentence we have denounced an agreement to prevent full and free competition in the importation of the articles described, and this necessarily means that the agreement shall precede the final act of importation. For it is certain that an agreement made after the act of importation is complete cannot have any effect on that past and completed transaction. It is not in the power of man to change or affect the past. What has occurred is not a matter in action; it is only a matter of history.

So that we have this contradictory enactment contained in the same sentence, that the agreement denounced by the bill shall precede importation, and that it shall also come after importation.

There is only one other conceivable meaning, and that is the phrase "agreements, etc., made with intention to prevent full and free competition in the importation, transportation, or sale of articles imported into the United States," means, with reference to importation, that the agreement must precede the act of importation, and, with reference to "transportation and sale," this agreement refers to those acts done after importation. With this meaning, if we are allowed to conjecture it in a criminal statute, the bill would be plainly unconstitutional. It would then include transportation and sale generally, there being no words to limit them. Transportation and sale generally are not within the jurisdiction of Congress, but only transportation and sale in interstate and foreign commerce. It is an undeniable rule of constitutional law that where the language of a statute embraces matters within and without the constitutional power of Congress the whole of it is unconstitutional.

But, if we were allowed to do this in this case, the result would be to demonstrate in the clearest manner the utter worthlessness of the bill as a remedy for the evils which afflict our country. For in this view we would have the prohibited agreement so far as importation is concerned preceding that event. As importation is the result of a transportation of goods from a foreign country, the agreement in relation to it would generally be made there, and would always be made there if such agreements were prohibited and punishable by law here. And as to the transportation and sales here, they would take place or could be made to take place after the articles imported ceased to be imports in the constitutional sense of the term or after the original package in which they were imported had been broken. An agreement made with reference to them in that connection would be beyond the jurisdiction of Congress.

There is another trouble—a very serious obstacle—in enforcing the bill as a law. The agreement or combination must be made with a certain specified intent. A combination or arrangement between two or more in relation to the business mentioned in the bill is altogether an innocent and lawful transaction, unless it be made with the intent named in the bill. The unlawful intent therefore is the gist of the offence. Without this intent the act is lawful, even meritorious. With it, the act is unlawful and criminal.

In such cases it is settled law that the specific intent which constitutes the crime must be proven on the trial to exist as is stated in the statute. A lawful act, made unlawful when done with a specific intent mentioned in the statute, remains still lawful, so far as that statute is concerned, if not done with that specific intent, though it may have been done with some other intent, which may be recognized in morals and even in law as equally objectionable as the specific intent named in the statute.

In all such cases the specific intent named in the statute must not only exist, but must on the trial be proven to exist beyond a reasonable doubt or the party indicted must be acquitted; the proof of a different intent, though it be also unlawful, will not do. So that, under the first branch of the statute relating to imported goods, it must be proven that the intention was to prevent competition in the transportation, when it is not purely internal and domestic, or in the sale of the article while it was still an import in the constitutional sense; that is, before it has been sold by the importer or before the original package in which it is imported has been broken. If the combination relates to sales to be made by others than the importers or even by the importers themselves after the original package is broken, then it is with different intention from the one included in the statute, and with an intention that can not be constitutionally included in it and therefore there can be no conviction under the statute.

So that all the benefits of this bill, so far as preventing increased price coming from combinations to prevent free competition in the sale of imported goods, come to naught if the parties making the combinations will only make them with the intent to operate on sales taking place after they have ceased to be imports by either having been sold by the importer, or he, still being owner, has broken the package in which they were imported. Of course, if the bill becomes a law, the combinations and arrangements will be made outside of it, when that can be so easily done.

I pass now to the second branch of the bill: combinations and arrangements "with intention to prevent full and free competition in the production, manufacture, or sale of articles of domestic growth or production or domestic raw material" that competes with any similar article upon which a duty is levied by the United States, intended for and which shall be transported in interstate commerce for sale.

This is a most remarkable provision, possibly unparalleled in penal legislation.

To constitute the crime under this part of the bill there must be combined three intents, entirely distinct, two of them not unlawful, and one act which may be done by a third party in no wise connected with the party who is made criminal. This act of such third party is not only not criminal, but is even meritorious and the subject of encouragement by law. That is, a crime is by statute compounded of three intents, two of them lawful, and of the separate and independent and subsequent lawful act of another, all of these concurring to constitute the crime.

To convict a party indicted under this clause of the bill, it must be proved beyond a reasonable doubt—

First. That he entered into the combination or arrangement named with another, or others, with the specific intent to prevent the full and free competition in the production, manufacture, or sale of domestic articles which compete with dutiable foreign goods;

Second. That these domestic articles must be intended for transportation in interstate commerce for sale; and

Third. That these goods have been so transported for sale.

Suppose the United States succeeds in proving the unlawful combination or arrangement to permit full and free competition. This alone will not do, as under the first branch of the bill something further must be proven. It must be further shown that the articles in relation to which the combination was made do actually compete with the dutiable foreign article. The language is that the domestic article ''competes'' with the foreign article, not that it may compete or has the tendency to compete. There must be actual competition. If we may, as this bill does, apply the action indicated by the verb ''to compete'' to inanimate and insensible subjects, as articles of merchandise, we can do it only in the sense that the separate owners of these articles are maintaining a contest, seeking and striving for the same thing; that is, each is striving to sell his own article, as against the other, in the same market and to the same set of customers or buyers.

This actual competition in the sense above named must be proven as stated. The statute is a penal one and must not only be strictly construed in favor of the alleged violator, but the acts constituting the crime must be proven beyond reasonable doubt. It must be shown, then, that the domestic article, in the language of the bill, ''competes'' with the foreign article; that this competition must be actual, a real, substantive fact actually transpiring and capable of observation, not a mere potentiality or possibility or even probability of competition. This it will be impossible to prove unless both articles should be actually in a particular market, as New York, and their owners are seeking and striving against each other to sell them. If the foreign article be absent and not offered in the market, there is no competition. If the domestic article be absent there is no competition, for in neither case can it be said the domestic article, in the language of the statute, ''competes'' with the other. And it makes no difference what may cause the absence of the foreign article, except that such absence shall not be caused by the combination. For if the foreign owner will not on any account bring or send his goods to our markets, there can be nothing here which competes with them. And so if the foreign goods be excluded by a law of the United States denouncing them as unlawful objects of commerce, for then they can not be brought here at all.

Is not the same thing true if their entrance into our ports be excluded by the imposition of a duty so high that it is prohibitory? In either case it is prohibition of competition, complete and effectual. In the one case the prohibition is absolute and *eo nomine;*[1] in the other it is equally effectual, though prohibition is not expressly and by that name enacted. In both cases there is no actual competition, nor does the *casus* named in the bill, that the domestic articles "compete" with the foreign article, arise.

So it appears that in a large majority of instances under our protective tariff, enacted expressly, as the friends of it claim, to prevent full and free competition between foreign and domestic goods, this bill, if enacted, will furnish no remedy. It will be a sham and nothing more.

But suppose the difficulty is surmounted and the actual competition is proven beyond a reasonable doubt, then it must also be proven that the domestic goods or raw materials were intended by the parties to the combination for transportation from one State or Territory to another for sale.

The intention to transport for sale must be the intention of the parties to the combination and the party on trial. However we may make one man responsible for the open and overt acts of another, I believe it has never been contended that we could make one man liable for the secret and uncommunicated intention and thoughts of another. So it must be proven that the combination was made not only with the intent to prevent full and free competition between the goods produced under it and the foreign article, but that the intent was that the goods produced should be transported from State to State for sale. These intents must coexist at the making of the arrangement in the minds of the parties to it. If either is wanting there can be no crime under this bill.

Parties, therefore, entering into these combinations after this bill becomes a law will of course make them according to law. It will be presumed that they did so conform to law

[1] "In that name."

XI—2

unless the contrary is proven. Seeing, then, when the bill passes, that it is not unlawful to make combinations and arrangements in the production, manufacture, and sale of goods, with intent to prevent the competition denounced by the bill, unless is shown the further intent that these goods shall be transported for sale from one State to another, they will limit the intention to selling them or exchanging them in the State in which they are produced. They will refuse to sell except at their doors. They will agree to make and produce goods to sell to whosoever will there at that very place and in that State buy them. Calling to mind the rule of law that when the specific intent is the gist of the crime it must exist and be proven to exist, specifically as stated in the statute, we see that no crime is established.

That a part of the goods produced may and actually does go into interstate commerce will not do to prove the specific intent mentioned in the bill, for that would only prove that the intent of the combination was to produce goods which parties to whom they were sold and over whom the combination had no control might or might not put into interstate commerce as circumstances of trade might afterward indicate as most profitable. This is a very different intent from the specific intent named in the statute, the intent solely to transport in interstate commerce.

But, Mr. President, if this trouble should be removed, it must also be shown that the goods produced were actually so transported, and that, too, with another specific intent, namely, for sale.

It is not stated in the statute who shall entertain this last intent, whether the persons making the combination, or of any person to whom they may have sold the goods, or the consignor on the transportation, or the consignee in the State in which the transportation ends. But though doubtful we must assume that the intent of sale was the intent of the party on trial, for one man can not be punished for the secret and uncommunicated intent of another.

But if this obstacle, insurmountable as it appears to be, should be found in fact removable, then we will find that the statute will nevertheless be a worthless remedy against the evils arising from these combinations. For, as the transportation must be for sale, and not for anything else, it must be negatived in the proof that it was for exchange or for consumption.

But up to this point, if all the proof be made as required, there must be proven a superadded or fourth intention; that is, it shall be the intent of the parties to the combination to advance the cost of the articles described to the consumer. The intent to advance the price to the wholesale or retail dealer alone will not do; it must be to advance it to the consumer. This leaves unpunished and perfectly lawful all these combinations, which have proven so disastrous, that have for their object a decrease in the price to be given to the producer, and also those speculative movements, now so common, by which there shall be a temporary advance in the market, to last till a day not far off, when there shall be a settlement.

These arrangements, combinations, or corners, or whatever else they may be called, are made wholly for speculative purposes—intended alone to squeeze those who are "short," as the saying is. It is true they do, as an incident, sometimes affect, while they last, the price paid by the consumer, but that is not the intent, the specific intent with which they are formed, and they are, therefore, not embraced in the statute. Nor are such combinations made in reference to articles intended for interstate transportation and sale, for such speculations are made wholly without expectation of a delivery of the articles, and settlements are made by merely paying the price on the day agreed upon.

Mr. President, up to this point I have been considering the bill in its aspect as a punisher of crime. But there is a section which gives the injured party a civil action to recover a penalty; that is, double damages. If we suppose that such a suit would ever be brought, an event almost certain not to occur, the plaintiff would encounter all the difficulties of a criminal prosecution, with one single exception. That exception is that he would not be compelled to make out his case beyond a reasonable doubt. He would, however, be compelled to prove every fact shown to be necessary in the criminal proceeding by clear evidence to the satisfaction of the court and jury. He would not be allowed to rely on mere conjecture or supposition, but he must establish his case affirmatively so as to satisfy the court and jury that all the facts and all the intents existed which I have shown to be necessary in the criminal prosecution. That this would be impossible is seen from what I have stated, and is also shown more clearly even by what follows.

The right of action against the persons in the combination is given to the party damnified. Who is this party injured, when, as prescribed in the bill, there has been an advance in the price by combination? The answer is found in the bill itself in the words, "intended to advance the cost to the con-

sumer of any such articles.'' The consumer is the party
''damnified or injured.''

This is the express provision of the bill, as I think is clear
from the last clause of the first section. But, even if it were
not the express language of the bill, it so˙results as a logical
necessity. An advance in price to the middleman is not mentioned in the bill, for the obvious reason that no such advance
would damnify him; it would rather be a benefit, as it would
increase the value of the goods he has on hand. He buys
to sell again. He buys only for profit on a subsequent sale.
So whatever he pays he receives when he sells, together with
a profit on his investment, and so of all of them, including the
last, who sells directly to the consumer. The consumer, therefore, paying all the increased price advanced by the middle-
men and profits on the same, is the party necessarily damnified
or injured.

Who are the consumers? The people of the United States
as individuals; whatever each individual consumes, or his
family, marks the amount of his interest in the price advanced
by the combination. It is manifest that in nearly every instance
the damage by the advanced price of each article affected by
these combinations would be—though in the aggregate large,
indeed—so small as not to justify the expense and trouble of
a suit in a distant court.

I do not hesitate to say that few, if any, of such suits will
ever be instituted, and not one will ever be successful.

Mr. President, I have proven this bill to be worthless even
if it be constitutional. These trusts and combinations are great
wrongs to the people. They have invaded many of the most
important branches of business. They operate with a double-
edged sword. They increase beyond reason the cost of the
necessaries of life and business and they decrease the cost of the
raw material, the farm products of the country. They regulate
prices at their will, depress the price of what they buy, and
increase the price of what they sell. They gather to themselves great, enormous wealth by extortion which makes the
people poor. Then making this extorted wealth the means of
further extortion from their unfortunate victims, the people of
the United States, they pursue unmolested, unrestrained by law,
their ceaseless round of peculation under the law, till they are
fast producing that condition in our people in which the great
mass of them are the servitors of those who have this aggregated
wealth at their command.

The people see this and they are restless and discontented.

THE TRUST GIANT

Cartoon by Homer Davenport in the Hearst papers

21

The farmers especially have been the victims of this and other policies which have brought them to the verge of ruin. Debts and mortgages accumulate. The home, the farm, the workshop, are becoming the properties by encumbrances of lordly creditors, who, by methods encouraged and fostered by law in some instances and permitted by law in others, have extorted their ill-gotten gains from the poor and then used the money thus obtained to complete the ruin of the people. The people ask us for redress. They plead for security against these wrongs. What is offered them is this bill, which, even if it be constitutional, is, as I have shown it to be, utterly worthless. It will aggravate rather than diminish the evils.

Mr. President, I do not charge the committee with bad faith in the presentation of this bill. I have faith in the fairness and justice of their intentions. The truth is, sir, the committee, by its methods, undertook to accomplish the impossible. They have undertaken to compound from reserved and granted powers a valid bill, and the result is the incongruities I have pointed out, that curious commingling of inconsistent and inefficient provisions which has produced this abortion. There is one power in the Constitution which would have been efficient if it had been resorted to. It is the power to levy taxes, duties, imports, etc. The author of this bill at one time concurred in the opinion that this was the only power in Congress on the subject which would be efficient. Speaking of legislation to suppress trusts, on August 14, 1888, Mr. Sherman said:

> Whether such legislation can be ingrafted in our peculiar system by the national authority there is some doubt. If it can be done at all it must be done upon a tariff bill or revenue bill. I do not see in what other way it can be done.

That, sir, is exactly my position. There is no other way under the Constitution.

And to show what he meant by legislation on a tariff bill the same great Senator, on January 2, 1888, commenting on a passage in President Cleveland's message recommending lower duties to prevent trusts, said:

> Where such combinations to prevent a reduction of price by fair competition exist I agree that they may, and ought to, be met by a reduction of duty.

But that distinguished Senator and the great Committee on Finance who have produced this bill believe in high duties, in

protective duties, in even prohibitive duties. They are wedded
to the conviction that the home market is the best market, and
that the American manufacturer is entitled to this American
market as against the world. They are unwilling to give up
this theory. Notwithstanding they see "that combinations to
prevent a reduction of price by fair competition do exist," and
that a fair and effectual "way to meet them is by a reduction
of duty," they can not make up their minds to do this. So,
contrary to the views expressed, as above quoted, by Mr. Sherman, they have sought another power in the Constitution to
suppress trusts. But they have sought in vain, as Mr. Sherman said they would. They seek to make two inconsistent,
even repellant, things coexist and harmonize, to wit: a high
protective tariff, which shuts out foreign competition, and the
vain prohibition that the protected parties shall not avail themselves of the advantage thus given them. They throw the
coveted sop to the hungry and greedy Cerberus and then say
to the dog, "You shall not eat it."

The attempt to do this must fail. Success is impossible.
You can no more make moral contradictory laws coalesce and
work in harmony than you can construct a system dependent
on contradictory physical and mathematical laws. The power
of Congress is impotent to reconcile and harmonize truth and
error. It is powerless also to make truth error or to make
error truth. We can not enact that the three angles of a
triangle shall be more or less than two right angles. We
can not repeal the law of gravity. We can not enact that vice
shall be virtue, that falsehood shall be truth. We can not
change human nature. We can not by our tariff laws administer
to and stimulate the greed of men, and then, without removing
the stimulant, enact successfully, as is attempted by this bill,
that this greed shall be generosity and self-abnegation. By
our tariff laws we hold out to the owners of the protected
industries the offer of 47 per cent. advance in price. We tell
them they are entitled to it; that it is right and just. By this
bill we say to them, you must not take the offer.

Of course, Mr. President, a bill framed with these utterly
contradictory and irreconcilable ends will be inefficient, the
miserable sham I have shown this to be.

Mr. President, I now proceed to show that the bill is utterly
unconstitutional.

This task is an easy one, since the principles applicable
to this examination have again and again been settled by the
Supreme Court. I warn Senators now that no attempt will

be made to show the bill unconstitutional upon that narrow
and strict theory of State rights which they may suppose is
entertained by the Southern people and by them only. In all
I shall say on this subject I shall plant my argument on an
exposition of the Constitution made by the tribunal which
the Constitution itself appoints to perform that duty.

The power to enact the bill is claimed in the bill itself
under the commercial clause of the Constitution: the power
"to regulate commerce with foreign nations and among the
States."

A statute enacted under this grant must be the exercise
of a power of regulation, a regulation of commerce, either foreign
or interstate. It must be this and nothing else.

The transactions which take place before this interstate or
foreign commerce begins and the transactions occurring after
it ends, though they be strictly commercial, do not constitute
interstate or foreign commerce nor any part of it. They are
only domestic commerce in the State in which they take place,
and are beyond the power of Congress to regulate. They belong
exclusively to the State in which they originate and are con-
summated. The power of Congress commences with the initia-
tion of interstate or foreign commerce and ceases with its
termination. The regulation, therefore, must be of things done,
transactions taking place, after this initial point and before
the point of termination. The acts which constitute interstate
or foreign commerce embrace purchase, sale, exchange, barter,
transportation, and intercourse for the purpose of trade in all
its forms. (See Welborn *vs.* Missouri, 91 U. S. R., and Mobile
vs. Kimball, 102 U. S. R., 702.) Of these acts this bill specifies
and claims jurisdiction over importation (purchase and transportation combined), transportation, and sale of imported
articles. This jurisdiction relates to foreign commerce. So far
as interstate commerce is concerned, the bill specifies transportation for sale only.

But, Mr. President, among these commercial acts are not
manufactures or any other kind of production, nor sales, nor
transportation purely within a State or wholly outside the
territorial jurisdiction of the United States? The bill proceeds
on the idea that as to interstate commerce the jurisdiction of
Congress extends to the regulation of the production and manufacture of articles taking place in a State, if only it be intended
that, after such manufacture or production shall be complete,
all or a portion of the articles shall become subjects of interstate
commerce, and shall in fact be transported as such.

This basis of the bill is expressly confuted by the decisions I shall quote.

The Supreme Court, in 1852, in Veazie *vs.* Moor, 14 How. R., speaking of the commercial clause of the Constitution, says it can not "be properly concluded that because the products of domestic enterprise in agriculture or manufactures or in the arts may ultimately become the subjects of foreign" (or interstate) "commerce, the control of the means or the encouragements by which enterprise is fostered and protected is legitimately within the import of the phrase 'foreign commerce,' or fairly implied in any investiture of the power to regulate such commerce. A pretension so far reaching as this would extend to contracts between citizen and citizen of the same State; would control the pursuits of the planter, the grazier, the manufacturer, the mechanic, the immense operations of the collieries and mines and furnaces of the country, for there is not one of these vocations the results of which may not become the subject of foreign" (interstate) "commerce."

The court further condemns the position that Congress has jurisdiction over a commerce "which . . . is unquestionably internal, although intermediately or ultimately it might become foreign."

This case was very recently (in 1880) confirmed by the Supreme Court in Lord *vs.* Steamship Company, 102 U. S.

This case expressly condemns that provision in the bill which seeks for jurisdiction in Congress over production and sales in a State merely upon the ground that the articles so produced or so sold might be afterwards transported in interstate commerce. There are other cases to the same effect.

But the bill places the power of Congress on such subsequent transportation, combined with an intention existing in the mind of the parties to these arrangements or trusts, at the time of production and manufacture, that the articles should be so transported.

That the conjoining of this intent in the production with the subsequent transportation does not help the case for the validity of the bill I now proceed to show.

Production of all kinds, manufactures of all kinds, as we have seen, are subject to the jurisdiction and power of the State in which they are carried on. Whatever regulations, therefore, may be made for carrying on these must be made by State authority. The methods of these operations of industry and art are exclusively for the States to regulate.

What is lawful by the State regulation can not be made

unlawful by the United States. The bill concedes this, for it professes not to undertake to condemn these operations as carried on under State authority. So far as this bill goes, these manufactures and productions are perfectly lawful, even when made with the intent of subsequent interstate transportation. Nor is interstate commerce in them interdicted or even regulated in any manner or to the smallest extent.

The question is, Can Congress, in the exercise of the power to regulate commerce among the States, make a law—prescribe a regulation—which punishes the intent with which an article is produced in a State and then permit it to be a lawful subject of interstate commerce, with no regulation whatever of that commerce in that article? That is exactly what this bill undertakes to do, neither more nor less. The result is that there is no regulation of interstate commerce, but there is a regulation of something else. That something is the domestic and internal production and business of a State. The power to do this will not be contended for.

Mr. President, if it be conceded that the punishment of an intent with which goods are produced, and which, when produced, are lawful subjects of interstate commerce, exactly as all other goods are, is a regulation of commerce, and not of production merely, still the bill is unconstitutional. This results from the fact that the acts and the intent with which they are associated, and which are punished by the bill, are not the carrying on of interstate commerce, but precede the commencement of that commerce, and therefore are not subject to the jurisdiction of Congress.

I now, therefore, proceed to inquire when goods intended for interstate commerce become subject to the jurisdiction of Congress. The answer to that is furnished by well considered decisions of the Supreme Court.

In Coe *vs.* Errol (116 United States) the articles of commerce were logs cut in the State of New Hampshire for transportation by floating on the Androscoggin River to Lewiston, in the State of Maine. So in that case the production of the article, the cutting of the logs, was with the intent to transport them to another State. But the logs were not only cut with this intent, but they were actually transported to the river with the intent to transport them as soon as the water should rise. They had gone through the initial domestic transportation necessary to enable them to be started on the final journey from New Hampshire to Maine. In that condition they were taxed by New Hampshire. If they were the subjects of interstate commerce, if the jurisdiction of New Hampshire had ceased and the power of the United States had commenced, the tax was unconstitutional.

The decision is that when the article of commerce has begun to move—not begun to be produced with an intent to move— from one State to another, then at that time interstate commerce in that commodity has first commenced.

That case, Mr. President, would seem to settle this question forever.

The case of Coe *vs.* Errol was confirmed in the late case of Kidd *vs.* Pearson (128 U. S. R., page 1), decided in 1888.

In that case the attempt was made to bring the production of goods in a State within the jurisdiction of the commercial clause of the Constitution, because they were manufactured with the intent to export them in interstate commerce. The court, after alluding to the right of the State to regulate the manufacture of an article of commerce as being settled beyond dispute, say:

> Is this right overthrown by the fact that the manufacturer intends to export the liquors when made? Does the statute, in omitting to except from its operations the manufacture of intoxicating liquor within the limits of the State for export, constitute an unauthorized interference with the power given to Congress to regulate commerce?
>
> These questions are well answered in the language of this court in the License Tax cases (5 Wallace, 462, 470). Over this commerce and trade (the internal commerce and domestic trade of the States) Congress has no power of regulation or control. This power belongs exclusively to the State.
>
> The manufacture of intoxicating liquors in a State is none the less a business within that State because the manufacturer intends, at his convenience, to export such liquors to foreign countries or to other States.
>
> This court has already decided that the fact that an article was manufactured for export to another State does not of itself make it an article of interstate commerce within the meaning of Section 8, Article I, of the Constitution, and that the intent of the manufacturer does not determine the time when the article or product passes from the control of the State and belongs to commerce.

There is but one remaining point in this part of the bill— referring to domestic production with the intent named—which may be considered as pointing to a fact giving Congress jurisdiction. The point is embraced in the language which describes the goods as competing with dutiable goods imported into the United States.

The question on this point is, Has Congress jurisdiction, under the power to regulate commerce, to regulate the manufacture, production, and sale in purely internal State commerce of goods because they compete with dutiable goods imported into the United States? An answer is found in the proposition that if the power exists as to production, to regulate by prescribing the rule laid down in this bill as to full and free competition, it may prescribe any other regulation. There is nothing in the prevention of full and free competitions in the manufacture and production of goods which of itself would give Congress jurisdiction as to goods competing with dutiable goods which would not authorize Congress to make any other regulation they might deem wise in such production of such goods.

If competition with dutiable goods gives jurisdiction for one regulation, it gives it for all regulations deemed wise by Congress. It results, therefore, that, if such competition be a ground of Federal jurisdiction, then Congress can assume or acquire the jurisdiction over the manufacture and production of all goods whatever manufactured and produced in any State by simply levying a duty on the competing foreign articles, and in this way would the whole internal business of the State be brought within the jurisdiction of Congress to regulate and control as Congress might deem proper. The two facts, dutiable foreign goods and competing domestic goods, coexisting, would, in this view, give Congress full jurisdiction as to the manufacture and sale of the latter. As the power of Congress is unlimited as to the selection of articles on which duties are to be levied, so by the exercise of this power its jurisdiction over domestic production and manufactures would be unlimited, and nothing would remain to the States of their ancient and undoubted jurisdiction over their internal business.

This *reductio ad absurdum* is a sufficient answer. But there is another answer as full and complete by direct argument. It is that the power of Congress is simply a power to regulate interstate and foreign commerce; that is, a power to prescribe rules for carrying on this commerce where it exists and as it is being actually carried on as between States and between the United States and foreign countries. This statute prescribes no rule for carrying on this commerce. On the contrary it prescribes a rule for carrying on something else; that is, for carrying on the business of manufacturing and producing domestic articles within the limits of a State and the sale of them even in the State of their origin.

I come now, Mr. President, to consider the power of Congress as proposed to be exerted in this bill in its first clause in relation to imports.

This clause makes it criminal to enter into a combination

or arrangement "with intent to prevent full and free competition in the importation, transportation, or sale of articles imported into the United States."

This is, to say the least of it, a singular provision. It is difficult to extract the meaning of the draughtsman.

Evidently as to "importation" preventing full and free competition in the importing of goods, the combination must precede the act of importation; otherwise it could not affect the importation. A combination to affect importation could not by any human power change or alter that which has already transpired, an act of importation already complete. So, if the bill be not absurd and impracticable on its face, we must make the unlawful agreement precede the act of importation. What, then, are we to do with the other words of the sentence, "transportation or sale of articles imported into the United States"? "Imported" means an act of importation already taken place. Note that the phrase "articles imported" means articles already imported. If it does not mean this, but is to be construed as if written "articles which shall be imported," then the agreement condemned must not only precede importation, but must precede the transportation and sale, which must also precede importation.

Then we have a provision which makes criminal an agreement to prevent competition in the transportation or sale of an article produced in a foreign country by whomsoever made and wheresoever made, and as to the time of the making indefinite and unlimited, except only that it shall precede the transportation and sale affected by it, which transportation and sale may have taken place anywhere on the face of the globe and at any time within the lives of the parties to the agreement. Of course a statute of that sort, embracing within its provisions transactions wholly without the territorial jurisdiction of Congress, can not stand. It will not help it that it may also embrace transactions within the jurisdiction of Congress, for in such a case, as I will show hereafter, the courts can not restrict the plain meaning of the words used, by running a line which Congress itself would not run, excluding the unconstitutional part and giving the statute operation and effect on those transactions which might fall within congressional power.

There is only one other conjectural meaning of this language, and that is that as to transportation and sale of the imported articles the meaning is: that the transportation and sale of the articles shall be after they are imported. This would confine the acts of transportation and sale to the United States—a place at least in which Congress has some jurisdiction. But here again we encounter the difficulty above alluded to, that the language embraces too much, embraces transactions within the power of Congress and transactions beyond or outside of this power. It embraces both interstate and domestic transportation; that is, transportation generally. Besides, the words "articles imported" are not the same as, nor equivalent in meaning to, the word "imports" in its constitutional sense. Articles once imported from a foreign country, always, as long as they remain in the United States, wherever situated and in whosesoever hands they may be and in whatsoever condition, as to being in the original package or not, continue to be "imported articles." That is, they are articles not of domestic production, but foreign articles which have been imported into the United States.

But "imports" in a constitutional sense are imported articles in the hands of the importer and in the original package. When they are sold to another or the package is broken, though there be no sale, then they cease to be "imports" in the constitutional sense; they cease to be within the jurisdiction of Congress to regulate and control, and become subject to State jurisdiction exclusively. They might be regulated as to interstate transportation, but, as we have seen, this is not provided for, but only transportation generally.

Senator George here cited on this point Brown *vs.* Maryland, reported in 12 Wheat. R., 419; License Cases, 5 Howard R., on pages 575 and 592, and Woodruff *vs.* Parham, 8 Wall.; Hinson *vs.* Lott, *ib.*

Mr. President, tested by these principles all that part of the bill that relates to these combinations in reference to the importation, transportation, and sale of goods imported into the United States must be unconstitutional, unless we restrict the plain meaning of the general language employed in the bill and confine it to transportation and sale of goods imported while they still remain imports; that is, to sale or transportation of the goods while they remain in the hands of the importer and also in the original bale or package in which they were imported. If we so restrict the meaning of the bill, it is utterly worthless, for the agreement may be made to relate only to the transportation of the goods after they have been sold by the importer, or being still owned by him after he has put them in a different bale or package from the one in which they were imported.

How worthless such a provision would be to suppress trusts is so evident as to need no comment. So of the sales of such articles. The combination need only relate to such sales by a purchaser from the importer, or even by the importer himself if he will only take the trouble to sell them in bales and packages made and put up after importation, to be wholly without the restraint of this bill. How near these transactions when they are beyond the jurisdiction of Congress may come to the act of importation is shown by the decision of the Supreme Court in Waring *vs.* Mayor (8 Wall. R., 110). In that case it was held that a purchaser of goods in transit from a foreign country to the United States and while at sea was not an importer if the agreement was that they should be at the risk of the seller till delivery. This purchaser not being an importer, the goods even in his hands and in the original packages after delivery remained no longer a part of the foreign commerce and subject to the jurisdiction of the United States.

But, Mr. President, we are not allowed to so restrict the language of the bill in this provision nor in the others which I have pointed out. (See United States *vs.* Reese, 92 U. S. R., 214, and Trade-mark cases, 100 U. S. R., page 82.)

This settles the unconstitutionality of the whole bill. That there are some things included in the general words of the bill which, if separately stated and disconnected from the great mass of the provisions of the bill, Congress can constitutionally enact is admitted. But they are not so separated, and, if they were, they are utterly without efficacy in remedying the great evil of these trusts and combinations, as has been shown.

But, Mr. President, there is another ground upon which the bill is clearly unconstitutional.

The bill is a proposition for the enactment of a penal or criminal statute. It does nothing but inflict penalties, either by civil or criminal procedure.

There are but few express powers granted by the Constitution for the enactment of criminal laws. They relate to punishing the counterfeiting of the coin and the securities of the United States and piracies and felonies on the high seas and offences against the law of nations. These are all the express powers for enacting criminal and penal legislation by Congress found in the Constitution.

Every other exercise of the power must be as an incident to some express power. In the language of the Constitution it must "be necessary and proper for carrying into execution" an expressly granted power. Congress must first determine to execute an express power before it can consider the propriety and necessity of assuming the incidental power. If the express power is found, that does not authorize Congress to exercise a power which might of itself be necessary and proper to the execution of that express power, if in fact there be no attempt to exercise the express power. The express power in this case is the power to regulate commerce among the States and with foreign nations.

Is there such a regulation in the bill? This question is easily answered. Recurring to what has been said—that regulation is prescribing a rule for doing the acts which constitute this commerce—we look in vain to the provisions of this bill to find such a regulation or rule.

Bearing in mind, Mr. President, that interstate commerce begins—so far as Federal jurisdiction over it comes from property, and not from the citizenship of the parties—with the beginning of transportation and ends with its completion, and that foreign commerce ends with the breaking of the original package or with a sale by the importer; that neither embraces production, manufacturing, or fitting articles for this commerce, with intent that they should be so afterwards employed, but that both relate only to articles already made and already actually embarked in interstate or foreign commerce, we see that there is not the slightest attempt in this bill to prescribe a rule by which such commerce shall be carried on.

Acts done with reference to the production of articles which are intended for such commerce—acts done with reference to articles which have been the subjects of such commerce—are by this bill made criminal, while that very commerce in these very articles which were so produced, brought into existence, or imported in violation of the provisions of the bill is wholly untouched. If the bill becomes a law, that commerce in these very articles will go on, or, as Chief Justice Marshall expresses it, will be carried on exactly in the same way in all respects whatsoever as if this bill had never been passed, and without the slightest variation or change, as in all other articles. Can that be a regulation of interstate or foreign commerce which regulates nothing done in that commerce, but something else? The something else is production and selling in a State, which all agree can not be regulated by Congress. Being such a regulation and being as such undoubtedly beyond the power of Congress, the bill can not be made constitutional as an incident to a regulation of interstate or foreign commerce, which is not only not regulated at all, but is left wholly untouched.

The Constitution is a reasonable instrument, designed to specify powers delegated to a general government. So far as these powers are granted expressly or by necessary implication for the execution of express powers, they are full and complete, as well as supreme, but the Constitution neither authorizes nor tolerates the absurdity of the exercise of a power as a necessary incident to and in aid of the execution of an express power when no attempt is made to execute the express power. We can not, therefore, assume a power which would be proper in the execution of an express power, and then pervert it, so that it will not be an execution of the express power, but will be, as exercised, a regulation of something else not within the jurisdiction of the Federal Government. For no incidental power is given as a separate and substantive power, independent of the execution of an express power to be exercised by Congress whenever and wherever it may seem desirable.

Such a power is always subordinate and conditioned for its existence on the necessity for its exercise for the proper execution of an express power; that is, for making effectual the actual exercise by Congress of the express power. All incidental powers are dormant, even non-existent, except in the promise of possible life to begin when their exercise is necessary to do their proper work in the actual execution of an express power. If the express power is not executed or not executed on the point to which an assumed incidental power is directed, then the alleged incidental power can not be evoked, for it can be constitutionally evoked only for execution, and only when its exercise is necessary and proper for executing the express power, and not for something else.

The bill regulates, not interstate or foreign commerce, but regulates, by penalties, contracts and agreements, etc., that are conspiracies of a certain character with the intent to do something else. That something else, or the end sought by the conspiracy, is not regulated at all. It remains perfectly lawful; lawful not only as a principal end, but lawful in the methods by which it is sought to be attained; lawful notwithstanding the criminal conspiracy. There is, be it remembered, no prohibition of the importation or transportation or sale of the articles imported, produced, manufactured, or sold by the conspiracy. Interstate and foreign traffic transportation and full and free commerce in them are wholly unregulated, but remain perfectly lawful and unrestrained. They remain not only unprohibited, but even meritorious—things fostered and promoted by our laws.

A criminal conspiracy is a combination or agreement of two or more to do an unlawful act or to do a lawful act in an unlawful manner. But here in this bill we have a criminal conspiracy made out of an agreement to do a thing, with the intent that it shall result in another thing, which is not only not unlawful, but meritorious, not only as to the act to be done, but as to the methods named in the bill as the gist of the crime. In other words, Congress usurps, as an incident to the power to regulate interstate and foreign commerce, the power to punish a thing, a conspiracy, over which it has *per se* no jurisdiction, and, at the same time and by the same law, the results of this conspiracy, when they become a part of that commerce and thereby become for the first time subject to the jurisdiction of Congress, are not only not criminal, but are encouraged and protected by our laws. Can such a usurpation stand?

The States may punish the conspiracy denounced in the bill without going further and declaring that commerce in the articles so produced shall be unlawful, because the States have full jurisdiction over the main or principal thing, the production, without reference to any subsequent commerce in them.

Senator George, in support of these positions, here cited United States *vs*. Fox, 95 United States Reports, 692.

Mr. President, I have shown that this bill is utterly unconstitutional, and, even if constitutional, utterly worthless. If we pass it we do not only a vain and useless thing; we do a wicked thing. We give to a suffering people, as a remedy for a great wrong, that which will not only prove utterly inefficient, but will prove an aggravation of the evils. There is, however, a power we can exercise: the power to reduce or abolish duties on the foreign competing articles. At the proper time I shall offer as a substitute for this bill an amendment looking to the exercise of that power.

On March 21 Senator Sherman submitted from the Committee on Finance an amendment to the bill. It substituted for section 2 the following section, adding it to section 1:

And the circuit court of the United States shall have original jurisdiction of all suits of a civil nature at common law or in equity arising under this section, and to issue all remedial process orders or writs proper and necessary to enforce its provisions. And the Attorney-General and the several district attorneys are hereby directed, in the name of the United States, to commence and prosecute all such cases to final judgment and execution.

It substituted for section 3 the following section, making it section 2:

SEC. 2. That any person or corporation injured or damnified by such arrangement, contract, agreement, trust, or combination defined in the first section of this act may sue for and recover, in any court of the United States of competent jurisdiction, without respect to the amount involved, of any person or corporation a party to a combination described in the first section of this act, twice the amount of damages sustained and the costs of the suit, together with a reasonable attorney's fee.

Senator Sherman supported the bill as amended.

The bill does not announce a new principle of law, but applies old and well recognized principles of the common law to the complicated jurisdiction of our State and Federal Government. Each State can and does prevent and control combinations within the limit of the State. This we do not propose to interfere with. The power of the State courts has been repeatedly exercised to set aside such combinations, but these courts are limited in their jurisdiction to the State, and, in our complex system of government, are admitted to be unable to deal with the great evil that now threatens us.

These two sections of the bill are distinct and different in their scope and object. The first invokes the power of the National Government in proper cases, to restrain such a combination, by mandatory proceedings, from interfering with the trade and commerce of the country, and the second section is to give to private parties a remedy for personal injury caused by such a combination.

The first section defines a civil remedy, and the courts will construe it liberally; they will prescribe the precise limits of the constitutional power of the Government; they will distinguish between lawful combinations in aid of production and unlawful combinations to prevent competition and in restraint of trade; they can operate on corporations by restraining orders and rules; they can declare the particular combination null and void and deal with it according to the nature and extent of the injuries.

In providing a remedy the intention of the combination is immaterial. The intention of a corporation can not be proven. If the natural effects of its acts are injurious, if they tend to produce evil results, if their policy is denounced by the law as against the common good, it may be restrained, be punished with a penalty or with damages, and in a proper case it may be deprived of its corporate powers and franchises. It is the tendency of a corporation, and not its intention, that the courts can deal with. Therefore the amendments first reported to the first section are not in the substitute.

The third section is a criminal statute applicable to individuals only, which would be construed strictly and is difficult to be enforced. In the present state of the law it is impossible to describe, in precise language, the nature and limits of the offence in terms specific enough for an indictment. It has therefore been omitted.

It is sometimes said that without this section the law would be nugatory. I do not think so. The powers granted by the first section are ample to check and prevent the great body of illegal combinations that may be made, but if not it is easy enough hereafter to provide a suitable punishment for a violation of this statute. Every corporation engaged in business must be responsible for the tendency of its business, whether lawful or unlawful, but individuals can be punished only for criminal intentions. To require the intentions of a corporation to be proved is to impose an impossible condition and would defeat the object of the law. To restrain and prevent the illegal tendency of a corporation is the proper duty of a court of equity. To punish the criminal intention of an officer is a much more difficult process and might be well left to the future.

This bill, as I would have it, has for its single object to arm the Federal courts within the limits of their constitutional power that they may coöperate with the State courts in checking, curbing, and controlling the most dangerous combinations that now threaten the business, property, and trade of the people of the United States. And for one I do not intend to be turned from this course by fine-spun constitutional quibbles or by the plausible pretexts of associated or corporate wealth and power.

It is said that this bill will interfere with lawful trade,

with the customary business of life. I deny it. It aims only at unlawful combinations. It does not in the least affect combinations in aid of production where there is free and fair competition. It is the right of every man to work, labor, and produce in any lawful vocation and to transport his production on equal terms and conditions and under like circumstances. This is industrial liberty and lies at the foundation of the equality of all rights and privileges.

The right to combine the capital and labor of two or more persons in a given pursuit with a community of profit and loss under the name of a partnership is open to all and is not an infringement of industrial liberty, but is an aid to production. The law of partnership clearly defines what is a lawful and what is an unlawful partnership. The same business is open to every other partnership, and, while it is a combination, it does not in the slightest degree prevent competition.

The combination of labor and capital in the form of a corporation to carry on any lawful business is a proper and useful expedient, especially for great enterprises of a quasi-public character, and ought to be encouraged and protected as tending to cheapen the cost of production, but these corporate rights should be open to all upon the same terms and conditions. Such corporations, being mere creatures of law, can only exercise the powers specially granted and defined. Experience has shown that they are the most useful agencies of modern civilization. They have enabled individuals to unite to undertake great enterprises only attempted in former times by powerful governments. The good results of corporate power are shown in the vast development of our railroads and the enormous increase of business and production of all kinds.

When corporations unite merely to extend their business, as connecting lines of railway without interfering with competing lines, they are proper and lawful. Corporations tend to cheapen transportation, lessen the cost of production, and bring within the reach of millions comforts and luxuries formerly enjoyed by thousands. Formerly corporations were special grants to favored companies, but now the principle is generally adopted that no private corporation shall be created with exclusive rights or privileges. The corporate rights granted to one are open to all. In this way more than three thousand national banks have been formed with the same rights and privileges, and the business is open to all competitors. In most of the States general railroad laws provide the terms on which all railroads may be built, with like rights and privileges. Corporate rights open to all are not in any sense a monopoly, but tend to promote free competition of all on the same conditions. They are mere creatures of the law, ordained to exercise only well defined powers, and they are not in any way interfered with by this bill.

This bill does not seek to cripple combinations of capital and labor, the formation of partnerships or of corporations, but only to prevent and control combinations made with a view to prevent competition, or for the restraint of trade, or to increase the profits of the producer at the cost of the consumer. It is the unlawful combination, tested by the rules of common law and human experience, that is aimed at by this bill, and not the lawful and useful combination. Unlawful combinations made by individuals are declared by the several States to be against public policy and void, and in proper cases they may be punished as criminals. If their business is lawful they can combine in any way and enjoy the advantage of their united skill and capital, provided they do not combine to prevent competition. A limited monopoly secured by a patent right is an admitted exception, for this is the only way by which an inventor can be paid for his invention.

Any other attempt by individuals to secure a monopoly should be subject to the law of restraint applied to partnerships and corporations. A partnership is unlawful when its business tends to restrain trade, to deal in forbidden productions, or to encourage immoral and injurious pursuits, such as lotteries and the like, but, if its business is lawful and open to competition with others with like skill and capital, it can not be dangerous. A corporation may be, and usually is, a more powerful and useful combination than a partnership. It is an artificial person without fear of death, without a soul to save or body to punish, but if other corporations can be formed on equal terms a monopoly is impossible. If it becomes powerful enough to exercise an undue influence in one State it is met by free competition with producers in all the other States in the Union and by importation from all the world, subject only to such duties as the public necessities demand.

But associated enterprise and capital are not satisfied with partnerships and corporations competing with each other, and have invented a new form of combination commonly called trusts, that seeks to avoid competition by combining the controlling corporations, partnerships, and individuals engaged in the same business, and placing the power and property of the combination under the government of a few individuals, and often under the control of a single man called a trustee, a chairman, or a president.

The sole object of such a combination is to make competition impossible. It can control the market, raise or lower prices, as will best promote its selfish interests, reduce prices in a particular locality and break down competition and advance prices at will where competition does not exist. Its governing motive is to increase the profits of the parties composing it. The law of selfishness, uncontrolled by competition, compels it to disregard the interest of the consumer. It dictates terms to transportation companies, it commands the price of labor without fear of strikes, for in its field it allows no competitors. Such a combination is far more dangerous than any heretofore invented, and, when it embraces the great body of all the corporations engaged in a particular industry in all of the States of the Union, it tends to advance the price to the consumer of any article produced, it is a substantial monopoly injurious to the public, and, by the rule of both the common and the civil law, is null and void and the just subject of restraint by the courts, of forfeiture of corporate rights and privileges, and in some cases should be denounced as a crime, and the individuals engaged in it should be punished as criminals. It is this kind of a combination we have to deal with now.

If the concentered powers of this combination are intrusted to a single man, it is a kingly prerogative, inconsistent with our form of government, and should be subject to the strong resistance of the State and national authorities. If anything is wrong this is wrong. If we will not endure a king as a political power we should not endure a king over the production, transportation, and sale of any of the necessaries of life. If we would not submit to an emperor we should not submit to an autocrat of trade, with power to prevent competition and to fix the price of any commodity. If the combination is confined to a State the State should apply the remedy; if it is interstate and controls any production in many States, Congress must apply the remedy. If the combination is aided by our tariff laws they should be promptly changed, and, if necessary, equal competition with all the world should be invited in the monopolized article. If the combination affects interstate transportation or is aided in any way by a transportation company, it falls clearly within the power of Congress, and the remedy should be aimed at the corporations embraced in it, and should be swift and sure.

Do I exaggerate the evil we have to deal with? I do not

think so. I do not wish to single out any particular trust or combination. It is not a particular trust, but the system I am at. I will only cite a very few instances of combinations that have been the subject of judicial or legislative inquiry, to show what has been and what can be done by them.

Here the Senator cited the opinion of Judge Baxter, in the case of Handy *et al.*, Trustees *vs.* Cleveland and Marietta Railroad Company, Federal Reporter, Volume 31, pages 689 to 693, inclusive. This case related to discrimination in rates in favor of the Standard Oil Company against George Rice, its competitor.

It also appears in an equity suit in which the Commonwealth of Pennsylvania was complainant and the Pennsylvania Railroad Company was defendant, filed in the Supreme Court of Pennsylvania for the Western District, in 1879, and where A. J. Cassatt, then third vice-president in charge of the transportation department of the Pennsylvania Railroad Company, testified that the Standard Oil Company were receiving over and above current drawbacks certain rebates and allowances.

Another case of unlawful combination was the case of David M. Richardson *vs.* Russell A. Alger *et al.*, recently decided in the supreme court of the State of Michigan. I have the opinion by the chief justice which sufficiently states the nature of the combination and the view taken of it by that court. This is quite a leading case.

November 15, 1889.

SHERWOOD, C. J. I think no one can read the contract in question and fail to discover that considerations of public policy are largely involved. The intention of the agreement is to aid in securing the objects sought to be attained in the formation and organization of the Diamond Match Company. This object is openly and boldly avowed. Its articles provide for the aggregation of an enormous amount of capital, sufficient to buy up and absorb all of that kind of business done in the United States and Canada, and to prevent any other person or corporation from engaging in or carrying on the same, thereby preventing all competition in the sale of the articles manufactured.

The sole object of the corporation is to make money by having it in its power to raise the price of the article or diminish the quantity to be made and used at its pleasure.

Thus, both the supply of the article and the price thereof are made to depend upon the action of a half dozen individuals, more or less, to satisfy their cupidity and avarice, who may happen to have the controlling interest in this corporation—an artificial person—governed by a single motive or purpose, which is to accumulate money, regardless of the wants and necessities of over sixty millions of people.

Monopoly in trade, or in any kind of business in this country, is odious to our form of government. It is sometimes permitted to aid the Government in carrying on a great public enterprise or public work under governmental control in the interest of the public. This tendency is, however, destructive of free institutions and repugnant to the instincts of a free people, and contrary to the whole scope and spirit of the Federal Constitution, and is not allowed to exist, under express provision in several of our State constitutions.

Indeed, it is doubtful if free government can long exist in a country where such enormous amounts of money are allowed to be accumulated in the vaults of corporations, to be used at discretion in controlling the property and business of the country against the interests of the public and that of the people for the personal gain and aggrandizement of a few individuals.

It is always destructive of individual rights and of that free competition which is the life of business, and it revives and perpetuates one of the great evils which it was the object of the framers of our form of government to eradicate and prevent. It is alike destructive to both individual enterprise and individual prosperity, and therefore public policy is, and ought to be, as well as public sentiment, against it.

All combinations among persons or corporations for the purpose of raising or controlling the prices of merchandise or any of the necessaries of life are monopolies and intolerable, and ought to receive the condemnation of all courts.

In my judgment, not only is the enterprise in which the Diamond Match Company is engaged an unlawful one, but the contract in question in this case, being made to further its objects and purposes, is void, upon the ground that it is against public policy.

CHAMPLIN, J. Such a vast combination is a menace to the public; its object and direct tendency is to prevent free and fair competition and control prices throughout the national domain. It is no answer to say that this monopoly has in fact reduced the price of friction matches. That policy may have been necessary to crush competition. The fact exists that it rests in the discretion of this company at any time to raise the price to an exorbitant degree. Such combinations have frequently been condemned by courts as unlawful and against public policy:

Hooker *vs.* Vandemater, 4 Denio, 349, etc.

It is not necessary that the parties, or either of them, should rely upon the fact that the contract is one which it is against the policy of the law to enforce. Courts will take notice of their own motion of illegal contracts which come before them for adjudication, and will leave the parties where they have placed themselves.

Campbell, J., concurred with Mr. Justice Champlin.

Senator Sherman cited similar decisions of courts in other States, and stated that all the State courts had so decided.

And now it is for Congress to say, when the devices of able lawyers and the cupidity of powerful corporations have united to spread these combinations over all the States of the Union, embracing in their folds nearly every necessary of life, whether it is not time to invoke the judicial power conferred upon the courts of the United States to deal with these combinations, when lawful to support them and when unlawful to suppress them.

I have seen within a few days in the public prints a notice of a combination intended to affect the price of silver bullion, as follows:

WITH A CAPITAL OF TWENTY-FIVE MILLION DOLLARS.

CHICAGO, *March* 2.

The *Herald* to-day says that, with the exception of five companies, all the refining and smelting companies of the United States have formed a trust, with a capital of $25,000,000, of which $15,000,000 is to be common stock and the remainder preferred.

If such a combination is formed it will enable a few corporations in different States to corner the Government of the United States in its proposed effort, by a bill pending in the Senate, to purchase silver bullion as the basis and security for paper money. Can any one doubt that such a combination is unlawful, against public policy, with power enough to control the operation of your laws, and destructive to all competition which you invite?

It is scarcely necessary on this point to quote further from the law books. Every decision or treatise on the law of contracts agrees in denouncing such a combination.

Judge Gibson, in the case of the Commonwealth of Pennsylvania *vs.* Carlisle, states the general principle in terse and vigorous language:

A combination is criminal whenever the act to be done has a necessary tendency to prejudice the public or to oppress individuals by unjustly subjecting them to the power of the confederates, and giving effect to the purpose of the latter, whether of extortion or of mischief.

The solicitor of the Standard Oil Trust, Mr. Dodd, in an argument which I have before me, admits that certain combinations are null and void. He says:

The law is properly very jealous of certain classes of combinations, such as—

First. Where the parties combining exercise a public employment or possess exclusive privileges, and are to that extent monopolies.

Second. Where the purpose and effect of the combination is to "corner" any article necessary to the public.

Third. Where the purpose and effect of the combination is to limit production, and thereby to unduly enhance prices.

.   .   .   .

These things are just as unlawful without combination as with it. In other words, the evil is not in the combination, but in its purposes and results.

I accept the law, as stated by Mr. Dodd, that all combinations are not void, a proposition which no one doubts, but I assert that the tendency of all combinations of corporations, such as those commonly called trusts, and the inevitable effect

THE VULTURES' ROOST

By E. W. Kemble in "Collier's Weekly"

of them, is to prevent competition and to restrain trade. This must be manifest to every intelligent mind. Still this can not be assumed as against any combination unless upon a fair hearing it should appear to a court of competent jurisdiction that the agreement composing such combination is necessarily injurious to the public and destructive to fair trade. These modern combinations are uniformly composed of citizens and corporations of many States, and therefore they can be dealt with only by a jurisdiction as broad as their combination.

I admit that it is difficult to define in legal language the precise line between lawful and unlawful combinations. This must be left for the courts to determine in each particular case. All that we, as lawmakers, can do is to declare general principles, and we can be assured that the courts will apply them so as to carry out the meaning of the law, as the courts of England and the United States have done for centuries. This bill is only an honest effort to declare a rule of action, and if it is imperfect it is for the wisdom of the Senate to perfect it. Although this body is always conservative, yet, whatever may be said of it, it has always been ready to preserve, not only popular rights in their broad sense, but the rights of individuals as against associated and corporate wealth and power.

It is sometimes said of these combinations that they reduce prices to the consumer by better methods of production, but all experience shows that this saving of cost goes to the pockets of the producer. The price to the consumer depends upon the supply, which can be reduced at pleasure by the combination. It will vary in time and place by the extent of competition, and when that ceases it will depend upon the urgency of the demand for the article. The aim is always for the highest price that will not check the demand, and, for the most of the necessaries of life, that is perennial and perpetual.

But, they say, competition is open to all; if you do not like our prices, establish another combination or trust. As was said by the supreme court of New York, when the combination already includes all or nearly all the producers, what room is there for another? And, if another is formed and is legal, what is to prevent another combination? Sir, now the people of the United States, as well as of other countries, are feeling the power and grasp of these combinations, and are demanding of every legislature and of Congress a remedy for this evil, only grown into huge proportions in recent times. They had monopolies and mortmains of old, but never before such giants as in our day. You must heed their appeal or be ready for the socialist, the communist, and the nihilist. Society is now disturbed by forces never felt before.

The popular mind is agitated with problems that may disturb social order, and among them all none is more threatening than the inequality of condition, of wealth, and opportunity that has grown within a single generation out of the concentration of capital into vast combinations to control production and trade and to break down competition. These combinations already defy or control powerful transportation corporations and reach State authorities. They reach out their Briarean arms to every part of our country. They are imported from abroad. Congress alone can deal with them, and if we are unwilling or unable there will soon be a trust for every production and a master to fix the price for every necessity of life.

But it is said by the Senator from Mississippi [Mr. George] that this bill is unconstitutional, that Congress can not confer jurisdiction on the courts of the United States in this class of cases. I respectfully submit that, in his subtle argument, he has entirely overlooked the broad jurisdiction conferred by the Constitution upon courts of the United States in ordinary cases of law and equity between certain parties, as well as cases arising under the Constitution, laws, and treaties of the United States. Much the greater proportion of the cases decided in these courts have no relation to the Constitution, laws, or treaties. They embrace admiralty and maritime law, all controversies in which the United States are a party, controversies between two or more States, between a State and citizens of another State, between citizens of different States, between citizens of the same State claiming lands under grants of different States, and between a State, or the citizens thereof, and foreign states, citizens, or subjects.

This jurisdiction embraces the whole field of the common law and of commercial law, especially of the law of contracts, in all cases where the United States is a party and in all cases between citizens of different States. The jurisdiction is as broad as the earth, except only it does not extend to controversies within a State between citizens of a State. All the combinations at which this bill aims are combinations embracing persons and corporations of several States. Each State can deal with a combination within the State, but only the general Government can deal with combinations reaching not only the several States, but the commercial world. This bill does not include combinations within a State, but if the Senator from Mississippi can make this clearer any proposition he will make to that effect will certainly be accepted and I will cheerfully vote for his proposition. Can any one doubt the jurisdiction of the courts of the United States in all cases in which the United States is a party and in all cases between citizens, including corporations, of different States? I will read a note from Story on the Constitution:

It has been very correctly remarked by Mr. Justice Iredell that "the judicial power of the United States is of a peculiar kind. It is, indeed, commensurate with the ordinary legislative and executive government and the powers which concern treaties. But it also goes further. When certain parties are concerned, although the subject in controversy does not relate to any special objects of authority of the General Government, wherein the separate sovereignties of the separate States are blended in one common mass of supremacy, yet the General Government has a judicial authority in regard to such subjects of controversy; and the Legislature of the United States may pass all laws necessary to give such judicial authority its proper effect."

The judicial power of the United States extends to all questions of law and equity which arise between citizens of different States or between the other classes named. The jurisdiction of the courts of the United States may depend either upon the nature of the causes arising under the Constitution, laws, or treaties of the United States, or upon the parties to the case. [See decisions of Chief Justice Marshall, in the case of Cohens vs. Virginia, 6 Wheaton, page 378, and Osborn vs. Bank of the United States, 9 Wheaton, page 738.]

By the Constitution of the United States this jurisdiction or the courts of the United States extends to all cases in law and equity between certain parties. What is meant by the words of "cases in law and equity"? Does this include only cases growing out of the Constitution, statutes, and treaties of the United States? It has been held over and over again that, by these words, the Constitution has adopted as a rule of remedial justice the common law of England as administered by courts of law and equity. [See Judge Story, in his work on the Constitution, Volume 2, page 485.]

I submit that this bill as it stands, without any reference to the specific powers granted to Congress by the Constitution, is clearly authorized under the judicial article of the Constitution. This bill declares a rule of public policy in accordance with the rule of the common law. It limits its operation to certain important functions of the Government, among which are the importation, transportation, and sale of articles imported into the United States, the production, manufacture, or sale of articles of domestic growth or production, and domestic raw materials competing with a similar article upon which a duty is levied by the United States.

If this bill were broader than it is and declared unlawful all trusts and combinations in restraint of trade and production null and void, there could be no question that in suits brought by the United States to enforce it, or suits between individuals or corporations of different States for injuries done in violation of it, it would be clearly within the power of Congress and the jurisdiction of the court. The mere limitation of this jurisdiction to certain classes of combinations does not affect in the slightest degree the power of Congress to pass a much broader and more comprehensive bill.

Nor is it necessary to limit the jurisdiction of the courts of the United States to suits between citizens of different States. It extends also to suits by the United States when authorized by law. It is eminently proper that when a combination of persons or corporations of different States tends to affect injuriously the interests or powers of the United States, as well as of citizens of the United States, the proceeding should be in the courts of the United States and in the name of the United States. The legal process of *quo warranto* or *mandamus* ought, in such cases, to be issued at the suit of the United States. A citizen would appear in such a suit at every disadvantage, and even the United States is scarcely the equal of a powerful corporation in a suit where a single officer with insufficient pay is required to compete with the ablest lawyers who are encouraged with compensation far beyond the limits allowed to the highest Government officer. It is in such proceedings that the battle with these great combinations is to be fought.

But, aside from the power drawn from the third article of the Constitution, I believe this bill is clearly within the power conferred expressly upon Congress to regulate commerce with foreign nations and among the several States and its power to levy and collect taxes, duties, imposts, and excises.

And here, Mr. President, I wish to again call attention to the argument of the Senator from Mississippi [Mr. George]. He treats this bill as a criminal statute from beginning to end, and not as a remedial statute with civil remedies. He says:

The first thing which attracts our attention, therefore, is that if the agreement or combination, which is the crime, be made outside of the jurisdiction of the United States it is also without the terms of the law and can not be punished in the United States.

It is true that if a crime is committed outside of the United States it can not be punished in the United States. But if an unlawful combination is made outside of the United States and in pursuance of it property is brought within the United States such property is subject to our laws. It may be seized. A civil remedy by attachment could be had. Any person interested in the United States could be made a party.

Either a foreigner or a native may escape "the criminal part of the law," as he says, by staying out of our jurisdiction, as very many do, but if they have property here it is subject to civil process. I do not see what harm a foreigner can do us if neither his person nor his property is here. He may combine or conspire to his heart's content if none of his co-conspirators are here or his property is not here.

Again he says:

But suppose, what I think, however, is highly improbable, some of these great combinations should be made in the United States. Will the case be any better for the people in whose interest we profess to legislate? The combination, agreement, or trusts, etc., must, under the bill, be made "with the intention to prevent full and free competition in the importation, transportation, or sale of articles imported into the United States."

The word "intention" is not in the bill. It was proposed as an amendment.

SENATOR GEORGE.—When the bill came back from the committee it had the word in it.

SENATOR SHERMAN.—But the bill as it comes from the committee now has certainly no such word in it. The language is: "made with a view or which tend." The *"intention"* can not be proved, though *"tendency"* can. The tendency is the test of legality. The intention is the test of a crime.

All through the Senator's speech he quotes the phrases of a "certain specified intent," "specific intent," "penal legislation," "reasonable doubt," "indicted must be acquitted." He treats this bill very much as he does the Constitution of the United States, something to be evaded, to be strictly construed, instead of being what it is, a remedial statute, a bill of rights, a charter of liberty. He no doubt is partly justified in this by the amendments proposed, but not adopted, and by the third section, which would be subject to his criticism, and which I will join him in striking out.

Now, Mr. President, what is this bill? A remedial statute to enforce by civil process in the courts of the United States the common law against monopolies. How is such a law to be construed? Liberally with a view to promote its objects. What are the evils complained of? They are well depicted by the Senator from Mississippi in this language, and I will read it as my own with quotation marks.

SENATOR GEORGE.—I am very much obliged for the compliment.

SENATOR SHERMAN read the paragraph of Mr. George beginning, "These trusts and combinations are great wrongs to the people."

One would think that with this conception of the evil to be dealt with he would for once turn his telescope upon the Constitution to find out power to deal with so great a wrong, and not, as usual, to reverse it, to turn the little end of the telescope to the Constitution, and then, with subtle reasoning, to dissipate the powers of the Government into thin air. He overlooks the judicial power of the courts of the United States extending to all cases where the United States is a party, or where a State may sue in the courts of the United States, or where citizens of different States are contesting parties with full power to apply a remedy by *quo warranto, mandamus,* judgment, and execution. He treats the question as depending alone upon the power to regulate foreign and domestic commerce and of taxation. I submit that, without reference to the judicial power, they are amply sufficient to justify this bill. What are they?

Congress shall have power to regulate commerce with foreign nations and among the several States and with the Indian tribes.

The want of this power was one of the leading defects of the Confederation, and probably as much as any one cause conduced to the establishment of a Constitution. It is a power vital to the prosperity of the Union, and without it the Government could scarcely deserve the name of a National Government and would soon sink into discredit and imbecility. It would stand as a mere shadow of sovereignty to mock our hopes and involve us in a common ruin. [Story on the Constitution, Volume 2, page 2.]

What is the extent of this power? What is the meaning of the word "commerce"? It means the exchange of all commodities between different places or communities. It includes all trade and traffic, all modes of transportation by land or by sea, all kinds of navigation, every species of ship or sail, every mode of transit, from the dog-cart to the Pullman car, every kind of motive power, from the mule or horse to the most recent application of steam or electricity applied on every road, from

XI—4

the trail over the mountain or the plain to the perfected railway or the steel bridges over great rivers or arms of the sea. The power of Congress extends to all this commerce, except only that limited within the bounds of a State.

Under this power no bridge can be built over a navigable stream except by the consent of Congress. All the network of railroads crossing from State to State, from ocean to ocean, from east to west, and from north to south are now curbed, regulated, and controlled by the power of Congress over commerce. Most of the combinations aimed at by this bill are directly engaged in this commerce. They command and control in many cases and even own some of the agencies of this commerce. They have invented or own new modes of transportation, such as pipe-lines for petroleum or gas, reaching from State to State, crossing farms and highways and public property.

Can it be that with this vast power Congress can not protect the people from combinations in restraint of trade that are unlawful by every code of civil law adopted by civilized nations? It may "regulate commerce"; can it not protect commerce, nullify contracts that restrain commerce, turn it from its natural courses, increase the price of articles, and therefore diminish the amount of commerce?

It is said that commerce does not commence until production ends and the voyage commences. This may be true as far as the actual ownership or sale of articles within a State is subject to State authorities. I do not question the decision of the Supreme Court in the case of Coe *vs.* Errol, quoted by the Senator from Mississippi, that property within a State is subject to taxation though intended to be transported into another State. This bill does not propose to deal with property within a State or with combinations within the State, but only when the combination extends to two or more States or engages in either State or foreign commerce. It is said that these combinations can and will evade this bill. I have no doubt they will do so in many cases, but they can do so only by ceasing to interfere with foreign and interstate commerce.

Their power for mischief will be greatly crippled by this bill. Their present plan of organization was adopted only to evade the jurisdiction of State courts. They still maintain their workshops, their mode of production, by means of partnerships or corporations in a State. If their productions competed with those of similar partnerships or corporations in other States it would be all right. But to prevent such competition they unite the interests of all these partnerships and corporations into a combination, sometimes called a trust, sometimes a new corporation, located in a city remote from the places of production, and then regulate and control the sale and transportation of all the products of many States, discontinuing one at their will, some running at half time, others pressed at their full capacity, fixing the price at pleasure in every mart of the United States, dictating terms to transportation companies, controlling your commerce, and yet it is said that Congress, armed with full power to regulate commerce, is helpless and unable to deal with this monster.

Sir, the object aimed at by this bill is to secure competition of the productions of different States which necessarily enter into interstate and foreign commerce. These combinations strike directly at the commerce over which Congress alone has jurisdiction. "Congress may regulate interstate and foreign commerce," and it is absurd to contend that Congress may not prohibit contracts and arrangements that are hostile to such commerce.

Congress also has power "to lay and collect taxes, duties, imposts, and excises." It may exercise its own discretion in acting upon this power, and is only responsible to the people for the abuse of the power. All parties, from the foundation of the Government, have held that Congress may discriminate in selecting the objects and rates of taxation. Some of these taxes are levied for the direct and some for the incidental encouragement and increase of home industries. The people pay high taxes on the foreign article to induce competition at home, in the hope that the price may be reduced by competition, and with the benefit of diversifying our industries and increasing the common wealth.

Suppose one of these combinations should unite all, or nearly all, the domestic producers of an article of prime necessity with a view to prevent competition and to keep the price up to the foreign cost and duty added, would not this be in restraint of trade and commerce and affect injuriously the operation of our revenue laws? Can Congress prescribe no remedy except to repeal its taxes? Surely it may authorize the executive authorities to appeal to the courts of the United States for such a remedy as courts habitually apply in the States for the forfeiture of charters thus abused and the punishment of officers who practice such wrongs to the public. It may also give to our citizens the right to sue for such damages as they have suffered.

In no respect does the work of our fathers in framing the Constitution of the United States appear more like the work of the Almighty Ruler of the Universe rather than the conception of human minds than by the gradual development and application of the powers conferred by it upon different branches of the Federal Government. Many of these powers have remained dormant, unused, but plainly there, awaiting the growth and progress of our country, and when the time comes and the occasion demands we find in that instrument, provided for thirteen States, a thread along the Atlantic and containing four millions of people, without manufactures, without commerce, bankrupt with debt, without credit or wealth, all the powers necessary to govern a continental empire of forty-two States, with sixty-five millions of people, the largest in manufactures, the second in wealth, and the happiest in its institutions of all the nations of the world.

While we should not stretch the powers granted to Congress by strained construction, we can not surrender any of them; they are not ours to surrender, but whenever occasion calls we should exercise them for the benefit and protection of the people of the United States. And, sir, while I have no doubt that every word of this bill is within the powers granted to Congress, I feel that its defects are in its moderation, and that its best effect will be a warning that all trade and commerce, all agreements and arrangements, all struggles for money or property, must be governed by the universal law that the public good must be the test of all.

George G. Vest [Mo.] opposed the bill.

I take it that there will be no controversy with the Senator from Ohio as to the enormity of the abuses that have grown up under the system of trusts and combinations which now prevails in every portion of the Union. What we desire is one thing; what we can accomplish under the autonomy of our Government is another.

I deprecate as much as the Senator from Ohio can possibly do that spirit of hypercriticism which would consider the Constitution of the United States as a bill of indictment. I believe that it is a great bill of human rights, conservative, liberty-preserving, liberty-administering; and it is conservative, it preserves and administers liberty because it is a written Constitution and not because it is given to Congress to legislate as it sees proper, under the general and nebulous presumption of the general welfare, without regard to the grants that are made by the people to them as their legislative servants.

The grants of power to the courts of the United States are limited also by this written Constitution, and the grants of power in the judicial clause of the Constitution consist of two sorts: first, the jurisdiction which comes from the character of the litigants; and, secondly, the jurisdiction that comes from the subject-matter involved.

As I understand the provisions of the original bill reported by the Senator from Ohio and the amendment which he offers now as a substitute, the attempt is made under one or the other of these two classes of jurisdiction, and then, permit me to say respectfully, by an uncertain and nebulous commingling of the two to give the power to Congress to pass this proposed act.

I know how ungrateful and dangerous it is now for a public man to object to this kind of legislation against this terrible evil, this enormous abuse of trusts and combines which the whole country is properly denouncing. I appreciate fully the significance of the remark of the Senator from Ohio when he says that unless relief is given, to use the language of Mr. Jefferson, "worse will ensue."

But, sir, even in the face of the popular indignation which may be visited upon any one who criticises any measure that looks to the destruction of this evil, I can not violate my oath to support the Constitution and all the habitudes of thought which have come to me as a lawyer educated and trained in my profession.

For Congress to pass a law which will be thrown out of the Supreme Court under the terrible criticism that any such law must invoke is simply to subject ourselves to ridicule and to say to our constituents that we are powerless to enact laws which will give them relief.

This bill, if it becomes a law, must go through the crucible of a legal criticism which will avail itself of the highest legal talent throughout the entire Union. It will go through a furnace not seven times, but seventy-seven times heated, because the ablest lawyers in this country, it goes without saying, are on the side of the corporations and of aggregated wealth.

Without invoking this spirit of hypercriticism, which the Senator from Ohio deprecates, let us look at the provisions of the original bill and then of the amendment which he proposes shall take its place. In the original bill the Senator from Ohio undertakes to derive jurisdiction in Congress, not from the character of the litigants, but from the subject-matter in litigation.

For the able argument of the Senator from Mississippi [Mr. George] against the original bill I have no words to express my admiration as a lawyer. I was exceedingly glad that it was made, because it is just through that species of argumentation that this legislation must pass.

It must be subjected to the crucible which was brought here by the Senator from Mississippi in that admirable dissertation upon constitutional power. After that argument was made the Senator from Ohio found it necessary to amend this original bill, and he did so by putting into it another element of jurisdiction, and that was the character of the litigants, in addition to the jurisdiction he had already invoked as to the subject-matter.

It is plain that the Senator from Ohio, recognizing the weakness of the original bill, attempted to invoke that idea which is found in the Constitution of the United States and the judiciary act of 1789, that citizenship in different States conferred Federal jurisdiction.

Now, let us see if the Senator by any such process as that can evade the argument made by the Senator from Mississippi. Sir, I shall not attempt to make any elaborate argument, but will simply read the Constitution and then inquire under what clause the legislative jurisdiction to enact this bill can be found. The Constitution of the United States provides as to the judicial power as follows:

> The judicial power shall extend to all cases, in law and equity.

If it had stopped there much of the argument of the Senator from Ohio would have been pertinent, but it goes further:

> All cases, in law and equity, arising under this Constitution,

That is to say, you must find the jurisdiction within the limits of this instrument——

> the laws of the United States—

There is another grant—

> and treaties made, or which shall be made, under their authority.
> To all cases affecting ambassadors, other public ministers and consuls; to all cases of admiralty and maritime jurisdiction; to controversies to which the United States shall be a party; to controversies between two or

more States; between a State and citizens of another State; between citizens of different States,—between citizens of the same State claiming lands under grants of different States, and between a State, or the citizens thereof, and foreign States, citizens or subjects.

Mr. President, let us take these clauses separately and see whether the power to pass this bill can be found under all or any of them. I shall reserve until the last my comments upon the first clause, because I think it can be established beyond any doubt that the jurisdiction is not found in the other clauses that follow. If this bill can be sustained at all, it is because there is a clause in the Constitution which authorizes it outside of the other clauses, which I shall proceed to enumerate. For instance, the next clause is:

To all cases affecting ambassadors, other public ministers, and consuls.

Unquestionably the power is not there. No minister, no consul is involved in this legislation.

To all cases of admiralty and maritime jurisdiction.

Unquestionably it is not found there, because the bill proposes only to affect contracts made upon land. Next:

To controversies in which the United States shall be a party.

Unquestionably it does not affect that unless it be in that uncertain and unsatisfactory statement of the Senator from Ohio that he means in one clause of his amendment to give to the United States the power to proceed by *quo warranto,* injunction, or otherwise. In his original bill he had a direct criminal proceeding on the part of the Government of the United States against these trusts and he struck it out in the substitute. He has eliminated from this discussion the direct criminal proceeding in the name of the United States against the parties composing this trust and against the trust itself. There is no machinery provided for any proceeding by the United States in his amendment, but only the uncertain state‧ ment that the United States may proceed by remedial process. There is nothing else to lead us to believe that he intends that the United States shall do anything else except proceed in some fashion by information against the persons composing these trusts or the trusts themselves.

To controversies between two or more States.

Unquestionably the bill is not under that clause.

Between a State and citizens of another State.

There is nothing in this amendment which gives jurisdiction under that clause.

Between citizens of different States, between citizens of the same State claiming lands under grants of different States, and between a State, or the citizens thereof, and foreign states, citizens, or subjects.

Of course there will be no contention that the jurisdiction is found under that clause. It must be then found under the clause——

SENATOR SHERMAN.—I have stated that the jurisdiction is sufficiently conferred in the ordinary language of the judiciary act of 1789, in all controversies in which the United States is a party and in controversies between citizens of different States. I did not claim any other power.

SENATOR VEST.—Unquestionably where there is any litigation between citizens of different States the Federal courts have jurisdiction, no matter what is the subject-matter. But here is a bill which is put upon no such ground. The bill says:

All arrangements, contracts, agreements, trusts, or combinations between two or more citizens or corporations, or both, of different States, or between two or more citizens or corporations, or both, of the United States and foreign states.

Not where there are litigants, not where one is plaintiff and the other is defendant. There is where the Constitution gives Federal jurisdiction. If the corporation itself is composed of citizens of different States then this jurisdiction attaches. Any citizen can sue, although he lives in the same State with the corporation. There is the distinction.

Let me say that it excludes all the remedy that can be given to any citizen of the United States against the enormous evils depicted by the Senator from Ohio, because, if this bill be passed and the Supreme Court of the United States decides it constitutional, you will never hear of the corporation which proposes to create or manipulate a trust that does not have the personnel of its stockholders all in the same State. That goes without saying, and it is to impute idiocy to the men whose schemes and machinations we are now attacking to suppose that they would do anything else. The idea that they, with the best counsel in the United States and even in the world, with the highest legal talent upon their side, will not immediately construct their corporations so as to nullify such a law is to impute to them a degree of mental imbecility that is simply ludicrous.

The Senator makes no distinction between the parties to the suit and the composition of the corporation which is itself a plaintiff or a defendant. He puts this jurisdiction upon something unknown to the Constitution, and the result would be (and it can be read between the lines) that if we enacted this into law the Supreme Court of the United States would immediately confront us with that clause of the Constitution and the judiciary act of 1789 and throw the case out of court.

It is very obvious that this attempt to invoke the web and woof of the judiciary act of 1789, which was made in pursuance of the clause of the Constitution that I have read, is an uncertain commingling of two elements utterly incongruous and utterly inconsistent.

SENATOR SHERMAN.—Does the Senator from Missouri say that there is anything in the bill that confers jurisdiction when they are citizens or members of a corporation of different States? There is nothing of that. The language of the bill is plain. I have read it. I do not see what the Senator is driving at.

Between two or more citizens or corporations—

The corporation is considered as a unit and the citizen as a unit—

or both, of different States.

This must be some persons and some corporations, distinct and separate personalities, not citizens who are members of the corporation.

SENATOR VEST.—Here is what I mean, and I think the Senator must agree with me: The Constitution of the United States makes one basis of jurisdiction to be the diverse citizenship of the litigants.

SENATOR SHERMAN.—This points that out. They must be citizens of different States or corporations of different States, or both.

SENATOR VEST.—Of course. Although it is so simple a matter that it hardly needs elucidation, I may put it thus: If Mr. Brown lives in the State of Missouri and Mr. Smith lives in Ohio they can sue each other without regard to the subject-matter, provided it comes within the limits which were fixed in the judiciary act as to the jurisdiction of a Federal tribunal. The Senator does not put his bill upon that ground at all. He undertakes to put it upon the composition of one of the litigants alone. He does not say, if one of these citizens lives in one State and one in another, which we would all admit to confer Federal jurisdiction, but he gives Federal jurisdiction because the corporation which makes the trust is composed of citizens of different States. If it does not mean that, then the English language has lost all its flavor and I have lost my power to understand it.

Here is what he says. I will read it again *ad nauseam:*

All arrangements, contracts, agreements, trusts, or combinations between two or more citizens or corporations, or both, of different States.

And that gives jurisdiction, provided they go on and undertake to do the other things enumerated in the other part of the section as to goods brought from foreign countries or goods carried from one State to another.

The Senator does not follow the Constitution, which says that when a suit shall be brought by a citizen of one State against a citizen of another State for doing the thing which he enumerates afterwards, which is another matter of argument, but he says if the corporation offending is composed of people living in different States, then the Federal courts have jurisdiction, which I submit is an unheard-of proposition and no lawyer ever advanced it before. As I undertook to show, how easy is it for these corporations to evade any such provision by simply having their stockholders all living in the limits of any particular State? It affords no remedy, even if the argument of the Senator from Ohio could stand for a moment, which it can not.

But, Mr. President, I proceed now, for it is not my disposition to make any elaborate argument, to the latter clause of the amendment, disregarding entirely the original bill, which for the purposes of discussion has been removed. If a corporation is composed of two or more persons living in different States or if it is composed of citizens or corporations, or both, in the United States and a foreign country, and they make a combination to prevent full and free competition in the importation, transportation, or sale of articles imported into the United States, then this proposed law takes effect, and they become subject to the jurisdiction we invoke legislatively.

I do not propose to make any hypercritical argument, but

I do insist that unless we adhere to the opinions of the Supreme Court, especially in the great case of Brown *vs.* The State of Maryland, we are at sea without rudder or compass in this whole discussion.

The Senator invokes the commerce clause of the Constitution, that clause which gives to Congress the power to regulate commerce with foreign countries, among the States, and with the Indian tribes. The first question that meets us *in limine,* which any lawyer would be ashamed to confess that he did not invoke at the very beginning of his argument on this commerce clause, in the material question, what is commerce? What is commerce with a foreign country? There is the point in this whole legislation, the point that has given me the most trouble after long and exhaustive thought to the extent of my ability.

I will confess now, parenthetically, but honestly, that in all my experience as a lawyer I have never encountered a subject so full of difficulty as that now before the Senate. I can very well understand how it is full of difficulty. Notwithstanding the eulogium in which I cordially unite with the Senator from Ohio upon the framers of the Constitution, it is simply impossible, unless we attribute to the framers of this instrument the intellect of gods, that they in the thirteen original colonies, poor, struggling for existence, limited in their territorial area to the Atlantic seaboard, should ever have contemplated the immense country for which we are now legislating, and the enormous aggregation of wealth which startles and amazes the world. They undertook in the Constitution to meet contingencies, but here is one which beggars Aladdin's lamp in the reality that is before us and with us to-day. It is no reflection, then, upon their intellect or their patriotism to say that they could not have contemplated an emergency such as that which now rests upon the people of the United States.

Mr. President, I come back to the question, What is commerce? We have the power to regulate it, but we must first find what commerce is in order to exercise our legislative power. I shall not undertake to read the decisions of the Supreme Court of the United States, which are elementary law upon this subject. In the great case of Brown against The State of Maryland, which leads upon this subject, and to which every lawyer goes first, decided by the most eminent men who ever sat upon the bench in this country, and the equals of any in the world, the regulation of foreign commerce was declared to be the regulation of the importation and sale of articles brought from a foreign country before they had left the hands of the importer and been broken as to the original package. I state crudely, but I think accurately.

The Supreme Court in that case settled the question of foreign commerce by declaring, as to the power of a State to tax foreign importations, that so long as the original package remained in the hands of the importer unbroken it was the subject of foreign commerce. When it left his hands and the package was broken, and the goods went into the common mass of the property of the people of the State, then the commercial clause of the Constitution as to foreign commerce ceased to operate.

Mr. President, apply that decision to the provisions of this bill. Here is one clause of the amendment which provides that if a corporation composed of citizens of different States does any act "with a view or which tends to prevent full and free competition in the importation, transportation, or sale of articles imported into the United States," this proposed law shall take effect.

Does the Senator from Ohio pretend that, after the importer has brought in the goods and the package has been broken and the merchandise has been mingled or commingled with the other goods of the people of the State into which the importation is made, under this clause of the Constitution we can enact such a law as is proposed? I take it that the statement of the case is sufficient to answer the proposition. But it is undertaken to get this jurisdiction under another clause of the Constitution. The bill proceeds:

Or with a view or which tends to prevent full and free competition in articles of growth, production, or manufacture of any State or Territory of the United States with similar articles of the growth, production, or manufacture of any other State or Territory, or in the transportation or sale of like articles, the production of any State or Territory of the United States into or within any other State or Territory of the United States.

I shall not repeat the argument, made by the Senator from Mississippi as lucidly and conclusively as any argument could have been made, that we have no power under any clause of the Federal Constitution to legislate as to any article simply because it is manufactured in any State of the Union and may be at some time carried to another State. That clause in the Constitution of the United States which affects interstate commerce, or, to speak more accurately, commerce among the States, has been defined by the Supreme Court in three leading cases to mean the power to regulate commerce in articles, whether manufactured in the State or not, after they have gone into commerce and are *in transitu* from one State to another.

The Supreme Court of the United States has decided that it is not for the manufacturer or the owner to say, "I intend these goods to go into another State." They must actually be *in transitu;* they must be in the hands of the common carrier, or in his depot or warehouse, with the impression distinctively made upon them that, to use the expression of one judge, they are dedicated to commerce among the States.

The Senator from Ohio makes the fatal mistake as a lawyer that, because goods manufactured in one State may be at some time or other taken into another, which as a matter of course is possible in every contingency, therefore he can invoke the general interstate commerce clause of the Constitution. He can not do it. If we pass this bill upon any such assumption and it goes to the Supreme Court of the United States, we shall simply be told that all we have done here is *vox et præterea nihil,* sound and fury, signifying nothing.

Mr. President, one year ago the Senator from Ohio struck the keynote as to all these trusts and combinations in the United States. It was in the expression made in this Chamber that whenever he was satisfied that any trust or combination was protected by a high tariff duty he would be in favor of reducing that duty. This is the remedy, and any other remedy, without an amendment of the Constitution of the United States, any remedy such as is proposed in this bill, will be absolutely nugatory and ineffectual.

The Senator from Ohio has drawn an eloquent picture of the operations of trusts in the United States. Sir, these trusts— and every intelligent man knows it, whether a legislator or a citizen—are protected by your high tariff, and are enabled to work their iniquitous purposes under that buttress which the tariff law erects around them.

We have been told in some directions that the trusts and combines have nothing to do with the tariff. Mr. President, that reminds me of a very suspicious old gentleman, who, when the Siamese twins were in this country, thought he would invest twenty-five cents in looking at this great natural curiosity. He was very suspicious and examined the ligament that bound them together, and he found in it the pulsation which indicated animal life to the fullest extent. He stepped back, still suspicious, and said to them, "Now, boys, tell me the truth; are you brothers?" [Laughter.] So with the connection between the trusts and the tariff.

William M. Stewart [Nev.] opposed the bill.

The difficulty in dealing with this question is well illustrated by hundreds of years of experience in Great Britain, where Parliament was supreme, where they could pass and enforce any law they pleased on this subject. They found after all this experience that such laws were simply hurtful, and so they passed an act repealing the law, changing the common law with regard to it, and leaving trade and commerce free.

The difficulty in the whole subject is in reaching any precise evil or defining the offence. If you say there shall be no combination the tendency of which shall put up prices, how far would that reach? It would reach to nearly every transaction in life and would be particularly oppressive upon the struggling masses who are making combinations to resist accumulated wealth. Accumulated wealth has the power to prosecute, and if the laborers combine in any form to protect themselves there will be means found of prosecuting them.

Suppose all the people of the different States should combine together and say, "We will stand against this Chicago combine that is attempting to get our produce for nothing," why would not they be liable to prosecution, the whole of them, if it were a constitutional law? But have they not a natural right to hold their products back until they can get a better price?

It is very probable that if this bill were passed the very first prosecution would be against combinations of producers and laborers whose combinations tend to put up the cost of commodities to consumers. It would be a weapon in the hands of the rich against the poor, and if you will trace the history of such legislation you will find that the experience of Great Britain was that such laws have always been turned against the people.

I believe that the true remedy against such trusts is that of counter combinations among the people. I believe in co-operation. Take, for instance, the most notorious trust in the West that there has been so much said about—the beef trust in Chicago. You can not reach that by such legislation as this. But suppose five thousand consumers in Chicago would form an association and supply themselves. Would not that break the trust? If you pass this proposed law, however, and such a combination were attempted in Chicago, it would be prosecuted the next day.

These evils of combination, of course, are great, but the question is, do they not grow out of civilization itself, the foundation of which is organization, and without organization men would be savages? Should we not rather encourage organizations among the people to meet the grasping disposition of the favored few?

On March 25 John T. Morgan [Ala.] opposed the bill as a *brutum fulmen* (an idle thunderbolt), a "tub to the whale."

It is not expected that it will ever yield any fruit in the way of checking conspiracies or combinations or forestallings or regrating or any other of the crimes against the market which the old common law furnished us with rules for defining and punishing also.

Monopoly is an intricate question. It taxed the powers of the British Parliament with all of its omnipotence about two centuries to meet these combinations and conspiracies in trade and about trade, relating chiefly, however, to the material subsistence of the people, articles of grain and provisions and the like, and every once in a while we find the brush of oblivion drawn by the English Parliament across all these enactments; they are all swept from the statute books. Why? Because of the vain, futile effort on the part of legislators after all to do very much in controlling men in making their agreements.

We hear the argument made here, and I think it is a perfectly sound one, that the way to get rid of troubles in trade in the nature of conspiracies and combinations is to remove the temptation. We probably could not reach the Standard Oil conspiracy or combination, and several other various important trusts, as they are called, in the United States by a modification of our protective tariff, but it is very certain that we should reach 90 per cent. of them. As long as we enact these temptations in the statute book we can hardly denounce that as immoral or criminal which men do under our invitation.

There is a great deal of danger—I think I can see it in almost every direction—in legislating upon questions of this kind. The Senator from Nevada [Mr. Stewart] has called attention to a very important topic in this connection. I do not know of anything that has a greater or a more direct impression upon our foreign commerce and our interstate commerce than the price of labor. There are combinations among our laboring men of various different fraternities continually being made for the purpose of raising the price of labor. The price of labor when raised by combination—or, if you please so to call it, by a conspiracy, or in the nature of a trust confided to the hands of some managing committee, some steering arrangement—combinations of that kind to raise the price of labor must necessarily increase the price of commodities in interstate commerce and international commerce, at least to the extent of the exports that we send abroad.

Labor is a commodity bought and sold every hour in the day. It is so much a commodity as that we forbid its importation here when it comes under contract; we treat it just as we would spurious medicines, or base coin, or something of that sort; we tax it as we do oleomargarine. We treat labor precisely as if it were a commodity, and it is a commodity that is imported into this country.

If we pass a law here to punish men for entering into combination and conspiracy to raise the price of labor, what is the reason why we are not within the purview of the powers of Congress in respect to international commerce? Who can answer the proposition as a matter of law?

There is a feature in this case that nobody has ever suggested, so far as I have heard, that has always struck me with a good deal of force. I think a proceeding *in rem* can be had under a libel for condemnation of goods, wares, and merchandise carried between the States, to seize, condemn, and confiscate goods that may have been manufactured under a conspiracy or bought and collected together under a conspiracy to control the markets. Why could not that be done? It seems to me that is as easy a way to get at it as any you could mention, certainly far better than the declaration of nullity of the contract or referring some poor fellow who bought ten pounds to a Federal court somewhere to recover double damages according to the percentage of loss he sustained in the amount taxed upon him through the conspiracy.

Mr. President, I belong to what is called the State-rights school of politicians, and in season and out of season, I suppose, I stand here for the purpose of trying to protect the States of this Union against encroachment on the part of the Federal Government. But, sir, in respect of this matter concerning trusts and combinations and conspiracies, I must say that I think the States are utterly derelict. They have the unquestioned power to handle and to punish every one of these conspiracies and combinations.

Why they do not do it is more than I can understand, unless I am prepared to accept the unpleasant allusion frequently made here that the legislatures and the authorities of the State governments have not the virtue to withstand the power of the great corporations. My judgment is that to average them they are just as honest as Congress is, and as little likely to be corrupted as Congress is, and I think it is the mere lethargy of the different governments, inspired by a too confident reliance upon the powers of Congress to remedy public evils, that is leading us to-day into this effort to do what the States themselves ought to do.

SENATOR SHERMAN.—How could the authorities of Alabama punish, say, a cotton-seed oil combination formed in New York?

SENATOR MORGAN.—When they came to Alabama and made a proposition to a man that unless he sold out they would establish their business and break him up they committed an offence against the laws of Alabama.

SENATOR SHERMAN.—They would probably send some poor clerk down there to make that declaration.

SENATOR MORGAN.—Suppose they did. Probably he would have better sense the next time if he served a short term in the penitentiary for it.

SENATOR SHERMAN.—Yes; all that Alabama could do would be to take the clerk and send him to the penitentiary.

SENATOR MORGAN.—It may be so, and we shall not get anybody but clerks practically out of this measure that the Senator from Ohio has put in here. All the big fish will escape. The little fish are the men who will have the trouble. There will not be a suit brought in twenty-five years to come under the bill of the Senator from Ohio, if it becomes a law. This bill is a good preface to an argument upon the protective tariff when that comes up: "We have sunk the trust question out of sight by a bill that has smothered it for the present."

SENATOR SHERMAN.—Why could not the man in Alabama sue the combination in the courts of the United States and make them pay for all the damages he suffered?

SENATOR MORGAN.—He would find, as everybody else would find under the bill of the Senator, that it is cheaper not to sue.

Senator Morgan moved that the bill be referred to the Judiciary Committee, as in his opinion it was constitutionally and practically unsound.

ZEBULON B. VANCE [N. C.].—Mr. President, I never have a bill in which I feel any interest referred to this grand mausoleum of Senatorial literature, the Judiciary Committee, without feeling that I have attended a funeral. This occasion

XI—5

is no exception to that feeling. The grand air of magisterial dominion which surrounds those gentlemen who constitute that committee, the awful profundity and gravity with which they are enveloped, naturally tend to produce a funereal impression upon a serious mind, and the whole atmosphere seems to me resonant with the strains of that familiar old hymn:

> Hark! from the tombs a doleful sound;
>   Mine ears attend the cry.
> Come, living men, and view the ground
>   Where your bills must shortly lie.

[Laughter.]

Mr. President, I feel an interest in this bill. I feel that one class of the community in this American country of ours has not partaken of the general prosperity which the country has enjoyed for the last twenty years. A step has been taken to remove some of the obstructions to this prosperity which a portion of our fellow-citizens fail to enjoy. It may not be the proper step; there may be a better step, but it is a beginning, at all events.

Mr. President, I think if it were not so late in the evening and the Senate would give me its patient attention that I could demonstrate the fact that if a man desired to go to any given point he must start, and that he never would get there until after he did start, and my opinion is that we never shall get a bill for the suppression of the trusts and combinations which oppress a large portion of the American people so long as we consign all of our bantlings to the fostering care of the Judiciary Committee. I say it with all due respect to that great committee, of course. I am a man too cautious of my personal safety to desire to do anything that would bring upon me the enmity or the disregard of that august body. [Laughter.]

So, if it is the determination of the Senate to send this bill to the Judiciary Committee, to deliver the child for nurture to the persons having most interest in its death, I shall have sorrowfully to submit myself to that state of things, but I hope I may be pardoned for saying that I feel a good deal as we are given to understand the Apostle Paul felt when he took leave of the elders at Ephesus.

> They all wept sore and fell on Paul's neck, sorrowing most of all for the words which he spake, that they should see his face no more.

I am satisfied, sir, that when this bill does come back it will be so mutilated that it will have everything that can possibly be of any benefit to the people of this country so entirely eliminated and eradicated that it will for practical purposes not be worth the paper that it is written upon, and the country will so accept it. The country knows the receptacles where we deposit our dead by this time. We can no longer hope to conceal them.

I heard of a Senator who once occupied a seat in this body who boasted that he was no milk-and-cider man, that he was a man of decision on all subjects. Said he, "When a question comes up before me I either vote for it or I vote against it, or I squat like a man." [Laughter.] Mr. President, the country has found out that when we desire the death of a bill and are not particularly anxious to put ourselves on record as having directly struck the blow which caused the demise, we refer it to the Judiciary Committee [laughter], where it sleeps the last sleep known to the literature of this Senate.

By a vote of 15 yeas to 28 nays the motion of Senator Morgan to refer the bill to the Judiciary Committee was defeated.

John H. Reagan [Tex.] had offered an amendment to the bill, providing that a person violating a provision of the act be fined not more than $10,000 or imprisoned not more than five years, or suffer both penalties, and that each day's violation be held a separate offence.

This was passed by a vote of 34 to 12.

Senator Sherman moved a proviso offered by Senator George, excepting from the application of the bill combinations between laborers for lessening hours of labor or increasing wages, and combinations between farmers for enhancing the price of their produce. This was agreed to.

An amendment offered by Senator Reagan that any person injured by a trust might sue in a State as well as Federal Court was agreed to.

An amendment offered by George F. Hoar [Mass.] that trusts formed in different States, as well as the same State, be punished was agreed to.

John J. Ingalls [Kan.] offered an amendment penalizing dealers in "options" and futures. It was agreed to.

Richard Coke [Tex.] offered an amendment of the

nature of a substitute, penalizing persons connected with organizing trusts in the Territories, or conveying thither from a State where trusts are prohibited the products of these unlawful combinations. It also authorized the President to suspend duties on trust products.

Senator Coke supported his bill.

You may take the bill of my colleague [Senator Reagan], you may take the bill of the Senator from Ohio [Mr. Sherman], examine them and test them under the rulings of the Supreme Court which we have heard cited here, and they are clearly and, as it seems to me, grossly unconstitutional. I want a bill that will stand. I want a bill that shall not be a promise to be broken, that shall not be a delusion and a sham.

Mr. President, the bill of my colleague is infinitely better and stronger than that of the Senator from Ohio. There is greatly more force and vitality in it, and yet I challenge any man to answer the arguments which can be made against its constitutionality. If you read the different propositions contained in the first, second, third, fourth, and fifth clauses they are plausible, but will not bear analysis or close inspection.

We are all working for the same end. We are all desiring the same purpose. We all want a bill that will accomplish some good, that will relieve the people of the robbery being perpetrated on them, one that the Supreme Court will sustain, and hence we have been offering amendments and suggestions with reference to the subject.

The measure which I have offered I believe to be clear of any constitutional objection. I believe it would be sustained by the Supreme Court. It coöperates with the States, it invokes the power and authority of the States in their own behalf, and does not act upon a State except in aid of her own action.

If there is a State that has not acted, the people of that State will see that they should act in order to get the benefit of the protection of this law if it shall be passed by Congress. If they want the protection, they will enact statutes on this subject.

We have all seen that Congress has not the power to deal fully with this subject. My amendment exhausts the power of Congress, and then uses all the aid the States can give in order to carry out its purpose.

Senator Coke's substitute was laid on the table by a vote of 26 to 16.

On March 27 the bill was referred to the Committee on Judiciary by a vote of 31 to 28.

The committee reported on April 2. Its bill was as follows:

Section 1. Every contract, combination in the form of trust or otherwise, or conspiracy in restraint of trade or commerce among the several States or with foreign nations is hereby declared to be illegal. Every person who shall make any such contract or engage in any such combination or conspiracy shall be deemed guilty of a misdemeanor, and, on conviction thereof, shall be punished by fine not exceeding $5,000 or by imprisonment not exceeding one year, or by both said punishments, in the discretion of the court.

Sec. 2. Every person who shall monopolize, or attempt to monopolize, or combine or conspire with any other person or persons to monopolize any part of the trade or commerce among the several States or with foreign nations, shall be deemed guilty of a misdemeanor, and, on conviction thereof, shall be punished by fine not exceeding $5,000 or by imprisonment not exceeding one year, or by both said punishments, in the discretion of the court.

Sec. 3. Every contract, combination in form of trust or otherwise, or conspiracy in restraint of trade or commerce in any Territory of the United States or of the District of Columbia, or in restraint of trade or commerce between any such Territory and another, or between any such Territory or Territories and any State or States or the District of Columbia, or with foreign nations, or between the District of Columbia and any State or States or foreign nations is hereby declared illegal. Every person who shall make any such contract or engage in any such combination or conspiracy shall be deemed guilty of a misdemeanor, and, on conviction thereof, shall be punished by fine not exceeding $5,000 or by imprisonment not exceeding one year, or by both said punishments in the discretion of the court.

Sec. 4. The several circuit courts of the United States are hereby invested with jurisdiction to prevent and restrain violations of this act, and it shall be the duty of the several district attorneys of the United States in their respective districts, under the direction of the Attorney-General, to institute proceedings in equity to prevent and restrain such violations. Such proceedings may be by way of petition setting forth the case and praying that such violation shall be enjoined or otherwise prohibited. When the parties complained of shall have been duly notified of such petition the court shall proceed, as soon as may be, to the hearing and determination of the case, and, pending such petition and before final decree, the court may at any time make such temporary restraining order or prohibition as shall be deemed just in the premises.

SEC. 5. Whenever it shall appear to the court before which any proceeding under section 4 of this act may be pending that the ends of justice require that other parties should be brought before the court, the court may cause them to be summoned, whether they reside in the district in which the court is held or not; and subpœnas to that end may be served in any district by the marshal thereof.

SEC. 6. Any property owned under any contract or by any combination or pursuant to any conspiracy (and being the subject thereof) mentioned in section 1 of this act, and being in the course of transportation from one State to another, or to a foreign country, shall be forfeited to the United States, and may be seized and condemned by like proceedings as those provided by law for the forfeiture, seizure, and condemnation of property imported into the United States contrary to law.

SEC. 7. Any person who shall be injured in his business or property by any other person or corporation by reason of anything forbidden or declared to be unlawful by this act may sue therefor in any circuit court of the United States in the district in which the defendant resides or is found, without respect to the amount in controversy, and shall recover threefold the damages by him sustained and the costs of suit, including a reasonable attorney's fee.

SEC. 8. That the word "person" or "persons" wherever used in this act shall be deemed to include corporations and associations existing under or authorized by the laws of either the United States, the laws of any of the Territories, the laws of any State, or the laws of any foreign country.

Amend the title so as to read: "A bill to protect trade and commerce against unlawful restraints and monopolies."

The bill came up in the Committee of the Whole on April 8, and was passed by a vote of 52 to 1, Rufus Blodgett [N. J.] being the sole voter in the negative.

The House referred the bill to the Committee on Judiciary, which reported it on April 25. It came up for action on May 1 and, by the operation of the House rules, was forced to a vote on that day. The bill was amended and passed on May 1.

The bill as amended was referred in the Senate to the Committee on Judiciary. It reported it with further amendments in which the House refused to concur. Two conferences were held before an agreement was reached (on June 18) that the two Chambers recede from their respective amendments. The conference report was unanimously adopted on June 20, and President Harrison approved the act on July 2, 1890.

CHAPTER II

CONTROL OF THE TRUSTS: BY NATION OR STATES?

[PROPOSED CONSTITUTIONAL AMENDMENT AND LITTLEFIELD BILL]

John J. Jenkins [Wis.] Proposes in the House Constitutional Amendment Giving Congress Control of Trusts—Charles E. Littlefield [Me.] Introduces Bill in the House to Amend Sherman Anti-Trust Act—Debate on the Amendment (Incidentally on the Bill): In Favor, John Dalzell [Pa.], George W. Ray [N. Y.], Mr. Littlefield; Opposed, James D. Richardson [Tenn.], Joseph W. Bailey [Tex.], William L. Terry [Ark.], Samuel W. T. Lanham [Tex.], John W. Gaines [Tenn.], B. T. Clayton [N. Y.], David A. De Armond [Mo.], Samuel W. McCall [Mass.]— Amendment Is Defeated; House Passes Bill; It Is Committed in the Senate.

ON January 26, 1900, John J. Jenkins [Wis.] proposed in the House a constitutional amendment empowering Congress to pass laws regulating combinations in trade. It was referred to the Committee on Judiciary, which reported it, with amendment, on May 15.

On April 7, 1900, Charles E. Littlefield [Me.] introduced in the House a bill to amend the Sherman anti-trust law of July 2, 1890. It was referred to the Committee on Judiciary, which reported it, with amendment, on May 16.

On May 31 the Committee on Rules proposed that the constitutional amendment be discussed that day and the next, when it should be brought to a vote, without amendment, and that then the Littlefield bill be taken up and discussed until 4 p. m., June 2, when the vote should be taken. This recommendation was adopted by a vote of 141 to 118. As a consequence there was virtually one continuous debate on the general subject.

72

The Amendment submitted by the majority of the Judiciary Committee was as follows:

1. All powers conferred by this article shall extend to the several States, the Territories, the District of Columbia, and all territory under the sovereignty and subject to the jurisdiction of the United States.

2. Congress shall have power to define, regulate, prohibit, or dissolve trusts, monopolies, or combinations, whether existing in the form of a corporation or otherwise. The several States may continue to exercise such power in any manner not in conflict with the laws of the United States.

The minority presented a report the nature of which will transpire in the debate.

TRUST CONTROL BY CONGRESS

HOUSE OF REPRESENTATIVES, MAY 31-JUNE 2, 1900

James D. Richardson [Tenn.] opened the debate.

Mr. Speaker, we are confronted by a somewhat unique condition here. The Republican party came into control of the Government on the 4th of March, 1897. They placed in the White House their President; they have had the Senate and they have had the House of Representatives since that day. Within eleven days after that time the President convened Congress in extraordinary session, the object being, as stated in his message, to repeal the then existing law and to pass a new revenue law. Notwithstanding the party had won the canvass the preceding year upon the monetary issue, Congress was convened to legislate upon the tariff. The result of that session was the passage of what is known as the "Dingley bill," which I state here in my opinion has done more to create, foster, and propagate trusts than any other bill put upon the statute book in our history.

Mr. Speaker, that was in the Fifty-fifth Congress. That entire Congress, three sessions, passed into history and not one step was taken by the dominant party to legislate to protect the country from the injurious effects of trusts. No statute was altered or changed. The Fifty-sixth Congress commenced to sit last December, and now, after six months, in the dying hours of this session of Congress, after we have already passed a resolution to adjourn within less than one week from this hour, we are presented with this resolution from the Committee on Rules bringing us to the consideration of a constitutional amendment.

The independent papers, as well as party organs, have all characterized the effort now being put forth by the dominant party in respect to this proposed amendment, and they all unite in saying the only object is to make cheap political party capital.

Mr. Speaker, I undertake to say that the country will not be fooled by this legislation. The Democratic party has taken action in respect to this matter of trusts. We will vote for any proper constitutional amendment to the end, if one be necessary. We are ready to vote even for the bill now pending, if we can do no better, in order to put something on the statute books to enable Congress to do, and the States to do, what is necessary to suppress trusts, but this constitutional amendment presented to us will not, in the opinion of the Democratic party, serve that purpose. On the other hand, we have solemnly decided as a party that it will have the opposite effect.

It will, in our judgment, take away from the States the power which they now possess to suppress trusts, or at least greatly impair that power in the States. The most effectual remedy so far for the suppression of trusts, and their control and regulation, has been in the States. Mr. Speaker, this constitutional amendment, if passed, will serve to excuse Congress from acting and break down the power of the States to control these trusts. I trust every Democrat who loves constitutional law and order, who believes in the rights of the State, will stand with his party here and vote down this constitutional amendment. [Applause on the Democratic side.]

Joseph W. Bailey [Tex.] also opposed the Amendment.

That you can never put this amendment into the Constitution of the United States is plain to every thinking man. You have purposely drawn it so that three-fourths of the States can never be induced to adopt it. You know as well as we do that no State in this Union that believes in the preservation of the right of local self-government will ever vest in the Congress of the United States the power to come within its borders and take control of its domestic industries. [Applause on the Democratic side.] You know that the trusts understand that there is not the remotest danger to them in this constitutional amendment. If you had sincerely desired to make it a part of our organic law, you could have accomplished your object by a very slight amendment. If you had merely added to the phraseology which it now contains, and, after enumerating the trusts, combinations, and monopolies which Congress should

THE GREAT REPUBLICAN CIRCUS
Cartoon by F. Opper in the Hearst papers

have the power to dissolve, you had merely added the words "engaged in commerce among the several States or with foreign nations,'' you would have received every vote on this side of the Chamber and the sanction of every sovereign State in this Union. [Applause on the Democratic side.]

For one, I will never vote to vest in the Congress of the United States the power to deny the State of Texas the right to define and punish her own domestic conspiracies against her own trade. If she has a corporation that in her wisdom ought to be permitted to engage in a given business, the States of Illinois and Pennsylvania ought to have no right to say her nay. If there be one that in her own imperial will she desires to crush, the States of Pennsylvania and New York have no right to stay her arm. Your safety consists in the fact that whenever an article of merchandise or manufacture produced within her borders is loaded upon a train or ship to become the subject of interstate or foreign commerce, then the power of Congress attaches. If you will limit the power of Congress over these organizations to those engaged in interstate and foreign commerce, which is as far as Federal jurisdiction ought to extend, you can pass your amendment by a unanimous vote; and I venture to record the prophecy here that, if you do not amend it in some such sensible manner, it can never become a part of the Constitution of the United States.

There are two ways to encourage crime. One is to close your eyes against the existence of it, and another is to propose an impracticable and impossible method of its punishment. You have chosen to do the latter, and you have chosen deliberately, because nobody doubts that you know exactly what you are doing. I have many times doubted your sincerity, I have sometimes doubted your absolute political integrity, but I have never doubted your ability. You may sometimes be hypocrites, and a few of you may sometimes be rascals, but none of you are ever fools, and you knew your purpose when you framed this amendment so as to prevent its adoption. [Laughter and applause on the Democratic side.]

JOHN DALZELL [Pa.].—Mr. Speaker, there is no political party in this country, nor any individual who has any care for his political future, who is not against the trusts. [Derisive laughter on the Democratic side.] The difference between the two parties or the three parties upon this subject is that the Democratic party and the Populist party confine their opposition to trusts to mere speech. The Republican party addresses itself to legislation. [Applause on the Republican side and manifestations of derision on the Democratic side.] The interstate commerce law is the product of Republican legislation.

The Sherman anti-trust law of 1890 is the product of Republican legislation. When in 1892 the Democratic party entered the field for the presidency, and nominated Grover Cleveland for President, it declared in its platform:

We recognize in the trusts and combinations, which are designed to enable capital to secure more than its just share of the joint product of capital and labor, a natural consequence of the prohibitive taxes which prevent the free competition which is the life of honest trade, but we believe their worst evils can be abated by law, and we demand the rigid enforcement of the laws made to prevent and control them, together with such further legislation in restraint of their abuses as experience may show to be necessary.

And yet for four years the Democratic party, in control of legislation, entered upon no legislation in further repression of trusts, and, being in control of the executive departments, took no steps to enforce the law that a Republican Congress had put upon the statute books. [Applause on the Republican side.] The great Populistic leader, after whom the Democratic party trails to-day, on the stump and at the trust conference in Chicago, declared that a constitutional amendment ought to be passed putting in the power of Congress the regulation of trusts, concurrently with the States.

He said:

As to the constitutionality of such a law my thought is that Congress should enact it, and if it should be declared unconstitutional by the Supreme Court, then I am in favor of so amending the Federal Constitution as to give Congress the power to destroy every trust in the country.

[Applause on the Republican side.]

But when we come here to-day and offer you the remedy suggested by your own leader, the leader upon that side of the House addresses himself in impassioned terms to his Democratic colleagues to stand together and oppose this proposed legislation. You say that we are hypocrites; that we are not acting in good faith. Why, we are exercising every power that is within our reach to put upon the statute books that which we believe will end the power of these great combinations.

The remedy proposed by the gentleman from Texas in respect to interstate commerce is a remedy that already exists. The Supreme Court of the United States, on several occasions, in several cases, have declared that with that remedy alone Congress is powerless to resist these trusts, and so now, following those decisions, following the way pointed out, we propose to remedy the evil by this new legislation. The gentleman from Texas [Mr. Bailey] says the trusts are not frightened by this proposed legislation. The trusts are not frightened because they know that between them and the proposed legislation in solid phalanx stands the Democratic party in their protection. [Applause on the Republican side.]

I conclude, Mr. Speaker, as I began. The fundamental difference between you gentlemen on that side of the aisle and us upon this side of the aisle is that you believe in mere demagoguery upon the stump. We believe in effective legislation upon the statute books. [Applause on the Republican side.]

George W. Ray [N. Y.], of the Judiciary Committee, supported the Amendment.

The necessity for this proposed amendment grows out of the fact that the Supreme Court of the United States has decided that the word "commerce" as used in the Constitution does not include manufacture or production within its legitimate meaning. All articles of commerce are subjects of commerce, but not a part of it. Therefore the constitutional provision, section 8, Article I, that "The Congress shall have power . . . to regulate commerce with foreign nations, and among the several States, and with the Indian tribes," gives Congress no power whatever over corporations, combinations, associations, or conspiracies organized or formed for the purpose of monopolizing manufacture and production, or which by illegal means do monopolize manufacture and production and so control prices, really dominate commerce, and wring unjust exactions from the people.

Combinations or so-called trusts formed for monopolistic purposes may be classified as follows:

1. Those created by a union or a combination of two or more corporations, associations, or companies.

2. Corporations or associations that have acquired control of other corporations or companies by purchasing their stock or by having their stockholders of the central corporation or association purchase the stock, etc., of the other corporations or companies, and so bringing all under the control of the same persons.

3. Corporations or associations which purchase the plants, including the real estate, personal property, stock in trade, and good will of a number of corporations, firms, or individuals engaged in a particular branch of business.

In the first class mentioned the stock of the combining corporations or associations is usually transferred to a board of directors or trustees. In lieu of the stock surrendered to this board the stockholders receive trust certificates. These directors or trustees thus become clothed with the absolute control of the entire business of the combination. They represent the holders of the stock certificates and are answerable only to them.

The second class mentioned is quite similar to the first. The effect is the same, but this form of combination is resorted to to escape the holdings of the courts that corporations can not enter into partnership. But few, if any, of the first class remain.

The third class referred to is even more dangerous than the others. When the mother corporation or association in the manner referred to gets hold of the stock, plants, property, etc., of the others, payment therefor is made in the stock or certificates of the corporation or association. The business is then carried on with reference to the interests of all. The mother corporation or association holds the legal and equitable title of all the property of all the corporations and companies brought in, and all the plants may be run at the same time or only one or more may carry on operations, and so the output of that business throughout the entire Union, and consequently the price, is controlled by the directors of this mother corporation or association or ''combine.''

It is readily seen that the purpose of such a combination is to limit production, where such limitation is profitable to the stockholders, as well as to create a monopoly and control prices.

These or similar combinations can be made by joint stock companies and even by partnerships, although there is more difficulty in forming and sustaining such combinations.

It is readily seen how powerful these combinations with unlimited capital become. Care is taken to have the stock owned by men of wealth and influence in every State of the Union so far as possible, by the editors and owners of leading newspapers, and by men of both political parties, and the result is that the political influence wielded by such a combination is sufficient many times to prevent in a State, or possibly in several States, the enactment of any law restraining, controlling, or prohibiting the combination.

No one can deny with reason that all such combinations tend to the creation of monopolies and result in the control of production as well as prices, and that therefore their existence is against public policy.

This was held in substance in:

State vs. Standard Oil Company, 49 Ohio St., 138.

Aggregated capital in the hands of corporations and combinations honestly formed and conducted is the friend of labor and of all mankind. So formed, they are desirable, and, in fact, indispensable. Modern civilization demands their existence. What is the Government itself but a vast corporation, an aggregation of millions of people and billions of wealth. Thus organized, it becomes a vast power for good in the world. Each enfranchised citizen is a director and every citizen is a stockholder. Unorganized, the people would accomplish nothing. Aggregated capital in honest hands and applied by intelligent minds has reared and sustained institutions of learning, affording opportunities for intellectual development and culture which, embraced by thousands, have given to the world inventive and mechanical genius in its most finished form.

Aided by this, combined capital has applied itself to the improvement and uplifting of mankind. The result has been that our country is united with a network of railroads, affording easy and speedy means of communication; the business man in Boston converses with his agent or co-worker in San Francisco; ocean has been connected with ocean; continent with continent, for purposes of communication, and, utilizing great discoveries made possible by it, combined capital has brought education and the comforts and many of the luxuries of life to the doors of all. Capital has erected and endowed charitable institutions throughout the land, and thereby alleviates human misery. Combined capital, encouraging and utilizing modern improvements, has erected great factories, employed labor, builded cities, created markets for farm products, and added to the industrial, intellectual, and moral wealth of our country. [Applause.]

It is not the existence, but the abuse of corporate powers and combined capital that merits condemnation or denunciation and calls for remedial legislation. When combined capital in any hands abuses its legitimate powers, becomes oppressive, or assumes the form of gigantic monopolies, it becomes detrimental and dangerous to the nation. It then affects injuriously every citizen, unless it be the very few who fatten at the expense of the many. It then becomes greedy, extortionate, monarchical in its tendencies and practices, and invades the political field and legislative halls, and corrupts, or seeks to corrupt, both.

The mere denunciation of these combinations, monopolies, and conspiracies by the press, on the floors of Congress, or in party platforms neither prevents their organization, operations, nor the evils flowing from their existence.

How frequently do we hear the demagogue in Congress and elsewhere denouncing trusts, monopolies, and conspiracies in speeches, but obstructing and opposing the consideration of legislation designed to suppress them.

In season and out of season, sometimes when relevant, but always when irrelevant, we have heard denunciations of the Administration, of party policy, and of trusts and combinations, always accompanied with assertions that the Republican party is responsible for and the protector of trusts. Accused of not doing anything, not intending to do anything, we were met at the very outset of active legislation to control and repress these illegal monopolies with Democratic objection, even to consideration of the subject. We have adopted a course of procedure that will compel the minority members of this House to register themselves in favor of this resolution, and therefore against trusts, combinations, and monopolies, or against the resolution, and therefore in favor of them and in favor of their continuing operations.

Equally groundless and untrue is the insinuation of the Democratic minority that they were excluded from the consideration and framing of the proposed legislation. The subcommittee, consisting of four Republicans and three Democrats, was appointed and directed to report. Days passed, to enable every gentleman opportunity to formulate and present his views. The subcommittee was called together and all given full opportunity to present proposed measures. But, aside from the presentation of the majority measures, but little, if anything, was presented, except words and denunciation of proposed legislation and lengthy advocacy of the doctrine of "State rights."

It is noteworthy that the "views of the minority" contain no substitute for, propose no amendments to, the joint resolution; do not deny our legal contentions or conclusions; do not assert that efficient laws can be enacted by Congress under its present constitutional powers. The main argument, if dignified by that name, is that under the proposed amendment the States are called upon to surrender some of their power. At the same time the monopolies are referred to as "the growing and most burdensome evil, popularly known as the trust." The minority also concedes that there "is a loud and imperative call.'' But the ''views of the minority'' propose no response to that call.

It is true that it is urged that the protective tariff is responsible for the existence of monopoly, and that free trade will remedy the existing evils. But this amounts to little more than denunciation of a system advocated and established by the Republican party. It is but a repetition of the stale and oft-refuted charge that protective tariffs are onerous and destructive of the prosperity of the country. It is also true that the ''views of the minority'' complain that the proposed amendment does not leave the States free to legislate in opposition to Congress, annul its laws. ''Concurrent jurisdiction'' is what is wanted, so that if a State can get ahead in its legislation the rule may be applied that ''first come, first served''; the one first taking jurisdiction shall hold it.

But all this trash of ''views'' is intended as denunciatory of the proposition of the majority to control and repress combinations and monopolies operating to the injury of the people and of the country. It is not designed to throw light on the subject or suggest wise action. The whole tenor of the ''views of the minority'' is in that vein of sarcasm, abandoning truth or reason, for which some writers are noted. It is a mere attempt to give an excuse for preventing the adoption of this joint resolution, if possible, by drawing the State rights lines taut on the party. The minority well know that two-thirds of each House must vote in the affirmative or action will fail.

Mr. Ray then discussed the question of the power of the States in regard to the trusts.

The States can not protect themselves against monopoly, combinations, and conspiracy to monopolize manufacture and production and fix and control prices, for the following reasons:

1. The State has no power whatever over interstate commerce; interstate transportation of persons or property.

2. The State has no power to prevent the corporation, associations, companies, or citizens of another State from coming into it and doing business therein if engaged in interstate commerce.

3. No State has power over the corporations, associations, companies, or citizens of another so long as they remain outside of her territorial limits.

4. No State has power to prevent the sending or bringing

into her limits the manufactures or products of corporations, associations, companies, or individuals, organized, doing business, or residing in another State, for use, even with the consent of Congress, or for any other purpose without such consent.

5. No State can prevent the purchase or control of the stock, property, etc., of its corporations, associations, companies, or citizens by those chartered, organized, or residing in another State.

The result is that a monopoly existing in one State and controlling the production, ownership, and price of an article of general use and necessity may, unless Congress intervenes when sent for (and the State legislature controlled by the monopoly may not ask the interference of Congress), send its productions into every State and supply the market there. The only way by which a State can protect her citizens against the unjust exactions of such a monopoly, combination, or conspiracy is to obtain laws on the part of Congress and supplement them by laws of her own, denying the citizens the power to purchase such articles in the State. This denies to the citizens the right to purchase in the State, but not the right to purchase of the monopoly without the State and send the articles into the State for use.

Only twenty-five of the forty-five States have anti-trust and anti-combination laws denouncing such combinations, conspiracies, and monopolies, and the result is that they flourish in some of the States and even meet with protection and encouragement by the legislatures. It is true that in creating a corporation or corporations the legislature of a State may forbid it to enter into any such combination or conspiracy, but it can not prevent its stockholders from selling their stock and thus passing under the control of a corporation or combination existing in another State. It is apparent, then, that capitalists desiring to monopolize any manufacturing business may incorporate under the laws of a State imposing no restrictions and, under the protection of that charter, monopolize a particular business throughout the Union.

In the exercise of the police power a State may say that certain articles shall not be sold because their use or consumption is detrimental to the citizens and consequently to the State. But can it prohibit the use of such articles by the citizen if in such use he interferes with no other person, injures no one but himself? If, then, a citizen has the constitutional right to bring intoxicating liquors into the State of his residence for his personal use (and if it be a constitutional right, the State and, perhaps, the United States can not interfere to prevent), the State can not, even with the consent of Congress, prohibit the introduction for use by the citizens of a State of the products of a monopoly or combination existing in another State, especially if such products be necessaries of life or articles of daily or frequent use and necessary for the prosecution of a lawful business or lawful occupations.

Can it be claimed that such power exists in Congress as incidental to the right to regulate commerce? No, for such action does not regulate commerce, but prohibits it. Can it be justified as a national police power? Perhaps; to come within the police power of a State or of the United States, the act need not relate to the public health, the public morals, or the public safety, but may "increase industries and develop resources." (Barbier *vs.* Connolly, 113 U. S., 27.)

This power to monopolize manufacture and production or the sale of articles of commerce is of the highest interest to the general Government itself.

In times of war sudden emergencies arise, and if any corporation or combination is permitted to so monopolize manufacture or production or control prices, the Government itself may be compelled to submit to unjust exactions and great inconveniences when purchasing supplies for its armies.

Every consideration of public policy demands that Congress have power to regulate, repress, and dissolve all such combinations and monopolies and leave competition open and free. If it would be improper and unwise to create monopolies by law, it is unwise to permit their existence and most unwise to leave the general Government without power to regulate and repress them.

I assert that the Congress of the United States should have the power to maintain an open field for honest competition in all industrial enterprise and occupation throughout the entire Union; that in efforts to accomplish this we should not be compelled to act by indirection, or resort to methods of questionable expediency or to legislation of doubtful constitutionality. I assert that when corporations or associations of individuals so conduct their business as to become a menace to the welfare of the people generally throughout this Republic, or in the territory belonging thereto, the Congress of the United States, representing that people and answerable to them, should possess the constitutional power to control, repress, and dissolve the illegal and dangerous organization. [Applause.]

William L. Terry [Ark.] opposed the Amendment as
intended by the Republicans not to be enacted but to
serve simply as political capital.

PROMISE AND PERFORMANCE
Cartoon by Bradley in the "Chicago News"

Even now the trust magnates who fill your campaign coffers
are laughing at the high antics you are cutting up.   [Applause
on the Democratic side.]

Mr. Terry then spoke against the Littlefield bill.   Of
the Sherman law, to which it offered amendment, he said:

It is a curious commentary on a law against monopolies
and trusts that it has found its most numerous victims in the
ranks of those who are themselves the victims of trusts and

monopolies. I can not believe that it was the intention of Congress to have this law applied to laboring men, as the courts have applied, and at least one Federal judge, reviewing the whole history of its enactment, has ruled that it was never intended to be so applied (see case of United States *vs.* Patterson, 55 Fed. Rep., 641), and the United States Supreme Court, in the Debs case, expressly refused to rest their decision upon its applicability to such a case. But other Federal judges have directly held that it was applicable. (See United States *vs.* Workingmen's Amalgamated Council, 54 Fed. Rep., 994.)

To relieve the law of such construction this amendment has been offered. The main amendment the committee offer to the Sherman law is to increase the punishment upon criminal convictions, but what trust magnate, agent, or officer has ever been put behind the bars? We have no doubt but that every trust magnate, and all their officers and agents, will "tremble in their boots" when they learn that a Republican Congress proposes to increase the punishment for criminal convictions under the Sherman anti-trust law.

Samuel W. T. Lanham [Tex.] opposed the Amendment and the bill.

Mr. Speaker, I can not give my approval to any proposition that may deprive the States of any power they now possess—to take away from them any rights which the fathers thought they ought to retain and enjoy, or to impair that eunomy which adorns the best and grandest instrument ever "struck off by the hand of man." Power is always aggressive. The tendency of the Federal Government is to magnify itself and extend its dominion. The hope of the country rests in the vigor, the energy, the development, the upbuilding of the States.

Mr. Jefferson has left on record for our guidance and for the instruction of generations yet to come, as an essential principle, "the support of the State governments in all their rights, as the most competent administration for our domestic concerns and the surest bulwarks against anti-Republican tendencies." The liberties of the people have found, and will continue to find, their best refuge within the "sacred circle" of the States. That refuge has been and will always be

> Our ready help in ages past,
>   Our surest hope for years to come,
> Our shelter from oppression's blast—
>   The freeman's ever welcome home.

The indissolubility of the Union has been firmly established. Let the indestructibility of the States be forever maintained, and may their autonomy never become less! [Loud applause.]

John W. Gaines [Tenn.] quoted a portion of a speech delivered by William J. Bryan at a trust convention held in Chicago on September 13-16, 1899.

A PLAN TO CURB THE TRUSTS

WILLIAM J. BRYAN

My plan is this: First, that the State has, or should have, the right to create whatever private corporations the people of the State desire.

Second, that the State has, or should have, the right to impose such limitations upon an outside corporation as the people of the State may think necessary for their own protection. That protects the right of the people of the State to say, first, what corporations they shall organize in their State, and, second, what corporations they shall permit to come from other States to do business in their State.

Third, that the Federal Government has, or should have, the right to impose such restrictions as Congress may think necessary upon any corporation which does business outside of the State in which it is organized.

In other words, I would preserve to the people of the State all the rights that they now have, and at the same time have Congress exercise a concurrent remedy to supplement the State remedy.

When the Federal Government licenses a corporation to do business outside of the State in which it was organized, it merely permits it to do business in any State, under the conditions imposed by that State in addition to the conditions imposed by the Federal Government. I would not take away from the people of the State any right now existing, but I would have the Federal Government and the State government exercise the powers that may be necessary to annihilate every monopoly.

I do not agree with the gentleman that you can not annihilate a monopoly. I believe it is possible to do so. While the gentleman was speaking, I could not help thinking of the lines of a song. While he was destroying every remedy suggested, and yet presenting no other, I thought of the lines:

"Plunged in a gulf of deep despair,
Ye wretched sinners lie."

Now, it is a great deal easier to find fault with a remedy proposed than to propose a remedy which is faultless. Macaulay —I think he is the author of the remark—has said that, if any money was to be made by disputing the law of gravitation, able men could be found to write articles against the truth of that law. I have no doubt that any remedy that is proposed will be assaulted. But those who believe that the trusts must go will accept the best remedy they can find, try it and then accept a better one, if a better one is proposed, and keep on trying until the people are protected.

I am sure that the Constitution would prohibit such an act of Congress as I suggest. Suppose that Congress should say that whenever a corporation wants to do business outside of the State it must apply to and receive from some body, created by Congress for the purpose, a license to do business. Suppose the law should provide three conditions upon which the license could be issued:

1. That the evidence should show that there is no water in the stock;

2. That the evidence should show that the corporation has not attempted in the past and is not now attempting to monopolize any branch of industry or any article of merchandise; and

3. Providing for that publicity which everybody has spoken of and about which everybody agrees.

Suppose that is done. Who is here to say that such a law would be unconstitutional? The Supreme Court, in deciding the Knight case, did not say that a broader law than the present one would be unconstitutional. It is true there are things in the decision which suggest that, but until that question is presented to the court you can not say that the court has passed upon it.

It is also true that Justice Harlan, in his dissenting opinion, assumed that a broader law would be held unconstitutional, but no one has a right to say that, if such a law as I suggest were passed and reviewed by the Supreme Court, it would be held unconstitutional. But, suppose the law is passed and held unconstitutional, *then we can amend the Constitution.*

The gentleman suggests that it is a difficult thing to get two-thirds of both Houses and three-fourths of the States to favor such an amendment.

That is true; it is a difficult thing, but if the people want to destroy the trusts they can control two-thirds of both Houses and three-fourths of the States. But what is the alternative? sit down and do nothing? Allow them to trample upon you, ride roughshod over you, and then thank God that you still have some life left? The people are told to be contented, but I think contentment may be carried too far.

I heard of a man once who had been taught to be contented with his lot, and finally became very poor and traded off his coat for a loaf of bread. Before he had a chance to eat the bread a dog came along and snatched it away from him. The unfortunate man felt a little indignant at first, but finally that feeling of contentment came back to him, and, as he watched the dog turn around a corner in the road carrying the bread away, he said: "Well, thank God, I still have my appetite left."

Let me suggest one other thing that I believe will be a step in the right direction. The great trouble has been that, while our platforms denounce corporations, corporations control the elections and place the men who are elected to enforce the law under obligations to them.

Let me propose a remedy—not a remedy, but a step in the right direction. Let the laws, State and national, make it a penal offence for any corporation to contribute to the campaign fund of any political party. Nebraska has such a law, passed two years ago. Tennessee has such a law, passed two years ago. Such a measure was introduced in the State of New York, but so far it has not become a law.

You remember the testimony taken before a Senate committee a few years ago, when the head of the sugar trust testified that the sugar trust made it its business to contribute to campaign funds, and when asked to which one it contributed replied that it depended upon circumstances.

"To which fund do you contribute in Massachusetts?" was asked. "To the Republican fund." "To which fund in New York?" "To the Democratic fund." "To which fund in New Jersey?" and the man replied, "Well, I will have to look at the books; that is a doubtful State."

If the people are in earnest they can destroy monopoly, and you never can do anything in this country until the people are in earnest. When the American people understand what the monopoly question means, I believe there will be no power, political, financial, or otherwise, to prevent the people from taking possession of every branch of Government, from President

to the Supreme Court, and making the Government responsive
to the people's will.

On June 1 B. T. Clayton [N. Y.] quoted the views on
trusts of Bird S. Coler, comptroller of the City of New
York.

A PLAN TO CURB THE TRUSTS

BIRD S. COLER

Whatever the State creates it should either supervise or
control. Every corporation should have a definite period of
existence and the right of renewal should rest with the State
and not with those in interest. Business that requires secrecy
of management and manipulation of securities is not entitled to
the protection of the State, and corporate powers should be
refused it.

No corporation should be allowed to issue securities except
for actual value, and these should not be placed upon the public
market until the end at least of one actual business year, and
then only after public reports by certified accountants under
employment of the State and bearing its seal. This to check
stock jobbing and to foster legitimate business and investment,
and also to provide definite information upon which to base
assessment and taxation, thus simplifying tax collecting and
abolishing tax dodging.

Places of business and location of factories should be named
at time of incorporation, and no removal of same should be
allowed without consent of the State. This to prevent the
destruction of communities, and for the protection of employees
who have invested their savings in homes contingent to factories,
and in many cases upon the recommendations of employers.

From its beginning the accounts of every corporation obtaining a charter privilege from a State government should be
open at all times to examination and regulation by properly
appointed public officers.

One of the most intelligent and plausible defenders of trusts
recently said that such concerns were of great advantage to the
people because they divided up their capital into small shares
in which the poor could invest their savings. Assuming that
such might be the fact, the argument advanced at once becomes
an imperative reason why such corporations should be subject
to Government inspection and regulation. If they receive
charters conferring exceptional privileges, such grants become

a part of their assets or capital and give them a financial and commercial standing in the business world, amounting to an advantage over each and every individual competitor. In addition, the charter conveys to them a semi-public or Government indorsement, that may materially affect the market value of their stock or bonds.

They have obtained a privilege that enables them to bid for the surplus capital of the public by the offer of interest-bearing securities. The Government, having made it possible for a few citizens to obtain the capital of the many for investment, should exert all its power to protect that capital and confine the use of it to legitimate business and the employment of labor.

It may be urged that such a system would extend the functions of State government to the regulation of private business. If that be so, no business that requires secret manipulation should receive the privileges of a charter from the people.

The United States Government charters national banks, reserving the right to inspect the methods and examine into the condition of such institutions at any time. This system has never been classed as usurpation of extraordinary functions of government, nor has it retarded the proper and safe development of the banking business. The State of New York has for many years exercised, without question, the right to license and examine the business of life, fire, and marine insurance. Depositors rely upon the State wholly for protection of savings banks.

Every chartered corporation that offers its securities to the people as an investment becomes a semi-public institution, and should be inspected and regulated by the same power that created it. Such control would not in any way oppress or retard legitimate business. Chartered companies should be compelled to confine their investments and development to the legal and proper conduct of the business for which they were created and for the prosecution of which they have received from the Government special privileges and powers.

Under existing conditions there is no safety and little protection for outside investors who buy the securities of great corporations. They must trust largely to the reputation of a company or that of its officers, and recent events in Wall street show how confidence is often misplaced and abused.

Our present system of laws puts a premium upon stock-jobbing. Recent developments in trust stocks put emphatic emphasis on this danger, so long pointed out by political economists. We have had many instances of late where officials of trusts, holding only a small interest, have run the business of their concerns in the interest of stock speculation instead of legitimate development. Mills have been shut down and men thrown out of work simply to affect prices on the exchange.

Corporations seeking legitimate business ends by honest methods and observing the time-honored principles that insure success in private enterprises invariably possess public confidence and are entitled to the protection of the State from which they derive their corporate power. Corporations of this class will gladly welcome legislation that will further safeguard and protect them in the enjoyment of their rights. They do not shun publicity; they court it.

On the other hand, these irresponsible cliques of individuals, for selfish ends and by doubtful methods, have secretly grasped chartered rights, and, by juggling manipulation of stocks and bonds in their merciless pursuit of gain, brought commercial ruin to thousands. The aggregation of their combined interests threatens the existence of free government. They dread more than anything the light of day, knowing publicity would be their downfall. They pursue their designs secretly. The vast fortunes thus acquired are largely—in fact, almost entirely— due to their corrupt control of legislatures. The sworn representatives of the people themselves, in State and municipal bodies, have venally yielded to them, one by one, the people's rights.

The power thus obtained has been used solely to augment the fortunes of a few insiders and their political allies. It is not the enormous size of these fortunes, but the fact that they were dishonorably obtained, that has proved a demoralizing example to our youth and a menace to our institutions.

The sovereign State has the power to grant charter privileges for purposes that are in consonance with the general welfare and not in violation of the constitutional rights of the individual. The power of regulation is implied in the act of creation.

The abuse of the privileges derived from the people by these favored combines merits severe punishment, and necessary legislation for such purpose is clearly within the scope of the legislative power of the State. The opinion that Congress is powerless to remedy this evil without constitutional change is generally conceded, but the right of the sovereign State in the premises is unquestioned.

The different sections of our country having varying industries, such as cotton and its products in the South, know best how to control them. The nominal attempt to turn over this

power to the Federal Government by the Republican party is
an evasion, because they know that the power of creating, regulating, and, where public interest demands it, of destroying
these corporate creatures is a State right that will never be

JUDGE PARKER AND THE TRUSTS
From the collection of the New York Public Library

yielded to the general Government with the consent of the
Democratic party, which from Jefferson to Tilden has steadily
opposed such centralizing tendencies.

In the presidential campaign of 1904 Judge Alton B.

Parker, the Democratic candidate, advocated curbing the trusts along the line laid down by Mr. Coler, namely, by State regulation rather than Federal.

David A. De Armond [Mo.], from the Judiciary Committee, opposed the Amendment and bill.

A short time ago, when this question of where the Constitution might go and how it might be restrained, what might be the medium of the conveyance of it—when these questions were up, I remember well how the gentleman from Maine [Mr. Littlefield] thrilled this House, how his speech and his logic sounded and resounded throughout the United States. I remember how a new hero was born, how a man from Maine was covered with plaudits of "Well done, good and faithful servant," for being at once able, brave, and conscientious.

I have not forgotten how that man arose above his party when his party was wrong; how that man pleaded with his party when his party in its blindness would not choose the right; how that man, with courage to determine his course by the chart of judgment and conscience, won fame. An able man, with an eye for the national life, he rose high in the estimation of the American people at a time when others were ready to throw the Constitution away, and after offering pitiful little arguments and excuses continued to shrink and shrivel until the public no longer could see them. [Applause.]

The great question then was whether this old Constitution of ours, this venerated Constitution, possesses power over Congress or whether Congress possesses power over it, whether the Constitution is still to be the supreme law of the land or be dropped into the minor position of a local law for the guidance of the justices of the peace, while Congress swells into omnipotent power over many lands. Then it was refreshing to behold Littlefield, of Maine, as he left Republican partisanship for American statesmanship.

Now, then, fresh from that picture, still enraptured with that scene, drinking in still that American sentiment which knew no party, no section, no race, I am waiting and I shall be watchful to hear from the gentleman from Maine how it is that there should be put into the Constitution of the United States, or submitted to the people for putting into it this provision: "All powers conferred by this article shall extend to the several States, the Territories, the District of Columbia, and all territory under the sovereignty and subject to the jurisdiction of the United States.'' I wait for the revelation upon that point. [Laughter on the Democratic side.]

I do not know, but I have had a kind of suspicion (I hope it will not prove to be well founded) that our eloquent and distinguished friend from Maine who will close the debate has been buncoed. His Republican brethren whom he chastised then have now circumvented him. I think I can see the smile of satisfaction broadening into shouts of exultation as they contemplate the gentleman from Maine laboring at the task they have set for him, that of trying to explain how it is advisable or necessary to send this article abroad. [Laughter on the Democratic side.]

If I had before me the most forceful and eloquent and convincing speech of the gentleman from Maine, and if time would permit the reading of it, I would prove conclusively to any doubter that the Constitution does not need to be carried anywhere by congressional legislation; that wherever congressional legislation goes there will be also the mighty, supervising, ever-controlling Constitution to guard the rights of the people and curb the power of the Congress.

Now, gentlemen, in all sincerity, what do you think of this amendment, so sacred that nothing shall be offered to better it? Why do you refuse to allow an amendment to be considered here?

You do not even disguise your purpose. You are trying to carry yourselves through a campaign. You are trying to make the people believe that you cannot do anything unless you have a constitutional amendment.

And then when the people point to the mighty trusts that have grown up since March 4, 1897; when they call to your attention the fact that these trusts have grown up under the shelter of your laws and that the men in them, in many instances, are the men who control the destinies of your party, who control your conventions and buy your elections, you are going to say, "Why, my good fellow; why, my dear sir, we have gone just as far as we could go until we get increased power by a constitutional amendment." Your object is to shelve the trust question. Your object is to delude the people.

Considering what a monster the trust is; considering how men, women, and children are perishing before it; considering how liberty is going out in individual instances, how individual enterprises are blighted and crushed and individual lives wrecked and ruined by the mighty trusts, would it not be well enough to see how far constitutional power does go?

How many trusts are sheltered behind the protective tariff? How many trusts are created by it? How many trusts could not live independent of it? Are you ready to pick out a single article upon which there is a heavy duty, which is controlled by a trust and by the sale or monopoly of which the American people are robbed, and take that protective tariff duty off of it? No; not one.

You have been asked in this Congress; you have been asked by the press of the country; you have been asked upon the hustings; you have been asked over and over to do that, and you will not do it. What is your reason? Is it a good one? You talk about a "protective system." Do you wish to be understood that the protective system is designed to build up and maintain trusts? If that be true, proclaim your purpose boldly. Say that you love the tariff for the trusts it makes. [Applause on the Democratic side.]

Now, there is a little device known and tried in this country for years with considerable success, that of excluding from the mails certain matter, such as lottery tickets and correspondence about lottery tickets. Could not that be applied to trust correspondence and trust business carried on through the mails?

Would it be unconstitutional to extend that to trusts, to denominate them robbers when they are robbers, to call crime crime when it is crime? Would it be unconstitutional to extend the provisions of the anti-lottery law, of the anti-swindling and anti-green goods and anti-bogus operator law, to the operator of the trusts? Who says that would be unconstitutional? Why, as I understand, the majority of the Committee on the Judiciary say that. Why would it be unconstitutional? They have not told, and they cannot tell. They rejected amendments to that effect. The trusts must not be hampered thus.

Take the monopoly of the patent law. How easy it would be while legislating against trusts to fix a shorter term during which the patentee shall have the exclusive use and control of his patent, and then Congress can easily fix an additional term during which the patentee shall have complete control, subject to the limitation that he shall, upon reasonable terms, permit the use of the patented article and grant the right to manufacture it on a reasonable royalty. Would that be unconstitutional? I think not. Who says it would be? Is there not a remedy there?

Then we have demonstrated under the law how another power can be used and how effective it is. Once there were in this country State banks of issue. It was thought advisable to destroy these State banks as banks of issue and have none but national banks of issue. The Congress of the United States placed upon the issue of State banks a tax of 10 per cent. Of course no State bank could pay 10 per cent. for the issue of notes and do business. The result was that from the hour that law took effect not another State bank note was issued, and if that law remains in force not another State bank note will be issued between now and judgment day.

Could not that power be applied to the monstrous abuse that constitutes the trusts? Could not the taxing power reach them? Surely it could, but you will not apply it. For another example, consider the oleomargarine law.

Control over the traffic in intoxicating liquors has been given to the States. A bill was passed by the House a few days ago to put convict-made goods under State control. Why not trust-made goods also? Simply because the party in power will not pass any law that might be effective against trusts.

These are some of the means that might be employed constitutionally, without doubt, because they have been sustained by the decisions of the courts on laws now in operation, and effective operation, in many instances beneficently operating; yet with this greatest of evils, with the hideous oppression of the grossest of despoilers, you will not deal effectively. Instead of honest effort to reach the trusts by approved legal methods, you pretend that you must have a constitutional amendment, and try to delude the people into the belief that they can have no relief except through a constitutional amendment, saying to them that relief must be denied because the power to extend it does not exist.

Put your amendment into the Constitution, and then Congress would have a monopoly of corporation making. It would create them by special acts, and in making many corporations the trusts which it would create would not be few. And, if you doubt whether these law-created trusts would have the power to maintain themselves and stifle competition, note that there is but one railroad road bridge over the Potomac at Washington, and that many efforts to get Congressional leave to build others have been defeated, to perpetuate a monopoly. Note how corporations which Congress has fastened upon the District of Columbia are influential enough to prevent competing companies from securing an opportunity to compete. This amendment would prove a breeder of trusts.

That is putting off the resurrection a long while; that is prolonging imprisonment through life; that is inflicting the death penalty without benefit of clergy. "Wait until you get this amendment!'' When? Who believes you are ever going to get it? None of you—none of you. What in the meantime? To every attack made upon you, to every appeal directed to you, to every cry for relief from those in distress, the one answer, stereotyped, will come: "My God, dear people! We can not do anything until we get this constitutional amendment"; and then aside, "which, thank God, we never will get." [Laughter and applause on the Democratic side.]

Pretence, hypocrisy, successful delusion of the people, only invite more of the same thing. Let this deception be rewarded, let the people be blinded by such pretences, let them forget their best interest, and forego their present opportunity, and the time, perhaps, will not be far distant when the gentlemen who now talk about the trust not being "necessarily bad" and the gentlemen who say there is no trust, and the gentlemen who say that if the trust is bad they will deal with it, may be emboldened, as they see the people more helpless and the power of the trust greater and the trust more exacting, and its contributions for party purposes more satisfactory—they may be encouraged and emboldened to say: "The trust has come to stay; the trust is not to be fought; the trust is not to be disciplined; the trust is a modern development; the trust is a product of this great and mighty power called 'progress,' and is the evidence of prosperity."

Some gentleman talked about "prosperity and the trust." He conceded that the trust lately has grown as never before. He conceded that the growth of the trust has been phenomenal in McKinley's three years, and he said its growth is due to the prosperity of the country.

You mean that the trusts are prosperous, that those who bask in their smiles and enjoy their favors are prosperous. But there are many who are under their ban, who are damned by their curse, who are robbed at will by the trust as it goes its way. The people do not regard that as prosperity.

For three and a quarter years you have been trifling with the people while the trusts grew and waxed stronger and stronger and more numerous and still more numerous. Now you are about to be called to account. You would like very much to get another four years' lease of power. You know you can not get it upon the record which you have made, and so you offer a fake record. Have you forgotten what Lincoln said?

You can fool all the people some of the time and some of the people all the time, but you can not fool all the people all the time.

We need not summon witnesses to prove your guilt; you are confessing it right here and now. Bow your heads and submit to the sentence of your indignant sovereign, the people. Vacate—make way for Bryan and reform. [Great applause on the Democratic side.]

Samuel W. McCall [Mass.], Republican, opposed the Amendment and supported the bill.

Mr. Speaker, with regard to the two propositions pending before the House, I intend to vote in favor of the bill which Congress has the power to enact, and which will immediately have effect, and I intend also to vote against this proposed amendment to the Constitution which at the most will keep the word of promise to the ear, but break it to the hope. [Applause on the Democratic side.]

Let us not deceive ourselves about this proposition. This amendment is not simply aimed at trusts and monopolies, but it has application to every form of individual combination, and in my judgment it confers upon Congress the power to strike a most deadly blow at individual liberty. [Applause.] Just consider for a moment the phraseology of the second section. It seems to me there can be no doubt that it covers almost the entire field of business and production. That section declares that Congress shall have the power to define, regulate, prohibit, and dissolve trusts, monopolies, or combinations, whether existing in the form of corporations or otherwise.

If two blacksmiths or two tailors combine together in their trades, or if two owners each of $10 unite their capital in a common venture, that clearly is a combination. That is within one of the primary meanings of the word and, if there is any doubt about it, there is this singular provision in this amendment that Congress shall have the power to "define" what a combination is, and, if it declares anything to be a combination and uses the term in any sense in which it has ever been fairly employed, that will be held to be a combination. So that this amendment involves practical control of all the capital of the country; it involves control of all the labor organizations of the country, and of any co-partnership or union of two or more men for any business purpose whatever.

Now, the wealth of this country to-day is nearly $90,000,-000, most of it in some form of combination or other. And then there is that far more magical and potent capital which is found in the brains and bodies of our people, and we propose, and it seems to me it is an amazing proposition, to confer upon the Congress of the United States full and complete jurisdiction over all these productive energies. Even with these enormous interests dealt with in forty-five different capitals and dissipated and scattered throughout the country, they are yet strong enough too often to break down the resistance of human nature and produce corruption. And what will be the effect if we concentrate upon one body of men more than one-third of all the capital of the world and all these other tremendous influences?

Why, Mr. Speaker, is there a gentleman here who does not believe in his heart that if this power is conferred upon Congress the most corrupt, the rottenest place in the universe will be found right here in the city of Washington? [Applause on the Democratic side.] Mr. Speaker, it will be time enough to talk about constitutional amendments when we shall have employed all those weapons against trusts that now exist in our constitutional armory. [Applause.] I think we are bound to use our best judgment in a matter of this importance; I think that we who begin the process of amending the Constitution are just as much charged with responsibility as they who end it, and even more, because, having cast our votes for it, there goes with our votes the influence of our example. I find myself, therefore, unable to consent to put in our organic law this proposed amendment, which, if finally adopted, would, it seems to me, have the effect of ultimately overturning free institutions in this country. [Applause on the Democratic side.]

Mr. Littlefield closed the debate on the Amendment.

I trust, Mr. Speaker, in the discussion of this question, that I shall not find it necessary to become delirious or hysterical over the question of trusts. I have been sitting here and listening to the debate upon the other side. I have heard trusts characterized as "hydra-headed monsters," "robbers," "thieves," and the awful combinations that were grinding innocent women and children into the earth and bringing down prematurely Cimmerian darkness over the firmament. Assaults upon aggregations of capital have been inflammatory, intemperate, and unstinted.

Notwithstanding all this, I think it is proper to say at the outset that there are aggregations of capital, that there are corporations in this land which are legitimate and useful. The prevailing phase of modern business development undoubtedly involves the aggregation of extensive capital. It contemplates small profits and large volume of sales. It also requires the consolidation of separate interests, and these work out economies. It is sometimes the result of the coöperation of individuals representing the smaller units. This condition of things has advantages, and is subject to disadvantages. The advantages are that the consumer to-day, with this peculiarity of development which exists, receives and buys his goods cheaper than he ever did before. The disadvantages are that it eliminates individual competition and tends to sink individualism in the great aggregation or corporation.

It is perfectly competent and proper for a legislative body to fulminate its denunciation against an evil aggregation, or against the corporation that violates the purposes of its organization, and undertakes to oppress the people. But where there is one aggregation, where there is one corporation that is what might be called a "hydra-headed monster," or, to use the expressive and beautiful language of my friend from Missouri [Mr. De Armond], that "has its villainous clutch on the throat of American energy," I desire to say, Mr. Speaker, that there are hundreds, aye, I may say thousands, that are legitimate elements of enterprise, that conserve the interests of the people, that are in fact indispensable to the general welfare, and they are not to be railed at on this floor or in any campaign. Without great aggregations of capital no railroads could exist, no water power could be developed, no spindles could turn, no manufactories could turn out the multitudinous products of human ingenuity. The earth could not be compelled to surrender up its magnificent treasures for the uses of men, and it ill becomes this great body to make a general and universal assault upon capital because it is aggregated or consolidated. It is not enough to show that large dividends are paid, that the business is widely diffused, or that it is centralized and subject to the control of a president or board of directors.

It is only when it is injuriously aggregated, it is only when it is improperly aggregated—when it crushes or seeks to crush out competition, when it is operated to restrain trade and commerce and oppresses the public—that it becomes a proper subject of legislation, a proper subject of judicial attention.

The Republican party suggests as an affirmative legal remedy for this condition of things, in addition to those which already exist, two propositions—a constitutional amendment and an amendment to the existing law—and upon both of these propositions they are met by the Democratic party—a party that has been uniformly and always one of obstruction and never of construction.

I address myself, in the first instance, to the constitutional amendment. First, let me say one word in relation to my friend from Massachusetts [Mr. McCall], who, in my judgment, is unnecessarily disturbed in relation thereto. He seems to labor under the impression that this constitutional amendment has concealed within it such tremendous possibilities that it is liable to obliterate the liberties of mankind—that is, that portion of it included within the United States.

Let me suggest for his consideration that the construction of the word "combination" would be a trifle more apt and proper if he would construe it in the connection in which it is used, rather than divorce it from its connection and look to the dictionary for some other literal application and construction. Let me illustrate.

This amendment provides that Congress shall have power to dissolve "trusts, monopolies, or combinations." The gentleman from Massachusetts sees trouble in that word "combinations" for blacksmiths, carriage makers, etc. Now, let me ask him this question and let me suggest it to any other doubting friend; let me suggest it to my Democratic friends. What does the word "trust" mean in this constitutional amendment? Every man here knows what it means in its ordinary use. Has it any other meaning? Every man here knows that it has. Will the courts, however, hold under this constitutional amendment that the word "trusts," collocated as it is, is intended to apply to the relation existing between a trustee and his *cestui que trust,* which in legal parlance is a trust—that Congress would have power under this amendment to define or dissolve such a "trust"? That would be absurd. The court would construe that word "trust" in connection with the position which it occupies in the amendment and the purpose for which it is obviously used, and would construe the word "combinations" in exactly the same way. If Congress undertook to act capriciously in defining the court would unquestionably restrain such action.

Be not unduly disturbed; the country will still live and the liberties of the people be preserved. Have no apprehension about that. The obvious meaning of that language as used in that connection would be the rule of construction. No objection is made to this amendment by my friends on the other side on that ground. But their objections are what? They are two: First, the constitutional amendment suggests indirectly that the Constitution does not control Congress in legislating outside the limits of the forty-five States, and therefore no loyal Democrat can vote for it; second, this constitutional amendment interferes with and infringes upon the sacred doctrine of States' rights.

The gentleman from Missouri [Mr. De Armond] claims that the Constitution does extend to our new possessions, and he apprehended that I differed from the majority on that proposition. I say here and now that in that respect I adhere to my view of the Constitution. I believe it to be right; I believed it to be right when I announced it, but I do not think I am situated perhaps quite as the gentleman from Missouri and my other Democratic friends are. I apprehend that there is a possibility that I may be mistaken! It is entirely possible that the Supreme Court when they come to pass upon this great question may determine it otherwise than I think it should be determined. I doubt very much if it was necessary to mention any place or places over which this amendment was to operate. If the language, however, does not add to, it certainly does not take from or narrow, the scope of the amendment. If it does no good it can do no harm. It is idle to assert that language that some may think it necessary to use, in order to make this amendment universal in its operation, can have any legitimate interpretative force in determining the proper construction to be placed upon the language used in framing the Constitution and the original amendments.

The other objection of the opposition is that they ought to have the privilege of amending this constitutional amendment, so that it would be concurrent. I ask the attention of the House to an analysis of that beautiful proposition. The power that exists to-day over this subject between Congress and the several States is divided. Between them they possess it all. Congress exercises its powers solely by virtue of the interstate commerce clause of the Constitution, which reads as follows:

To regulate commerce with foreign nations, and among the several States, and with the Indian tribes.

When persons, corporations, trusts, or syndicates avail themselves of the facilities of interstate commerce, then they subject themselves to Congressional control. When any article becomes an item of interstate commerce, then the national power operates upon it. Until then Congress has no control, and its control ceases when the article ceases to be an item of interstate commerce. Upon the other hand, the State has the sole control until the line of interstate commerce is reached, when its power ceases. The State has no power to obstruct, interfere with, or control interstate commerce. The line which divides interstate and local commerce is the line of division between the two jurisdictions.

It is simply a legal impossibility to increase the power of Congress upon any practicable plan without decreasing the powers of the State, and this amendment does undertake to and will, if adopted, decrease to the extent of its terms the powers of the States; and hence the objection by men who believe in State rights, and hence the suggestion by my friends on the other side that concurrent power is what they want. Concurrent legislative power in this particular is simply a legal absurdity. That means equal power, power in the same degree, to the same extent. What would it mean when applied to these different things we are undertaking to remedy? It means the State could exercise the power, and the United States could exercise the same power to the same extent and to the same degree. Both have equal power. Now, if they happened to be inconsistent, one was in conflict with the other, which under that proposition would prevail?

If New Jersey saw fit to declare that a certain corporation was legitimate, innocuous, and wise, and the United States Government should undertake to say that they would dissolve that corporation, which one of these concurrent and equal powers would prevail? Neither; and you would have paralysis of legislative action. That is the Democratic theory of amending the Constitution; putting in a power that could not be effectively exercised by either, unless it was exercised on exactly parallel lines. If conditions that now prevail continue to prevail, and there is no reason to expect otherwise, there would be inconsistent legislation throughout the length and breadth of the land, and you would have a worse condition than exists to-day. And now they rail because they haven't been allowed to vote for that proposition. These are the only objections that our Democratic friends have to the constitutional amendment.

I want to call your attention now to a suggestion made by a gentleman for whom I suppose my Democratic friends have the greatest respect. I refer to our distinguished fellow-citizen who, during the last four years, has apparently been standing upon a mental eminence looking out over the country and crying out: Oh, America, America, how often would I have gathered thee "as a hen gathereth her chickens under her wing, and ye would not!" And she will not. [Laughter and applause on the Republican side.]

I have great admiration for Mr. Bryan. He is an orator of great ability and a distinguished public character; a man

"MR. BRYAN OPENS HIS CAMPAIGN"

Cartoon by Charles Nelan in the "New York Herald"

upright in his private character. I have no doubt upon his lines he may be sincere, but I can not say that I think my friend Bryan is really a great lawyer. His remedy for the great trust problem is that Congress can control a local corporation in a State by reason of the mere fact that it happened to be organized in another State. Every lawyer knows that the Congress of the United States has no more control over such a corporation, under such circumstances, than it has over the precession of the equinoxes. There happened to be a man in the audience who knew that, and this followed:

"A VOICE———"

I suppose it was the "voice of one crying in the wilderness."
[Laughter.]

A VOICE. Colonel, would such a law be constitutional?
MR. BRYAN. I was coming to that. I am glad you mentioned it.
What I mean to say is that Congress ought to pass such a law. If it is
unconstitutional, and so declared by the Supreme Court, I am in favor of
an amendment to the Constitution that will give to Congress—

I want to commend this to the distinguished gentleman from
Texas [Mr. Bailey], who is ready to adopt a constitutional
amendment provided he can have it in the homeopathic form.
He does not want it in the allopathic, to apply to every trust,
but he wants it in the homeopathic, to apply to only those engaged in interstate commerce. What is there about trusts that
will drift around in States and not engage in interstate commerce, that they should be protected by the suggestion of the
gentleman from Texas? I submit this to the consideration of
the gentleman from Texas.

Mr. Bryan says:

I am in favor of an amendment to the Constitution that will give to
Congress the power to destroy every trust in the country.

This amendment will do it. Under the Constitution as it
is Congress can not do it. Now, our Democratic friends have
this proposition: "Choose you this day whom ye will serve."
Choose you whom ye will serve—Colonel Bryan, the gentleman
from Texas [Mr. Bailey], or the gentleman who heads the minority on the Judiciary Committee—when you come to vote upon
this constitutional amendment.

I now come to the favorite panacea of our friends, the
Democracy, for this gigantic disease, the trust.

It is the abolition of the tariff on trust-controlled articles at
the discretion of the President.

My first objection—it may be a Democratic objection—is
this: There never was attempted to be written into the statute
books of any State or of the United States a provision so
violently imperial and czar-like as this proposition. It gives
to the President of the United States the power to enforce
upon an organization which is assumed to be criminal, for the
express purpose of punishment, and that punishment is expected
to be business ruin, the penalty of the law without even giving
the offending party the right to be heard. The President brings

the charge; he tries the cause; he renders judgment, and he executes the sentence. If that is not Cæsarism, if that is not imperialism, if that is not centralization run mad, I ask you to distinguish it.

This arbitrary power is in no sense parallel with the power vested in the President under a reciprocal clause in a treaty, where he only has to perform an act dependent upon the existence of a fact over which he has no control, as its existence is determined by the action of an independent power. Under this section he has the power to determine *ex parte* whether a crime had been committed, and then proceed to punish on the Democratic theory by ruining the criminal. As the tariff must be suspended upon all such articles, innocent parties who were dependent upon the tariff for success would have to meet the fate of the guilty. Again, it is only to be suspended when the "price is enhanced," but the great weapon of the trust is to crush competition by lowering prices, and while this interesting process was going on under this section they would have the benefit of the tariff, as it can only be suspended while the "price is enhanced." I deny wholly the efficacy of this legal nostrum.

Now, I want to call your attention to the author of the sugar trust, an eminent Democrat, Mr. Havemeyer, who, in his testimony before the Industrial Commission, states this proposition:

The mother of all trusts is the customs tariff bill.

And then he has the monumental assurance in that same statement to say that the tariff upon sugar should be doubled.

The Standard Oil Company has never had the protection of a cent upon petroleum or oil. But go into England, free-trade England, and the trusts and aggregations of capital in England exceed the aggregations of capital and the formation of trusts in the United States under the protective tariff. It is literally covered with them. They create no surprise. But where is the creator of trusts in England? Have we creatures without creators? Can it be possible that they are like Topsy, they simply grow, or are they like the original protoplasm in the theory of evolution, they come and nobody knows how they come? I take the report drawn by the gentleman from Missouri [Mr. De Armond], in his magnificent English, and I find that he states that the tariff is the mother of trusts. This is his language:

Consider for a moment how the tariff operates to make and perpetuate the shameful monopoly known as the paper trust.

I went on and read his report to see *how* it operated. Did he tell how? Did he tell why? No. Did he show how it was brought about? No; and no other man who has made that assertion has ever told. It reminds me of the lawyer in the West who was arguing a case before a justice on the frontier, and was pictured by Bill Nye as standing up before the justice, with his clenched fist uplifted in the air, his mouth wide open, saying: "When I holler, it's law." [Laughter.] So it is with my friends upon this proposition, when they say it is so, it is so, but the man doesn't live who has yet given a reason why it is so.

Now, I want to quote to my friends what Colonel Bryan the Great said upon this proposition that our Democratic friends say that they believe in.

While some relief may come from modifications of the tariff, we can not destroy monopoly until we lay the ax at the root of the tree and make monopoly impossible by law.

Now, in view of his last suggestion, when we have the adoption of a constitutional amendment pending here, the question is whether our friends will follow the lead of the Colonel or will they follow the suggestion of my friend from Missouri, who says that it has been so long since the Constitution has been amended that it can not be amended, or my friend from Texas [Mr. Bailey], who objects to the amendment because it would take away all the powers of the State, or my friend from Texas [Mr. Lanham], who says the Constitution can not be amended except by bayonet and saber stroke, and shot and shell, and the spilling of blood. I had hoped it was not as bad as that. We have not reached the period of blood, except the blood that my friends on the other side are sweating in connection with the vote that they expect to have to cast here in a few minutes. [Loud laughter on the Republican side.]

The joint resolution to amend the Constitution was put to vote, and resulted in 154 yeas to 132 nays, thereby failing of the two-thirds vote required for its passage.

The anti-trust bill was passed by the House on June 2 by a vote of 274 to 1. After considerable debate in the Senate it was referred to the Committee on Judiciary, which failed to report it during the session.

CHAPTER III

BOUNTIES

[THE COD-FISHERIES BILL]

Debate in the House on Granting Bounties to Cod-fishers: In Favor, Fisher Ames [Mass.], Elbridge Gerry [Mass.], Samuel Livermore [N. H.]; Opposed, William B. Giles [Va.], Hugh Williamson [N. C.], James Madison [Va.], John Page [Va.]; Bounties Are Granted.

THE subject of the constitutionality of bounties came first before Congress in February, 1792, in connection with a cod-fisheries bill. Those in favor of such grants were Fisher Ames [Mass.], Elbridge Gerry [Mass.], and Samuel Livermore [N. H.]; those opposed were William B. Giles [Va.], Hugh Williamson [N. C.], James Madison [Va.], and John Page [Va.].

ON BOUNTIES

HOUSE OF REPRESENTATIVES, FEBRUARY 3-9, 1792

Mr. Giles moved to strike out the section in the cod-fisheries bill granting bounties. In support of his motion he said:

The present section of the bill appears to contain a direct bounty on occupations, and, if that be its object, it is the first attempt as yet made by this Government to exercise such authority, and its constitutionality struck him in a doubtful point of view, for in no part of the Constitution could he, in express terms, find a power given to Congress to grant bounties on occupations; the power is neither directly granted, nor (by any reasonable construction that he could give) annexed to any other power specified in the Constitution. It might perhaps be brought in under a mode of construction already adopted by the House, viz.: that of "ways and ends" by which any power

109

whatever might be equally implied, but he wished ever to see some connection between a specified power and the means adopted for carrying it into execution. There is a great difference between giving encouragement and granting a direct bounty. Congress have a right to regulate commerce, and any advantage thereby resulting to a particular occupation connected with commerce comes within that authority, but when a bounty is proposed to a particular employment or occupation, this is stepping beyond the circle of commerce, and such a measure will affect the whole manufacturing and agricultural system. In all cases the revenue to be employed in this bounty is drawn from all the sources of revenue in the United States and confined to a particular object. He was averse to bounties in almost every shape as derogations from the common right, and he thought there would be no great difficulty in proving that a government is both unjust and oppressive in establishing exclusive rights, monopolies, etc., without some very substantial merit in the persons to whom they are granted, although even in that case the propriety of such grants is still questionable. Under a just and equal government every individual is entitled to protection in the enjoyment of the whole product of his labor, except such portion of it as is necessary to enable government to protect the rest; this is given only in consideration of the protection offered. In every bounty, exclusive right, or monopoly, government violates the stipulation on her part, for, by such a regulation, the product of one man's labor is transferred to the use and enjoyment of another. The exercise of such a right on the part of government can be justified on no other principle than that the whole product of the labor of every individual is the real property of government, and may be distributed among the several parts of the community by governmental discretion; such a supposition would directly involve the idea that every individual in the community is merely a slave and bondman to government, who, although he may labor, is not to expect protection in the product of his labor. An authority given to any government to exercise such a principle would lead to a complete system of tyranny.

He entertained fewer doubts respecting the principle as it regards political economy. All occupations that stand in need of bounties, instead of increasing the real wealth of a country, rather tend to lessen it; the real wealth of every country consisting in the active product of useful labor employed in it. It is therefore bad policy to encourage any occupation that would diminish, instead of increasing the aggregate wealth of the community, and, if an occupation is really productive and augments the general wealth, bounties are unnecessary for its support, for when it reimburses the capital employed and yields a profit besides it may be said to support itself. When it fails in these points any forced advantage that is given to it by the Government only tends to decrease the wealth of the country.

The subject, however, might be considered in a more favorable point of view, and that is, whether the provision was essential to the defence of the United States, and whether the bounties proposed in the bill were more than equivalent to the portion of defence that would be procured by them. The bill does not (in his opinion) contain that kind of encouragement which is essential to the national defence. Any man who takes a view of this country must be convinced that its real support rises from the land and not from the sea, and the opposite mistake must have arisen merely from a servile imitation of the conduct of Great Britain; the inhabitants of this country heretofore thought favorably of her Government, and the Revolution has not yet altered their former ideas respecting it. But the circumstances of the two countries will, on examination, be found widely different; Britain, surrounded by the sea on every side, finds a navy necessary to support her commerce, while America, possessed of an immense territory, and having yet ample room to cultivate that territory, has no occasion to contend by sea with any European power; her strength and her resources are all to be found within the United States, and, if she but attends to her internal resources, the object of national defence will be much better answered.

From a comparison between the bounty and the number of sailors employed in the fisheries he showed what an expense each man would be to the United States, and, after other remarks, observed that even Great Britain, whose whole national support and defence depend on her navy, had found that the men employed in the fisheries, though so necessary for that defence, cost her too much; that America, whose consequence as a nation does not depend on a navy, ought to take a lesson from the experience of Britain; that he did not wish to enter into a competition with Britain and France in supplying the different markets with fish; that, as those nations are able to hold out greater encouragement to their fishermen than we can to ours, we would, by such a competition, only exhaust the treasury of the United States to no purpose, and upon this principle alone he thought there was some reason to doubt the policy of the measure proposed in the section under consideration.

MR. AMES.—The more fish we catch the cheaper; the English fish will need a greater bounty; whereas, if we should yield, the English would probably need no bounty at all; they would have the monopoly. For example, suppose the English can fish at two dollars the quintal—we catch so much that we sell at one dollar and two-thirds; the loss to them is one-third of a dollar on each quintal. They must have that sum as a bounty. Whereas, if we increase our fishery, a greater and a greater bounty is needed by foreign nations. The contest so painfully sustained by them must be yielded at last, and we shall enjoy alone an immense fund of wealth to the nation which nature has made ours, and, though foreigners disturb the possession, we shall finally enjoy it peaceably and exclusively. If the lands of Kentucky are invaded, you drive off the invader; and so you ought. Why not protect this property as well?

Another view has been taken of the subject which is drawn from the naval protection afforded in time of war by a fishery. The coasters and other seamen, in the event of a war, would be doubly in demand, and could neither protect themselves nor annoy the enemy to any considerable degree, but the fishermen, thrown out of business by a war, would be instantly in action. They would, as they formerly did, embark in privateers; having nothing to lose and everything to hope, they would not dishonor their former fame. Their mode of life makes them expert and hardy seamen. Nothing can be more adventurous. They cast anchor on the banks three hundred leagues from land, and with a great length of cable ride out the storms of winter. If the gale proves too strong they often sink at their anchors and are food for fish which they came to take; forever wet, the sea almost becomes their element. Cold and labor, in that region of frost, brace their bodies, and they become as hardy as the bears on the islands of ice; their skill and spirit are not inferior to their hardihood; familiar with danger, they despise it. If I were to recite their exploits the theme would find every American heart already glowing with the recollection of them; it would kindle more enthusiasm than the subject has need of.

Some gentlemen think of a navy, but what navy could do more? What nation would provoke a people so capable of injuring them? Could fifty ships of the line afford more security? and yet this resource of the fishery, always ready, always sufficient, will cost nothing. The superior naval force of our

Fisher Ames

foes should not discourage us; our privateers would issue like so many swordfish to attack the whale.

MR. GERRY.—The State of Massachusetts asks nothing more than equal justice. We do not come forward to request favors from the United States; we only wish that the same system which is applied to other parts of the Union may be applied to us.

We have laid on hemp a duty of fifty-four cents per hundred-weight, and on beer, ale, and porter five cents per gallon. Now, I ask, gentlemen, whether the professed design of those duties was to raise a revenue, or to prevent the importation of those articles? They were laid for no other purpose than to prevent foreigners from importing them, and thereby to encourage our own manufactures, and was not that encouragement a bounty to the persons concerned in producing such articles in this country? If the duties had not been laid, the importer could sell much cheaper than he now can, and the landed interest would be under a necessity of selling cheaper in proportion. If those prohibitory duties operate as a bounty in favor of raising hemp and of brewing beer, ale, and porter, I ask whether, if a bounty were proposed on every quintal of fish, it might not, with the same propriety, be granted? If we have not a right to grant a bounty in the one case, we have as little right to grant it in the other.

MR. WILLIAMSON.—In the Constitution there are two or three remarkable provisions which seem to be in point. It is provided that direct taxes shall be apportioned among the several States according to their respective numbers. It is also provided that all duties, imposts, and excises shall be uniform throughout the United States, and it is provided that no preference shall be given, by any regulation of commerce or revenue, to the ports of one State over those of another. The clear and obvious intention of the articles mentioned was that Congress might not have the power of imposing unequal burdens; that it might not be in their power to gratify one part of the Union by oppressing another. It appeared possible, and not very improbable, that the time might come when, by greater cohesion, by more unanimity, by more address, the Representatives of one part of the Union might attempt to impose unequal taxes, or to relieve their constituents at the expense of other people. To prevent the possibility of such a combination, the articles that I have mentioned were inserted in the Constitution.

But we have been told that Congress may give bounties for useful purposes; that is to say, they may give bounties for all imaginable purposes, because the same majority that votes the bounty will not fail to call the purpose a good one. Establish the doctrine of bounties and let us see what may follow. Uniform taxes are laid to raise money, and that money is distributed—not uniformly; the whole of it may be given to the people in one end of the Union. Could we say, in such a case, that the tax had been uniform? I think not. There is certainly a majority in this House who think that the nation would be stronger and more independent if all our labor were performed by free men. Establish the general doctrine of bounties, and all the provisions I have mentioned become useless. They vanish into air, and, like the baseless fabric of a vision, leave not a trace behind. The common defence and general welfare, in the hands of a good politician, may supersede every part of our Constitution, and leave us in the hands of time and chance. Establish the doctrine of bounties, set aside that part of the Constitution which requires equal taxes and demands similar distributions, destroy this barrier, and it is not a few fishermen that will enter, claiming ten or twelve thousand dollars, but all manner of persons—people of every trade and occupation—may enter at the breach, until they have eaten up the bread of our children.

MR. LIVERMORE.—The article of the Constitution which says that taxes shall be equal in all the States can only respect the *rates* of the duties, *i. e.*, the *same* duties shall be paid in Virginia as in New York—at the North as well as at the South. It surely can not mean that every individual shall pay exactly the same sum in every part of the Union.

MR. MADISON.—It is supposed by some gentlemen that Congress have authority to grant bounties under a power by virtue of which they may do anything which they may think conducive to the general welfare! This, sir, in my mind, raises the important and fundamental question whether the general terms which have been cited are to be considered as a sort of caption, or general description of the specified powers, and as having no further meaning and giving no further powers than what is found in that specification, or as an abstract and indefinite delegation of power extending to all cases whatever—to all such, at least, as will admit the application of money—which is giving as much latitude as any government could well desire.

I, sir, have always conceived—I believe those who proposed the Constitution conceived—it is still more fully known, and more material to observe, that those who ratified the Constitution conceived—that this is not an indefinite government, deriving its powers from the general terms prefixed to the specified powers—but a limited government tied down to the specified powers, which explain and define the general terms.

It is to be recollected that the terms "common defence and general welfare," as here used, are not novel terms, first introduced into this Constitution. They are terms familiar in their construction, and well known to the people of America. They are repeatedly found in the old Articles of Confederation, where, although they are susceptible of as great a latitude as can be given them by the context here, it was never supposed or pretended that they conveyed any such power as is now assigned to them. On the contrary, it was always considered clear and certain that the old Congress was limited to the enumerated powers, and that the enumeration limited and explained the general terms. I ask the gentlemen themselves whether it was ever supposed or suspected that the old Congress could give away the money of the States to bounties to encourage agriculture, or for any other purpose they pleased. If such a power had been possessed by that body, it would have been much less impotent, or have borne a very different character from that universally ascribed to it.

The novel idea now annexed to those terms, and never before entertained by the friends or enemies of the Government, will have a further consequence, which cannot have been taken into the view of the gentlemen. Their construction would not only give Congress the complete legislative power I have stated; it would do more; it would supersede all the restrictions understood at present to lie in their power with respect to a judiciary. It would put it in the power of Congress to establish courts throughout the United States with cognizance of suits between citizen and citizen, and in all cases whatsoever.

There are consequences, sir, still more extensive, which, as they follow clearly from the doctrine combated, must either be admitted, or the doctrine must be given up. If Congress can apply money indefinitely to the general welfare, and are the sole and supreme judges of the general welfare, they may take the care of religion into their own hands; they may establish teachers in every State, county, and parish, and pay them out of the public treasury; they may take into their own hands the education of children, establishing in like manner schools throughout the Union; they may undertake the regulation of all roads, other than post roads. In short, everything, from the highest object of State legislation down to the most minute object of police, would be thrown under the power of Congress, for every object I have mentioned would admit the application of money, and might be called, if Congress pleased, provisions for the general welfare.

Several arguments have been advanced to show that, because, in the regulation of trade, indirect and eventual encouragement is given to manufactures, therefore Congress have power to give money in direct bounties, or to grant it in any other way that would answer the same purpose. But surely, sir, there is a great and obvious difference which it cannot be necessary to enlarge upon. A duty laid on imported implements of husbandry would, in its operation, be an indirect tax on exported produce, but will any one say that by virtue of a mere power to lay duties on imports Congress might go directly to the produce or implements of agriculture, or to the articles exported? It is true, duties on exports are expressly prohibited, but, if there were no article forbidding them, a power directly to tax exports could never be deduced from a power to tax imports, although such a power might directly and incidentally affect exports.

In short, sir, without going further into the subject, I venture to declare it as my opinion that, were the power of Congress to be established in the latitude contended for, it would subvert the very foundation and transmute the very nature of the limited Government established by the people of America.

Mr. Page.—We are asked, Is it not of great consequence to the United States to employ those bold, skillful seamen in our service that we may enjoy the commercial advantage they give us in peace, and their powerful assistance in war? To this I reply that it ought first to be proved that Congress has the power and authority to give them the encouragement demanded, and, even if Congress have that power, it ought to be shown that it can be extended to the benefit of the sailors of some of the States, and not to those of every State. It may be said that Congress may with as much propriety give bounties to our hunters in the Western country, to raise up a nursery of soldiers as a barrier against the Indians, and to promote the fur trade, as to give drawbacks and bounties to the fishermen of the Eastern States, with a view to encourage fisheries, and to raise a nursery of seamen for their defence against enemies who may invade our Eastern frontiers. Indeed, if defence be the object in view, we might as well give bounties to sturdy landsmen to be in readiness and constant training for war. A nursery of virtuous families which will produce soldiers, sailors, husbandmen, and statesmen must be preferable to a mere nursery of sailors, who generally live single and often perish at sea. I always look upon the loss of a crew to an infant republic as the loss almost of a new State.

Is it politic and wise, then, Mr. Chairman, to exert the power contended for, even if it be authorized by the Constitution? May not Congress, with equal propriety, undertake to regulate the tobacco, the rice, and indigo trade, as well as that of the fisheries? If they intermeddle in the business of sailors, why not in that of manufacturers and farmers? As a member of this House I shall think it my duty to protect the fisheries and every other branch of our commerce, the fisherman as well as every other citizen, as far as may be within my ability, but I am not permitted, as a member of Congress, I humbly conceive, to select the fisheries and fishermen as objects of more consequence than any other branches of trade, or persons employed in them, lest Congress should not only show a mistaken attachment, or, even if judiciously placed, excite jealousies and discontents between the States, and distrust, destructive of their weight and influence. My constant wish has been to see Congress confined to such acts as would form a more perfect union, promote the general welfare, insure domestic tranquillity, and engage the confidence of our fellow-citizens.

Let the legislatures of the different States encourage, as far as in their power, the commerce, agriculture, or manufactures of their respective States, and let Congress, as far as can be consistent with the most steady impartiality, patronize their patriotic exertions, by wise regulations of their commerce with foreign nations, such as may open as full an intercourse with those nations as the States may desire. The emulation of the sister States in commerce, manufactures, or agriculture would lead to the early establishment of that branch of either to which each State might be best adapted. This rivalship could produce no jealousy, no general national discontent in the States, no localities in Congress. Virginia would not attempt to rival Massachusetts in her fisheries or carrying business, nor will South Carolina and Georgia rival the manufactories of New Jersey and Pennsylvania. Each State may rejoice to see its sister States enjoying the advantages with which Heaven has blessed them, and Congress, if confined to subjects which admit not of local considerations, may debate with temper and decide with unbiased judgment.

The question on striking out the first section was taken and negatived—32 to 26.

CHAPTER IV

SHIP SUBSIDIES

ON January 21, 1873, Samuel Shellabarger [O.] introduced in the House a bill to create a Board of Commissioners of Commerce to execute Government contracts for the encouragement of commerce. The bill provided that the commissioners be authorized to offer bounties for the construction of ships in the United States (not over $15 a ton for iron ships and not over $12 for other ships) to be engaged in foreign trade, and that the total tonnage thus subsidized should not exceed 500,000, nor 100,000 a year.

Mr. Shellabarger said in support of his bill:

A nation which surrenders or becomes incapable of carrying on and controlling its own exchanges of commodities in its own vehicles and channels of trade is one which, at the very beginning of that surrender or incapacity, has commenced to sink in a vital respect to the rank of an inferior and dependent nation, and is one which must cease to hold any material commerce or rank in the community of nations.

Here the speaker went at great length into ancient, medieval, and modern history to prove his contention. He then discussed the reasons why maritime power is essential to our national prosperity.

The sum of our exports and imports last year reached within a fraction of $1,071,000,000, excluding gold and silver. What was paid out for the mere freight of this enormous shipment in and out was about $100,000,000, including American passengers. Now, let the United States surrender its right or lose its ability to earn this hundred million a year, which must be paid by us to somebody, simply for carrying our own freights and passengers in and out, and the transaction is exactly the same as payment by the United States of an annual tax of $100,000,000 to such nations as we hire to do this, our own carrying work. The labor, or the cost of the labor, of carrying an axe to its market is as much part of the cost of the axe as is the making of it. That nation is simply mad that makes $1,000,000,000 worth of products a year, makes them nine-tenths done, then stops, stands idle, and pays another nation $100,000,000 per year for completing the manufactures. In the light of your common mother wit, tell me how long will it be before this libation of seventy-one and a half millions a year, drawn from the blood of the people, will make us poor indeed, and those who feed upon us rich indeed. Take this fact alone, and do you wonder that history should tell you that the merchants of Babylon, of Tyre, of Venice, of Lisbon, of Antwerp, and of London, who drew this seventy-one and a half millions each year, got rich, and that they of India, who paid it, became poor?

The most familiar experiences of this nation show the values coming from owning our ships. Passing by, for want of time, the new and vast markets given to our own and, in part, wrested from other nations by the establishment of American lines to Brazil and Japan, take, as a sample, the results of the establishment, through the patriotic agency of a single citizen of New York, of a line of American steamers from San Francisco to the Hawaiian Islands, New Zealand, and Australia. Already such amounts of the mechanical and agricultural production of our people have been carried to a before unknown market by this line that the tariff revenues derived from the imports for which they paid is already estimated at $1,138,577.09 for little more than six months.

Mr. Speaker, it is in this stupendous affair, which lies at the foundation of our very civilization and of every material greatness—in this thing, the great Republic is perishing. Why, sir, to defend your flag throughout the globe you to-day pay two hundred and fifty diplomats and consuls near a million a year. And yet that flag has nearly vanished from the seas! The permanent exemption of the United States, as of every other nation, from war is to be found only in perpetual readiness for war. This proposition, so self-evident as to make one of the maxims in public economy, is of the very first moment in this great discussion, and must be thoroughly comprehended.

The next proposition which must be kept ever in mind is that it is a traditional and fixed policy of the United States that in time of peace it will not keep up either its army or navy to such magnitudes as are required in case we are at war. In other words, our policy is to maintain readiness for war by always maintaining the nucleus of an army and navy, and by a constant state of readiness to increase these to every requisite of war from the reserved forces of the people. This policy results mainly from the nature of republican institutions, which forbid the keeping up of vast armies and navies in time of peace, and the policy cannot and ought not to be changed.

The next thing which we should instantly and fully comprehend as a nation is that in a great commercial navy the United States would have constantly a great war navy, commensurate with all the wants and exigencies of war, and we can consistently, with our policies, have an adequate war navy, ever at hand, in no other way. The immense importance of this proposition demands us to look into its truth, but my time admits of my naming but few of the proofs of that truth. No living authority is higher upon this point than our gallant Admiral Porter. In imploring Congress at once to create a great commercial marine, he testified in 1870, before one of your committees, that this identical proposition in all its parts was true—true in science, in theory, and by the huge experiences of the recent war. As to the capacity of merchant vessels, like the Cunard line, being speedily changed into powerful war ships and made ample for every defensive and aggressive purpose of a great war, he declares the following things, found on pages 183-85 of Executive Document No. 28, second session, Forty-first Congress.

These merchant ships could be quickly changed into powerful

warships, rigged with masts, and made capable of remaining at sea three years without coal. Had we possessed only thirty such steamers as the Cunarders at the beginning of the Rebellion, not a bale of cotton would have escaped the Southern ports, and the war of the Rebellion would have been far shorter than it was. Thirty such vessels, changed to warships, would have proved twice as effective as was the entire navy of the United States.

That in case of war with a foreign nation, like England and France, our great power would be in cutting up their commerce, and England could not stand a war six months with a fleet of such vessels. That nearly every effective warship we used during the Rebellion was a merchant ship, and but two or three rebel boats, roughly fitted up, had sufficed to drive our commerce from the seas, destroy eighty-six American ships and $70,000,-000 of our property, and he asks if two could do this what could two hundred do?

Besides the momentous facts above stated from Admiral Porter, the nation will not fail to remember forever what that navy did for the succor of the Republic, and the memory of the Republic itself will perish from history as soon as will the names of Farragut and his compatriots. But, remembering these deeds of the navy, the sleepless and winged ally and companion of our vast armies, remember also the words of its gallant Porter. He declares "nearly every ship that was used during the war was a merchant ship."

Mr. Speaker, by proofs like these it is completely fixed and sure that the creation and support of a great merchant marine are absolutely vital to the Republic.

These coasts are by far the vastest possessed by any existing State. Your readiness for their defence must every hour be in exact proportion to your continental proportions. Like as a huge chain measures its strength by that of its weakest link, so a navy, protecting nine-tenths of your vast circle of seashore, but leaving the supplies and disasters of war to go freely in at the uncovered tenth part, would, in that particular species of service, be no navy at all. Now, I solemnly declare to the House and nation that in the presence of such a fact as this one—the vital relations of a merchant marine in furnishing an adequate and ceaseless supply of trained sailors and ships for the national defence—to hesitate in the adoption, at whatever cost, of the requisite and best means for the creation of such a marine is a crime against the national safety and life, and, with the lessons of the present decade before us, becomes, in the rulers of this people, a weakness and wrong unapproximated in our history.

But now, sir, add to the terrible logic of such facts as I have now passed over the force of those yet to come. The Secretary of the Treasury a year ago said that you are paying annually an enormous sum in cash as a direct undisguised subsidy to the very lines which burnt and banished your ships from the sea, and which now rule over that $1,100,000,000 worth of the products of the labor of this people which passes through our ports each year.

But this is not all nor the worst. The decay of your carrying trade with foreign nations is still going on at appalling rates. In 1826 you carried ninety per cent. of your own commerce. You slowly lost, relatively, up to the beginning of the war, when you still retained sixty-five per cent. At the end of the war you had thirty-seven per cent. Now you retain only twenty-eight per cent. of your own carrying commerce. Your surrender, even since the war, has been at the rate of a million dollars per year in this single item of foreign freights. Speedily, unless this process is arrested by removal of its causes, the United States flag will disappear from the ocean.

Mr. Speaker, this House now enters upon a momentous duty. That duty is the speedy adoption of the best measure for the rescue of the country from this immense and impending peril. The commercial growths of your three great rivals are already three centuries old, and are the result of governmental fostering and guardianship that have not had a day or hour of sleeping in the three hundred years.

The substitution of iron for wood is a cause hitherto against us, but one which we may, owing to our superiority in iron and coal, make immensely in our favor. The girdling of the globe with the telegraph is another, and by enabling the avoidance of fruitless voyages has enormously lessened the mileage assessed upon the aggregate of the ocean trade. The tunnel of Mont Cenis has shortened the way of central Europe to India, and is abolishing the power of England at Gibraltar. The Suez canal brings India and the East thousands of miles nearer our east coast, and is emancipating the rest of the world from British warehouses, commission men, and bankers. The Pacific railroads are sending streams of commerce and even European mails for Asia across our Republic.

Russia is pushing her conquests and her railroads to the walls of China. Germany, Prussia, England, Austria, and Italy are enormously extending and strengthening their commercial machinery and resources, and are grasping eagerly each new accession to the resources of the international trade. Their statesmen comprehend the situation, and they have seized the new wealth which the impending commercial revolution tenders them.

It remains yet to be disclosed whether they who rule our country shall arise to this comprehension and the action to which in all other nations it has already impelled them.

Because of the abolition of differential duties and the adoption of reciprocity treaties by our own and all other commercial nations, the competition on the seas between these nations for the world's carrying trade is reduced to substantial equality, and, since the great bulk of this trade is permanently transferred to iron from wooden ships, other nations can supply the elements which enter into the creation and running of these iron lines at less outlay than the United States, and can therefore, under present conditions, underbid us for this international trade, and they do underbid us. Hence we rapidly disappear from the ocean. This is the whole of the sad story, and has in it neither mystery, uncertainty, nor doubt.

The ability of foreign lines to underbid us in the competition for carrying the world's commodities, including our own, is approximately indicated by the following differences in the cost of the things entering into the creation and running of the great lines:

1. England can build the ship of iron for nine and a half per cent. less than we, after we are allowed the drawback of duties on ship materials.

2. The capital required to build and run the ship costs but two to three per cent. interest in England, while in the United States it costs from six to seven per cent.

3. The cost of ship supplies in the United States, in absence of rebate of duties, is about twenty per cent., in the aggregate, in excess of foreign supplies.

4. The cost of the labor for officering and manning the ship is with us, as contrasted with England, about as seventy-two is to one hundred and one; this as estimated in 1870.

5. The taxes, State and national, levied upon what enters into the creation and maintaining of an American line did heretofore exceed the tax on British lines about as fifteen to one.

6. England grants a rebate of duties upon imports used on shipboard amounting to an annual subsidy to her ships of $2,328,762 in gold. We have allowed none.

7. England pays in direct annual subsidies to nine lines

$4,201,866 in gold, and France pays $4,732,267. We allow none to any line with Europe.

Great as we are compelled to confess these differences against us now seem, I know there is not an American heart so cowardly or lost to the impulses of patriotism, or of mere self-preservation, as to sink beneath this danger of our commercial extinction, or which does not prompt the instant exclamation: ''These obstructions shall be overcome and the nation rescued.'' The question you ask is not whether the obstacles to our commercial greatness shall be overcome, but is how surest, quickest, and best shall we remove them.

Most glad am I, Mr. Speaker, to assure the House and country that some of these differences against us are rather adventitious and temporary than real or enduring, and are already either disappearing or removable by agencies not involving the voting of any direct subsidies. Others have already been removed, in whole or part, and the residue are such as can be removed without the infliction of unbearable taxation.

Those taxes on commerce which have not already been removed by the abolishment of taxes upon shipping interests by the law of June 9, 1872, granting rebate on ship materials, etc., and by abolition of internal revenue taxes, should be speedily removed.

The advance, within a year, of the cost of iron, labor, and supplies for ships in England has materially reduced their advantages over us in iron ship-building, and the boundless and easy supplies we hold of both iron, coal, and wood, added to the ten per cent. of superiority in the tensile quality of American iron for ships, together with our either attained or attainable progress in the application of machinery in producing ships, has abolished, or soon will abolish the advantages hitherto held by England over us in the production of the iron ship. The differences which remain, and which must be met, are mainly in the cost of our labor and capital, added to the direct subsidies annually voted by other nations. How best to overcome these is the momentous practical problem submitted now to the American people and to their Congress.

But two policies have been materially pressed for adoption. These two rival plans may be stated thus: one proposes to procure for American ships from foreign countries, at their prices, whatever is required to make and maintain those lines under our flag. The other plan, and that on which the bill of the committee is founded, is to permit ship supplies and materials for ships to have the benefit of rebate of duties, or equivalent bounties, but to insist that the building of the ships and procurement of the officers and men thereof, and the controlling ownership, shall be American and not alien, and that the differences now against us in cost resulting from insisting that these shall be American shall be overcome by direct Government aid.

My time precludes an attempt at giving even an epitome of the argument on which the committee rests its adoption of this policy. Some of my own reasons I condense thus:

First of all, any policy wholly refusing all Government aid, and trusting for the creation of an American marine to the procurement of the things, even should these be everything required to create and maintain it, in cheap foreign markets will never give us any lines or ships under our flag, simply because such lines would still have to compete with lines subsidized enormously by their governments, as in case of England, at the rate of $4,201,866, and France, at the rate of $4,732,267 per year in gold.

Next, a policy which involves our making an American merchant marine out of nothing American except what can be procured at as low prices as our rivals would be willing to supply us at, so long as we are rivals, would be marvelously un-American. The iron ship would be foreign; its supplies would be foreign; the capital in it would be foreign; insurance risks upon it would be foreign; the labor which created it would be foreign; the profits of its building would be foreign; the profits of its running would be foreign; the sailors and officers upon it would be foreign; its shapes and capacities would be foreign; its movements and control would be foreign; the docks for its repair would be foreign; and the bunting for its flag and the dyes for the colors thereof would be foreign; and the residue thereof would be American! What that residue is and the services it would render the Republic as the "American" part of our marine after we had created it they will tell you who think American lines can be created, officered, manned, and owned by our alien rivals. I have no arithmetic adequate to detect what that remainder is.

Again, political economy is preëminently the science taught by experiment—is tentative. Here a statesman is surely insane who follows mere theory and rejects what is taught by the experience of all other nations. Looking to this source of learning, I pray to be informed what commercial State has ever gone abroad for all her ships, seamen, and the capital which creates and guides them? Passing by, however, the teachings

on this point furnished by all other States, let us take the
example of England. Let us take this one, not only because
of this being the highest example in history of commercial
success, and because it is the power we must now combat, but
also because this is the example we are all pointed to as the
one exhibiting the benefits of free trade in ships. From the
date of the commercial code of Cromwell she not an hour ceased
to enforce a policy which is summed up in a single sentence. I
quote from an able report from one of your departments:

"It seems as if British statesmen were for two hundred years haunted
by a dread lest in all the wide world a loophole of advantage might be
left to the ships of other nations, which, by any possibility, an act of
Parliament could secure to the British flag."

In the light of that three hundred years of government
fostering it is no wonder that Mr. Levi—the last chronicler of
England's commercial annals—declares her commercial greatness to be the product of "superhuman" effort and care, and
that he should boast that the opening of her ports and ship
business to foreigners in 1849 has not taken from British
subjects over six-tenths of one per cent. of their monopoly in
the creation and manning of her enormous merchant marine.

But, sir, by far the gravest reasons are yet unnamed which
forbid the adoption of policies making this Republic for an
hour dependent for its ships, their officers or seamen, upon their
supply by other nations. These unnamed reasons are the
political and commercial degradation and vassalage which such
policy involves in time of war. I have named the degradation
and endangerment of peace which our banishment from the
ocean brings in time of peace. Add to this degradation what
comes to us when come the disasters of war—and, forsooth, war
with the powers on whom we have decided we will depend for
ships, seamen, and their officers. These ships, and the yards
that produce them, and the inured and trained men who command and run them, are the production not of an hour, but
years. War is now upon us—a war invited by our chosen,
chronic, and insane feebleness; and what is the spectacle we
see? A nation invited to accept empire on the ocean by the
vastest possibilities ever bestowed of God on a single state;
one whose seat is a continent; whose coast two oceans; whose
material in wood, iron, coal, and every other wealth is simply
inconceivable; whose home lies in the very pathway of the commerce of the globe; whose people have genius, force, science,
skill, and every resource of power in degrees unsurpassed, if

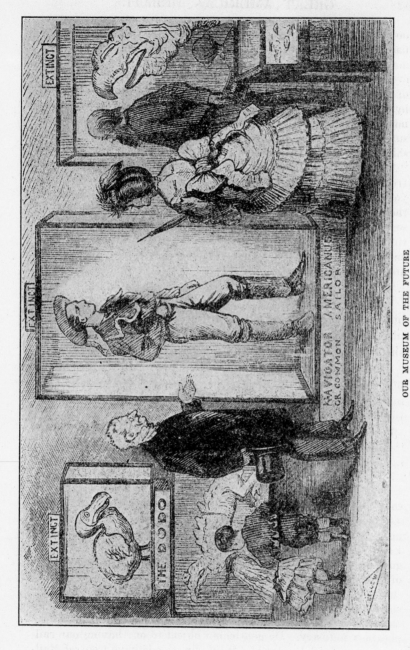

OUR MUSEUM OF THE FUTURE

Learned Professor. "THESE ARE THE RESTORED REMAINS OF A NOBLE CREATURE LONG SINCE EXTERMINATED BY THE RAVAGES OF PESTILENT INSECTS KNOWN AS POLY TICKS",

From "Punchinello"

not unmatched, on the earth—that people is now at war and
has no shipyards of her own, no ships of her own, no ship-
makers of her own, no ship commanders of her own, no sailors
of her own; nothing upon the seas of her own, save billions
of dollars of her people's products, and these in ships mocked
by the presence of a flag over them giving them neither direction
nor defence; and this flag to be instantly, that war has come,
supplanted by that of the alien foe that owns and mans the
ship. And with your foreign-owned, made, manned, commanded
"American" merchant marine transformed with all its precious
freights, by the touch of war, into whole fleets of foes, and
you incapacitated, by your chosen feebleness, to reproduce
them in years! Such, without painting, is the spectacle presented by a nation whose rulers have deliberately elected, for
times of war as well as peace, to put out to the nursing and
culture of its traditional foe the very elements of its safety
and of its sublime being!

Samuel S. Cox [N. Y.] offered an amendment to the
bill, repealing the act of December 31, 1792, and all sup-
plementary acts forbidding the registry of foreign-built
ships, provided their owners were American citizens.

John Lynch [Me.] objected that this amendment was
not germane to the bill, which was for the encouragement of shipping, since it would destroy American shipping.

Mr. Cox replied that the gentleman was confounding
"shipping" with "commerce," and that the larger interests of commerce would be benefited by his amendment.

We are the only nation, Mr. Speaker, on the face of the
earth which cannot go where it pleases to procure its ships.
The gentleman from Ohio a few moments ago challenged us to
point out a nation that sent abroad for its ships. I point to
France, which goes to Glasgow. I point to Germany, which
goes to Scotland also. England herself goes to different ports
of her own country, although much the greater proportion of
the ship-building is done by Glasgow. Every nation goes, or
should go, in the interest of humanity and of its people, to
that place where it can find the cheapest commodity or the
cheapest industry. Do gentleman object to our having our railroads owned in England? Why, sir, the Illinois Central Railroad is owned in England.

William D. Kelley [Pa.].—I would ask the gentleman whether the railroads are built in England, whether the work on them is done there?

Mr. Cox.—The gentleman knows that a great many of the rails are constructed there, but of course Pennsylvania has almost had a monopoly of that business under the outrageous system which he has always championed. We would have had a revival of our commerce and shipping were it not for the miscalled protection which the gentleman advocates. It is a protection to the foreigner, as I could show, yet the gentleman from Maine [Mr. Lynch] says that my amendment for free shipping is not germane to this bill. I could show you, if I had time and if the House were in the humor, that $40,000,000 are earned annually at the port of New York alone by foreign vessels and foreign citizens in the carrying trade of the Atlantic; that we lose from seventy-one to seventy-two million dollars annually by the protective policy taking from the people the right to buy ships and run them and man them with American seamen, is already confessed in the treasury reports quoted by my friend from Ohio [Mr. Shellabarger].

I know, Mr. Speaker [James G. Blaine, of Maine], that in your State an effort has been made under the specious guise of drawbacks and under cover of our recent legislation to revive your shipping interests. Perhaps some little good may result in promoting the building of wooden ships in Maine and on the Delaware. But, sir, bounties have failed in every guise and device, whether by drawbacks, bounties, postages, or otherwise, to revive our commerce and shipping interests. We have a large coasting trade; we have an immense area of inland navigation; we have made great efforts to foster these interests here. But there is one interest so eulogized by the gentleman from Ohio [Mr. Shellabarger] that has not been fostered by this Congress, and all that that interest cares for is that they shall be "let alone." They do not care about protection. They are, and long to continue, free men, and to trade free. Was there any difficulty about our shipping or commerce up to 1860? We had no bounties, or scarcely any, except to one line [Collins], up to that time. Was there ever such an increase known in ship-building as up to 1856 in the United States? We not only built all our own ships, but we built ships which were sent into English ports to be sold. Why? Because by even a partial repeal of your odious tariff taxes, responding to the repeal of the corn laws in 1846, we were enabled to interchange, and through the increase of commerce to command, the carrying

XI—9

trade of the world. Why, sir, we grew under the magic of our industry and of our comparative freedom from taxation from $2,180,000 in 1840 to over $3,000,000 in 1850, and to $5,258,000 in 1860!

I am simply ashamed to show our decline since 1860. It would look partisan. I am almost ashamed to discuss the causes of that decline. The talk about the *Alabama,* so far as decline in shipbuilding is concerned, is a fraud. The more ships destroyed, the more demand for shipbuilding.

When the gentleman from Ohio [Mr. Shellabarger], so learned in history, goes back to the Phœnician and other pirates of old times, and comes down, as I think he does by his bill (of course unintentionally), to the pirates of this time, who have ever preyed by tariffs and what not upon our industry, you will find that, as the result of our historic and economic experience, Pennsylvania, or its narrow selfish policy, rules us with a rod of iron. As the result of this State and local dictation, our people have degenerated in prosperity, and by the reverse policy our people would have grown in prosperity. Their growth would have been in proportion as they were released from commercial shackles. England to-day is an illustration of the splendid benefits of the repeal of navigation and all other restrictive laws. If we would be just to ourselves we would copy her example. We would make the sea free and common to our enterprise. A free sea, free as the winds and waves, is the emblem of that grandeur of nations which the irrelevant speech of the gentleman from Ohio has even aggrandized by his rhetoric.

But gentlemen by their insane tariffs as well as by their corrupt bounties have nearly destroyed commerce. All we can do now is to mourn over it as men mourn over the ruins of Rome or of Athens. They are splendid in their ruins, but they are ruins still. Our vessels, our shipyards, and our harbors speak of your former grandeur and your present selfish fatuity. Dislocated and unrecompensed labor, paralyzed and alienated labor, tell the tale of feeble and senseless Federal legislation!

There are only two ways of reviving shipping. One of them is to reduce your taxes on articles that enter into the construction of shipping, iron, steel, timber, cordage, etc. Thus you may, perhaps, revive shipping. There is another way, and that pointed out by the substitute which I hope to bring before the House. That is to allow our merchants to buy ships freely wherever they may or can. Do not, as is proposed by this bill, create a new bureau, a bureau of commerce, with certain men at the head of it, for the purpose of intervening in business. You want them to supervise the construction of ships. Do you not propose to give them the privilege of giving bounties to a few at the expense of the many? Is there anything more unrepublican or undemocratic, more illiberal or unjust? Agriculture and commerce join hands in advocating the largest liberty in commerce. They are interdependent, and thus they make nations, ay, even the world, better and greater!

It has often been suggested to me by our leading men, and by our great newspapers in New York City, that there was no way possible for Congress to help shipping or revive commerce except by giving free registry. The unprotected classes, ever the victims of selfish spoilers, have begged that they may go abroad to buy the instruments of commerce. You allow other trades and other people to buy the instruments of their handiwork abroad, if so be they can so buy, and buy, of course, with advantage. Why is a ship, iron or wood, different from an adze or a woolen fabric? If a tariff is demanded, very well; levy it. But why prohibit entirely one kind of adjutants to industry and transportation and let others in, even under heavy burdens?

Now, the bill before us discriminates in favor of certain classes. Where do we get our right to discriminate in favor of a half dozen lines of steamships to the exclusion of all others? Is it in the Constitution? In economy? In morals?

I presented a petition here two or three years ago signed by Charles H. Marshall, of the Black Ball line to Liverpool, and other shippers and owners, asking that they might not have the competition which was fed by subsidies to contend with. They asked no aid from the overtaxed farmer or mechanic. They did not believe, of course, in the bounties given by Congress to other lines. Why should they ask Congress to help their competitors? What right have we to build up a dozen lines at the expense of a hundred? Why help a few by hindering many others who do not get bounties? What right have we to help one line running to one country, when we do not help the lines running to another country? All the laws of piracy, from Carthage down to the pirates of Algiers, cannot sanction such inequitable and swindling devices. If that be our policy, where and when shall we stop? Look at the details of this bill. I cannot now stop to consider them. I tell you, Mr. Speaker, and fellow-members, that this bill has no limit to its power of plunder. It will drain your treasury dry. If it is not piracy, it is something worse, and namelessly worse, because done by Government. It is not only "inequality before the law," but, if it is a law, it will draw every dollar from your treasury.

Not to refine too much, the proposition is that the Government shall help out of the treasury a few men that they may venture into this peculiar line of business, while others have to foot their own losses without the aid of the taxpayer.

Such a measure is not just. It is not equal. Being unjust and unequal, it will not foster prosperity. It cannot help commerce or shipping. It has no precedent in honest history when properly analyzed and studied. I oppose it *in toto* as the beginning of another era of corruption. I oppose it as I did in other years the connection of Government with railroads. Where is the natural right or justice, where the constitutional right by which we can, as Congressmen, connect Government with private business and fortune? Experience shows that the less we connect such private enterprises with authority the purer is the Government and the greater the prosperity of the individual and the nation.

The absurdity of the pretence that the *Alabama* destroyed shipbuilding is evident enough. If the ships destroyed by that cruiser were worth being replaced by others, would not their very destruction have given an impetus to shipbuilding? The truth is that, iron steamships at that precise epoch superseding wooden sailing ships, their destruction was no loss. They were generally insured and paid for by the underwriters with the proceeds of extra premiums, wrung from the community. Our ship owners were fortunately induced to sell their wooden ships to England, and the beneficial rather than the disastrous result is that they have been rotting in English dockyards instead of in ours. As to the bounty passed last session, it was all for the coasting trade, an already absolutely unapproachable monopoly; for it is susceptible of proof that at least seventy per cent. should be allowed on the cost of every American vessel in order to make the builder even with the Scotsman. The decadence of American coastwise navigation is owing simply to the facts that railroads are their successful competitors, and that, steamers taking the places of sailing vessels and making their voyages more frequently, less tonnage is required.

The decadence of American ocean navigation, the almost entire extinction of it, is owing partly to the latter cause, but chiefly to another one that is all-powerful. All other people of the world being allowed to purchase their ships in the cheapest markets, and the ocean being the common property of all nations, they are enabled to underbuild and consequently to undersail us. That is the whole story.

Now for the true remedy. It does not lie in subsidies which are only for the benefit of a few companies. Every individual American citizen who wishes to own a ship has as much right to a bounty as a steamship company. It does not lie in bounties; for all bounties, to be just, must be general. Then the amount to be drawn from the treasury would be so enormous that the scheme would be impracticable. The true remedy is just this and nothing else: give every American the privilege, as my substitute does, and which every foreigner now enjoys, of buying ships where he pleases.

A few ship builders, whose theory is that government should promote a great monopoly shop for their exclusive benefit, tell us that, the duty on foreign material being removed, they can build ships as cheaply here as they can be built abroad. Simple arithmetic exposes this fallacy. Given equal cost of material (which would be impossible even if duty-free, on account of freight and other charges), what of a considerable item, labor? If in this country we must still be taxed on all the necessaries of life, so that it takes two dollars to buy here what one dollar buys in Scotland, must not the price of this kind of labor be greater here? The difference in cost of labor alone on a three-thousand-ton steamship two years ago was $200,000. It has been but little modified. I propose a bill of perfect fairness to the ship builder and the ship owner. It is a bill which shall at the same time admit materials and ships duty-free. Give the ship builder a fair chance. Let him try. If with these facilities he can build the ship, surely the merchant will have no occasion to go to a foreign market. Why should not the merchant provide himself abroad with what the builder cannot furnish him at home? Once more, Mr. Speaker, let our countrymen own ships, as once they did, that we may acquire wealth instead of giving it to strangers. Thus, reassuming our rank as a commercial nation, we may have sailors to man our fleets in case of war, and not, by a hotbed growth, make war by subsidies, as proposed by the gentleman from Ohio. In such a war we should inevitably fail.

The gentleman from Ohio has intimated, while emitting his statistical demonstration, that the price of labor in foreign countries is approximating our own. But in the business of shipbuilding I imagine that some discrepancy still exists. At least two years ago there was so great a difference that I was informed that a steamship of three thousand tons would cost more, according to the labor and materials, in Scotland than in this country by $200,000. We know that owing to our tariff it costs more by thirty-three per cent. to build in New Brunswick than in Maine. Let the fact be understood. We cannot build ships here because of your impracticable and, I was about to say, infernal tariff. You will not, because of your tariffs, let us build ships; and you will not let us buy. It is simply a dog in the manger. I ask by my amendment, since the privilege of building ships is not allowed us, that we may buy them where we can buy cheapest.

WILLIAM D. KELLEY [Pa.].—Will the gentleman yield to me for one moment?

MR. COX.—I know what the gentleman is about to say. He is going to tell me that on the Delaware River they are building ships.

MR. KELLEY.—I wish to inform the gentleman that among the many industries of this country none is growing so rapidly as the building of iron ships.

MR. COX.—I knew the gentleman was going to say that. [Laughter.]

MR. KELLEY.—It is a square contradiction of the gentleman's assertion.

MR. COX.—If this industry is so prosperous, why does it need these extraordinary bounties? If it is so healthy and is growing, why administer to it this poison of subsidies? Why tax the body of the people throughout the country to help a special business? Why, especially when this "industry is growing so rapidly"? Why compel the farmer in Illinois to pay an extra amount for his plow by reason of your tariff to pay such subsidies? Why—when men out West are burning their prairie-raised corn for fuel—why do you keep up your taxes on coal for fuel? Why on iron for transportation by rail?

MR. SHELLABARGER.—There is one point in reference to which I think the gentleman has fallen into an error, and upon that point I would like to hear him.

MR. COX.—I ask my friend to be a little forbearing. He has made here an elaborately prepared speech of nearly two hours. He has sent over to England for statistics. I had no idea this matter was coming up to-day. I speak without my papers, and without preparation. I have not the figures I should like to dilate upon to meet the gentleman. Do not take advantage of a poor blind boy by asking statistical questions. [Great laughter.]

MR. SHELLABARGER.—We are told by Mr. Joseph Nimmo,

Jr., chief of the division of tonnage in the Treasury Department, our price would be reduced to nine and a half per cent. more than the assumed English price if our builders are allowed the benefit of drawback of duties.

Mr. Cox.—I wish to get at the drift of the gentleman's argument. He says there is a great difference between shipbuilding in this country and shipbuilding abroad. Yes, there is. He says that difference is constantly being reduced, and yet, while that is his argument, at the very time when we are equalizing the cost of labor in Great Britain and in this country, at this very time, in comes the gentleman, asking us to make a grand, monstrous, moneyed, and subsidized monopoly for the benefit of a few people at the expense of many. As I have often said in this House, so I say again, I am in favor, as Tittlebat Titmouse [1] was on one occasion, of giving something to everybody. [Laughter.] I wish every man, woman, and child to have a subsidy, or else I wish nobody to have a subsidy, and I prefer the latter. Is it the function of government to help one class of people at the expense of another?

Omar D. Conger [Mich.].—I should like to inquire why the gentleman in his argument asks that importers alone, of all the people of the United States, shall have the privilege of buying ships and bringing in their imports free of duty when everything else is required to pay its proper duty? He asks for the protection of the importers, and not for the protection of every other interest in this land. Why is it that he is in favor of giving this privilege to only one class, and that the importers, which class he represents upon this floor?

Mr. Cox.—The gentleman is arguing with his heels and standing on his head. [Laughter.] I wish to convince him he is wrong in attributing to me any such idea. I represent no special class. If my remarks seem to free the importers from undeserved burdens, and thus free others, I ask why should they not have the privileges of fair government as well as other people? They do not ask bounties or tariffs. Why not let them have free registry? If you choose to tax by way of tariff the ships they would buy and import and register, very well. Fix your tax. But do not make it prohibitory. Now the gentleman from Michigan [Mr. Conger] can see how he has mistaken my point, when he attributes to me a desire for special legislation.

Mr. Conger.—I do not think I understand the gentleman's point.

Mr. Cox.—I cannot help the gentleman to see, but if he will

[1] A character in Samuel Warren's "Ten Thousand a Year."

take my spectacles I think he will be able to see it. The gentleman from Michigan is like other gentlemen in this House who urge and obtain protection for their respective local industries. He has his lumber to take care of, and shipbuilding enhances the home market for lumber. Why not, on principles of equal justice, allow the importer to buy his ship or medium of transportation abroad? Why not allow him to go for lumber to Canada? Why not allow this without paying tax or tariff? Oh! I wish that I could make an enlarged, liberal, say a cosmopolitan, emphasis on the gentleman. But he is a Michigander. He is a man who stands by his constituents and their timber. He is limited by the interests of his own State. Well, some of the best men in this House are thus bound. Yet they know the general interest.

When I present a large, far-reaching amendment becoming the Representative of the commercial metropolis, the entrepôt of the commerce of the country; when I speak in the interest of the largest body of generous commercial men from the source and center of nearly the whole of our importing and exporting commerce; when speaking for a city which nature and enterprise have made; and into which three-fourths of our commerce goes out and comes in, the grand and proud gateway of a people of forty millions; when I consciously represent the best intellect, industrial, mercantile, economical, and liberal, in our land, and which does not ask protection or bounties, or anything in the shape of taxes to be levied on other localities or industries for their aggrandizement—a very genius of enterprise which asks only to be let alone that it may go with its ships on the free, common sea, free as its wild waves and winds, free to draw from all the world to their own country the riches of other lands, and free to send out our products in glad and golden interchanges—when I propose these generous policies, lo! the gentleman says he cannot see the propriety of my representing a selfish class of importers on a measure fraught with commercial and economical liberties.

If he will only rise to a higher plane he may perceive the meaning of my thought. I would speak for the best economy. Good economy is the highest morality. Morality approaches very near the Christian throne. If the gentleman will allow me to lead him gently along I will bring him within the consecrated pale of that fair, beautiful, and true religion which extended itself through the world and still extends its benignities —on the wings of commerce, even as in the early days on the blue Mediterranean. Ah! if the gentleman had lived in those simple and early days on one of those islands in that blue sea which Paul traversed for the evangelization of the heathen and the barbarian, and, if Paul had landed on his island and had seen him, I have no doubt that the first man whom Paul would have ''gone for'' would have been the gentleman from Michigan. [Great laughter.]

Why, sir, the honest importer is a laboring man; he labors in the highest sense. What does he not do by his work? He brings the products of other climes here. He asks no favor. He would bring them cheap. He would buy ships in the cheapest market. He thus makes transportation cheap. He thus makes all the necessities and comforts of life cheap. He is a benefactor, under God, to all! He would do it best by getting rid of your odious tariffs upon his business. He would do it best by free trade with all. Perhaps now the gentleman can see that the interest of the importer is the interest of the whole people. Perhaps he can see how I reconcile all the interests of my city and district. But I do not speak here, sir, for the importers only; I do not speak for my own constituents only; I speak for yours, and for all the tax-ridden people. I speak as well for the consumers of carpets, dry goods, and woolen cloths; for those who use lumber, leather, and iron. I would have everything that you tax by your tariffs relieved of excessive burden by the cheapest freights. If I do represent importers, I represent also the honest and poor people of all parts of the country. They deserve, as they desire, cheap transportation, which cheapens commodities. I am opposed to scarcity; in favor of abundance. I want competition by sailing ship or steamer, by locomotive or stage. I am against subsidies. They injure and debauch. Therefore I am against this bill, because it will drain the treasury to help a few at the expense of the people, who are the many.

The bill was tabled on January 22 by a vote of 121 to 65.

President Harrison, in his annual message December 1, 1890, repeated former recommendations in regard to the development of American steamship lines.

The reciprocity clause of the [McKinley] tariff bill will be largely limited, and its benefits retarded and diminished, if provision is not contemporaneously made to encourage the establishment of first-class steam communication between our ports and the ports of such nations as may meet our overtures for enlarged commercial exchanges. The steamship, carrying the mails statedly and frequently and offering to passengers a comfortable, safe, and speedy transit, is the first condition of foreign trade. It carries the order of the buyer, but not all that is ordered or bought. It gives to the sailing vessels such cargoes as are not urgent or perishable, and, indirectly at least, promotes that important adjunct of commerce. There is now both in this country and in the nations of Central and South America a state of expectation and confidence as to increased trade that will give a double value to your prompt action upon this question.

On December 10, 1890, John M. Farquhar [N. Y.], from the Committee on Merchant Marine, introduced in the House a substitute for a ship subsidy bill [the Frye bill] passed by the Senate during the previous session. It came up for discussion on December 18.

Ship Subsidies

House of Representatives, December 18, 1890-February 27, 1891

Mr. Farquhar supported the bill.

I was very sorry to-day to hear a characterization from the other side of the House which seemed to me somewhat gross and malicious, that somewhere in this bill, somewhere in the management of bringing this bill before the House, there was a "job." There has never been one suspicion in the committee that there was any particular interest standing persistently there as job makers for this bill or for the substitute. The only organization of which I have any knowledge, if I may say it is an organization, that ever appeared before the committee was the American Shipping League, of which the gentleman from Alabama, General Joseph Wheeler, was the president for three years.

Mr. Wheeler.—I was elected three times, each time for a year, against my protest. On the last occasion I resigned and kept on resigning until they finally accepted my resignation.

Mr. Farquhar.—I was present at a meeting of that association on one occasion when it passed very complimentary resolutions to him for the interest he had taken in a bill of the very character that is now under consideration.

Mr. Wheeler.—At that time this bill had not been introduced. I am in favor of reviving American shipping, but that is not involved in this bill. There are other ways of reviving American shipping.

Joseph H. Outhwaite [O.] asked if the bill did not favor the Pacific Mail Company.

Mr. Farquhar.—This is a bill that cares no more for the Pacific Mail Company than it does for the owner of a coal schooner sailing out of the harbor of Philadelphia, and the man never read the bill and does not know its merits who claims that any corporation or organization in this country gets one dollar more out of this bill than it is fairly entitled to in sailing on even keel in competition with its neighbors.

Mr. Outhwaite.—Can the gentleman inform us how much the Pacific Steamship Company will receive the first year as a subsidy under this bill?

Mr. Farquhar.—If the gentleman will read the hearings he will find all the figures he desires.

Mr. Outhwaite.—I will ask the gentleman another question. Can he tell us how many points Pacific Mail Steamship stock went up yesterday in expectation of the action of this committee to-day?

Mr. Farquhar.—Not being interested in the Pacific Mail—not nearly so much as some Ohio men—I do not know anything about it, and I do not intend to have any interest in it.

A Member.—It went up four points.

Mr. Farquhar.—If we intend by legislation or otherwise to put the American merchant marine on a footing to defy the world and even to reach England in the course of twenty years, all we have to do is to go back to the protective policy of our fathers with differential duties. By this policy 12½ per cent., which is the beggarly amount of the commerce of our country that we are carrying to-day, can be increased to 90 per cent. in twenty years.

That is what is wanted. But it seems that under the courtesy of reciprocal relations with other nations this cannot be done. The nearest way to reach the result is, instead of placing differential duties in favor of American bottoms, to pay this bounty to every American vessel engaged in that trade. That is the exact position our committee has taken after full deliberation.

Some say you cannot trade with any nation unless they

trade back. That is what they call the "goods-for-goods" theory.

JAMES R. WILLIAMS [Ill.].—That is good Democratic doctrine.

ALEXANDER M. DOCKERY [Mo.].—Or reciprocity, in other words.

MR. FARQUHAR.—No; reciprocity, properly understood, carries with it amity, friendship, and strength. There is no reciprocity on the high seas where every nation fights for an advantage. Not a single American ship to-day travels the wide ocean but has to compete with a parallel subsidized line, and the American ship receives not a dollar of assistance.

Now, under the "goods-for-the-goods" theory, whether we pass a bounty bill or not, we cannot get the trade; and I want to call the attention of the House for a minute to a single fact in that connection.

Look at the excess of imports from Mexico, Central America, the West Indies, and South America. Look what a tremendous balance of trade there is against us there. Now, what inducement can this country give to these Latin-American countries if to make trade there is a difference of $80,000,000 in the rough at once? We have now a carrying trade that extends to only two main lines; all the rest is in the hands of foreigners.

There are only two great propositions in the carrying interest of the merchant marine in the foreign trade. Will you take care of your own marine and will you ship by ships built here, or will you buy your ships anywhere you wish and put the American flag over anything of foreign manufacture?

Under the French building bounty law a large proportion of the French lines were owned by Englishmen. They reaped the benefit of the French bounty. The French did, however, make a total gain in tonnage of 10 per cent. from the start. They have now as fine a class of tonnage as can be found anywhere on the face of the sea, and instead of extending the ten-year bounty law, as was expected, they simply extended the bounty, but cut out foreign-built ships from receiving any more bounties on building, and they intend to abrogate their reciprocity treaties. That is just what I said some time ago would be the proper thing to do in this country in order to build up a merchant marine.

HILARY A. HERBERT [Ala.].—During the first period of ten years after the bounties were granted the steam tonnage of France rapidly increased, but for the last five years her steam tonnage has rapidly fallen off, so that she has lost her second place and declined to the third; and the cause of this falling off was a fear on the part of the ship owners and shipbuilders that the French Government might not continue the subsidy for another term of ten years.

When this policy is once begun, like the tariff, there is no possible end to it; it must go on with a continually increasing demand. Why do you ask us to be guided by the example of France and undertake a policy here which would result necessarily in the same condition of things? For, after ten years, as the example of France shows, we would have to do the same thing over again; while a country without any subsidy at all, like our own, can outstrip a country like France which has a subsidy, as the figures show.

Mr. Farquhar.—Mr. Chairman, I recur to the problem of free ships.

This bill proposes, by paying bounty on every new steamship that makes more than 12 knots an hour and shall come under the supervision and inspection of the Navy Department, to build up the American merchant marine. It provides that such ships shall be certified and enrolled. How much cheaper are you going to make your defences on the ocean than that? let me ask. At the very beginning, at the very genesis of this bill, it is made conditional that the tonnage shall be of first character.

Again as to the postal matters. They offer now under this bill to turn in the sea and inland postage, amounting to hundreds of thousands of dollars a year, and instead of paying a profit to other nations running a ship this bill proposes to carry every mail free. What better proposition can you have than that every port in America can be a port for the mails?

James H. Blount [Ga.].—How do you carry the mails free when you take the money out of the Treasury and turn it over in the shape of bounty to these ships?

Mr. Farquhar did not answer this question but continued his line of discussion.

Mr. Chairman, I want to say a word further about this free-ship matter.

Under the present tariff act there is not anything that enters into the construction of an iron ship, or a wooden one, either, but what can be imported into this country free of duty. What more do you ask in the way of free ships? Do you want also to constitute a foreign-built ship simply a piece of "shelf goods," or is the mechanic to be shipped to the other side if he cannot get work here, to do the work on a foreign ship? We have all of the material free and the bill covers everything down to a ten-penny nail, and yet because the friends of the American shipyards and the American sailor and carpenter do not see, in addition to what is conceded them, that you shall import the whole ship, assembled as a ship, why then we are under "restraints" in American commerce, and there is no relief to any man who is engaged in that business!

Why, it would seem that such complaints are absolutely childish when such a law as that is on the statute books. Now, your free traders and free shippers have for years knocked at the door of Congress, as they claim, and got this legislation; yet when they get it, oh, the organs of British opinion say, "No, you will have to take the whole ship, labor as well as material," buy it as shelf goods and run up the American flag to the peak as a lie.

I say it is time that we arrested the strides of a nation that claims everything for herself and finds supporters even in high bodies in this land.

Newspapers that are supported by Americans, with a few crumbs of foreign advertisements, turn their editorial columns to favor the abolition of the American sailor, the American navy, the American mechanic, and American trade. Oh, it is a fearful spectacle, that of men who, forgetting the land of their birth and the blood in their veins, have taken a partisan line that leads to the destruction of American pride and American honor. [Applause on the Republican side.]

On January 6, 1891, Gen. Joseph Wheeler [Ala.], of the Committee on Merchant Marine, opposed the bill.

We are told that we ought to pass this bill because England adopts a similar policy. There has never been a more flagrant misrepresentation uttered in this House than a statement of that character. England, with her magnificent tonnage, her great fleets engaged in foreign commerce, pays to her 8,235,854 tons of steamers but $3,184,435 a year, while were this bill in operation in England she would be compelled to pay about $300,000,000 in bounties; so far from England paying anything for maintaining her shipping, she simply pays out for steamship lines a certain amount of the postal revenues, and the total aggregate of the postal revenues is more than fourteen millions in excess of her expenditures.

In 1883 I had the honor to make a speech in this hall, when the bill was up to increase the tariff, and I alluded then to the threats of retaliation by European governments and the possible effect it would have upon the exports of the products of American farms.

At that time we exported $225,000,000 of wheat, and the threats were carried out. The tariff was raised by Germany and other foreign countries against our wheat exports, and in the seven years since that these have fallen off so that we export about $50,000,000 of wheat. Of this California supplies $17,-000,000. Now these California wheat growers will buy ships for themselves to transport it when this tremendous bounty is given; a ship sailing from a California or Oregon port to England or France would draw from the treasury from 20 to 25 cents per bushel, and that, too, when they are already successfully competing with the wheat of Kansas, of Nebraska, of Illinois, of Ohio, of Indiana, and New York. That being so, what will be the pitiful condition of those States?

With the fertile soil of California upon which to raise their wheat, they can produce it almost without limit and send it to Europe, being paid by the Federal Government a bounty upon the transportation which is almost equal to the cost of production.

Again, under this bill it might be a profitable business to bring wheat from India. It would land in New York. There they would have simply to make it into flour and then ship it to England, and it would draw two bounties, a bounty for the voyage to the United States from India, and a bounty for the voyage from the United States to England.

Take the case of iron ore. Spain and Italy have iron ores of a very superior character. It is now being brought to this country as ballast.

Under this bill, iron ore coming here as ballast will draw at the minimum 83 cents per ton and at the maximum the sum of $4 a ton. Coal from Nova Scotia will draw twice as much bounty as the duty; and the consequence will be that ships bringing iron ore from these foreign countries will enable manufacturers to make iron on our coasts cheaper than it can be made anywhere in the interior.

GENERAL CHARLES H. GROSVENOR [O.].—Would not that produce free raw material substantially?

MR. WHEELER.—It would produce much more than free raw material. The bounty would pay back the duty and give a large sum besides.

MR. GROSVENOR.—And are you not in favor of free raw material? [Laughter.]

MR. WHEELER.—I am in favor of a general revision of the tariff for the benefit of American industries, but I am not in favor of selecting one material that one section of the country is interested in and making that worse than free by giving a bounty to bring it from abroad, while leaving the tariff on everything else to stand for the enrichment of other sections of the country.

MR. GROSVENOR.—But would it not have had the same sort of effect upon free raw material produced abroad? Would it not, according to your doctrine, stimulate our industries along the seacoast?

MR. WHEELER.—It would certainly stimulate many industries. Take, for instance, lime. When a ship coming from St. John with a load of lime receives this bounty, the tendency will be to bring foreign lime to this country in competition with the lime produced here. I contend, from a careful calculation, that the bounty will entirely wipe out the duty under the existing tariff bill, and it would much more than wipe out the duty exacted by the tariff law which the McKinley bill supplanted.

Again, take lumber. All you have to do is to establish a lumber industry at some place in Maine, then bring in your lumber from Canada, simply plane it on the edge; that makes it "manufactured," and you get a rebate on the duty, and then you get a bounty for bringing it to this country, and, again, a bounty for carrying it to England.

The report of the chairman of the committee quotes evidence tending to show that ships built abroad are no better nor are they any cheaper than those built at home. If that be true, what is the harm to have a free-ship bill? The only effect would be this: That it would make the shipbuilders of America build ships at a reasonable profit, while without free ships they can, by having a "combine" or entering into a "trust," so arrange their business as to have the power to charge any price they please; and that is contended for and made possible by the prohibitory laws regarding American ownership of foreign vessels.

If we had free ships none, or very few, would be imported, but ships would be built in America and sold cheaper than anywhere else on earth, and cheap enough to make it profitable to use them in the foreign trade, which alone would contribute more than this bill possibly can to build up American shipping.

SETH L. MILLIKEN [Me.].—Has the gentleman ever heard of

a shipbuilding trust in this country and does he not know that there is no such thing?

MR. WHEELER.—The shipbuilding interests are combined by a tacit understanding, which is the same as a trust, and they maintain their prices, which are some 30 per cent. above the price of foreign ships, when I have abundant proof that ships can be made in this country at a cheaper price, and better ships, than anywhere else in the world. Lumber is cheaper here, iron is cheaper, hemp is cheaper, cotton for sails is cheaper here than in any other shipbuilding country.

On January 29 of last year Charles H. Cramp stated to the Committee on Merchant Marine that his yard could build a ship like the *City of Paris* for 8 or 10 per cent. more than such a ship would cost in England.

The above shows that the cost of building ships in this country under the old tariff was but little greater than in England, and with a revision of the tariff it would seem that we could build ships cheaper in America than in England.

Mr. Cramp also, before the Senate committee, in reply to a question propounded by Senator Morrill as to the average rate of duty upon materials used in the construction of ships, said:

About 40 per cent.; and if our shipbuilders could be relieved from that they could compete successfully with foreign builders. The difference in the cost of labor would be overcome by the superiority of American mechanics. Wooden ships will no longer be built, since iron ships are superior in every respect.

It will be seen these shipbuilders were quite well satisfied at one time to work upon their own resources, but when the Republican party advertised that the purpose of their party was to make the rich man richer by subsidizing industries controlled by monopolies, it was natural for them all to come and ask for their part of the spoils.

It will also be observed that John Roach also sustains me in my statements regarding the cost of American labor, and refutes the assertions we hear so often repeated by high-tariff advocates upon that subject. Mr. Roach says:

The labor question is misstated. We are prepared to meet that difficulty, and to ask no further legislation on that subject.

Here General Wheeler summarized former debates on the question of ship subsidies.

XI—10

I invite attention to the confident and positive opinion of that distinguished lawyer and legislator, Senator Edmunds, of Vermont, that it is as much a violation of the Constitution to grant such subsidies to Americans as it would be to grant them to foreigners.

I think with the great Daniel Webster that it is not by protection and bounties that a people's maritime supremacy is to be established.

I concur with General Butler in the conviction that it is not a good business proposition for any set of men to build up any great enterprise on a subsidy by the Government.

I unite with that great statesman, Senator Lot M. Morrill, of Maine, in the decided negative, not a dollar of subsidies, and earnestly second his demand for cheap materials as an indispensable prerequisite to success in the effort to regain our lost supremacy on the ocean.

I agree with Senator Zach. Chandler, of Michigan, in the assured belief that subsidies will never restore our flag to the ocean.

In conclusion, let me say there is no member of this House who desires more sincerely and earnestly than myself the rehabilitation of American prestige on the ocean. I want to see our flag, that emblem of energy, progress, and human liberty, float on every sea; I want to see it wave over prosperous fleets in every port; I want the products of American skill and industry to find their way unfettered to every country and to the people of all nations; I want the moral influence of American character, American thought, and American principle to penetrate to every clime.

To accomplish these objects it is not new legislation that we need so much as the repeal of old laws which have been a hindrance to our progress.

Give American pluck, enterprise, and skill, unhampered, untrammeled, and unchecked, their rightful opportunity and legitimate sway, and their triumph upon the ocean will be as grand and signal as have been their victorious achievements in all other fields of endeavor.

Hilary A. Herbert [Ala.] opposed the bill in a speech which extended over parts of two days (January 6 and 7).

You propose to give these subsidies for twenty years. That is your legacy to the American people as you go out of power.

You impose upon them this burden which you undoubtedly hope they will be unable to shake off for that period, and why? Why do you make your bill run twenty years? The answer is plain. The testimony of Mr. Cramp, which you did not see proper to allude to in your report, seems nevertheless to have influenced your action. He shows that the result in France demonstrates that ten years of subsidy is not enough. The shipping that is propped up on a general subsidy will begin to decline as soon as there is a prospect that the prop is to be taken away. The infant that is fed with a subsidy, as soon as it gets strong enough to use its legs, will walk up to the Government crib and ask for more, and when he gets strong enough to do it he will enforce his demands with a club in hand. It is true, Mr. Chairman, that we have never before tried a wholesale subsidy like this, but never before did we have such a Congress as this; never did we have a Congress that would appropriate a million and a half of dollars for a World's Exposition, inviting foreigners to bring in their wares for display, and then immediately afterward pass another bill [the McKinley Tariff] avowing its purpose to be to prevent these same foreigners from selling us their wares.

But, Mr. Chairman, we have tried subsidies to shipping three different times, and three different times have we abandoned them. Every time, or, if not every time, certainly twice, the American Congress was disgraced by the efforts put forth by the parties who received the subsidy to perpetuate their hold upon the Government bounty. This struggle always was and always will be desperate, a death struggle, because it always was and always will be the case that shipping that comes into existence as the result of bounties must have those bounties continued or it must die.

What else besides disgrace was the result of the experiments we made? Did you build up any trade with China? No. Did you build up your trade with Brazil? No. Did you build up your commerce with any nation anywhere? No. If there is any period of time prior to 1860 during which the proportion of the American carrying trade done in American vessels was dwindling away, when we were losing in the race with England, it was that period from 1850 to 1860, as your own figures show, and this was at the very time of our first experiment with subsidies. I admit that if you subsidize everything and put plenty of money in the hands of ship owners you can build up a merchant marine, just as you can raise elephants in Boston if you appropriate money enough to keep them under glass and supply them with steam heat; but you must keep on paying the bounty. The moment you stop it your hothouse fabric crumbles and falls to pieces.

The money to defray the expenses of this scheme upon which you are entering is to be raised by taxing all the people. The immediate benefits, the direct benefits of the system are to be reaped by the favored class. The people at large are to bear the burdens. The theory of the bill is that those burdens are to constantly increase. From year to year you say the shipping will grow, and from year to year the subsidy will grow, and the people's burden will be heavier and heavier. If that is not to happen, then you would not want and nobody would want the subsidy. Well, I will not say that. It is perhaps going a little too far. I was thinking, gentlemen, of you who advocate this bill and the magnificent plans you have in view. I think you will be willing to admit that you favor the plan because you think it will build millions of tons of shipping and cost the people hundreds of millions of dollars, and I suppose you are further willing to admit that, if it will not do that, then you do not want it. But I was forgetting the lobby that is behind you, gentlemen. I was forgetting your friends who own the ships that are now on the seas. It is fair to presume that the ships are there because they are making a profit. These gentlemen want the Government to add to these profits. In the language of Mr. Flanagan, that is what they are here for. Whether the tonnage of the American marine is ever increased by a single vessel does not affect the question with them. They want government money—they want it now—and your bill proposes to give it to them.

But you gentlemen, statesmen, looking ahead as you should look to the interests of this country in the future, do you want the subsidy if the American merchant marine is to stand as it is now? All of you say no. You wish to tax the American people this unknown amount because you think that the American merchant marine would double, treble, or quadruple under its operation. You wish the amount of the subsidy annually to double, treble, and quadruple, aye, to increase ten and even twenty fold, and you declare by this act if you can have your way that the taxpayers shall foot the bill. That is what you mean. It is either that or nothing. And yet you have the amazing effrontery—I beg gentlemen's pardon; that seems to be a strong word, but it seems only a proper characterization of the act—to get up here from your seats, two of you almost at the same time, and interrupt a gentleman in debate that you may tell the taxpayers of the country that you do not expect that this bill will result in any reduction of freight rates; that it is not intended to have that result; that its only purpose is to help the ship owner; that all these taxes are to be paid by the people simply to put the American on the same footing and help him carry your freight at the same rates that the foreigner does. In the face of this declaration, where is the representative of the farmers on this floor who will dare vote for this bill? That seems to me to be the whole question in a nutshell.

Now, Mr. Chairman, I spoke for a moment of subsidizing ships which would be a burden to us in time of war. Those who have studied this question know well that one of the principal uses a nation has for a navy is to protect its merchant vessels, and that the size of a navy ought to be measured, to a certain extent, by the number of merchant vessels it is required to protect. The value to Great Britain of her navy, for instance, is often estimated by saying that she has one cruiser for so many merchant ships and one line of battleship for so many merchant ships. But you propose here to subsidize our sailing vessels, which are not fit for any purpose in time of war, except to be an incubus on the navy, and to call on the navy for more ships to convoy and protect them against the enemy in time of war. [Applause on the Democratic side.]

Now, then, let me discuss this catch phrase, "Trade follows the flag." Trade, like water, runs in natural channels, seeking always the lowest level of prices to get to the best markets; and, when untrammeled by law, trade knows no more about a flag than water does. Let me illustrate. We have a trade with Brazil, a somewhat extensive commerce; but it is nearly all on one side, and this onesidedness is not affected at all by the flag or flags which carry it, but entirely by other considerations, as I shall show.

We imported from Brazil last year $59,000,000 worth of goods. Our people wanted the coffee, the rubber, the sugar, and other products of Brazil and they were willing to pay for them; hence these products came to us. There was no lack of transportation. There are five lines of regular steamers plying between the two countries, one of these at least, if not more, being American. Then many tramp steamers engage in the same trade. Those who ship goods send them, of course, by the vessels which will bring them cheapest. When the vessels come here what do they have to carry back?

Altogether they carried $11,000,000 worth of goods; that is, we bought more than five dollars' worth from Brazil where we sold only one dollar's worth. And why? Not for lack of transportation, but because we did not have the goods Brazil wanted to buy. The agricultural products needed in Brazil are very largely supplied by the Argentine Republic and by Uruguay. They cannot get return cargoes of manufactures, because the manufactured goods of this country cannot compete with the manufactured goods of Europe, and especially of the United Kingdom.

The difference between the European prices and prices here is measured by the McKinley bill. That bill says in effect that 47 per cent., the average of the old law, does not measure the difference. It was not sufficient to enable the American manufacturer to compete with the foreigner. On that ground the McKinley law raised the average rate to 61 per cent. So 61 per cent. measures the difference between our goods and the goods that Brazilians can buy from across the water. And so they will not buy of us. We have no power to compel the Brazilians or any foreigners to buy high-priced goods. We have the power to compel our own people to do it, and unfortunately we exercise it. But, inasmuch as these South Americans are not under our laws and inasmuch as they do not agree with some of our statesmen who say that cheap goods are nasty goods, they buy their wares from the points where they can get them the cheapest.

Thus is established the route known among mercantile men and shippers as the "mutton-leg route." It describes a mutton leg, coming up from Brazil to our ports to bring us what we want, then for want of a return cargo going over to Europe to get cheap goods that are needed in Brazil, and then carrying them straight to that country. So we see that, as long as our manufacturers are denied, by our tariff laws, the benefit of free raw materials which would enable them to compete with these foreign manufacturers, the United Kingdom and France and Germany all reap a profitable trade with Brazil, which geographically belongs to us. Now, what has the flag to do with trade? Does it influence in any way? Whose flag is it that causes us to buy from Brazil five times as much as we sell to her? Yet the hope is held out to our taxpayers, and our farmers especially, that by an indiscriminate subsidy of this kind some new markets somewhere are to be opened to them. How and at what price?

Mr. Chairman, I oppose such legislation as this, and I will always oppose it, come from whatever quarter it may. I stand upon the doctrines of the old Democratic party, the party that it has been justly said is enduring because it is right and invincible because it is just. That party demands equal and exact justice to all men and special favors to none. He who once departs from this great foundation principle, he who demands for any set or class of men privileges or favors from the Government that are denied to others, cannot stand upon its doctrines.

But there is a measure which in my opinion would help the carrying trade and help the shipping of this country. That is the scheme that was adopted by England in 1849 when she found that America was outstripping her in the race upon the ocean. She then enacted a law for free ships, giving her people the right which they enjoy to-day of buying ships wherever they could buy them cheapest. Germany does that, Norway does it, Italy, France, and Germany all do it. No civilized nation in the world except this has any such law as that which we maintain, a law that is a relic of that semibarbarous policy by which nations once sought to build themselves up by striking other nations down. We began to lose our carrying trade when iron ships superseded wood. Other nations build iron and steel ships more cheaply than we do and they always buy ships now where they can buy them cheapest; but here is a bill which starts out with the avowed purpose of equalizing the shipping of America with that of other countries, and yet it fails to repeal that old law, and its authors refuse to remedy this defect.

Why profess in the title of the bill to equalize when you refuse to equalize? Oh, no; the men who are lobbying for this bill prefer a subsidy; they prefer to hold onto the law which compels them to buy ships at home and call on the people to equalize, as they call it, by paying the money from their pockets; and all this on the plea that they could not compete, even if they had free ships. That this is not true is demonstrated by figures furnished by the Government authorities, which show that, as against all other countries of the world, we do two-fifths, or 40 per cent., of the shipping in sail vessels simply because we can furnish sail vessels as cheaply as other countries. This fact demonstrates that when we have the vessels on as favorable terms as other countries we can afford to run them in competition with foreigners. What we do with sailing vessels we could do with steamships if we only had free ships.

In conclusion, Mr. Chairman, let me say that I hope that this bill may not pass. But it may be better for the country that it should, for it will, in my opinion, be hastening the end. The people have condemned bounties and subsidies by unheard-of majorities, and they will complete in 1892 what was only half done at the November election, the destruction of the Republican party.

Nelson Dingley [Me.], of the committee, supported the bill.

MR. DINGLEY.—Mr. Chairman, the gentleman from Alabama entirely overlooked the vital fact that a merchant marine and shipyards and trained seamen and skilled shipwrights are essential to commercial independence and national defence.

Readers of the debates in the early Congresses that assembled after the framing of the Constitution must have noticed that those great men who laid the foundations of this Government dwelt largely, in their discussions and in their legislation, upon the vital importance to the preservation of the nation of a merchant marine and shipyards, of trained seamen and skilled shipwrights. I am sure that any gentleman upon this floor who has read the celebrated report made by Jefferson upon this very question has noted that that great statesman, the founder of the true Democratic party, laid it down as a fundamental proposition that the care of the merchant marine of the nation and the preservation of her shipyards, to which the nation might resort in time of war for the construction of transports and cruisers, were as vitally important as the maintenance of forts and navies.

Unless some steps shall be taken by the Government of the United States looking to the support of this interest until it can be intrenched as the British shipping was intrenched under the assistance given by the British Government, within ten years nearly every vessel engaged in foreign trade which floats the Stars and Stripes will have been driven from the ocean.

I desire at the very inception of this discussion to disabuse the mind of every gentleman present of any impression that he may have received that tariff changes or tariff policies or any question at issue between our political parties have had anything to do with the decline. If some one asks what is the proof of this, I point to the fact that our shipping in the foreign trade prospered equally well under the protective tariff of 1842 and also the revenue tariff of 1846 for nine years until 1855, and that then, in the midst of the operations of the revenue tariff of 1846, the decline commenced and went steadily on through the remaining years of both the revenue tariffs of 1846 and 1857; and the decline has gone on, not at quite so rapid a rate, but it has gone on continuously under the protective tariff since the war.

The suggestion has been made in the progress of the debate that under the existing tariff policy of the Government we are depriving our vessels of cargoes; that if we could go back to a revenue tariff the cargoes would increase, and as a consequence our shipping interests would increase with them.

There were never so many cargoes as there are to-day, 50 per cent. more per capita in the last decade than in the decade between 1850 and 1860. But the trouble is that British and

PROTECTED TO THEIR OWN RUIN

[Tariff on Raw Materials]

Cartoon by C. J. Taylor in "Puck"

other foreign vessels, admitted to participate on equal terms with American vessels in the carrying trade of the United States, have been able to distance our shipping, and carry the cargoes which ought to have been carried by our own vessels and to our manifest disadvantage.

Again, Mr. Chairman, the suggestion has been made in the progress of the debate, and elsewhere, that changes of tariff have increased the duty on shipbuilding materials, and, therefore, because of these duties, we cannot construct vessels for foreign trade in competition with the British. Now, in reply to that I simply desire to call the attention of the committee to the fact that in 1872 a law was passed putting upon the free list all materials necessary for the construction of American wooden vessels to be employed in the foreign trade; that in the tariff of 1883 this law was reënacted and the list of materials enlarged; and that in the tariff of 1890 all the principal materials necessary for the construction of a vessel, whether of wood or iron, for the foreign trade were admitted with a rebate of duty or free of duty. So that the question of duty on the materials employed in the construction of vessels does not enter at all into the discussion. They are all free now, and the difficulty, so far as it lies against us, is entirely in the difference of wages of the labor employed in constructing and equipping the vessel, from the materials, here and on the Clyde.

This decline commenced in 1855. What great events having a bearing upon ship construction were then in progress? The revolution from wood to iron and steel in materials for construction, and from sail to steam in the propulsion of vessels. So long as the wooden sailing vessel controlled the ocean commerce of the world, so long the United States, as the possessor of cheaper shipbuilding materials than any other nation, requiring comparatively little labor to construct the vessel, and that vessel a sailing vessel requiring but a small crew, so that whatever additional wages might be paid to seamen were overcome by the advantage we had in the construction of the vessel—so long as that condition existed we could defy the world in the control of ocean carriage. But unfortunately for us, although not unfortunately for mankind as it will prove in the end, I trust, this great revolution, commencing about 1840 and culminating in success about 1850, became an accepted fact about 1855, when England, as the possessor of iron ore and coal in juxtaposition near the seashore, with cheap labor to work them, seized upon the advantage given her by this revolution, and the tables were speedily turned.

But this advantage, obtained by England in the ocean carrying trade, could not have seriously affected us if, in 1850, feeling entire confidence in our ability to maintain ourselves and not having carefully weighed the significance of this great revolution that was taking place in shipbuilding, we had not, by an arrangement with Great Britain, admitted her vessels to participate in our carrying trade on equal terms with our own vessels in return for similar participation in her carrying trade. We thought then it was a good bargain, but it marked the decadence of our shipping in the foreign trade. Previous to 1855 British vessels participating in our carrying trade were obliged to pay discriminating tonnage dues upon their vessels and upon the cargoes which they carried discriminating duties. These were all removed in October, 1849, to take effect on the 1st day of January, 1850.

But even this would not have brought about the rapid decline of our shipping that has followed if the Government of Great Britain, taking advantage of this revolution in shipbuilding, had not come to the aid of her shipping by a most gigantic system of subsidies.

The third cause of decline was the Civil War. That, to be sure, was temporary, but its malign influence cannot be overestimated. One-third of all our shipping in the foreign trade was swept from the ocean—captured by Confederate privateers or transferred to foreign flags for the purpose of avoiding capture. Not only that, but when our hands were thus tied during the four years of civil war Great Britain redoubled her efforts to intrench her own shipping. What did she do? She adopted the policy of building 80 per cent. of all her naval vessels in private shipyards for the purpose of encouraging the establishment of great iron and steel ship plants. More than that, on all or nearly all of the routes of ocean travel she offered large subsidies for the purpose of establishing British ship lines.

So that when we came out of the Civil War in 1865 we not only found that our shipping had been swept from the ocean, but we found on our own hands problems that engrossed the attention of the nation, while Great Britain was intrenching herself on all the ocean routes of commerce. Not only that, but immediately after the war, engrossed as we were with these great problems, with the new West opening and inviting such magnificent opportunities for capital and for labor, opportunities greater than could be offered by maritime pursuits, the attention of our people who had formerly been interested in shipping was transferred to the great West, so that we find to-day seven-eighths of all the great houses that were engaged before the war in shipping have had their interest and capital transferred into other channels.

Now, Mr. Chairman, in such a condition as this, with only 12½ per cent. of our imports and exports carried in American vessels, with Great Britain intrenched on every ocean route, with all the advantages that she possesses, it is obvious, or ought to be obvious, that it is utterly out of the power of private individuals, without assistance in some direction, to dislodge the shipping of Great Britain, which has obtained possession of and intrenched herself on all the seas.

Our ship owners have been trying since the war to recover

themselves, but they have found every route of commerce pre-empted by subsidized British steamship lines. They find that great shipbuilding plants have been established in Great Britain by government aid extended through contracts for the construction of government vessels at the most extremely liberal prices. In this situation it must be clear to anyone who will take the trouble to investigate this question that we have come to a pass where if we are to have shipping in the foreign trade built in American shipyards and flying the American flag something must be done outside of merely individual effort.

What is the remedy that is to revive our merchant marine and foreign carrying trade, which is proposed by gentlemen who oppose this bill? The gentleman from Alabama [Mr. Herbert], with his accustomed ability, has presented that remedy. It is that we modify our navigation laws so as to allow the importation and American registry free of duty of foreign-built vessels. That is the remedy, and the only remedy, suggested in this condition of things, either in the arguments of gentlemen on the other side or in the minority report of the committee.

This is proposed as an adequate remedy, but not a single fact has been presented to show that it would be adequate, even if it were safe and wise.

Mr. Chairman, I desire to call attention to the fact that if it is proposed to give the right of free importation and registry to foreign-built vessels, in order to be effective it cannot be confined to the foreign trade, but must include the coastwise trade also. Why? No man would ever think of buying a vessel built abroad and registering it as an American vessel if he could not use her wherever American vessels could be used. If he is to be restricted to one particular trade he never would think of investing his money in any such direction. Why, when the chief of free-ship apostles was before the joint select committee in 1882 I asked him the question, "Would any ship user think of buying a foreign-built vessel for American register if the use of such vessel was limited by law to the foreign trade?" and he replied, "No."

Mr. Herbert.—If I understand it, the Inman Steamship Line have had built abroad and are now having sailed under the British flag several of their steam vessels. An attempt was made to get a bill through Congress to allow them to do that thing, and it was defeated in the Senate. That was about three or four years ago.

Mr. Dingley.—So, Mr. Chairman, when we enter upon the free-ship policy—that is, the policy of the free importation and

American registry for a completed manufacture like a fully equipped steamship, the most wonderful piece of mechanism that has ever been made by human ingenuity—when we once enter upon that policy we provide an entering wedge for the free-ship policy for all our shipping; and it will be impossible, when we once enter upon such a policy, to prevent yielding to the force of the argument that, if you give the right of free importation of vessels for one voyage, you cannot deny it for another.

But without regard to that, Mr. Chairman, it is almost the universal judgment of gentlemen acquainted practically with this question of ship use that the free-ship policy would prove at this late day, whatever it might have done before the war, inadequate for the purpose contemplated. And why? The difficulty of competing with foreign vessels is not so much in the original cost of the vessel here and on the Clyde as in the difference of the cost of running the British and American vessel after it is completed. Within the last ten years the difference in the cost of a British-built and an American-built iron vessel has been reduced more than one-half; so that, while in 1882 this difference was about 30 per cent., it is now only about 15 per cent. in the cost of freighters, and from 10 to 12 per cent. in the cost of passenger steamships.

An iron or steel vessel has a lifetime of from thirty to fifty years. A difference of 10 or 12 per cent. in the original cost spread over fifty years is almost infinitesimal in the amount to be charged to any one year. Besides, it is claimed, and I think there is good ground for the claim, that as a matter of fact, comparing quality with quality, the American-built vessel now is practically as cheap as the foreign-built vessel for the reason that her plates are made of better iron; and, unless there shall be some step taken whereby American shipyards are driven to the wall by the adoption of a free-ship policy, the time is not far distant when our shipyards will be able to compete with foreign shipyards in the cost of vessels.

The growth of our iron and steel shipbuilding yards in the last ten years has been wonderful. We have to-day some of the finest iron-shipbuilding establishments to be found in the world, and they are rapidly diminishing the cost of construction of vessels that are shown to be the equal, if not the superior, of any in the world. The naval vessels which have recently been constructed in American shipyards have proved to be fine specimens of naval architecture and compare favorably with the best vessels of the British navy.

At this time, when we have almost surmounted the obstacles in that direction, when we are well-nigh able to construct iron and steel vessels as cheaply as any country in the world, when the builders of vessels for the foreign trade may lay their hands upon the foreign material free of duty, to seriously propose to abandon our shipyards and to go to the Tyne and the Clyde for the purpose of having our vessels constructed shows, it seems to me, a singular disregard of the best interests of the nation. Why, if we should do that to-day and do nothing in the direction of bringing together the cost of running American and foreign vessels, the experiment would be an utter failure and would result in the crippling to a serious extent of the shipyards which we now have, and would prevent the establishment of new shipyards to which the nation might turn in case of war in the future.

Some gentlemen may ask how it is that it costs more to run an American vessel than a British vessel. I refer them to the report on this subject of Mr. Russell, who was our consul at Liverpool, a prominent Democrat, agreeing entirely with the party on the tariff question. He made an investigation at that port as to the wages paid to masters, mates, and seamen upon American and upon British vessels respectively. The report was made to the State Department, under date of November 18, 1887. He sums up the situation as follows:

British vessels in domestic ports can procure crews for from 37 to 32 per cent. lower than those paid on American vessels. Then, again, the cost of maintenance on American ships is about 40 cents per day per man against the English 29 cents, or a difference of 27 per cent. in favor of the latter.

And this 27 per cent. higher cost of maintenance is not due to provisions costing more in this country than in Europe, but to the fact that our seamen and other laborers will not live as seamen and other laborers live abroad; for Consul Russell adds:

It is an acknowledged fact that the living on board our vessels is superior to that of other nations.

MR. OUTHWAITE.—That was the case thirty-five years ago, when we competed successfully with English shipping.

MR. DINGLEY.—But the gentleman must be aware that now, when the commerce of the world is being controlled mainly by steamships, the relative cost of labor in running a vessel becomes a much greater element than it was when wooden sailing vessels controlled this commerce, because it takes a great many more men to run a steamer than a sailing vessel. Forty years ago, whatever disadvantage we had in running a sailing vessel was compensated by the fact that we could supply wooden sailing vessels more cheaply than any other nation.

MR. DOCKERY.—Does the gentleman from Maine take into account the fact that, according to his own report made to the Forty-seventh Congress, 90 per cent. of the crews of American vessels are foreigners?

MR. DINGLEY.—That does not make any difference. When a foreigner comes to this country and obtains employment, he gets American and not foreign wages, and demands American and not foreign fare; and I am glad that it is so.

Now, with 32 to 37 per cent. higher wages, with 27 per cent. higher cost of subsistence on an American than on a corresponding British vessel, do not gentlemen see that the difference in the cost of running the two kinds of vessels is so great that unless this difference can be bridged over in some way or the wages of our seamen can be brought down to the foreign level (and I should regret to see the latter result), it is impossible for us to run our vessels in competition with British vessels?

MR. DOCKERY.—The gentleman stated a moment ago that the 90 per cent. of foreigners on our vessels receive American wages. Now, I desire to ask him why, if that is true, American wages will not command American seamen.

MR. DINGLEY.—The gentleman very well knows that in the long period since the beginning of the war, with our foreign carrying trade dying out in consequence of open foreign competition, our young men who love a roving life have had their minds diverted to the West; they have been turned to other pursuits, and we shall have to take a little time to draw them back to the old-time sea pursuits, which once had so great attractions to so many of your youth.

But, Mr. Chairman, the most vital objection to the free-ship proposition addresses itself to national interests, not simply to economical considerations. Why was it, may I ask gentlemen, that on the recommendation of Washington, with the earnest approval of Madison and Jefferson, the First Congress of the United States passed the law which my friend from Alabama [Mr. Herbert] has stigmatized as narrow and unstatesmanlike, providing that vessels registered as American vessels should be built in the United States and officered by American citizens?

Would that the statesmanlike views of Jefferson on this question might now animate gentlemen upon the other side and lead them to see that a merchant marine in the foreign trade, built in our own shipyards, to which the Government can resort for the construction of cruisers and transports in time of war, is as necessary to commercial independence and national defence as forts and navies; and that the adoption of the policy of relying upon a foreign country to supply us with vessels would be unwise, suicidal, and unpatriotic.

MR. HERBERT.—That law was passed at that time in retaliation for the then existing system of England. But in 1849, when England found that we were building better and cheaper ships than she was, she abolished her policy in that direction and allowed her ship owners to purchase from us their ships in order that she might outstrip us. Now, why should not her example be followed by us at this time in a bill the object of which, as stated in its title, is to place us on an equality with foreign nations?

MR. DINGLEY.—Is the gentleman willing to imitate Great Britain's policy of subsidies also?

MR. HERBERT.—I am willing to imitate her policy in respect to free ships; and I ask you why you are not.

MR. DINGLEY.—Now, a word in response to the suggestion of the gentleman that in 1849 Great Britain repealed her navigation laws and allowed her citizens to buy ships abroad and have them registered as British vessels free of duty. She did that; but she did not take that step until after she had adopted free trade as to every other industry in her country. The last thing that she put under the free-trade system was her shipping. More than that, she would not do even this until it had been demonstrated by the revolution in shipbuilding that she would be able to distance the world from that time forward in the construction of iron and steel vessels.

MR. BLOUNT.—Is it not true that in the debates in the British Parliament on the passage of the bill just referred to it was proclaimed on behalf of the shipbuilders and the ship owners and the naval officers of Great Britain that the adoption of the policy then proposed would result in the destruction of the commerce of that country?

MR. DINGLEY.—Some, it is true, made the claim that it would destroy the British shipping in the foreign trade, but the wiser heads who understood what progress had been made in iron shipbuilding knew otherwise. If the gentleman will read the history of British shipping he will find that, while on the occasion referred to some persons thought that England had not reached the point where she could defy the world in

this matter, yet those who had most thoroughly examined the
subject predicted that the British nation had reached a point,
in view of the revolution in shipbuilding, where they could
defy competition. But even this step was not taken until after
England had adopted free trade as to every other interest; for
they deemed their shipping interest the most vital for the safety
of the nation.

MR. BLOUNT.—The gentleman speaks of "wiser heads."
Did not Disraeli and many other distinguished English statesmen in the House of Commons and the House of Lords claim
that this new policy would ruin British commerce? The vote
was very close in both houses.

MR. DINGLEY.—If the revolution in shipbuilding from wood
to iron had not then been in successful progress, and if the
result had not been clearly seen, Great Britain would have
waited before lifting protection from her shipping, even after
having lifted it from every other industry of the land. After
we have adopted free trade as to every other industry in this
country, it will be time to consider whether we can safely do
it as to ships. At least England took that course.

But, Mr. Chairman, the gentleman from Alabama says that
all of the nations of the world have adopted the free-ship policy except the United States. In form many have, but practically none. Why, France, although apparently adopting the
free-ship policy, gives a construction bounty only to vessels
built in her own shipyards, and double the navigation bounty
to such vessels that she gives to foreign-built vessels. Italy,
after trying the free-ship policy for twenty years, became
alarmed at its unsatisfactory results, and in December, 1885,
practically superseded that policy by offering a construction
and navigation bounty for all vessels built in Italian shipyards.
And even Germany in her latest subventions insists that the
vessels receiving such bounties shall be constructed in her own
yards.

In 1850 Great Britain started off on a scale such as was
never before known in the history of any government upon
this policy of establishing steamship lines on all the great
routes of commerce by the aid of postal subsidies, as she calls
them. For instance, in 1868, when the British steamship line
to Brazil got into difficulty in consequence of competition with
a French line, the British Government came forward and entered into a contract with the company to guarantee it 8 per
cent. dividend upon its investment, or at least $360,000 a year,
to maintain that line. Here was the spectacle of Great Britain

XI—11

entering as a partner in the maintenance of a British steamship line when a French line was ready to carry the mail for less than one-half that amount. And yet we are told, "Great Britain has left her shipping to take care of itself." I wish that we could have a little of such care here.

But some one says, "What Great Britain did thirty years ago is of no consequence; to-day she is not expending so much. She is giving only fair mail pay."

MR. DOCKERY.—What the United States did thirty years ago is of some consequence, taken in connection with what Great Britain did.

MR. DINGLEY.—I will come to that in a moment.

JOHN F. ANDREW [Mass.].—That is the point of the argument.

A. J. HOPKINS [Ill.].—Granting that the English and the French governments do subsidize their lines, does not the gentleman's argument lead right to this, that if we subsidize our lines the English and French governments will increase their subsidies until it ultimately comes to a question of a paternal government where the United States will have to run her marine?

MR. DINGLEY.—All I can say in reference to that point is that I think it is the duty of the United States in her own defence, for the maintenance of her commercial independence, to maintain her merchant marine upon these great routes of commerce upon the ocean, and if she cannot do that she fails in a material regard in the duty of a government. And no one who has investigated the subject doubts that if we had continued the policy which was inaugurated in 1847-1850 and given up partly in 1855 and finally in 1858, and had extended this policy in other directions, we should have maintained our lines with an expenditure far less than that made by Great Britain.

MR. HOPKINS.—But why would it not be better for the Government at once to establish Government lines and pay for them out of the Treasury of the United States, and if there is any profit in it retain it in the Treasury?

MR. DINGLEY.—The obvious answer to that suggestion is found in the success of other maritime nations in successfully maintaining steamship lines on the great routes of commerce by postal subsidies far less expensive than Government lines would have been.

It is true that Great Britain is not now paying postal subsidies to the amount of $6,000,000 per annum, as she did in 1870, but the reason that she is not is because she has successfully established her lines upon all the great routes of commerce and, having intrenched them, they do not need the encouragement that they once needed. Yet last year she paid to her steamship lines a postal subsidy of $2,775,000 and a subvention of nearly half a million to ten steamships, constructed after naval plans, carrying up her expenditures for this purpose to nearly $3,250,000, or over a million more than her receipts from ocean postage.

MR. DOCKERY.—Her experience with infant industries is a little different from our own, then?

MR. DINGLEY.—More than that. Whenever the opportunity offers to extend her steamship lines by subsidies, Great Britain takes advantage of it. Only two years ago, when her mail was being carried satisfactorily by the Pacific Steamship Line from San Francisco to China and Japan for less than $40,000, when all her postal wants were being fully satisfied with a small expenditure on an American line, England and the Canadian Government agreed to give a subsidy of $300,000 a year to establish a steamship line from Vancouver to China and Japan.

BENJAMIN F. SHIVELY [Ind.].—That was in pursuance of her military policy, was it not?

JAMES BUCHANAN [N. J.].—But they got the money all the same.

MR. DINGLEY.—Referring to this project of Great Britain to open up this new steamship route, William C. Whitney, Secretary of the Navy under President Cleveland's Administration, in advocating an imitation in this respect of England's policy, said:

A notable illustration of the generosity and courage with which England pushes her shipping interests is seen in the manner in which she is at this moment dealing with the trade of the North Pacific. It has been thus far principally under the American flag and contributory to San Francisco and the United States. Under the new competition it is quite easy to conjecture what will become of the American flag and our resources in the North Pacific.

Would that more gentlemen on the other side could be brought with Ex-Secretary Whitney to clearly see the duty of the hour.

Why, any student of commercial history understands that when it was an open question as to who should control the great ocean routes of commerce by means of steamship lines Great Britain expended from her treasury everything that was necessary to intrench herself upon the seas. She has been wise in that policy.

JOSEPH WALKER [Mass.].—And economical.

MR. DINGLEY.—And economical, notwithstanding she has expended $250,000,000 since 1840. By this expenditure she has extended her trade, taken possession of the great ocean routes of transportation, obtained the largest merchant fleet that floats upon the waters, and secured hundreds of vessels that can be called to her aid in time of war as cruisers and as transports, and thus intrenched herself upon the ocean in such a way as she could not have done if she had spent ten times the amount in ordinary naval expenditures. It has, therefore, been a policy of economy as well as of national forecast. She has secured her commercial independence. Not only that. She has made Great Britain the greatest naval power in the world.

To all of her subsidies and subventions she has attached the provision that vessels thus subsidized shall be subject to purchase or charter by the British Government. So that, in case of war, within ten days' time the British Government can detach from her merchant marine several hundred steamers, on which guns can be placed, to reënforce her navy or to transport supplies. That is what makes her so specially powerful upon the ocean, and gives her control of the great routes of commerce.

All steam vessels built hereafter in order to obtain the benefit of this act must be constructed after naval plans in certain respects and be enrolled as auxiliary cruisers or transports, subject to purchase or charter by the Government. Thus in this respect the bounty provided by this bill will accomplish the same object as the British policy of subvention and largely increase our naval strength.

Now, the gentleman from Illinois [George W. Fithian] asks, why include sailing vessels in this bill when sailing vessels are not to be converted into cruisers in time of war? For these reasons: Sailing vessels are as important to ocean transportation and commercial independence as steam vessels. No great merchant marine can be said to be complete without an adequate proportion of sailing vessels, although the proportion of steam tonnage to sail tonnage is larger than formerly. Why? Because sailing vessels alone can be used in long voyages like those from our Pacific coast ports to Atlantic and European ports, and because, even on shorter routes, sailing vessels can carry a cargo cheaper than it can be carried by any other conveyance, and are essential for all those forms of traffic where speed is not an important factor. As a matter of fact, a very large proportion, even to-day, of the imports into this country are brought in by sailing vessels, because they are that kind of merchandise that will not bear the cost of steam transportation, and time, in their shipment, is no element of importance. To shut sailing vessels out of this act would be practically to deprive the Pacific coast States of much of the benefit which would flow from its passage.

But, secondly and more important still, the only vessel that can adequately train seamen for service in time of war on our naval vessels is a sailing vessel. Why, upon steamers the work is more like land work. No special training is required for much of such service. But upon sailing vessels men are trained to feats which demand courage, endurance, all those qualities which make a seaman valuable in the navy in time of war. Why, it was for half a century the policy of the true Democratic party, the party which had not departed from the teachings of Thomas Jefferson, and a wise policy, to give a bounty to fishing vessels engaged in fishing upon the ocean. And why? Because they were the nursery of seamen, who could be called upon whenever war was on our hands for service in our navy.

But, Mr. Chairman, a proper discrimination is made in this bill between the sailing vessel and the fast steamer. It is a mere pittance that the sailing vessel gets, just enough, in the judgment of the committee, to cover the difference in the wages and subsistence of the officers and seamen on the vessel as compared with the British vessel. The freight steamer of slower speed and even the sailing vessel are always specially useful as transports in time of war. Over three hundred British merchant vessels of less than 14 knots were used as transports by the British Government in the Egyptian and Abyssinian wars.

Mr. Dingley then prophesied that, by the provisions of the bill, which required an annual expenditure beginning with $2,000,000 the first year and rising gradually to $7,000,000 in the tenth, we would secure a merchant marine in the foreign trade of a tonnage of 1,000,000 tons, composed largely of first-class iron and steel steamships, enrolled as auxiliary cruisers, and add hundreds of fast steam cruisers to our naval strength in time of war, and maintain lines of American steamers connecting the ports of this country with foreign ports, for the transportation of our mails, and the promotion of our commerce. Could, he asked, a similar expenditure in another direction add so much to our naval power?

Mr. Chairman, the gentleman from Alabama [Mr. Herbert] contends that the establishment of American steamship lines to the countries of South America, for example, will not increase our foreign commerce; that commerce first exists independent of means of communication and transportation, and that when trade demands these they follow under natural laws.

It is surprising to me that, in the face of everyday experience, anyone should insist that the establishment of prompt and regular means of communication with any district or country does not of itself promote trade between the two centers or countries thus connected. Why is it that every city in this country invests money in the construction of railroads to other districts? Everyone knows that this is done because experience has taught them that prompt and regular means of communication with any other district promotes trade. Why, Chicago has been made by her railroad and water systems.

And yet gentlemen who admit the soundness of this view in its application to domestic trade seem to forget that foreign trade is controlled by the same principles as domestic trade. So long as we are destitute of regular steamship lines connecting the ports of the United States with the countries of South and Central America our trade with these countries must be small. So long as orders for goods and the goods themselves must be forwarded by way of England and subject to transshipment and great delays the American merchant will find it difficult to extend trade with South American countries, and our trade with those countries will not be developed till the means of regular and rapid communication exist.

We have a conclusive demonstration of the correctness of this view in the effect on American trade of the establishment of an American steamship line between New York and Venezuela. Our trade with Venezuela has increased from three and one-half millions in 1860 to fifteen millions in 1890.

In the long run, therefore, trade follows the flag. If, as is expected, reciprocity treaties shall be concluded with the independent countries south of us, the establishment of steamship lines to connect with them will be essential to reap any advantage from them.

Indeed, so important do the South American countries regard these that Brazil has for several years paid a subsidy to maintain the little steamship communication that we now have with her, while we have done almost nothing; and the Argentine Republic has been ready to aid, to the extent of $100,000 per annum, in establishing a direct steamship line to this country.

And I may add that all experience shows that the flag which floats at the peak of the steamers which furnish the means of transportation is the most effective advertisement that can be employed to promote trade with the nation which the flag represents.

The gentleman from Alabama [Mr. Wheeler] has intimated that it is not worth while to enact measures to increase our merchant marine in the foreign trade so long as a protective tariff remains, which (as he claims) discourages foreign trade.

This criticism assumes that because we favor a tariff that discourages imports of articles which we can and ought to produce or make for ourselves, and encourages imports of articles which we cannot produce by placing them on the free list, therefore we do not look upon foreign trade as desirable. The difference between us and such critics is that we believe in enlarging our foreign trade by increasing our imports of such articles as we cannot produce or make. They want to increase our foreign trade by enlarging our imports of such articles as we can and ought to produce for ourselves.

That the former method of increasing our foreign commerce gives us not only greater prosperity, but also a larger foreign trade than we should have under a contrary policy, is shown by the fact that our foreign commerce was 50 per cent. greater per inhabitant between 1870 and 1880 under the policy criticised than between 1850 and 1860 under the policy favored by the critic.

The objections to the pending bill which have been urged by the gentleman from Alabama [Mr. Wheeler], first, that vessels will run with only small cargoes to obtain the bounty, and, secondly, that the bounty will remove some of the protection which our coal and iron-ore miners and other producers now receive from the tariff, only serve to show the unsubstantial character of much of the opposition.

It is a conclusive answer to these objections, first, that the bounty paid will on the average only be 11 per cent. of the cost of running the vessel, and therefore that no vessel could sail with a small cargo without losing money, and, secondly, that the bounty covers only the difference in cost of sailing an American and a foreign vessel, and therefore only makes it practicable for an American vessel to accept a cargo at the rate for which a foreign vessel will carry the same cargo without in any manner affecting the protection now afforded by freight charges.

Undoubtedly the fact that American vessels would be able to successfully compete with foreign vessels in the transportation of our imports and exports would in the long run tend to reduce freight charges and to prevent foreign vessels from advancing rates. I am informed that the presence of American ships at San Francisco, competing with foreign vessels for cargoes of wheat, has the effect of lowering the rates of freight. So that even from this point of view the farmers of the country are deeply interested in the passage of this measure. Indeed, the National Grange has already indorsed it.

The objection which has been urged with so much apparent force, that bounties are hothouse expedients which promote an unhealthy growth that ceases when the bounty is withdrawn, does not apply where the object to be secured is of the highest importance and beyond the reach of unaided private enterprise, either on account of its magnitude or the disadvantage to which one country is placed by preoccupation of the field by another country or other cause.

No one seriously questioned the wisdom of the policy of aiding in the construction of transcontinental lines of railway. No one doubts the expediency of river and harbor improvements through Federal expenditures. The statesmanship of Napoleon's policy of fostering beet-sugar production in France by imperial aid has never been doubted. The foresight which Great Britain has shown in so intrenching her steamship lines on all the great routes of ocean commerce that unaided private enterprise cannot get a foothold to seriously compete with her is confessed even by those who stoutly contend that the Congress of the United States should not extend similar aid to American shipping in foreign trade.

When we see an enterprise too large for individual enterprise, and when competition or other cause is so intrenched that it cannot be dislodged by private effort, if the end to be attained is national and important the Government is justified in stepping in to aid. How many municipalities in this country have aided even in the building of railroads?

H. Clay Evans [Tenn.].—And in the building of manufacturing establishments.

Mr. Dingley.—And in the building of manufacturing establishments, as my friend from Tennessee says, by exempting them from taxation for a period of years.

The main argument on which the opposition to this bill seems to rely is that a bounty to encourage our shipping in the foreign trade cannot be defended unless it is proposed to extend the bounty system to other interests and industries.

What I have already said anticipates the conclusive reply to this objection. A merchant marine, especially the class of vessels required for the foreign trade, and shipyards and trained seamen and skilled shipwrights are essential to commercial independence and national defence; and expenditures from the Treasury, when needed to secure these, are to be justified in part on the same ground as expenditures for the mail service, in part on the same ground as expenditures for lighthouses, beacons, to improve rivers and harbors, and to aid in the construction of transcontinental railways, and in part on the same ground as expenditures for forts and a navy.

Commercial independence is impossible to a nation which does not build and control the marine which serves as a vehicle for its commerce. Gentlemen tell us that, if British ships are ready to serve us in transporting our exports and imports, it matters not that we have not American ships. But what would be our situation, what would be the straits of our farmers and mechanics and people generally if England should be engaged in war with a nation which could place commerce-destroyers on the ocean or if we should be at war with England herself?

There is no interest in this country that has more at stake in the preservation of the American merchant marine built in American shipyards than the Western farmers, who look to the maintenance of a marine on which they can have their produce transported, even in time of war, when Great Britain's vessels are being swept from the ocean. Commercial independence demands that we should maintain our own shipping and our own shipyards.

Not only commercial independence, but the safety of the nation itself may depend upon the possession of a strong merchant marine to aid our navy, and private shipyards to which the country may resort for the construction of cruisers and transports. The lessons of history point out to us the vital importance of a merchant marine to aid in the defence of the integrity of the nation.

Where would this country have been in 1861 and 1862 had we not possessed private shipyards to which the Government could go for the construction of the *Monitor* and other vessels to aid in the campaigns against the Confederates and to maintain the blockade? Why, to-day, instead of having a united country there would unquestionably have been two independent nations.

GEORGE E. ADAMS [Ill.].—With two great navies.

MR. DINGLEY.—Now, I say that we cannot, from the point of national safety, abandon our merchant marine in the foreign trade, and that we are justified—not only that we are justified in aiding, but that the obligation is upon us as representatives of the American people, to maintain an interest which will be our defence in time of war.

In the light of our own history, I appeal to the representatives of the American people to come to the rescue of our merchant marine in the foreign trade, and thus insure commercial independence and national safety before it is too late. [Prolonged applause on the Republican side.]

Alexander M. Dockery [Mo.] spoke against the bill.

When this question was being considered in the Forty-fifth Congress the gentleman from Illinois [Joseph G. Cannon] made this declaration on the floor of the House:

> The subsidizing of these steamship lines, from the Collins line in 1852 up to the present time, has bankrupted every prominent man that has favored it. The political ghosts of departed politicians that have squandered the money of the people for this kind of unwarrantable expenditure from the Treasury rise up and warn Representatives to avoid the errors heretofore committed by our predecessors.

DANIEL KERR [Ia.].—Can any objection of that kind be made against a subsidy or bounty which is to be appropriated according to a fixed rule and in regard to which there will be no discretion?

MR. DOCKERY.—Mr. Chairman, there will be no "discretion," so far as Congress is concerned, if this bill passes. The only "discretion" contemplated in the bill is the mandatory "discretion" of the accounting officers, compelling them to audit for payment the enormous sums that will be taken from the public treasury for the benefit of a few New England ship owners.

I care nothing about the details of these various subsidy schemes. They all work out the same result. It is wholly immaterial whether the amount be definitely specified or whether it be based on mileage; both mean one and the same thing: the taking of the people's money to aid private enterprise on the ocean; and against this the gentleman from Illinois [Mr. Cannon] protested in 1879, in language which I will now read:

And these subsidy seekers came into this House, or rather into Washington in 1872, and absolutely took the money which we paid them out of the Treasury and with it corrupted the officials about this House, your doorkeepers and your postmaster, to procure another subsidy. The soldiers of fortune swarm about the corridors of Washington; the lobby is on hand.

And perhaps, Mr. Chairman, some gentleman can now state whether there is a "lobby on hand" at this time.

Will the gentleman from New York [Mr. Farquhar], who has charge of this measure, in the light of the remarks I have just read from the chairman of the Committee on Appropriations of the House, tell us now how much of this appropriation will go to the Pacific Steamship Company? I await a reply. [After a pause.] I see the chairman of the committee present and again request this information. How much under your tonnage bill will go to the Pacific Mail Steamship Company annually, a corporation which in 1879, according to the statement of the gentleman from Illinois [Mr. Cannon], corrupted the postmaster and the doorkeepers of this body, and expended $900,000 to procure a renewal of the subsidy which they had enjoyed for ten years and which was then about expiring?

MR. FARQUHAR.—All I know is that this company gets simply what the bill allows them as their fair proportion for the work done; this and nothing more.

MR. BLOUNT.—Under the bill this amount is fixed at $607,-424.93.

MR. DOCKERY.—I am very glad to have the information from the gentleman from Georgia, since the chairman of the committee has failed to furnish it.

MR. FARQUHAR.—Whatever the amount may be, one thing is certain, they will not get a dollar more than the bill allows. [Derisive laughter on the Democratic side.]

MR. DOCKERY.—Does the gentleman from New York deny the statement that the Pacific Mail stock has increased in value since this bill was reported?

MR. FARQUHAR.—If it is an indication that the bill is going to pass I am very glad of it.

MR. DOCKERY.—Then the gentleman admits that it has so enhanced in value?

MR. FARQUHAR.—Yes; and I want the stock of every American steamship line to rise.

MR. DOCKERY.—I am very glad to have the confession of the gentleman from New York. I want the farmers of the West to know the effect of this legislation which is to take at least $5,000,000 annually from them in the way of additional taxa-

tion and expend it for the benefit of a few Eastern ship owners, and for no other purpose. [Applause on the Democratic
side.]

Mr. Chairman, the present attitude of Great Britain upon
this whole question of subsidizing, both in intent and in fact,
has recently received official verification which does not admit
of cavil upon the other side. Consul-General Harry S. New, a
Republican of eminence in the councils of his party, says in an
official report dated September 3, 1889, that—

> The British Government does not grant subsidies, in the general sense
> of that term, to any steamship company, but the post office authorities
> make contracts for the conveyance of mails to the different parts of the
> world with the steamship companies having steamers sailing to those ports.

Further, Mr. Chairman, I invite attention to the significant
fact that England contracts for her ocean mail service in the
open market to the lowest bidder, while we propose to pay a
bonus for no equivalent service. Sir, the lesson of this whole
question is so plain that he that runs may read. England's
amazing prosperity is the result of unfettered commerce and
free ships. The United States, by a policy of suicidal exclusion, has hampered and restricted her commerce, and thus crippled and virtually destroyed her merchant marine. It is an
impossible feat, sir, to attempt to build up a mercantile navy
of any great proportions and yet, at the same time, repel
that ocean commerce upon which it must depend for its
existence.

Mr. Chairman, a brief *résumé* of the experience of France,
after an ample test of the subsidizing and bounty policy, will
at once enlarge the scope of this question and convey its practical lesson. In 1881 the French Government offered a bounty
of $12 a ton on all iron or steel ships built at home, as well as
a subsidy of 30 cents per ton for every 1,000 miles sailed by
French vessels. The Government further offered half the latter
subsidy in the case of ships purchased abroad by her citizens
and carrying the French flag. There was consequently a fever-
ish stimulation at once given to her own shipbuilding, as well
as competitive activity in British shipyards. In two years the
tonnage of her steamers had increased from about 300,000 to
nearly 700,000, while, in a single year, the tonnage of her steamships engaged in long voyages leaped from 3,600,000 to over
4,700,000 tons. The ultimate result was one of profound dis-
appointment. The experiment proved a disastrous failure.
France had the ships idle upon her hands, as there was not

sufficient commerce to employ them, and they could not create it.

Indeed, sir, so far from building up a proportionate commerce it produced a competition for what trade already existed and rendered the dividends paid by ships before the subsidizing era impossible. France had this experience for her immense outlay: that while subsidies will produce ships—a truth which was as obvious before her vast expenditure as afterward—they cannot create commerce. On the contrary, the truth is the exact reverse; commerce invariably creates a demand for ships. The experience of the Austro-Hungarian Empire in the same direction has been almost identical with that of France. On the other hand, the policy of liberated trade and free ships enabled England, from 1878 to 1887, to contribute one-third of the entire increased tonnage of all the chief maritime nations, while of the added steam tonnage of those nations she has produced two-thirds.

Free-trade England is the carrier of the world, not only floating her own commerce, but in 1888 carrying as well 43 per cent. of the commerce of all the "protected" nations of the earth. Of these protected countries the United States easily holds the first rank in maritime degradation, the English flag floating, as it does, over vessels that carry 51 per cent. of her commerce.

Having shown by the experience of the past the inability of subsidies to establish upon a permanent basis our merchant navy, or even to arrest its decline, and having demonstrated by the kindred experience of commercial nations that ships must depend upon commerce for their support, I come now in the natural and logical order of my argument to a review of some of those real causes which have for so many years fettered our commerce and arrested its growth. All phases of the subsidy fallacy rest upon the assumption that it is the lack of American ships, and not the lack of commerce, which impedes the restoration and development of our mercantile marine, its advocates forgetting that our commerce has in fact trebled, although our flag has almost entirely disappeared from the paths of ocean traffic.

It is not, therefore, the flag of any particular nation which determines its ability to compete in the traffic of the world, but it is the ability to produce as cheaply or more so than any other nation those articles which are forced to seek a foreign market. It goes, indeed, without saying that such must be the fact; and if this fundamental fact be conceded it follows that

anything which enhances the price of such products must necessarily, and in the precise ratio of such enhancement, operate
to bar their entrance into foreign markets or to limit the profits
upon their sale should they be enabled to effect an entrance
into these markets at all.

Mr. Chairman, Senator Sherman, in a speech during a recent Ohio campaign, made no pretence that subsidy would advantage the farmer, but was frank enough to avow that the intent of subsidizing our ships plying to South American countries was "to furnish our manufacturers a market there." And
so, sir, our farmers are to be further borne down with at least
$5,000,000 taxes annually in the endeavor to give a foreign
market to the manufacturing interest, which has already under
tariff laws secured a monopoly of the American market, selling
as it does of its annual product, estimated at about $7,000,000,-
000, the entire amount to our own people, save about 2 per cent.

Mr. Chairman, the just and timely criticism of Mr. Blaine
upon the McKinley bill, that it did not "open the market for
another bushel of wheat or another barrel of pork," has been
recently indorsed by an amazing popular approval; but, sir,
that distinguished gentleman finds himself confronted in his
famous "reciprocity" scheme with the identical dilemma, that
it also wholly fails to "open the market for another bushel of
wheat or another barrel of pork." Reciprocity, Mr. Chairman,
to be of genuine avail to the farmer must not be limited to the
insignificant markets of the South American countries, but
must embrace within its scope all countries where our farmers
can buy and sell with mutual advantage the surplus they have
to sell and such commodities as they are compelled to buy.
[Loud applause on the Democratic side.]

Mr. Chairman, regardless of the causes which determine this
question, the Protectionists have to offer but a single infallible
prescription for all our economic ailments—the taxation of the
people. Indeed, sir, this wonderful panacea is strongly suggestive of the alleged methods of the allopathic physicians
of our earlier times. It mattered not what might be the appearance of the tongue, whether the complexion was florid
or sallow, whether the fever was high or low, whether the
circulation was anæmic or plethoric, the remedy was heroic and
invariable—blood-letting and calomel. [Laughter.] So, sir,
is it with our friends on the other side in their politico-economic
practice, for a subsidy is but a protective tariff with a different
name; the one securing its exactions under the insidious guise
of an indirect tax, while the other, bolder though none the less

objectionable, exacts its tribute directly from the public treasury.

Mr. Chairman, the opposing theories of exclusion and freedom of trade have contested for supremacy upon the seas at many periods in the world's history, and with always the result in favor of unhampered commerce. Let us return, then, to that propitious policy under which our merchant navy, crowned with an abundant and increasing commerce, explored every sea and cast anchor in every harbor. Divested of artificial impositions and hurtful restraints, our commercial marine can then renew and reassert its strength and importance upon the great deep. Sir, the incoming and refluent waves that make music on our shores seem themselves to woo us to resume our "pride of place" upon the glorious sea. The arms of old ocean extend themselves far into our interior, as if to meet and welcome those mighty rivers and inland seas which should bear to her embrace the wealth of our mines, our forests, our manufactories, and our fertile fields.

Mr. Chairman, strike off these shackles of exclusion which have "cabined, cribbed, confined" our commerce; give full scope and play to the inventive and adventurous genius of our people, and we shall see arise, as Venus from the waves, a splendid mercantile marine, pouring its treasures into the lap of our common country and restoring its prestige and its prowess upon the seas. [Loud applause on the Democratic side.]

George W. Fithian [Ill.] spoke on January 8 in opposition to the bill.

Government paternalism is a species of socialism. While men of wealth and intelligence insist upon Government aid for their own private enterprises they should not complain of the ignorant and unlearned, who learn from their more intelligent brothers to ask the Government's aid for themselves. The doctrine of the socialist is that the Government must care for the individual. That demand is as reasonable and is upon the same footing as the demand for subsidies to shipowners who are engaged in purely private enterprises. Good government should enact only good laws, such as would extend the benefits to all alike. A law that gives to one individual or class of individuals benefits to the exclusion of others and taxes the whole people to maintain the benefits for the few is vicious and is contrary to the fundamental doctrine of a free government, a government of the people, for the people, and by the people. Suppose this Congress subsidizes ships. Other industries will soon discover that it is easier to make profits by having Government aid. This policy throttles individual enterprise and removes all incentive to industry, and as a permanent system would be a curse to the thus favored industry, as well as a curse to the nation. The day laborer, the tradesman, the blacksmith, and all other classes of labor, will demand their share of Government aid under this system, and who then will be left to support the Government? This system carried to its logical conclusion would necessarily result in the ultimate destruction of any government that adopts it. Once fairly under way, there would be the greatest danger of reaching that period when all the people would look to the Government for support and none would be left to support the Government.

Nor is the claim that subsidized ships will furnish cheaper transportation founded in reason. It will be found that competition, unless combinations are formed to prevent the operation of natural laws, will regulate the price of transportation, as it does everything else when left free. Combinations may exist with or without subsidies, it is true, but it is certain that subsidies will not prove to be an agency to prevent combinations, and the truth is would more likely feed and stimulate them. The result would be, as reason will dictate, that after the subsidy was granted the subsidized shipowner would take his subsidy and charge current rates for transportation of freight.

On February 26 Roger Q. Mills [Tex.] opposed the bill.

Mr. Chairman, I am at a great loss to account for the change which has come over the spirit of the dream of our friends on the other side of the House. Within the space of a few short revolving moons our Republican friends stood in this hall and the other and before the American people, claiming that our home market ought to be protected against the introduction of the products of the labor of the people in all other parts of the world. The echoes of these patriotic speeches are almost resounding around the hall yet.

Gentlemen went back and brought up the old doctrines of their philosophers, of Mr. Henry C. Carey, who contended that the Almighty had not made this world right in leaving it with oceans which could be crossed with the products of the labor of one people to be exchanged for the products of another;

that these oceans ought to have been set on fire like that dark river that divides the finally impenitent from the blessed, which poets tell us is tossed with fires and with no sounds heard upon its bosom but groans that are groaned and sighs that are sighed, and where tears ever weep and ever fall, but not in mercy's sight. [Applause.]

Professor Robert Thompson, a late philosopher of that faith, contends that it would be better to hang every American sailor at the yardarm of his vessel than to permit him to be engaged in carrying the surplus products of the people of the United States to foreign countries to be exchanged for the products of the labor of other people that are calculated to satisfy the wants of our people.

And but recently the third illustrious disciple of that faith has been writing in one of the magazines inculcating the same doctrine. He says that foreign trade is a contemptible braggart that ought to be overthrown, yet that very same gentleman, a distinguished manufacturer of steel rails, has been appointed by this Administration as one of the members of the Pan-American Congress to negotiate for a reciprocity that will let his steel rails into South America. [Applause on the Democratic side.]

Why this great change? What does it mean? The earth rings in every direction with the acclamations of the same disciples of the same political party, the same zealous missionaries who want reciprocity and trade, reciprocity defined by lines of latitude. "We want reciprocity," they say, "for another bushel of wheat and another barrel of pork." If this is what they want, why do they not try to negotiate with England or with France or with Germany?

Why do they not try to negotiate a little with themselves? England has put down the bars and is ready to welcome the admission of every bushel of our wheat, every barrel of our pork. You feed from your Western farms the crowded populations that stand in her factories, and from the fields of the South we furnish the great staple that gives employment to her people to manufacture clothing for the population of the globe. She is willing to take more of our cotton, more of our wheat, more of our pork, more of our agricultural products if you will only take down the bars and extinguish the fire in the ocean, stop hanging your American sailors to the yardarms of your vessels.

You say you want foreign trade. But you have built up an intervening wall. Twelve months ago you said you did

XI—12

not want to come in contact with foreign paupers. Now you want to trade with them, and in order to get that trade you are proposing to pay out money wrung by exorbitant, wicked taxation from the laboring people of this country—money to build ships to go over the seas that you have set on fire—seas from which you have prohibited navigation by declaring that any vessel which sails the ocean displaying your flag must come back in ballast.

Why, sir, the distinguished leaders of the Republican party in the Senate made a report two years ago that we could not compete in the markets of the world with our wheat, that it was a melancholy fact confronting the American people that we must look to the home market alone for the consumption of our wheat, that we must cease speaking about sending wheat to Europe and exchanging it for their calicoes, their woolens, their iron, their steel. What did those Republican Senators propose to do in order to relieve the situation? Why they gravely proposed to send to Europe and import her population to come here and eat up our wheat!

We will assume that these foreigners coming here will eat five bushels of wheat per head annually. Then it will require 36,000,000 of people to be imported the first year to consume the surplus 180,000,000 bushels of the wheat of the United States. That is what you are building your ships for—to send over to Europe to transport those people to the United States to consume our wheat.

They tell us, besides, that this must be a non-agricultural people to do this. They say that if these are agriculturists they will only make more wheat and add to the surplus. It must, therefore, be the people who are brought here, in pursuance of the protective policy, who will consume and not add to the surplus—people who will eat wheat and not make it.

About one-third of all our people, as the census shows, are engaged in gainful occupations. Then one-third of those who must come under this protective policy must come and engage in gainful occupations, and the other two-thirds, being the women and children, are to be supported by the labor of the one-third.

Twelve millions of people, being the one-third of 36,000,000, the total number of people required to consume the surplus, are to be laborers engaged in the factories and other gainful occupations throughout the country. Well, 4,000,000 of our people, it is estimated, make the manufactured product of America, amounting to seven thousand millions annually.

Three times four are twelve, and the 12,000,000 of persons employed in manufacturing products, being the addition to our population under this policy, would make twenty-one thousand millions of manufactured products in place of seven thousand millions, and where will we get the market for their sale?

Why, you can not consume your own products now, and you are hunting markets for your manufactures under the name of a "bushel of wheat and a barrel of pork." It would take more than 250,000,000 of people to be brought from Europe to come here to consume the surplus of one year's cotton crop! What a magnificent development of statesmanship! [Applause on the Democratic side.] Instead of sending our surplus abroad, sending the things we do not want in exchange for the things we do want, to benefit ourselves and our fellow-men, they propose to break up all the habitations of all the people of the globe and bring them here to consume our surplus and hunt up employment here! [Applause on the Democratic side.]

You say you want ships. Why not build them? You have the protective policy. You say it develops American industries. You say it cheapens and brings down the cost of production. But there is one thing at least that the history of the last few months shows you have succeeded in cheapening, and maybe you think that is "nasty" too; you have succeeded in cheapening American labor in all parts of the country. [Applause on the Democratic side.]

Yes, Mr. Chairman, since the passage of the McKinley bill, if you will take up the papers of the country, you will see a string like long skeleton fingers pointing to factories which have curtailed—stricken down—the wages of their employees, and there is a reason for all of these things which I have not the time now to discuss.

Why is it, if you gentlemen do not like cheapness, that you will insist on cheapening the wages of the men you employ? If you want to compel people to pay manufacturers higher prices because they are American, why do they not, when there is no law to compel them to do it, do the same thing for the people they employ? Why do they not, out of the goodness of their hearts, practice the doctrines that they preach to others? I think they are somewhat like Dow, Jr., who, in preaching to his congregation, said, "Don't do as I do, my hearers, but do as I tell you." [Applause on the Democratic side.] That is your doctrine.

Now you want to subsidize ships; you want to have ships

built, and you think the way to do it is to destroy your commerce and then make ships to build it up again. Why do you not stand on one side of this fence and fight loyally on one set of principles all the time? Why are you now talking about extending your foreign commerce? These subsidies you are giving are not for your coastwise shipping. They are to encroach upon the dominion of that little braggart whom Mr. Andrew Carnegie says we ought to help dethrone. You are for building up foreign commerce. If you will tear down your wall, it will build itself up.

Now, if you will take off your duties and bring them down to a revenue standard, placing them upon articles where they will be the least possible burden upon the taxpayers, and permit your importations to come in overwhelmingly, what will be the result? I would welcome a double amount of importations, because it would mean a double amount of exportation. That increases the value of all farm products. That distributes wealth among 30,000,000 people, each dollar of which is behind a want. Each one demands employment of labor to satisfy that want. Each one of them sends joy and life into the heart of American industry and brings prosperity and peace, contentment and happiness, where now misery and want prevail.

But you say, "We do not want these pauper products of foreigners. We want our own products. Our policy is to send our surplus product to foreign countries and sell it for gold and silver and bring the gold and silver home, and then expend that gold and silver for the purchase of things made in this country by the labor of our own people."

Now, let us follow that absurdity a little. In the recent discussions before the Committee on Coinage, Weights, and Measures it was shown that there are seven and a half billions of gold and silver in all the world. Of that amount we have one billion. There remains then among the other people of the world the accumulated stock of four thousand years or more, six and a half billions of gold and silver. Well, suppose we send abroad a billion dollars' worth of products a year (we are sending abroad now about six hundred and thirty millions of agricultural products); in six years we would have in the United States the whole accumulated stock of gold and silver in the world. Then what would take place? Your trade would stop still. You could not export anything more. In six years the judgment day comes. [Applause on the Democratic side.] Six years and you go back to barbarism. No man can exchange his surplus. You then have a thousand million bushels of wheat, perhaps more than you can consume, but it ceases to be of any value. We have perhaps by that time seven or eight million bales of cotton more than we can consume. That vast amount is worthless. It can not be consumed in this country; it can not buy anything; it is as worthless as the water so far as commercial value is concerned, or as worthless as the wind. You can not buy it or sell it. All your products fall to the earth. And that period, when it comes, would be the final millennium of the great policy of American protection as foreshadowed and taught by the great American Republican party. [Applause on the Democratic side.]

This policy that you are teaching leads to making all the products of labor less valuable, leads to making everything that money measures and buys less valuable, leads to darker days, leads to more tears, more distress, leads to a more hopeless struggle by borrowing money to keep from sinking down into the depths of distress and woe, and at last the people must touch the last deep of distress and go through all the horrors of universal bankruptcy.

The Creator hath made us dependent upon each other for the satisfying of many of our wants. By living in harmony with that law which binds with threads the human heart, and by conforming to that law of the Creator we will obtain the greater satisfaction of our wants, the greatest distribution of comforts, and make the highest advance in civilization and the greatest growth in prosperity and happiness. [Applause on the Democratic side.]

Amos J. Cummings [N. Y.] supported the bill.

"Free trade and sailors' rights" is good old Democratic doctrine. [Applause.] Democracy is the true friend of labor. I am a Democrat upon principle and conviction. I see no power in Congress to tax one man for the benefit of another. If this bill were such a measure I would not vote for it. But it is not. It is not a protective measure. It is not a gratuitous subsidy from Government to shipowners, like the sugar subsidies and the privileges given to monopolist manufacturers. To those who say that it is I answer that it is rather like a patent—a contract between the Government and the citizen who takes advantage of it—a contract beneficial to both parties.

These ships are at the service of the Government if required. No manufacturing establishment holds that relation. The shipowners and shipbuilders are bound in return for the assistance which they receive from Government to build their vessels as the Government requires and to turn their ships over to it upon requisition in its hour of need. Thus we see that this is the readiest, the most efficient, and, I believe, the cheapest means of increasing our naval strength.

Sir, this bill is not only a measure of safety, but it will stimulate trade. Labor furnishes the means, but trade brings wealth. It is not only a measure of safety, but of prosperity. Its passage will bring trade. And it does follow, as the day the night, that every hindrance to trade is a barrier to national wealth as it does follow that every stimulant helps it. [Applause.] At the same time this measure will develop our shipping and shipbuilding interests to an enormous extent and be a boon to our workingmen. As a workingman, and as a representative of a district containing tens of thousands of hardy mechanics, I dwell upon this feature.

Shipyards would be planted on the shores of the Gulf of Mexico, on the Lakes, and on the Pacific coast, as well as on the Atlantic. A new army of laborers would be required to mine and to smelt the ore. New railroads would be built to convey the iron and coal to the seashore. The farmers would share in the prosperity. The demand for agricultural products at home would increase and new foreign markets open.

An iron steamship represents a wide range of trades and talents and labor. Few, if any, products of modern industry equal it in this respect. There are few in which so great a proportion of the whole cost goes to the workingman. On an average it takes $19 in labor to work up $1 in raw material into its place in the finished structure of the ship. In other words, 95 per cent. of the ship represents labor, and 5 per cent. raw material.

Sir, the passage of a free-ship substitute would not be a measure of defence, it would be injurious to national prosperity. It would throw upon the American market the tramp iron steamships now rusting in the waters of the Clyde, and pour millions of American gold into English pockets. It would give British shipowners an opportunity to save their merchant marine in case of war with Russia or any other naval power, and involve us in complications in which we would be measurably helpless. But this is not all. They could transfer their ships to nominal American owners and come out of such a war unscathed under cover of the Stars and Stripes.

No, sir; we want no such measure. What we must have is one that will practically increase our naval power and at the

same time develop anew our commerce by the building of
American ships, thus giving employment to thousands of
American artisans and sailors. Then, and not till then, shall
we have American sailors to man an American navy, and Amer-
ican designers, American builders, and American workmen employed in building American vessels in American shipyards
from American steel and iron, launched from American ways,
for the benefit of American commerce, to be used in reclaiming
our foreign carrying trade and in national defence.

John H. Rogers [Ark.] declared that the Republicans
were bound in honor to pass the bill, in order to fulfil
their contract with the shipbuilders.

Everybody knows that you bought the Presidency by buying
up the State of Indiana and the State of New York in the
last presidential contest. You have paid back all the parties
out of whom you "fried the fat" and got the means to do it,
except the shipbuilders.

You have paid off the manufacturers with the McKinley
bill; you have paid off the railroad corporations by impliedly
confirming to them their land grants; you have now on hand
a bill to pay back what you got from the shipbuilders and
the shipowners of the country. That this is so no less distinguished a person than the Speaker of the House [Thomas B.
Reed] himself announced some time ago when he said that—

Step by step we are fulfilling the pledges to the people.

[Laughter on the Democratic side.]
You can either go into political bankruptcy or else pass
this bill and keep your obligations and your contracts.

CHARLES A. BOUTELLE [Me.].—That is what we are going
to do. [Applause on the Republican side.]

MR. ROGERS.—I have another witness of the truth of what
I am saying. [Laughter on the Democratic side.] It comes
from Maine. It comes from one who is the right bower of the
Speaker, who tells us he is going to keep his contract and
pay back this money to the shipbuilders from whom he got
it to conduct the campaign. [Applause on the Democratic
side.]

Mr. Chairman, the Speaker ought not to repudiate that
testimony, for, if the gentleman [Mr. Boutelle] had served his
God as faithfully as he has the Speaker, his future hope of

salvation would be much better than it is now. [Laughter on the Democratic side.] There is only one thing that is left unsettled—and that is in entire harmony with all the balance of the legislation of this Congress—and that is, you repudiated the Blair bill, the money for which was going to educate the black man at the South, but where you get no support.

Now, Mr. Chairman, one word to my Democratic friends. A man can hardly get a seat at the House restaurant table to-day for the plethoric abdominal development of the lobby who are here for the purpose of advancing this bill. [Laughter.] Some of them are so big as to take one-half of a whole table, and they are down with their barrels as big as they are, I have no doubt. [Renewed laughter.] They have gone so far, I am told, as to tell some Democrats if they can not vote for this bill to leave the hall. I advertise the fact that no Democrat on this floor shall leave this hall on the final vote without the country's understanding why he is away from this Chamber. [Loud applause on the Democratic side.]

He must have the courage and manhood to vote his convictions upon this bill, either for or against it. Let him go upon record, but do not let him skulk if he is against it. Let him come here, state his views against it, and by his vote prove his loyalty to the country and to the people who have turned over the control of this House for the next two years to his party. [Loud applause on the Democratic side.]

On February 27 William McAdoo [N. J.] spoke against the bill. Replying to the charge that its opponents were acting in the interest of England, he said:

Whenever, Mr. Chairman, there is a raid contemplated upon the pockets of the taxpayers of the United States, whenever there is a measure advocated in the interest of some favored class, our friends on the other side protrude upon the public gaze this tremendous but unreal image of "bogy" John Bull, while under the shadow of this nebulous monster created for the occasion from the graveyard of lost character and blasted reputation come the choice spirits who are now using their jimmies on the national safe. [Applause on the Democratic side] I tell gentlemen that this figure is played out in our politics. It is an insult to the American intelligence, more especially to that portion of our citizens whom they seek to affect by it. How, to be sure, you hate John Bull when you want a bounty or a monopoly, and how you love him as you revel in your British castles bought with American money, or chase social recognition in London!

I hear men in this House and out of it howling like shrieking dervishes about John Bull, this figure whom they have created, whose open mouth and cavernous stomach are to take in the great Republic unless we give them the key to the United States Treasury; and yet we have seen that these men, both within and without this Chamber, who never uttered a protest while the veritable John Bull was stealing the territory of Venezuela, spoliating the people of India, and robbing and tyrannizing over the people of Ireland; and these same men must have the benefit of the taxes of the people, the hard-earned, scanty money of the people, because they are so intensely American when an opportunity is in sight or a monopoly is to be given them. And within the last few years we have seen the gentlemen who have gained their money by grants, subsidies, class legislation, and vicious laws, procured by devious ways from the people in this land, make our whole people seem inconsistent and ridiculous to foreigners by begging recognition of the debauchees and titled vagabonds of the mock courts of modern Europe, and then come here and talk about free America, "our glorious institutions," "America against the world," and the American flag.[1] [Laughter and applause.]

We are legislating not for these tuft-hunting bounty patriots, but for the plain, every-day, all-the-year-round, loyal Americans. We know we can best outrun and crush British domination by making ours a land of free homes and happy, prosperous people. The severest blow at England and all other foreign rivals is to make America great, strong, free, pure, and prosperous. This can best be done by honest, light-felt, economical government, low taxes, no bounties nor favors, and a freer commerce. An intelligent people, once humbugged, now only laugh at ranting "spell-binders," the fake conjurers of international spooks, and the circus-poster proclamations of trade circulars against lower tariffs.

This old piece of political theatrical property ought to go to the lumber room with the bloody shirt. [Renewed laughter.]

You will not take one waif out of an American coast city, you will not take your poetic boy off the farm and make a sailor of him by this bill. You will not, under existing conditions, float the American flag over an additional ship built for subsidy. Fifty hours after you take away the bounty you are going to pay great sums for old prehistoric Noah's arks

[1] This referred to Andrew Carnegie.

that disgrace rather than glorify the flag, and in my opinion
you are going to enter upon the suicide of republican government in America. It is un-American, it is unrepublican, it is
unfair, it is unjust for gentlemen in the closing hours of this
Congress to hand the key of the treasury, which contains the
hard-earned, toil-stained money of the American people, to the
men who are rearing a bastard "aristocracy" under the flag
of which you prate so much. [Prolonged applause on the
Democratic side.]

The bill was amended and then passed by a vote of
139 to 120. The Senate concurred in the House amendments, and President Harrison approved the act on
March 3, 1891.

On December 4, 1900, the Senate took up the discussion of the bill of William P. Frye [Me.], "to promote
the commerce and increase the foreign trade of the
United States, and to provide auxiliary cruisers, transports, and seamen for Government use when necessary."

Ship Subsidies

Senate, December 4, 1900-January 25, 1901

Senator Frye.—In 1891 I reported from the Committee
on Commerce two bills, one paying a bounty to all ships engaged in the foreign trade, the other postal subsidies. The
bounty was nearly double that contained in the pending
measure. It passed the Senate and was defeated in the House
by a majority of 3. The subsidy bill cost me several months
of hard work. The completed bill was submitted to capitalists
who were willing to consider the propriety of establishing steamship lines to South America, in the Pacific, and across the
Atlantic.

I received assurances that if the bill was enacted into law
six or eight lines would be established of ships from 14 to 21
knots an hour. The House crippled the bill by a large and
unscientific reduction of rates, returned it to the Senate too
late in the session for any contest, and it became a law. Of
course, it proved a dead failure. We did succeed under it
in securing the American line from New York to Southampton
by admitting the *New York* and *Paris* to an American registry
on condition that the company should build two ships here of

like tonnage and speed. But those four ships have ever since been run at a loss to the corporation, not to us, for their value as auxiliaries to our navy during the Spanish war was beyond computation.

Three years ago, instructed by resolutions of State legislatures, of political conventions, of commercial organizations, by recommendations of public officials, it seemed to me that our people were taking a greater interest in the restoration of our merchant marine than ever before, and that it was an opportune time to once more call the attention of Congress to the subject. I found, however, a great diversity of opinion among friends of the ship as to the remedy to be proposed. Discriminating duties had many advocates; bounties, subsidies, free ships each some. I knew that success was dependent upon united action. As a method of securing that I selected a committee of twenty-five, all friends of Congressional action; some of them shipbuilders and shipowners, experts, required for intelligent conclusions; a majority having no interest other than as American citizens; those interested hardly any two in the same trade or in the same type of ships, selected from every part of the country; some favoring each proposed remedy except that of free ships, a majority at the start for discriminating duties.

This committee was composed as follows: Senators Hanna, Elkins, Perkins, Frye, gentlemen who had shown great interest, and some of whom had had experience in shipping matters; Hon. Sereno E. Payne, then chairman of the House Committee on Merchant Marine; and the leading shipbuilders, and men with shipping interests, in the country. The subject-matter was committed to this committee in 1897.

Knowing that the subject to be considered would involve many important legal questions, I advised the employment of counsel. Hon. George F. Edmunds was very wisely selected. The committee was indefatigable in its labors, meeting many times in New York, Philadelphia, and Washington. After full, complete, and most careful consideration, this committee finally, with entire unanimity, decided against discriminating duties, against discriminating tonnage taxes, against bounties to be paid on the exportation of the products of the American farm, and in favor of sailing bounties for our ships, and in my opinion these conclusions were eminently wise.

None of the committee were in favor of free ships, and I do not know why any of them should be. The highest duty of the United States of America to-day is to provide more shipyards, more docks, more facilities for the construction of ships for the oceans. A great maritime nation like ours might just as well be without a constitution as without shipyards. And free ships would simply relegate all of our shipyards to doing Government work, or supplying the necessities of the coastwise trade and the Great Lakes. Besides, what benefit would a free ship be? What would you save by it? You would save the depreciation, the interest, and the insurance on the additional cost of the American ship over the English, and that is all. You would save, on the average, about $4.50 a gross ton. That you would save, I admit, but you would still be handicapped by the difference of operation, from 40 to 80 per cent. in wages, as between a foreign ship and your own. I assert, and I assert it without the slightest hesitation, that you can admit free ships to the United States to-day, and you will find no capital to invest in them. You will not be able to sail them on the oceans of the world in competition with the Norwegian ships or the English.

A bill was finally drafted embodying the views of this committee, was presented to the Senate in the last Congress by Senator Hanna, and to the House by Representative Payne, referred to the respective committees having jurisdiction, was carefully considered, evidence taken, discussion had, amendments adopted, and favorable reports were made, but for want of time the measure was not considered. The general committee agreed to the amendments proposed by the Congressional committees; the press gave the details of the bill to the country. The result was further criticisms, additional amendments. All were considered, and those seeming reasonable were adopted. At the last session of this Congress the amended bills were again referred, were again discussed in committee, additional amendments were adopted, and agreed to by a subcommittee of the general committee, which was continually in session here.

Finally the pending measure, with proposed amendments, was favorably reported to the Senate by the chairman of the Committee on Commerce. In regard to it I wish to say that there never was any other bill before Congress which received such close and critical consideration, on which was expended such careful, conscientious, and intelligent work. Nor was there ever one with this purpose in view which so generally commended itself to the friends of the American ship. Its critics and opponents are those who honestly believe in, and have always advocated, free ships, and the foreign lines who will not tamely submit to surrender the profits of their carrying trade. The former contest it from principle, but are not dangerous, for the country rejects their theory; the latter are inspired only by self-interest, one of the most powerful of all motives, and they will make a most determined, vigorous, and never-ending fight.

I now call your attention to the provisions of the pending bill. The first section authorizes the secretary of the treasury to pay to American ships registered and engaged in the foreign carrying trade of our exports and imports one cent and a half a ton for each 100 miles sailed up to 1,500; beyond the 1,500, 1 cent per ton for each 100 miles. Those figures were reached with the greatest possible care, the only purpose being to equalize the conditions of the British ship and the American ship. The committee did not take the ships which can carry at the lowest possible cost.

The Norwegian ships can beat the world to-day in cheapness of carrying. The committee did not take them, nor the German ships nor the Spanish. For its standard of comparison it took the English ship, which in wages and manner of living on shipboard leads the other nations, and it only intended by its bill to equalize the difference between the two. That provision applies to all ships, sail or steam, registered and engaged in the foreign carrying trade. It is the purest kind of democracy. A postal subsidy law is aristocracy; it is monopoly. The subsidy is paid to one great line, for instance, running between this port and the other port, thus practically excluding every other line from running between those ports. But the provisions of this bill seek to encourage the building of ships by any man who has money enough to build them, and the establishing of lines by any corporation that desires to establish them, and to run them between any ports they please.

The difference between the 1,500 miles and the balance of the long voyages was made on the principle of the long and short haul. The ship that sailed but 1,500 miles would make a great many more entries in a year than the one that sailed 10,000 miles, and the former would have to handle cargo a great many times more frequently than the latter. The ship on the long voyage would have a decided advantage over the ship on the short. It would pay less in port charges, because it would be less frequently in port. It would pay less lighthouse dues and other port charges abroad for the same reason. Therefore the committee believed that for voyages under 1,500 miles, which would be confined very largely to those between here and the Caribbean Sea ports and the West Indies, the rate fixed was wise, because we have for some time been losing trade there.

ORVILLE H. PLATT [Conn.].—The shorter voyage vessel gets the greater pay?

SENATOR FRYE.—Yes; for reasons which were very obvious.

Now, is the committee correct in its statement that it costs more to build and more to operate an American ship than it costs our commercial rivals to build and operate theirs? If the committee is mistaken in that respect, then the foundation of this bill falls through. If the committee is correct, then any Senator can see that we never will run American ships on the oceans against foreign ships until there is legislation which will equalize the difference.

Men say, "Suppose your American ship is in Liverpool; is she not to obtain sailors for Liverpool wages?" Not one bit of it, if she flies the American flag. Those sailors know just as much about wages as the men who run the ship, and they know the going wages under our flag just as well as the captain does. If you ask a man to go on an American ship, where he will have better living and better quarters, he will not do so in a foreign port unless he has the wages the other sailors on the American ship have. Sailor-like, he will take the poorer food, the poorer quarters, and the lower wages and sail under the British flag.

The best estimate which can possibly be made as to the difference in food between English sailors and Americans is that it costs 10 cents a day more for the latter than for the former, and as a matter of course it costs a great deal more than in several other countries of Europe.

On December 11 Alexander S. Clay [Ga.], of the minority of the committee, opposed the bill.

The majority of the committee tell us in their report that the most promising field for the future development of our markets for agricultural products is northern and temperate Asia, and that our grain fields and cotton plantations will gain in greater proportion from the enactment of this bill into law than the seaboard shipbuilding and shipowning States, whose benefits, they say, from its enactment are to the casual eye more clearly manifest. A more absurd proposition was never stated. How our grain fields and cotton plantations are to be benefited in greater proportion than the shipbuilding and shipowning States by legislation which takes from the public treasury

$9,000,000 annually for a period of twenty years and contributes this vast sum, collected by taxation from the people, to ship-owners to aid them in carrying on their private business, I must confess I am unable to see. The proposition stated by the majority of the committee is simply this: If you will tax all the people and raise $180,000,000, and take this sum and give it to the shipowners and aid them in developing their private business, you will benefit the people who pay the taxes more than the private individual who receives the donation. I presume the majority of the committee are going on the theory that it is more blessed to give than to receive. While the friends of the measure proclaim loudly that its real purpose is to increase our merchant marine, so as to promote the commerce and increase the foreign trade of the United States, a careful analysis of the bill—I desire to reflect upon no Senator who assisted in framing the bill, because the presumption is that all acted honestly—will show conclusively that it was not framed with the view of building up our merchant marine; at least, if enacted into law we can not hope to see such results follow. The bill provides that the owner or owners of any vessel of the United States now in existence, and completed and in existence January 1, 1900, shall be entitled to make application and draw the subsidy out of the public treasury without being compelled to build other ships to correspond in tonnage with the ships drawing the subsidy. This provision of the bill is not drawn with the view of encouraging shipbuilding and enlarging our merchant marine.

If the friends of this bill framed it with the view and for the purpose of encouraging shipbuilding, why did they not provide that the owner or owners of any vessel engaged in the foreign trade of the United States, before receiving the benefit of the subsidy provided in the act, should be required to obligate themselves to build new ships to correspond with those receiving the benefit of the subsidy? In such an event every owner of a vessel applying for the subsidy would have been compelled to have built a similar vessel, which would have resulted largely in building up the merchant marine and would have given a great stimulus to shipbuilding in the United States, but clearly, to my mind, this legislation in its present form can produce no such results. If Senators will examine the testimony taken before the committee, the conclusion will be reached that the shipowners have a thorough organization to carry through this legislation.

They were not seeking opportunities to build ships, but,

on the contrary, to secure legislation that will enable them
to go into the public treasury and draw nine million annually
and divide it among themselves.

It is true that before the foreign-built steamship can receive
any part of this subsidy a majority of the stock in such foreign-
built steamship now sailing under a foreign flag must be owned
by American capital. It is also true, under the provisions of
this bill, that the admission of all these foreign-built steamships is conditioned upon the construction within the United
States inside of ten years of vessels equal to the gross tonnage
of those receiving the subsidy. In other words, American
citizens who have invested their money in foreign-built ships
and who are now sailing them under foreign flags are permitted to admit these ships to American register, and to sail
them under our flag, and to participate in the subsidy fixed
in this bill, provided the American owners of such foreign-built
vessels will build other vessels to be used in our foreign trade
equal to the gross tonnage of the vessels receiving the benefit
of this subsidy. The difference between American citizens owning American vessels and those owning foreign-built vessels is
that the former are not required to build other vessels of like
capacity and the latter are required to build such vessels in
order to receive the subsidy. The owners of American vessels
registered for foreign trade will draw twice the subsidy for
operating their ships that those draw who may bring their
foreign-built ships under our flag and register them for foreign
trade.

It necessarily follows that American capital invested in
foreign-built ships will readily see the disadvantage under which
it labors. American citizens who have invested their money
in foreign-built ships, and who are sailing them under a foreign
flag, will not avail themselves of the provisions of this bill,
for the reason that they are not only required to build new
ships, but after they have done so they can only draw half
of the subsidy allowed ships of Americans flying our flag. They
can not afford to come in competition with a class of ships
drawing from the public treasury a sum twice as large as the
amount given to American owners of foreign-built ships. As
we proceed to analyze the bill, every step we take leads inevitably
to the conclusion that, any view you take of the different
features of the measure, no great stimulus will be given to
shipbuilding in the United States, and consequently our merchant marine will not be enlarged to any great extent by this
legislation.

Since I began the preparation of my argument two amendments have been adopted by the Committee on Commerce, which materially change the bill and render it much more objectionable than when the bill first came from the committee. The bill originally provided that no vessel shall be entitled to the full compensation unless she shall have cleared from a port of the United States with cargo to the amount of 50 per cent. of her gross tonnage. The bill, as amended, strikes out "gross tonnage" and inserts "capacity for carrying commercial cargo." This is a radical difference. There is quite a difference between the gross tonnage of a steamship and its commercial tonnage, or cargo capacity. Gross tonnage means the entire cargo capacity of a ship, not deducting any space for coal, fuel, crew, etc. Take, for instance, the *St. Louis*, a swift passenger steamer of 21 knots, and this ship has a gross tonnage of 11,629 tons and a cargo capacity of 3,500 tons.

This amendment provides that the swift passenger steamers can first deduct the space consumed by coal, fuel, crew, passengers, etc., and draw the full subsidy, provided such a ship shall convey a cargo equal to one-half of the space left, deducting the space consumed as above set forth. This is another evidence, to my mind, that the bill is not intended to increase our agricultural exports, but that its principal benefit is to go to the owners of the swift passenger steamers, engaged almost entirely in conveying passengers to foreign countries.

The other amendment confines the subsidy to such ships as were completed or in process of construction on February 1, 1899. How easily such an amendment could be utilized for the special benefit of a certain class!

Those who were not on the inside of this legislation and not realizing the time that would be fixed for making contracts for the construction of ships, not knowing that the time for such contracts would expire February 1, 1899, two years before the passage of the bill, would be shut out from making contracts for the construction of ships entitled to enjoy the benefit of this subsidy. Persons who may have completed ships since February 1, 1899, or who may have entered into contracts for the construction of ships since that time are not entitled to enjoy the benefit of this subsidy. This amendment, to say the least of it, is suggestive of favoritism, and would indicate that the persons who are to enjoy the benefit of the subsidy under this provision knew before the passage of this legislation that the subsidy would be confined to a certain class, to wit, those who had completed their ships or who had entered into contract for the construction of ships on or before February 1, 1899. Why were not the friends of this measure willing to extend this feature of the subsidy to the owners of ships in existence at the time of the passage of the act or that might be under contract for construction at the time of the passage of the act or for a certain time to be named in the future? Why not give an equal and a fair chance to all shipowners and builders who might be entitled to the subsidy under this feature of the bill?

There is another objection to this bill, to my mind, that carries with it great weight. Under the provisions of the bill any citizen of the United States who applies to the Secretary of the Treasury for the purpose of building a new ship and receiving the benefit of this subsidy must do so within five years after the passage of this act, and American owners of foreign-built vessels receiving the benefit of this act must, within ten years after the registry of any foreign-built vessel, build a new vessel of an aggregate gross tonnage equal to the gross tonnage of the foreign-built vessel receiving the benefit of this subsidy.

Now, American citizens, under this bill, who may desire to build ships to participate in this subsidy must do so within five years. American citizens who do not own ships before the passage of this act, and who build them within the next five years, will enjoy the benefit of this subsidy for twenty years. But ships built after this five years shall have elapsed can not participate in the subsidy. What will be the result? Those who may build ships during the next five years, enjoying the benefit of this subsidy, will have the advantage over those who may build ships after five years, one receiving a large subsidy from the Government every year and the latter class receiving nothing. The result will follow—every American ship built during the next five years will be under a bounty contract for twenty years, longer than it would last, while new ships, built after five years, will not be subsidized and can not compete with the ships built during the next five years enjoying the benefit of this bounty.

The stimulant gives out at the end of five years, but the ships built during this period enjoy the stimulant for twenty years. Americans, realizing that the ships already built during this five years will continue to enjoy this bounty, will see that it is impossible to build new ships, after a lapse of five years, to compete with these subsidized ships built under the provisions of this act. There certainly will then come in the history of our country a period when no American can afford to build a new ship to compete with those ships enjoying this large subsidy for twenty years to come. This is one of the serious difficulties which is always inherited from the bounty scheme and can not be avoided. History teaches us that such has always been the result. A bounty once begun, there is no good place for giving it up. The more bounty you give, the more the recipient wants.

In the language of the minority of the House Committee against the passage of this measure, "A bounty works on an industry like alcohol on the human system—the more you take, the more you want, and, after you have taken too much, it will kill you to stop and kill you if you do not stop." An American marine built up in this way will not remain long at a maximum point, but will decrease and go to decay so soon as the supply of the bounty ceases.

Mr. Clay declared that there was no natural reason why ships could not be built in the United States without aid of a subsidy.

Both iron and steel can be obtained in the United States as cheaply as in any country in the world and, regardless of restricted navigation laws, we will become at no distant day the shipbuilding nation of the world. It can be substantiated by unquestionable evidence that our shipyards on both the Atlantic and Pacific are now enjoying a degree of prosperity and a period of activity in business unparalleled in the history of our country. I am informed, Mr. President, that it will take these shipyards from three to five years to comply with and fulfill the contracts now on hand for the building and equipping of new ships.

Many years ago Mr. John Roach and Mr. Charles H. Cramp, two of our greatest shipbuilders, testified before a committee from the House of Representatives investigating the cause of the decline of our shipping interest, that if Congress would take off the duties from American iron, reducing it to the price of foreign iron, then we are prepared to compete with foreign shipbuilders.

The labor question is misstated. We are prepared to meet that difficulty and to ask no further legislation on the subject. Congress began the policy of free material for shipbuilding for the foreign trade in 1872 and has steadily pursued and expanded that policy. We all know that by sections 7 and 8 of the tariff act of 1894, which were repeated in sections 12 and 13 of the tariff act of 1897, the free list was extended so as to include all materials for the construction of ships. We all know that articles of domestic production, when used as supplies for vessels of the United States, are exempted from internal revenue taxes. In view of these special favors enjoyed by the shipowners, is it just and right that they should continue to clamor for additional assistance at the expense of the public treasury?

The argument presented by the majority of the committee that the American shipowners pay better wages to labor can be easily answered. We know previous to 1855, when American ships competed successfully with British ships in our foreign-carrying trade, we then paid better wages to our sailors than the English paid. Still we successfully met the keen competition of our rivals. An examination into the scale of wages paid by us, in comparison with British wages, coupled with the food and comforts of the sailors of both nations, shows a decided advantage to our sailors. While this is true, the nutritious food and superior treatment received by our sailors enable them to do much more efficient work than the British sailors perform. It is estimated that our sailors do from 17 to 28 per cent. more work than British sailors.

Thus far I have endeavored to point out the inequalities and favoritism running through the entire measure, but my objections to such legislation go still further, because, in my opinion, the bill is vicious in principle, and bounties have always been repugnant to the spirit of our free institutions. The $9,000,000 donated to a certain class of shipowners is necessarily taken from the entire people by taxation. If the shipowner is entitled to a bounty to aid him in his private business, can not the farmer, with equal justice, demand a bounty from the public treasury on his corn, his wheat, cotton, or other products?

Can not we, with as much propriety, take from the public treasury 20 cents a bushel for all grain raised by the farmer and donate it as a bounty, and with equal consistency, as we can make this donation to the shipowners? It is manifestly unequal and unjust to tax farmers, shoemakers, carpenters, blacksmiths, masons, dairymen, miners, and railroad men to pay a bounty to shipowners for every mile they sail upon the sea, unless you go into the public treasury and give a bounty to all forms of industry, which is impossible. In the United

States, with our free institutions, the people have a right to expect that all legislation will tend to equalize the conditions of human life. This bill, if enacted into law, will tend to build up a moneyed aristocracy and to reproduce in the United States the method of government which has for centuries controlled Europe.

Is the financial success of one class of our people of greater concern than that of another? What special service has the shipowner conferred upon his country that he should have the right to tax the farmer, the merchant, or the laborer to build up his private business and to enhance his private fortune? The principles of this bill are unjust, undemocratic, and absolutely indefensible.

On December 13 Marcus A. Hanna [O.] supported the Frye ship subsidy bill.

The remarks of the Senator from Georgia [Mr. Clay] on this measure brought into question somewhat the motives which prompted those who have acted in the preparation of this measure. I regret that the cause seemed to demand the reinforcement of an insinuation which challenged the motives of the men who had to do in an advisory way with the construction of the bill. Being a member of what is called the Maritime Committee, I felt it my duty, my right, and privilege, to explain on behalf of that committee the motives and the methods under which they acted. For my part I resent even an insinuation that any other motives, aside from those of public policy and for the best interests of this country, were beneath any such action.

Mr. President, the duties of this committee were many times found to be embarrassing. The difficulties presented were hard to overcome. But as the members were all bent upon the same object, attempting to accomplish the same result, after a few meetings a spirit of compromise developed. The disposition to find some middle ground, some foundation upon which this great measure might be constructed, grew and grew until at last a bill was perfected by the committee, which, with its amendments reported from the Senate Committee on Commerce, is believed to be the most practical measure that can possibly be devised.

I spoke of my connection with the great maritime interests of the lakes. In my short business career I have seen that business grow and develop within a little more than thirty years from a comparatively small business to a business of un-paralleled magnitude.

That industry has been developed largely by the direct aid furnished in its infancy by the United States Government. The protection of that interest first of all was because our navigation laws prohibited any other but an American vessel trading between American ports. We have north of us Canada with just as much water front as we, with cheaper material and cheaper labor. Canada would have become a formidable rival in the earlier stages of our enterprise had it not been for the protection of the navigation laws of the United States.

But even with that protection, Mr. President, the present condition as to rates of transportation could not have been attained. It is to the liberal policy of this Government in the matter of our rivers and harbors that we owe more than all else the growth of our merchant marine upon the lakes and the cheap transportation as a result.

What is true of the marine interests of the lakes is true of all other interests of that nature, and, whether or not the protection afforded by the laws of which I have spoken was the only reason for the development of this commerce, it at least was the foundation which led to it.

Mr. President, the time has not faded out of the memory of members in this Chamber when, during our war with Spain, the people of the Atlantic coast were shivering with terror and appealing to the departments of this Government for coast protection against the invasion of the Spanish navy and those unknown but much-dreaded torpedo-boat destroyers.

But, Mr. President, when it was known that those four ships of the American Line which had been chartered by the Navy Department, manned by their own crews, every man of whom had taken the oath of allegiance to the cause for which they proposed to fight, I say when it became known that those four swift steamers were on the picket line on the ocean, steamers that could show their heels to any man-of-war in the Spanish navy, ready to transmit to our fleet of warships any plans or information on the part of the supposed invaders, there was a feeling of confidence, of complete confidence, of safety, that if you would descend to measure it by a money value would be worth more than the whole subsidy proposed in this bill.

I say, Mr. President, that when we attempt to combat prejudice which is used against an enterprise that induces our people to go so far in that direction of sentiment, if you please to call it, as did those who built and who run those ships, we have got to appeal to the people of the country and go behind those missionaries of foreign shipowners who come to educate Congress.

I have noticed many newspaper comments and criticisms upon this measure, nearly all tending to the one point—that this whole measure is intended to be in the interest of certain lines or certain kinds of steamships. I deny it. I deny it because in all the discussion that has taken place during the construction of this measure by the so-called Maritime Committee every kind of a ship and every kind of trade was represented there. No one man or no one agency had any more power in shaping the policy embodied in the bill there framed than any other. I speak for myself, and I know I reflect the sentiment of the Maritime Committee when I state as the sole purpose and object that we started upon the hypothesis that something must be done to build up our merchant marine if we were to have one, and, as I said in the beginning, the spirit of conciliation and compromise prevailed at every meeting that was held and every discussion that was had.

I claim that the men who have and who take the responsibility of this measure before the country are entitled to just as much consideration for honesty of purpose and ability to accomplish the result as the people who criticise the measure as a subsidy. It was intended that the very class of vessels specially mentioned by the Senator from Georgia [Mr. Clay] as the most useful to this country should receive the first and the highest consideration at the hands of the committee. It is to the low-power ship, the economic ship, the ship that can bring to us the lowest prices of transportation, that the fullest consideration is given, and when it is said that all of the benefits of this provision will be given to lines already in operation, to the men already controlling certain lines and certain business facilities engaged in foreign trade, I say that it is not true.

Yet as you go to put into successful operation the provisions of the proposed law, where will you look for the accomplishment of its purposes, which is so earnestly desired, but to the men who have given their lifetime to the study and operation of each business which is peculiar unto itself? If we have a few ships engaged in foreign trade to-day, all the better. If we can induce the men who are conducting that business to build more ships, all the better; it accomplishes the result for which we are striving. If the upbuilding of the merchant marine of the United States depends upon the successful issue of the

measure, it must be through the hands and under the administra-
of the men who know and thoroughly understand the business.

The question of the admission of foreign tonnage to American registry is troubling many, and it troubled me. I have
always been opposed, as a matter of principle, to giving advantage to ships constructed abroad. I was inclined to take
a narrow view of that proposition when I was first called into
the councils of this committee, but there are none of us who
know so much upon any subject that we can not learn something, and I learned from those discussions that it was necessary to protect the property and the capital of American
citizens who had invested their money in foreign-built ships,
who in the conduct of their business found it absolutely necessary that they should have ships, and finding it impossible
because of the higher cost to build those ships in the United
States, in order to further their business interests, were obliged
to invest their capital in foreign-built ships and operate them
under a foreign flag.

In that way, owing to the rapid and continuous development of our export trade, in the growth of their business
in connection with our affairs at home, and through energy
and effort on their part, several important lines have been
established and maintained fairly well against all competition.
I speak now of foreign ships owned by American citizens and
operated under a foreign flag. When it came to the consideration of this question in perfecting the measure which was to
come before Congress and the people of the United States, it
was very important that consideration should be given to everybody alike, and there was no attempt to do otherwise and
no thought or desire to do otherwise.

We felt that it was our duty as much to those who had
acquired interests in ships under a foreign flag, without any
prospect of anything better, and in the protection and development of their own business interests had invested their capital
in that direction, that the only men who are experienced and
able to put into effective operation the provisions of this law
must receive just as much consideration as those representing
any other interest, and they did, but under different conditions. That was a concession made, and entirely made, to that
spirit which dominates the American people, that we shall first
take care of ourselves when considering the question of competition.

The condition was made that for every ship owned by
American capital and operated under a foreign flag, when

their owners availed themselves of the provisions of this bill, the contract would not be complete until they had constructed in the shipyards of the United States a tonnage equal to that coming under American registry. In that connection came the interest of the American shipbuilder.

Mr. President, one of the first objections that I met in the informal discussion of this bill among business men of my acquaintance in the East was that the measure was framed purely upon the plan of building our own tonnage, even although Congress might decide to give it exclusively to that class of vessels, owing to the fact that under the conditions which had existed in this country ever since the civil war the shipbuilding industry of this country had been confined entirely to the construction of coastwise and naval vessels. The shipbuilding industry of the United States has not been profitable since then, and capital has not sought that industry for investment.

What they wanted was immediate relief, the opportunity at this time, now, to take advantage of the conditions which seemed so favorable to make one more effort in this direction, and therefore the claim was that if you depend upon the limited capacity of the shipyards of the United States, already almost filled to overflowing in the construction of our magnificent navy, of which we are all so proud, before a merchant marine can be built which will be of any service or relief to the business of the country, our competitors, with the full knowledge of our purpose and intent, will, as they have always done, be ready to meet us and circumvent us if possible.

I said a moment ago that every time the question of subsidizing American ships was even mentioned in the newspapers of the United States there came a renewed effort and a continuing effort for the upbuilding of English and German ships, even to the extent that a credit almost unheard of was offered by the shipbuilders in Europe, saying: "We will build your ships; we will let you pay for them when you can; we will extend to you a rate of interest one-half what you would be obliged to pay in your own country; we will do anything; we will do everything, rather than have you invest your capital in ships built in the United States."

I say that the necessity for immediate relief in the direction which I have indicated was the one overpowering argument, because it appealed to my business sense as right, that if the Government of the United States was willing to take the responsibility of expending the money of the people in this direction, every man who is called upon to cast his vote upon this legislation would want to feel that the result would justify that vote.

No one can be blamed for considering that feature of this case. Therefore I say it was an argument that appealed to the business sense of that committee, and I believe to a large proportion of the committee of the Senate, that, having by our action adopted that policy, we felt it was necessary that the results should justify the act, and that those results should come quickly. In other words, the benefit to those who would avail themselves of the privileges in their export trade—I mean the shippers—if they found that as a result of this measure they would soon have the opportunity to ship their export goods in American bottoms and under the American flag, they would know further, and they would know it surely, too, that that would mean a competition which would result in lowering freights across the Atlantic and the Pacific.

There is one feature of this question which I desire briefly to touch upon, and that is from the standpoint of the ship-builder. The upbuilding of the merchant marine of this country means more than many can appreciate without a careful study of the situation. The privilege which we give to those American citizens who bring under our registry a foreign-built vessel, requiring that they must build a compensating tonnage in this country, will make a demand, without any doubt, in the next five years, for more capacity than we have shipyards in this country to supply.

By this bill 600,000 tons—300,000 tons in existence and 300,-000 more to be built—would be added to our merchant marine, because under the provisions of this bill it is intended—and rightly so—that the benefits shall not be confined to those who first avail themselves of this $9,000,000. Anybody and every-body can go on and build ships and then go to the Secretary of the Treasury and ask a contract under the same provisions, and, when he has complied with the features of the law, given bond, and signed the contract, his ship can be registered for the foreign trade and begin earning the same proportionate amount of subsidy as that given to the ships which were built and in operation before the $9,000,000 was absorbed.

It was intended and it is expected that that provision of the bill, as we grow in experience and ability, as we enlarge this sphere of industry, if it is found profitable, will attract idle capital not otherwise invested, and if it pays more than the normal rate of 2 or 3 per cent. interest—which has come to be the rate on the best securities in which money can be invested—then it will have served the purpose that is intended, to not confine the size of this merchant marine in tonnage or number within the limit of the $9,000,000—not that the $9,000,000 is to be increased, but that any man who builds a vessel after that amount has been absorbed can come under the provisions of the bill, and that the necessary percentage shall be taken from the others and given to him.

One word about our shipbuilding industry. I say, should this bill become a law, it will immediately affect that industry very perceptibly and very beneficially. What does that mean? Every ship that is built in a yard of the United States will be built wholly from materials furnished in the United States, beginning with the iron ore in the ground. Every additional ton that is demanded for this new industry will be an addition to the demand for labor in this country.

It will take that many more men to mine that ore—and I speak now more particularly of ores from Lake Superior, which is the source of our main supply—to handle it on the railroads to the lake shipping points and then on vessels to the distributing points on the lower lake, then to furnish additional ships needed upon the lakes, additional men to man them, additional men to handle that ore upon the docks in its reshipment, additional men to aid the transportation to the point of manufacture, then through all the ramifications of that manufacture to bring that iron ore into a condition to go into the ship and during the construction of that ship until she is slipped upon the waters and is a part of the merchant marine of the United States, thousands of men will find employment in an industry heretofore comparatively unknown to this country.

Our productive capacity is one-third greater than our consumption. So, either one of two things must happen: we must either find a foreign market for that surplus or we must curtail the production one-third. What does that mean? In the conditions existing to-day it would mean to throw out of employment thousands and thousands of our workingmen. Why, then, is it not better sense and better policy to study all the conditions from the American standpoint of bettering them for ourselves and bettering the conditions of the people who look to us?

It is just as much the duty of Congress to consider a question of that kind as it is for the manufacturer. When he finds his market will not consume his product he must consider what he had best do to first protect his own interest, which he does, and that of those who are dependent upon him, or, if he be public-spirited and enough of the philanthropist, he would consider those interests mutually, and would study the subject in order to avail himself of every opportunity to discover some method, even at less profit to himself, to find a market for that surplus product.   ·

There is no country on the face of this earth that is so richly endowed with mineral wealth as ours. There is no section of this country that has more undeveloped mineral wealth than the border States of the South.

The chairman of the Senate Committee on Commerce in his remarks the other day made a statement which has impressed me more than ever before, because I know it is true. He said we are on the eve of a war, not of arms, but on the eve of a contest for commercial supremacy in the markets of the world; the result of recent changing conditions, which have opened the door, and will keep open the door of those great markets of the Orient, where every nation that has any industries to protect, that has any industries to develop, is availing itself of the fullest opportunity at its command.

This country is endowed with the greatest natural mineral resources of any in the world. Already the markets are opening to her coal product. The Senator from Georgia stated—and truthfully so—that the development of the manufacture of pig iron has grown enormously. That is true of those infant industries in the South, where thousands of spindles are singing, where thousands and hundreds of thousands of tons of coal are being taken from beneath the soil, where the materials for the manufacture of pig iron lie within the circumference of a few miles. The industry in northern Alabama and Tennessee has grown so rapidly that almost 50 per cent. of its product is being exported to Europe.

Mr. President, the limit of that export to-day is reached by the inability to secure transportation upon the high seas. In order successfully to operate and carry out great industries of that kind, looking to a foreign market, it is not only important, but absolutely necessary that the manufacturer shall know what it will cost to deliver the goods. He must know what it will cost every month of the twelve months of the year if he attempts to predicate his operations upon the demand and the business that he can build up in the foreign trade.

Mr. President, the United States has changed its condition from a debtor to a creditor nation. We are not only loaning money to foreign countries, purchasing their bonds, but we are loaning to them millions of dollars which come to us as the balance of trade and which are left in their hands because there is greater remuneration abroad than at home. Is it not better for the American people that they shall invest that capital here in any of the variety of industries which will not only call capital into activity, but will furnish bread for thousands and thousands of men, women, and children, who are a part of us, depending upon us, and who in all conditions must be considered?

This question is broader than the lines of the bill can write it. It will be widespread in its benefits. It is not aimed at any class or any particular industry. It is one of those measures the influence of which will permeate every industry and every class in the length and breadth of the United States. When I am told that the people of the interior of this country are not interested in the shipping question—that the farmers take no interest in it—I say it is not true in fact. I know that every man, no matter what his vocation in life, is interested and will be benefited, directly or indirectly, because you can not create an industry like this, bringing about, as it must naturally, first the development of our raw materials and then a condition which ends with the construction of the ships, opening up the markets of the world, giving greater opportunities to our merchants and manufacturers, without benefiting every industry and every line of business.

There is a strange contradiction of interests that has crept into this matter since I have paid attention to it recently. I find that people in Boston and people in New York, engaged in the same business—what I would call a commission business—exporting, and otherwise, and who have built up a great business at each of those points, at this late day are bringing to our attention, in the way of an argument against this measure, the fact that it is detrimental to those interests.

It is claimed that if a regular line is formed between New York and Brazil or the Argentine, which would supply the needs of that trade regularly, in a short time it would become a monopoly, controlling the trade, and would put freight at an abnormally high price. It is claimed that that would be the result of admitting foreign ships. There is no objection on the part of those people to a subsidy being paid to American vessels. On the other hand, the Boston party contends that unless the door is opened wide enough in this measure to give him or anybody else the privilege at any time in the near future of bringing in as many foreign ships as he can or wants to bring in, after he has made a careful calculation as to the profits of the investment, it will injure his business. Thus it is claimed that in the same line and kind of business you do one thing and it will ruin one party, and you do the other thing and it will ruin the other party. I can not understand it. But I do say that the bill as framed is approved, so far as I know, by all the interests that have been consulted and advised with during the three years we have been considering the subject. If it fails to meet every demand and every condition which may arise, it is because we have not had an opportunity to see everybody and to consult everybody. I believe that it fully and completely answers the demand, and therefore I am in favor of its passage.

Mr. President, in making my appeal to the American people for this great industry, I want to put it upon higher grounds than that of dollars and cents. I want to put it upon the broad ground of a connecting link between the producer and the consumer, as an adjunct to our further growth and prosperity, which it is written must continue in the nature of things because of the conditions which control us and our future—conditions which rise above the speculative question whether one man will get a little more benefit than another man, conditions which appeal even to our benevolence in the responsibilities which we owe to the working people of this country.

I claim for every line in the bill that it is in the interest of the whole people of the United States, and particularly of those who must look to higher and more experienced authority to conduct the public affairs of our Government in their interest. Upon that basis I make my appeal, and I leave it in your hands. [Applause in the galleries.]

On January 23 George G. Vest [Mo.] opposed the bill.

Mr. President—and I do not want to assume the rôle of Cassandra and be taunted as a pessimist—I am warranted in the statement that the immense corporations, which are the principal beneficiaries, with unlimited capital and unparalleled business enterprise, will almost immediately constitute themselves into a syndicate or trust, as it is generally termed, and put enough of their own vessels under the flag of the United States to avail themselves of the provisions of this law and shut out all competitors.

The Senator from Ohio [Mr. Hanna] drew an eloquent picture of the vast increase of shipping upon the Great Lakes, and he ascribed it to the navigation laws and to the improvement of rivers and harbors. I saw the other day a statement in a Chicago newspaper, and it was repeated in a New York newspaper, that a syndicate has just been perfected under the laws of New Jersey which made a gigantic trust of every shipyard on the lakes, shutting out all competitors. Within three days afterwards a New York newspaper published the announcement that another trust or syndicate was being formed to embrace all the shipyards upon the Atlantic and the Pacific seaboards.

Everything in the country, from the cradle to the grave, is under a trust. The brood of trusts hovers over the land like birds of prey, and there seems to be no hope, no redress, from their inevitable grasp.

The House of Representatives during the last session passed a bill making more drastic the provisions of the trust law, known as the Sherman anti-trust law. That bill passed the House with one dissenting vote. It came to the Senate, our Republican friends by a party vote referred it to the Committee on the Judiciary, and they then assured us positively and emphatically that the first business at this session would be the passage of that bill. But it sleeps the sleep of death in the pigeonhole of the room of the Judiciary Committee, and never will be heard of again. This Congress will end and another season of riotous plunder will be given to these syndicates. The Republican party could not afford to attack them on the eve of the last canvass, for they wanted funds for campaign purposes and they dared not put up the black flag in the face of their pecuniary auxiliaries. Now, out of gratitude, I suppose, they will pretermit any legislation against them hereafter. So we are warranted in saying, without being charged with being critical or unjust, that the money of the capitalists engaged in railroad and steamship lines, dominating the business of the country on land and sea, will be applied for the purpose of securing the subsidies granted by this proposed legislation.

Mr. President, we have lost our merchant marine because we would not allow our people to buy ships where they could buy them cheapest. If the ships had been ours, the trade would have been ours and the sailors would have been ours.

But I do not care to pursue this discussion further. This bill will pass the Senate. It is a part of the great protective system which is sacred to the Republican party. Drunk with victory and under the belief, as they seem to be, that conditions will remain as they are, the Republican party seems determined to stop at nothing. The glamour of foreign conquest and the abundance of money produced by the recent enormous discoveries of gold have rendered them reckless as to consequences.

On January 25 Chauncey M. Depew [N. Y.] supported the bill. He closed as follows:

Those of us who have passed middle life remember as boys the pride with which we used to recite upon the school platform the great speech of Daniel Webster about the American flag seen in every port and the American ship upon every ocean. That inspiring effort of our greatest of congressional orators no longer appears in the American school book. The American schoolboy knows, if he finds it in an old volume in the library, that it relates to a glorious period of his country's history. He does not understand why he should be deprived of the privilege, in which his father took such patriotic interest, of exulting in the proud preëminence of the American ship and the Stars and Stripes upon all the waters of the earth. To-day the American makes the circuit of the globe. He sails into the harbors of Europe, of Asia, of Africa, and of South America, amidst the abundant shipping which fills those ports. He passes upon the different seas the argosies of commerce, carrying the products of his own and other countries. The flags of all nations fly from the mastheads of these steamers, except one. He sees nowhere the Stars and Stripes. He finds the merchants and the people of foreign lands familiar with every emblem but our own. If he wishes to address a letter home it goes from South America through Liverpool, from China through London, from the East through the mails and under the flag of every country but his own.

Under this bill, as new lines are established between our ports and lands across the Atlantic or the Pacific they must carry free American mail. With the enactment of this measure five years will witness a wonderful change in the relations of the United States to ocean transportation. Long before the limited period of the subsidy has passed we shall have returned again to the jubilant and patriotic feeling of Daniel Webster. We can again proudly boast that our ships are upon every sea, our flag in every port, and the name and fame of our country respected by all nations, and that the products and the goods of the United States are in successful competition in every market of the world with our rivals in production, trade, and manufactures. [Applause in the Senate and galleries.]

No action was taken upon the bill during the session.

XI—14

CHAPTER V

CHINESE EXCLUSION

Reports on the Committee to Investigate Chinese Immigration: Majority
Report; Minority Report, by Edwin L. Meade [N. Y.]; Thomas Wren
[Nev.] Introduces in the House Bill to Restrict Chinese Immigration;
It Is Reported from Committee by Albert S. Willis [Ky.]—Debate: In
Favor, Mr. Willis; Opposed, Martin I. Townsend [N. Y.]; Bill Is
Passed—Debate in the Senate: In Favor, Aaron A. Sargent [Cal.],
James G. Blaine [Me.]; Opposed, Stanley Matthews [O.], Hannibal
Hamlin [Me.]; Bill Is Passed; Vetoed, with Reasons, by President
Hayes—John F. Miller [Cal.] Introduces in the Senate a Chinese Ex-
clusion Bill; Bill Passed by Congress and Vetoed by President Arthur;
Amended, and Approved by the President May 6, 1882—Barclay Henley
[Cal.], in 1884, Introduces in House Bill to Amend This Act; William
W. Rice [Mass.] Presents Minority Report; Bill Is Passed by Congress
and Approved by President Arthur—Joseph N. Dolph [Ore.] Introduces
in the Senate a Bill to Exclude Chinese Laborers; It Is Passed—Debate
in the House on the Record of ex-Sen. Benjamin Harrison on the Chinese Question: William D. Bynum [Ind.], Joseph McKenna [Cal.],
Nelson Dingley [Me.], Benton McMillin [Tenn.], Joseph G. Cannon
[Ill.]; Bill Is Enacted.

WHILE the subject of restriction of immigration,
from a constitutional point of view, belongs to
the general topic of Civil Rights, nevertheless,
as the chief aim of its advocates has been to limit competition in the labor market, it is generally looked upon
as an industrial question, and therefore is treated in this
volume.

As we have noticed in various debates on Civil Rights,
particularly those relating to the Fourteenth and Fif-
teenth Amendments to the Constitution, during the decade following the Civil War great opposition to the further admission of Chinese developed in the Pacific States,
whither they had been brought in great numbers under
the provisions of the Burlingame treaty with China, in

order to work upon the railroads, etc., the price of white labor being very high owing to the opportunities afforded American citizens to take up homesteads, mining claims, etc., and so dig out of the land rich wages for themselves as well as be independent of employers. But when the more productive mining claims and homesteads were taken up, and the amount of these was further limited by Government grants to railroads, the product of land at the margin of cultivation, which, according to the law of David Ricardo, establishes the rate of wages, decreased more and more, until the hitherto independent American citizen was forced into the labor market. Here he met with the competition of the Chinese coolie, who, with a far lower standard of living, and with virtually the same ability as an unskilled laborer, underbid him as an employee. Obviously, thought he, the coolie is the cause of the low wages I am forced to take or starve, and therefore he began to demand, through his Congressman, the exclusion of his competitor from this country. The coolie, having no vote, had few political friends, and these were idealists who lived far to the east and, even there, commanded little influence in matters where their views ran counter to the interests of their constituents.

Upon the insistence of Representatives from the Pacific States, Congress, in July, 1876, appointed a joint committee to visit these States and investigate "the character, extent, and effect of Chinese immigration."

The committee made its report (a majority one) on February 28, 1877. This was as follows:

Report on Chinese Immigration

Joint Congressional Committee

The resources of the Pacific coast have been and are being more rapidly developed with the cheap and docile labor of the Chinese than they would have been without it. Profit is found by certain American citizens in their transportation to this country. Religious teachers opposed restriction of Chinese immigration, saying that the presence of these people among us imposes a duty and gives an opportunity for Christianizing them.

On the other hand, the committee found that laboring men and artisans, perhaps without exception, were opposed to the influx of Chinese, on the ground that hard experience had shown that they are thereby thrown out of employment and the means of decent livelihood are more difficult of acquisition. But the opposition to Chinese immigration was not confined to laboring men and mechanics. Lawyers, doctors, merchants, divines, judges, and others, in large numbers, say that the apparent prosperity derived from the presence of Chinese is deceptive and unwholesome, ruinous to our laboring classes, promotive of caste, and dangerous to free institutions.

There are 35,000 Chinese in San Francisco.

They live in filthy dwellings, upon poor food, crowded together in narrow quarters, disregarding health and fire ordinances, and their vices are corrupting to the morals of the city, especially of the young.

The testimony taken by the committee includes that of twenty operatives in as many trades.

It shows that the Chinese have reduced wages to what would be starvation prices for white men and women, and engrossed so much of the labor in the various callings that there is a lack of employment for whites; and young men are growing up in idleness, while young women, willing to work, are compelled to resort to doubtful means of support. The hardships resulting from these causes bear with especial weight upon women.

As a result of this competition there has sprung up among the white workingmen a bitterly hostile feeling to the Chinese, which has exhibited itself in abuse of individual Chinamen and sporadic cases of mob violence.

The better class of society holds the unlawful results of this feeling in check, but are only able to do so because of the general expectation that Congress will remedy the situation.

As the safety of republican institutions requires that the exercise of the franchise shall be only by those who have a love and appreciation for our institutions, and this rule excludes the great mass of the Chinese from the ballot as a necessary means to public safety, yet the application of the rule deprives them of the only adequate protection which can exist in a re-

THE YELLOW PERIL

From "The History of the Nineteenth Century in Caricature"

public for the security of any distinctive large class of persons. An indigestible mass in the community, distinct in language, pagan in religion, inferior in mental and moral qualities, and all peculiarities, is an undesirable element in a republic, but becomes especially so if political power is placed in its hands. There are, therefore, springing from this subject antagonistic considerations, the only way to reconcile which would seem to be that the laws should discourage the large influx of any class of population to whom the ballot cannot be safely confided.

The Pacific coast must become either American or Mongolian. The two races are already in active opposition. They can never amalgamate.

The American race is progressive and in favor of a responsible representative government. The Mongolian race seems to have no desire for progress and to have no conception of representative and free institutions. While conditions should be

favorable to the growth and occupancy of our Pacific possessions by our own people, the Chinese have advantages which
will put them far in advance in this race for possession. They
can subsist where the American would starve. They can work
for wages which will not furnish the barest necessities of life
to an American. They make their way in California as they
have in the islands of the sea, not by superior force or virtue,
or even industry, although they are, as a rule, industrious, but
by revolting characteristics and by dispensing with what have
become necessities in modern civilization. To compete with
them and expel them the American must come down to their
level or below them; must work so cheaply that the Chinese
cannot compete with him, for in the contest for subsistence he
that can subsist upon the least will last the longest.

Accordingly immigration is checked from the Eastern
States. The welfare of the whole country demands that
the Pacific States should be peopled by Americans, like
those of Iowa or Illinois, rather than Asiatics like those
of Pekin and Canton.

The Chinese have little regard for an oath, and hence
convictions of them for offences committed against themselves or the public are difficult.

They are unassimilative with Americans.

After a quarter of a century they still retain their peculiar
costume and follow their original national habits in food and
mode of life; they have no social intercourse with the white population; they work for wages which will not support white men,
and especially white families; and by the small amount and
poor quality of food which they consume, and their crowding
together in close quarters, reducing individual expenses of rent,
their having no families to support or educate, they are able to
compete with white labor in all departments and exclude it
from employment.

Ethnologists testified before the committee that the
Chinese have too little brain capacity to furnish motive
power for self-government. As a class they are inferior
morally to the Aryan race. Yet the committee found that
the Chinese merchants are honorable in their dealings
with other merchants. However, they evade to a considerable extent the revenue laws.

The Chinese are rapidly increasing in number, not by births, of which there are few, but by importations. These are of the same low coolie class. Their increase is greater than that of the American adult population.

The Chinese do not come to make their home in this country; their only purpose is to acquire what would be a competence in China and return there to enjoy it. While there is a constant and increasing incoming tide there is a constant outflow also, less in volume, of persons who have worked out specified years of servitude and made money enough to live upon in China, and who sever their connection with this country.

The Chinese do not desire to become citizens of this country, and have no knowledge of or appreciation for our institutions. Very few of them learn to speak our language. They do not desire the ballot, and there is danger that if they had it their "head men" would control the sale of it in quantities large enough to determine any election.

To admit these vast numbers of aliens to citizenship and the ballot would practically destroy republican institutions upon the Pacific coast, for the Chinese have no comprehension of any form of government but despotism, and have not the words in their own language to describe intelligibly the principles of our representative system.

Chinese women in California are bought and sold for prostitution, and are treated worse than dogs; they are held in a most revolting condition of slavery.

The Chinese have a quasi-government among themselves, independent of our laws, authorizing the punishment of offenders against Chinese customs, even to the taking of life. Violent hostilities exist between Chinamen from different parts of China, to the disturbance of the public peace. Large numbers of them, notwithstanding the difficulty of conviction, owing to the looseness of the Chinese oath, occupy the State's prison and jails.

They are cruel and indifferent to their sick, sometimes turning them out to die, and the corpses of dead Chinamen and women are sometimes found in the streets by the policemen, where they have been left by their associates at night. The climatic conditions of San Francisco are unfavorable to the prevalence of pestilence, but it was in testimony that the conditions existing in the Chinese quarter of this city, transferred to New York, St. Louis, Cincinnati, New Orleans, or other large cities east of the Rocky Mountains, would make those cities uninhabitable. The Chinese quarter already extends over a considerable area in the heart of San Francisco, and is growing year by year. The progress is steady and constant, and the business portion of the city is already cut off by the Chinese quarter from a portion where are many of the most elegant residences.

Such Chinese quarters exist in all the cities and towns of the Pacific coast. The tide of Chinese immigration is gradually tending eastward, and before a quarter of a century the difficult question that now arises upon the Pacific coast will probably have to be met upon the banks of the Mississippi, and perhaps on the Ohio and Hudson.

The committee believe that free institutions founded upon free schools and intelligence can be maintained only where based on intelligent and adequately paid labor. Adequate wages are needed to give self-respect to the laborer and the means of education to his children. Family life is a great safeguard to our political institutions.

This problem is too important to be treated with indifference. Congress should solve it, having due regard to any rights already accrued under existing treaties and to humanity. But it must be solved, in the judgment of the committee, unless our Pacific possessions are to be ultimately given over to a race alien in all its tendencies, which will make of it practically provinces of China rather than States of the Union.

The committee recommend that measures be taken by the Executive looking toward a modification of the existing treaty with China, confining it to strictly commercial purposes; and that Congress legislate to restrain the great influx of Asiatics to this country. It is not believed that either of these measures would be looked upon with disfavor by the Chinese Government. Whether this is so or not, a duty is owing to the Pacific States and Territories which are suffering under a terrible scourge, but are patiently waiting for relief from Congress.

Edwin R. Meade [N. Y.], of the committee, spoke upon the question. In his recommendations as to the proper action to be taken by this Government in the matter he referred particularly to our treaty obligations toward China.

While it is obvious that measures should be adopted restricting this growing coolie immigration a wise policy suggests due consideration and regard for existing treaty obligations with China. Location of the two countries favors the energy and enterprise of our citizens to monopolize the large and growing commerce with China. England has hitherto been the great power with that nation, but it is well understood that we are fast gaining the ascendency, and that the Chinese Government feels a keener sympathy and higher consideration for this nation.

The appointment of Anson Burlingame to distinguished honors was a signal indication of the kindly feeling which the Chinese entertain for us, as well as of the termination of the Chinese exclusive policy, which, for hundreds of years, has proved an insuperable barrier to western nations in establishing satisfactory relations with that empire.

The Burlingame treaty of June 18, 1858, contains the following provisions which at the date of their adoption received general approval:

ARTICLE V

The United States of America and the Emperor of China cordially recognize the inherent and inalienable right of man to change his home and allegiance, and also the mutual advantage of the free migration and emigration of their citizens and subjects, respectively, from the one country to the other, for purposes of curiosity, of trade, or as permanent residents. The high contracting parties therefore join in reprobating any other than an entirely voluntary emigration for these purposes. They consequently agree to pass laws making it a penal offence for a citizen of the United States or Chinese subjects to take Chinese subjects either to the United States or to any other foreign country, or for a Chinese subject or citizen of the United States to take citizens of the United States to China or to any other foreign country, without their free and voluntary consent respectively.

ARTICLE VI

Citizens of the United States visiting or residing in China shall enjoy the same privileges, immunities, or exemptions in respect to travel or residence as may there be enjoyed by the citizens or subjects of the most favored nation. And, reciprocally, Chinese subjects visiting or residing in the United States shall enjoy the same privileges, immunities, and exemptions in respect to travel or residence as may there be enjoyd by the citizens or subjects of the most favored nation. But nothing herein contained shall be held to confer naturalization upon citizens of the United States in China nor upon the subjects of China in the United States.

These provisions are the solemnly pledged faith of this nation and preclude us from entertaining the suggestion of the majority of the committee, that this Congress may pass laws prohibiting or restricting Chinese immigration or in other mode discriminating against its people without first obtaining the concurrence of the Chinese Government itself; for, while I believe that the government at Pekin would prefer that its population should not emigrate, yet in the face of these treaties any unfriendly legislation on our part would be justly regarded as their infraction and as a breach of good faith, implying a disrespect for the Pekin government; which would naturally seek reprisals, to the interruption of commercial relations, and the material injury of the several thousands of our citizens whose residence and business interests are within the Chinese Empire. That the Chinese ministry is not unmindful of the importance of treaty obligations is shown in the correspondence transmitted by Minister George F. Seward to Congress on the 4th of December last.

A judicious policy admonishes this Government to avoid the appearance of error in our present relations with China when it is apparent that the British Government seeks by every device known to its subtle policy and diplomacy to extend and perpetuate its power in that empire.

As at present situated, the main checks to English aggression in China are this country and Russia, and for the welfare of both these nations, as well as China, it is desirable that the counterbalance against England shall be maintained by frank, cordial, and intimate relationship with China, which no misunderstanding shall be allowed to impair. It may be said that I exaggerate the importance which would attach to the passage of a law by this Congress, prohibiting or restricting Chinese immigration; but we must bear in mind that our intercourse with China has scarcely assumed form, and that the Chinese Government yet views its relations with the western powers with much doubt and hesitation, while its national pride and self-respect are fostered by a history of more than four thousand years, distinguished by a literature and discoveries in arts and sciences before present empires and republics had a place in the world's geography.

In closing what in these limits must be an imperfect review of the subject, the following suggestions are prominent:

The immigration of merchants, men of education, students, and capitalists should be encouraged, and every unfriendly obstacle in the way of their residence here removed. The French Government has established a professorship of the Chinese language. We need to understand that people more thoroughly, and a liberal endowment for a similar purpose in this country would be of great benefit in developing our business and political relations with them. Entire justice is due the Chinese already on the Pacific coast according as guaranteed to them by existing treaties. A new convention should be held having for its object the strict regulation of coolie labor. The establishment by Congress of a bureau or department of immigration is requisite not only to a proper understanding and regulation of the subject with China, but also with European nations, and the proper reception and treatment of immigrants on their arrival in this country. With such a bureau properly organized, in accord with the State Department and its body of foreign officials, treaty stipulations respecting immigration may be made sufficiently flexible to admit of congressional and executive control, and thus to subserve at all times the interests of our people, eliminate objectionable features, and remove the difficulties which now exist respecting the subject generally.

In the improbable contingency that the Chinese Government will refuse to coöperate with us in proper limitations respecting immigration, then will be the proper time to consider what independent action for ourselves is necessary. For the present, the entire business should remain with the treaty-making branch of this Government. A permanent Chinese embassy soon to be established here, and a Chinese consulship in San Francisco, will be timely, and greatly facilitate in arriving at an intelligent disposition of questions under consideration.

A just and equable national policy respecting immigration is a present need, and great wisdom and prudence should characterize it, especially in the infancy of relations which are to create so many bonds of common interest between the oldest and the newest nations of the globe.

In the next session (1877-78) Thomas Wren [Neb.] introduced in the House a bill to restrict Chinese immigration. It was referred to the Committee on Education and Labor. During the following session (on January 28, 1879) it was reported from the committee by Albert S. Willis [Ky.].

RESTRICTION OF CHINESE IMMIGRATION

HOUSE OF REPRESENTATIVES, JANUARY 28, 1879

Mr. Willis read the report of the committee:

Briefly stated, this bill provides that no master of a vessel shall take on board at any port in China, or elsewhere, more than fifteen Chinese passengers with intent to bring them, or shall bring them, within the United States. The violation of this provision is made a misdemeanor, punishable by a fine of $100 for each passenger and imprisonment for six months. The master is required, under like penalty, to report on his arrival a sworn list of all Chinese passengers. The penalty is made a lien upon the vessel. The bill becomes operative on the 1st day of July, 1879.

Waiving for the present any consideration of the merits of the bill, the first question is whether such legislation is within the power of Congress.

The existing treaty with China gives its subjects an unlimited right of immigration to the United States. The second clause of article 6 of the Constitution provides that "this Constitution, and the laws of the United States which shall be made in pursuance thereof, and all treaties made under the authority of the United States, shall be the supreme law of the land."

It is contended that any law restricting Chinese immigration would contravene this provision of the Constitution, and would therefore be null and void.

Such a construction cannot be sustained either upon principle or authority. The objects for which the Constitution was formed are higher than any power granted under it. The general welfare, justice, domestic tranquillity, and the blessings of liberty are of supreme importance, and cannot be taken from the people by any treaty however solemnly ratified. The treaty-making power is limited by these objects. Moreover, both in nature and by international law, the first duty is self-preservation. If, therefore, it be true that the presence of the Chinese endangers the peace and prosperity of our people, no mere technical considerations should intervene to prevent an increase of the evil.

The clause of the Constitution above quoted does not, however, admit of the construction contended for. It elevates treaties from the status of mere compacts to the dignity of laws, but does not clothe them with any additional superiority.

Laws made in pursuance of the Constitution are equally as binding and authoritative as treaties, and, if last enacted, control any contravening treaty. This conclusion is enforced by numerous decisions both of the exclusive and judicial departments of the Government. In 1851, in the case of the Florida claims, an apparent conflict between a treaty and a subsequent act of Congress was decided by Attorney-General John J. Crittenden in these words: "An act of Congress is as much a supreme law of the land as a treaty. They are placed on the same footing, and no preference or superiority is given to the one or the other. The last expression of the law-giving power must prevail, and just for the same reason and on the same principle that a subsequent act must prevail and have effect, though inconsistent with a prior act; so must an act of Congress have effect, though inconsistent with a prior treaty."

These decisions of the Executive Department have been followed by the judiciary. In the case of Taylor *vs.* Martin, 2 Curtis, C. C. Rep., 454, the court says: "It is impossible to maintain that under our Constitution the President and Senate exclusively possess the power to modify or repeal a law found in a treaty. If this were true, no change in a treaty could be made without the consent of some foreign government. That the Constitution was designed to place our country in this helpless condition is a supposition wholly inadmissible. It is not only inconsistent with the necessities of a nation, but negatived by the express words of the Constitution. That gives to Congress, in so many words, power to declare war, an act which, *ipso facto*, repeals all treaties inconsistent with a state of war. It cannot, therefore, be admitted that the only method of escape from a treaty is by the consent of the other party to it or a declaration of war. To refuse to execute a treaty for reasons which approve themselves to the conscientious judgment of a nation is a matter of the utmost gravity; but the power to do so is a prerogative of which no nation can be deprived without deeply affecting its independence. That the people of the United States have deprived their Government of this power I do not believe. That it must reside somewhere, and be applicable to all cases, I am convinced, and I feel no doubt that it belongs to Congress."

Upon principle, therefore, as well as upon the authority of precedents, judicial and administrative, it would seem clear that Congress has the right, by appropriate legislation, to change or to abrogate any existing treaty. Indeed, Congress has in one instance expressly exercised this power. The act of July 7, 1798, declares that the existing treaties with France are no longer obligatory upon the United States.

The evils of Chinese immigration have been fully recognized upon the Pacific slope for many years. Welcomed at first as a unique addition to the society and a valuable ally in the development of the material resources of their new home, the Chinese, by their sordid, selfish, immoral, and non-amalgamating habits, within a very short time reversed the judgment in their favor and came to be regarded as a standing menace to the social and political institutions of the country.

The State laws which had been enacted having been declared unconstitutional by the Supreme Court, and every other means of relief proving ineffectual, it was finally determined to appeal to Congress. Accordingly, as early as the 22d of December, 1869, an effort was made, but without success, to secure restrictive legislation. In the Forty-second Congress, and also in the Forty-third Congress, numerous memorials, resolutions of public meetings, and petitions were presented to the same effect and with the same result. At the first session of the Forty-fourth Congress these renewed appeals for relief met for the first time with a favorable response. A joint resolution was introduced and passed calling upon the President of the United States to "open negotiations with the Chinese Government for the purpose of modifying the provisions of the treaty between the two countries and restricting the same to commercial purposes."

Subsequently, at the same session, another joint resolution was passed, requesting the President to present to the Chinese Government an additional article to the treaty of July 28, 1868, reserving mutually to the two governments the right to regulate, restrict, or prevent immigration to their respective countries. These authoritative requests on the part of Congress failed to secure the desired relief. In the meanwhile the question had assumed dangerous proportions. The conviction that Chinese immigration was a great evil was so deep-seated and unanimous that mob violence was openly threatened, and in many instances the arm of the law seemed powerless to protect. Recognizing the exigency, the legislature of California appointed a special committee, whose report, based upon the testimony of witnesses familiar with the subject, ably and graphically sets forth the objections to the Chinese. Subsequently to this a joint committee appointed by the Forty-fourth Congress collected voluminous testimony upon the same subject, and by a majority report urged upon the Executive Department the necessity for an immediate change of the Burlingame treaty, to the end that such immigration might be restricted or prevented. These reports, together with other official documents upon the subject, were laid before the present Congress.

Your committee consider that further delay would work great injustice to a large portion of our country, provided the evils whereof they complain are well founded.

This whole question is not one of right, but of policy. There is no principle upon which we are compelled to receive into our midst the natives of Asia, Africa, or any other part of the world. The character, source, and extent of immigration should be regulated and controlled with reference to our own wants and welfare. The difficult problems, economic and political, resulting from the presence of the red and black races would be renewed in a more aggravated and dangerous form by the yellow race. The Mongolian, unlike the Indian, is brought in daily contact with our social and political life; and, unlike the African, does not surrender any of his marked peculiarities by reason of that contact. It is neither possible nor desirable for two races as distinct as the Caucasian and Mongolian to live under the same government without assimilation. The degradation or slavery of one or the other would be the inevitable result. Homogeneity of ideas and of physical and social habits is essential to national harmony and progress. Equally grave objections may be urged against the Chinese from an industrial standpoint. Our laboring people cannot and ought not to be subjected to a competition which involves the surrender of the sacred and elevating influences of home and the sacrifice of the ordinary appliances of personal civilization. The question, therefore, is not one of competition, but of a substitution of one kind of labor for another.

No self-governing country can afford to diminish or destroy the dignity, the welfare, and independence of its citizens. Justice to the people of the Pacific slope, the dictates of common humanity and benevolence, as well as the plainest suggestions of practical statesmanship, all demand that the problem of Chinese immigration shall be solved while it is yet within the legislative control.

Governed by these views, your committee present and recommend the passage of the bill accompanying this report.

Martin I. Townsend [N. Y.] opposed the bill. He said that Dennis Kearney, the "sand-lot" labor agitator of San Francisco, who had started the anti-Mongolian movement with his cry, "The Chinese must go," had won over the Democratic party to the movement. He disclaimed speaking for the Republican party in the matter.

I have nothing to charge against the dominant party in this House, although the first treaty under which these immigrations have occurred was negotiated in good old Democratic days [under Buchanan], but it was in days when the light of heaven sometimes reached the brain of the Democracy. [Laughter.] And, sir, I credit to the Democracy not only the making of the treaty but the prosperity which has accrued to the Pacific coast from the adoption of it. California owes what she is in the agricultural world, her grains, her fruits, her agricultural prosperity, to the treaty of 1858 and the one subsequently negotiated. It was before Kearney came and before Kearney was represented in the national halls.

But it is said we must take unusual ground for the benefit of the laboring classes in this country. The laboring classes in this country, the gentleman from Pennsylvania [Hendrick B. Wright] said, are starving. "Two hundred millions of them" [laughter], said the gentleman from Pennsylvania, "are starving!" Two hundred millions in this country are starving! [Great laughter.] And he said, besides, that there are in Pennsylvania five thousand in the lunatic asylum from the hardness of the times. Let me say to the gentleman from Pennsylvania that lunatics sometimes are made by hardness of the times, sometimes by unrequited love, and lunatics are sometimes made from unsatisfied ambition [laughter] and the Pennsylvania lunatics made by the latter cause do not always stay at home within the State of Pennsylvania. [Great laughter.]

I stand here not to disparage, not to underrate, the suffering of the laboring classes or other classes in this country. It has been very great; it is very great to-day; it has been always very great in the world. The struggle to keep the wolf away from the door is the hardest struggle humanity has to make, and yet it is what has made humanity what it has come to be in the better portions of Christendom. The hard soils of Pennsylvania—there are some good soils there—the hard soils of the hardest part of New York, and the hard soils of New England have made a body of men whom we may be proud of before the world and before Heaven.

But, sir, do not let us forget another thing, that in the midst of these hard times the year 1878 in the United States of America was the year of the greatest prosperity that has ever occurred to any people since the dawn of creation. There never has been a period in any land when labor could buy with its rewards so much to eat, to drink, and to wear and with which to provide for its loved ones, as the year 1878; and all this has occurred to a great degree because we have overridden the fanatics of the olden time. It is the "Heathen Chinee" to-day that we are called to suppress. I say to the gentleman from Kentucky [Mr. Willis], who has charge of this bill and who represents Louisville, Kentucky, that I remember the day when the cry was against the Catholic Irish, against the condemned Germans, and when the streets of his city flowed with blood and when the streets of St. Louis, in Missouri, flowed with blood in the riots against the Irish and the Germans because they were coming here to take away the labor of the American citizen and rob his children of their bread. Those who got up those riots were overruled. Thank God, I had a hand in it. I was in a minority. The great men of the Democratic party, many of them of the State of New York, were on the other side. Erastus Brooks, of the *Evening Express,* a trusted leader of the party to-day, was, if I remember rightly, the head of what was called the American Order, organized to protect the country against the inroads of what they deemed hordes of Irish and Germans. But, sir, we put them down by the use of hard common sense. We beat them, though we were in a minority. My State gave 200,000 majority in favor of oppression and exclusion. But, sir, our unparalleled prosperity which has crowned us in this country has been due in a gerat degree to the sturdy, stalwart labor of the Irish and the Germans.

Some one says "demagogue." Is it Bill Nye that says it? [Laughter.] I have Bill Nye here [holding up a volume] [laughter], and I will allow Truthful James to read his dreadful indictment against the "Heathen Chinee."

Here the speaker read "Plain Language from Truthful James," by Bret Harte.

Now, sir, I did not join in that raid against the Irish and the Germans. I have never yet joined in a raid against anybody, and now that old age is upon me I hope that God will give me grace for the future hours I have to live to keep me from joining in a crusade against any portion of the race that has descended from Adam.

Sir, this Chinese immigration is put in a light that will bear a great deal of criticism. The census of 1870 shows the total number of Chinese in Oregon, in California, and in Nevada was in that year only fifty-five thousand. I do not believe that there are to-day more than seventy-five thousand men that we are called upon to legislate against.

What is the matter with these men? A gentleman in Washington now, a distinguished merchant of California, whom for political reasons I will not name, has said to me, within the last week, "I have dealt to the amount of more than half a million of dollars in small sums with the Chinese merchants in San Francisco. They never violated their word, and I never lost a dollar by them." Do not these men earn their fee and

XI—15

bounty? The charge is that they come and make us rich and do not take away money enough to pay for their services.

Ah, but we have a new school of philosophers; such as went before our labor committee and for weeks twaddled about over-production. They declared that the sufferings of the laboring people in this country arose from the fact that there was too much production; we were ruining our laboring people by furnishing them too much clothing; by furnishing them too much food; the country was getting to be all piled up with food, all loaded down with clothing, and hence starvation and nakedness.

Sir, these are not the laboring men. They are demagogues and idlers at corner groceries; men who are supported by the labor of their wives and never do a day's work from year's end to year's end. What labor does Kearney perform? He is hounding on his wild followers to the destruction of all we hold dear. What does he do to earn an honorable subsistence?

THOMAS RYAN [Kan.].—He passes round the hat.

MR. TOWNSEND.—It is said these Chinese are wicked. I have never known a people who were not wicked—if you listen to those who wish to do them wrong. In the Middle Ages it was said that the Jews stole children and crucified them.

It was said in 1854 that if we allowed Catholicism to come into our country our liberties would be gone. How many men on the opposite side of the House come here to-day except by permission of St. Patrick?

I have another thing to say about the Chinese. It is said by those who hound on the hoodlums to wrong and torture them in their quiet labor by which they shun your poorhouses that they cannot be induced to adopt the Christian religion. I say to such, and I say to all men, if you wish to make Christians of the Chinese treat them in a manner becoming Christians.

Sir, when James Buchanan negotiated that first treaty, which was afterward so much enlarged by the Burlingame treaty under Lincoln, he made a step forward in the advance of civilization, Christianity, and commercial prosperity, and a step in favor of the human race; and when the treaty of Japan was negotiated the two treaties together opened to Christianity and prosperity and fraternity a portion of the world which had been shut up for centuries.

I am not for taking a step backward. I am for going forward and treating the human race as brothers. I will quote upon this subject the language of a man whose lyre was always resonant with the best sympathies of humanity; I refer to the immortal Robert Burns:

Then let us pray that come it may,
As come it will for a' that,

. . . . . .

When man to man, the warld o'er,
Shall brothers be for a' that.

[Applause.]

Mr. Willis supported his measure.

Mr. Speaker, twice before in our history we have been called upon to determine questions arising from the difference of races. Our first experience was with the red face. Millions of money and thousands of valued lives have been sacrificed in the vain effort to make the Indian either an obedient subject or a willing citizen. He is to-day the same sullen, unconquered alien savage that he was in the earliest colonial history of our country. The "Indian policy" is as much a vexed problem of legislation in this as it has been in every preceding Congress since the organization of our Government.

Our next experience was with the black race. Need I recall the bitter animosities, the sectional strife, the political and religious dissensions which marked its progress, until the problems which the wisest statesmanship had failed to solve were finally determined by the arbitrament of arms?

And now before our trials and difficulties with the red and black races are fully ended we are invited to another and even more difficult experiment with the yellow race. If our experience has been a failure, or at best a doubtful success, with the African and the Indian, what can we expect from the Mongolian, who has neither the docility and humility of the one, nor the consciousness of inferior civilization which distinguishes the other. The bill which is now before the House puts an end to this third experiment with an alien race.

But two questions are involved in the passage of the bill: Have we the constitutional right to enact such a law? and, if so, ought we in this instance to exercise that right?

Upon the first of these questions the decisions which have just been read from the report are, it seems to me, conclusive. A treaty under the Constitution is not more sacred or binding than a law. The last expression of the legislative mind, whether by treaty or by law, is the controlling one. If, therefore, Congress passes this bill the Burlingame treaty, as far as it conflicts with its provisions, will become null and void. Admitting, then, the right, a right not founded upon any doctrine of higher law, but based upon the principles and precedents of the Constitution, the next and more practical question is, shall we exercise it? Is it good policy? Is it expedient or necessary to enact a restrictive law of this kind? Do the facts justify it?

The first fact to which I would call the attention of the House is that wherever the Chinese have gone the judgment of condemnation against them is almost unanimous. The States of our own country in which they have secured a foothold have been pronounced and often violent in their opposition. Their governors have issued messages and proclamations, their legislatures have enacted laws, their courts have rendered judgments, the avowed object and purpose of which were to put an end to Chinese immigration. There are to-day in the hands of our committee the joint resolutions of four State legislatures, the memorial of the constitutional convention of California, passed only a few days ago without a single dissenting voice, together with the proceedings of innumerable societies, religious bodies, labor conventions, and the petitions of over one hundred thousand private citizens, setting forth from different standpoints the evils of Chinese immigration, and urging upon Congress the necessity for prompt and vigorous measures of relief.

When it is borne in mind that the people of these States were not at first hostile to the Chinese, but on the contrary welcomed them as valued allies in the development of their material resources, the weight of this adverse testimony is greatly increased. If, as is contended for by some, the Chinese make useful citizens and worthy members of society, why this unanimous desire to get rid of them. If the evil of their presence did not exceed, did not far outrun the good, would not self-interest join with justice to prevent such a result? As it is, the free, unprejudiced, and deliberate judgment of so many different communities, not confined to any one but held by all classes, is certainly worthy of the gravest and most careful consideration. And especially, Mr. Speaker, should it be respected when it is confirmed and enforced by that of every country in the world where the Chinese have found a lodgment. In Java, in Siam, in Singapore, in the Philippine Islands, and in the Australian colonies, as has been shown by my esteemed friend from California [Horace Davis], the same opposition has been aroused and the same results realized long ago which we to-day see upon the Pacific slope. Everywhere they have made themselves obnoxious; everywhere heavy penalties and restrictive legislation have been found necessary means of protection. In Java the Chinese have lived for hundreds of years, but this long residence has neither diminished nor destroyed the objectionable features of their character. Years ago they were declared by the official authorities to be a very dangerous people, a pest to the country, for which the only remedy was their expulsion. We are not, therefore, the only people who object to the Chinese.

Nor, Mr. Speaker, if we pass this bill will we be the only nation that has set aside a treaty which worked injury and injustice to its citizens. Both France and England have treaties with China which, like our own, provide for free immigration, but neither government has hesitated to impose special taxes and restrictions upon them. As far back as 1855 the English colony of Victoria levied a capitation tax of $50 upon every Chinese immigrant. In 1861 a similar tax was imposed by the colony of New South Wales, and in 1877 by the colony of Queensland and also by the French colony of Saigon. We, sir, may well profit by the older and riper experience of these countries. If restrictive laws have been found necessary and have proved successful with them, why should we not use the same means for our own protection?

The briefest inquiry, Mr. Speaker, into the reasons for such legislation will show both its propriety and its necessity. The Chinaman, whether as a laborer, as a member of society, or of the body-politic, is an undesirable and dangerous element in any community. Crowded, huddled together, forty or fifty in a room not larger than would accommodate with decency and with comfort one man with a family, discarding or disregarding all the usual ordinary appliances of personal civilization as to diet and clothing, cooking, eating, and sleeping in the same apartments, they have succeeded in reducing the cost of living to its minimum and thus wherever located have forced the laboring classes to the wall. As laborers, therefore, the Chinese can only exist to the exclusion or degradation of all others in the community.

Nor as members of society are they less objectionable. The personal habits consequent upon their mode of life in these squalid dens, their low groveling ideas of virtue and religion, and their peculiar social views have been commented upon and condemned by every nation with whom they have come in contact.

As members of the body-politic the complaints against them have been equally strong and widespread. Nearly fifty years ago we find the Dutch government of Java complaining that the Chinese form a distinct class, refusing to mingle with or be absorbed by the society around them; preserving their own costume, their own habits, traditions, social organization, and nationality.

These objections to the Chinese, Mr. Speaker, whether from an industrial, social, or political standpoint, are worthy of serious consideration in any community. In a self-governing one, however, such as ours, they deserve especial attention. Here, if anywhere, it should be the aim of the Government, of its legislative representatives, to elevate the dignity and preserve the self-respect of all of its citizens. As are the people so will be the government. If the people are corrupt, if they are ignorant, selfish, or unpatriotic, the government will reflect these ignoble traits in its own features.

The introduction, therefore, of a class of men like the Chinese, who are without homes or families, whose education and habits disqualify them for citizenship, whose cheap wages degrade labor, and whose want of morality and self-respect unfits them for society, is fraught with great danger to our republican institutions, and should be promptly and effectually checked.

We say in theory to our citizens that they are to be protected in all their rights and privileges; we say to them in theory that the Government respects and honors labor—honors the bone and sinew of the land. How, then, can we hope to secure a bold, defiant, independent citizenship among the laboring men who comprise four-fifths of our population if we declare to them by our conduct, by our practical legislation that these generous theories are but myths, but glittering generalities? Shall we subject them to a competition—to a mode of life—that will make these grand and inspiring truths utter impossibilities? Shall we say to them that the rights and honors of American citizenship are one thing, and their possession, their enjoyment another and a different thing? Shall we, in other words, compel any class of our fellow citizens to surrender church, home, and school to become mere "hewers of wood and drawers of water," by subjecting them to the shame and degradation which curse the Chinese laborer?

I hope and believe that no such declaration will ever go forth from this body, but that we will recognize the equal rights and dignity of all of our citizens by the prompt passage of this bill.

Such a result is demanded by political no less than by industrial conditions. We welcome to our shores all who desire or intend to make this their home or who expect to become permanent citizens of our Government. The Germans, the Irish, the French, and other immigrants to our country have quickly

and successfully adapted themselves to our institutions. Prompt
to defend the honor and to promote the interests of their adopted
land, yielding ready and cheerful obedience to its laws and
customs, they have illustrated in their lives and vindicated by
their conduct the wise policy of immigration. As kindred drops
of water they have mingled and been lost in the great stream

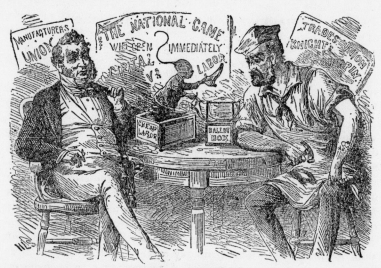

THE NEW PANDORA'S BOX

Representative Manufacturer, *(springing open Chinese surprise box)*— "There!—What do you think
of that little joker?"

Knight of St. Crispin.—"Pshaw! That's a mean trick! Wait till I open *my* box."

From the collection of the New York Historical Society

of American life. The Chinese have no such intention or experience. They do not come to seek homes. They disdain to accept our institutions; they look with contempt upon our social
customs; they defy the authority of our laws; they retain all the
distinctive features and characteristics of their national life.
Twenty-five years of residence and contact with our people
have left them unchanged and unimproved in any important
particular. The argument, therefore, which the gentleman
from New York [Mr. Townsend] bases upon a comparison of
this race with our Irish and German fellow citizens is utterly
without foundation. The Chinese, unlike them, have always
been and will always be an alien element in our midst. We
want no such indigestible substance in the body-politic. We
want a brave, patriotic, self-reliant, assimilative citizenship.

The bill was passed by a vote of 155 to 72. It was referred in the Senate to the Committee on Foreign Relations. On February 7 Hannibal Hamlin [Me.] reported the bill from the committee. It came up for discussion on February 13.

RESTRICTION OF CHINESE IMMIGRATION

SENATE, FEBRUARY 13-15, 1879

Aaron A. Sargent [Cal.] repeated the familiar arguments in favor of the bill. He dilated upon the conditions in "Chinatown," San Francisco.

There is in San Francisco a city within a city, a section cut out of Pekin or any other Chinese city that may be mentioned, an *imperium in imperio*. There is a population concentrated in certain blocks and squares of some forty thousand, varying at different times in the year. At great expense our people have been able to preserve something like cleanliness in that quarter. Left to itself it becomes so filthy that no white man can stand the stench. White people flee from the contact of that neighborhood, and property all around it depreciates. There is a strange people there. A newspaper or a book never penetrates within its precincts. They speak a foreign and impenetrable tongue. They are governed by their own tribunals which inflict penalties for the transgression of their laws, laws frequently in violation of the municipal laws, even to the extent of death; and upon that the testimony is uniform of our judges, our prosecuting officers, our clergy, and others who have had occasion to investigate the matter.

This China city needs but to grow to fill up and supplant the whole American city, and what is to prevent it? Its denizens are a very slight fragment of the four hundred million people behind them, pushed by famine outwardly, seizing every opportunity to come to California where, under any circumstances whatever, even of oppression, their lot is better than that in their own country. In that quarter of the city—and it is nearly a quarter of the city—there are nests of contagion which the utmost vigilance of our health officers can hardly break up. We can trace to them two or three epidemics of small-pox; on one of those occasions everybody in San Francisco who would take the smallpox had it; hundreds died in our pest-houses. Leprosy is found there; a friend of mine who employed Chinese in his family, and I suppose caught the contagion in that way, died of that horrible disease. Leprosy among the Chinese themselves is quite common, so that we have been compelled to deport them back to China, finding them in their haunts as we find smallpox patients in the last extremity of misery and disease, hid away under some stairway, perhaps put into the streets to die by unfeeling associates.

This vast horde of people bring no families; a family is an exception among them; probably not more than a dozen or two in San Francisco have families, and those the very highest merchants. They bring no women, except that out of one hundred and twenty thousand or one hundred and forty thousand of them in the State there may be six thousand women, held in most abject bondage and brought for purposes of prostitution.

Now, what are the morals of one hundred and forty thousand men without families? I cannot discuss in this presence a question like that. If Senators have any curiosity on it, let them read works on China. They are guilty of hideous immoralities wherever they are, so that they become offensive to any community where they go. I will read a short extract from Bayard Taylor in his work on "India, China, and Japan." Bayard Taylor was a Republican. He certainly was as strongly imbued with sentiment, the sentiments of my friends on my right, as any man ever in the country; but, more than that, he was a practical observing man, and he says with reference to the Chinese:

It is my deliberate opinion that the Chinese are, morally, the most debased people on the face of the earth. Forms of vice which in other countries are barely named are in China so common that they excite no comment among the natives. They constitute the surface level, and below them are deeps and deeps of depravity so shocking and horrible that their character cannot even be hinted. There are some dark shadows in human nature which we naturally shrink from penetrating, and I made no attempt to collect information of this kind; but there was enough in the things which I could not avoid seeing and hearing, which are brought almost daily to the notice of every foreign resident, to inspire me with a powerful aversion to the Chinese race. Their touch is pollution and, harsh as the opinion may seem, justice to our own race demands that they should not be allowed to settle on our soil. Science may have lost something but mankind has gained by the exclusive policy which has governed China during the past century.

Furthermore, they come and are worked so cheaply because there is a system of contract or coolie labor; they come from China consigned to one of six companies, great, powerful, wealthy corporations. They come, giving their labor in exchange for their passage money for a number of years, to work wherever they are sent, and they are sent wherever it is profitable to their masters to put them. They live on a few handfuls of rice. A dozen of them will be stowed in the space of four or five of these seats; a room of moderate height with a false floor put in it, and both covered all over with bunks and shelves one above the other, and in these quarters they cook, they sleep, they smoke their opium. They lay by a few dollars to send back to China, and they are rich. How can the American laborer compete with them? The American laborer has or desires a family; he has children that he wishes to educate. Upon his best room he wants a carpet. Decency requires that his daughters shall not sleep in the room with his sons or with the parents. He wants the little conveniences of life. He wants American civilization. This is not American civilization; this is filthy, squalid barbarism, and if anybody is disposed to sneer at this question from this latter aspect I tell him he cannot afford to do it. I have no sympathy with agrarian notions; I believe in the rights of property; I believe in peace and order; I have no sympathy with Kearneyism; I am speaking in no such interest.

It is not the laboring man, it is not the Irishman, the German, or the American uneducated man, who complains of these things merely. All classes of people on the Pacific coast who have observed this are of the same opinion. I hazard the assertion that there are not a thousand men in California who are not of the same opinion that I hold on this matter. There are great ranch holders, men who cultivate or attempt to cultivate ten, twenty, or thirty thousand acres of land, who say that without this cheap labor they cannot carry on farming. Such farming ought to stop, Mr. President. Those great domains, half covering counties, ought to be broken up. It is the highest policy of society to break them up and allow mankind generally to have homes. Small farms, cultivated by the owners, need none of this cheap servile labor.

It was the same argument that justified slavery; cheap labor was absolutely essential to carry on the industries of the South, it was said; and we know how fallacious that is in the face of a larger cotton crop this year than they ever raised before since the South was founded.

The fears of California and the other Pacific States are not peculiar in this matter. We are not alone in saying that this is an emergency and in begging Congress for some relief upon it. The Chinese problem is being discussed in England, in France, in Russia, in the English and French and Dutch colonies of the East Indies, by the ablest magazines of the world, and by the foreign press. I have here copied at considerable length an article from the London *Times,* which is so important that I am almost tempted to read it, wherein they show the effect of the Chinese upon the English colonies and in the United States, and say that in their belief, so far as the United States is concerned, there is a graver crisis arising from the influx of these people than there was from the slave trade and the abolition of slavery. The *Revue des Deux Mondes,* the great French magazine, says with regard to this matter:

If nothing happens to check this movement before the end of this century China will have completely overrun California, and, pushing forward her waves of emigrants, she will spread toward the rich and fertile plains of the center of the American continent. Only a war of extermination can then take from them what they will have peacefully conquered by the sole force of numbers, work, and slow, patient economy. What such a war will be one can easily imagine; and this new conflict of races will attain proportions hitherto unknown.

And, again, the same magazine says:

It is evident that, whenever the Chinaman becomes a permanent resident, the invasion will increase by giant strides and the American population will disappear in these compact masses of Asiatics. Without the reverse current homeward, California would have been long ago a Chinese colony.

Aside from the question of foreign influence and as to its influence upon California, I desire to call the attention of the Senate to the fact that at the recent Berlin congress, where the peace of Europe was again patched up, Count Shouvaloff, the Russian ambassador, called attention to this great Chinese problem threatening the civilization of the world, and said that unless "arms of precision"—as I translate his language—could be kept out of their hands they would overmaster civilization. I quote from his declaration:

If the countless hordes of China and India are to be permitted to arm themselves with modern weapons and to acquire a practical knowledge of the art of modern warfare, there will be nothing to prevent them from rolling forth into Europe and crushing Christian civilization out of existence. Especially were the Mongolians to be feared from this point of view, and he invited the congress to take the matter into serious consideration and to deliberate upon the practicability of a league of the European powers, binding them to abstain from employing Asiatic troops in Europe and to prevent, as far as possible, importation of arms of precision into Asia.

This is a problem more important than that of Tamerlane. The other foreigners who come to us are assimilated almost immediately in our midst. In the second generation their distinctive features disappear; at any rate, in the third they cannot be distinguished, no matter what nationality they may originally have been, from the common mass of our people. That is not so with the Chinese. Over a generation has elapsed since the Chinese came to the United States, and they are the same as they were when they first came, entirely, in every sense of the word, indigestible; and it is not merely so in California, it is so in the East Indies wherever they go. Japan fears them, and has made stringent regulations to keep them away. It was the effort of the Coreans to keep them out of their borders, persisted in for long, long years; and the restriction is not yet removed so that they can go to Corea, and the reason is because they are hated and feared. Sir Walter Medhurst in an article in the *Nineteenth Century* for September, an English magazine, after defending the Chinese from some accusations, showing that he is friendly toward them, says of them in conclusion:

It follows that, whatever may be the political changes that may transpire in the countries to which Chinamen resort, their condition will be the happiest for themselves, and safest for the country concerned, if they are dealt with as a subject people, and as a community possessing abnormal characteristics, and therefore needing otherwise than ordinary treatment.

Can we treat any people in our midst as "a subject people"? Is it possible? Is it not contrary to the genius of our institutions?

Now, for a moment I wish to call attention to what other nations have done to get rid of this Chinese invasion, for that is what it amounts to. I do not say that the means adopted by them were the wisest or were humane, but it simply shows an endeavor to get rid of them on some terms or other. That seems to be a necessity which apparently knows no law sometimes of mercy or humanity.

In Australia they do it by a heavy capitation tax or importation tax. The Dutch in Batavia levy a heavy and insulting tax; they tax the Chinaman's head, they levy a tax on his fingernails, on his cue proportioned to its length. The French in Saigon seek by oppressive legislation to keep them out. The Spanish in Manila tried the same thing by massacre, so much so that at one time, there being I think some fifty or sixty thousand Chinese there, they were reduced by a massacre to seven thousand—a most uncommendable way to get rid of them. But there is an instinctive aversion to them, arising from their habits and their peculiarities, above all other peoples; so that the consul of the United States at Singapore, writing to my able and excellent colleague in the other House, Horace Davis, says that the Hindus and other Asiatic races which we have been disposed to consider in the lowest scale of humanity will not associate with the Chinese, and have as great a prejudice against them as any other people, and in the case of the riots which have occurred at Singapore, raised by lawless Chinese, and which I have seen matched in California from their fighting among themselves, they always take part with the authorities against the Chinese.

In Siam and the Philippine Islands there is a heavy poll tax on them.

In conclusion, I simply wish to say that in the East this matter is being understood by the most enlightened of the public men, by clergymen, by professors of colleges, and by others. I hold in my hand, out of many letters that I have received from men of this class, two letters; one is written by Andrew D. White, president of Cornell University, and the other by the lately deceased and regretted president of Princeton Theological Seminary, Dr. Charles Hodge. And, when men like these can write upon this subject, it seems to me it would be well for those who would brush it aside from mere sentimentality to review the position in which they stand.

Stanley Matthews [O.] opposed the bill.

Mr. President, if I believed that the representations which have been made in respect to the evils to be remedied by this legislation were as true, as faithful to the fact as no doubt those gentlemen sincerely do who make them, I should still be compelled to vote against this bill. If I believed that we not only had the constitutional power but the moral right to keep out from our social and political body voluntary immigrants from the Chinese Empire or elsewhere on the face of the globe; if I believed that the good to be accomplished and the evil to be averted by keeping them out were as great as the gentlemen who represent on the floor of this body the States of the Pacific coast do believe them to be, nevertheless my respect for the sanctity of the plighted faith of the nation in a solemn treaty with a sovereign power would compel me to seek some other method of securing these results than this arbitrary act of legislation.

Why, Mr. President, we are discussing the passage of this bill and about, I fear, to pass it, in the face of a treaty, a treaty made by the constitutional treaty-making power of this nation, made with remarkable circumstances of exceptional solemnity, made by a special embassy sent for the purpose, in which, in the face of great difficulties and obstructions occasioned by the impenetrable character of these people, we solicited from them the covenants which we are now about to break; and we are to do it by putting upon that treaty the stamp of hypocrisy on our own part as a party to it, for we approached the Chinese Government in the Burlingame treaty with such expressions as these:

The United States of America and the Emperor of China cordially recognize the inherent and inalienable right of man to change, his home and allegiance.

And also:

The mutual advantage of the free migration and emigration of their citizens and subjects respectively from one country to the other for purposes of curiosity, of trade, or of permanent residence.

What has occurred since the date of that treaty to give the lie to that declaration? If none but our own convictions have changed either as to the right or the expediency, then by the same bonds with which we bound the parties let us seek to unloose them from the obligations into which we entered. Let us go to the Emperor of China and say that the experience of the nation and of the world since that time has convinced us of the error of that profession, and that notwithstanding the mistake under which we entered into the contract at that time we desire to make the correction with their consent, as with their consent we entered into it.

Suppose, Mr. President, this were a treaty with Great Britain; suppose it were a treaty with France or Germany or any other fighting nation; suppose it were a treaty with a Christian nation and not with pagans and heathens; would it be consistent with the obligations of international law, would it be consistent with the courtesy that prevails in international intercourse, would it be consistent with our own self-respect, would it be consistent with that wholesome fear which every man and people have when they are on the brink and verge of doing that which they are conscious to be wrong, that we should approach them in any other way than by the peaceful way of amicable negotiation? Would we dare, in the face of the opinion of the civilized world and in the fear of the consequences of exciting the indignation and just anger of a proud and high-spirited people, be guilty of this act of Punic faith, repudiating the obligations of a treaty, without the ordinary and poor politeness of giving an antecedent notice of our intention, much less soliciting the consent which binds nations by a moral obligation as strong, as high, as great, as those which affect the consciences of private individuals?

We have the constitutional power to do this thing, Mr. President. I do not question that. We have the right by law to repeal any other law, and we have the power by law to violate all our treaties; and when it has passed into the form of an enactment, and received the sanction of the whole law-making power of the body-politic, it is then the binding law of the country, but it is a law nevertheless in breach of a treaty and in violation of solemn and plighted faith.

Whenever we wish to make war we break treaties of peace; and doubtless there are occasions when the cause and provocation are sufficient, and when the emergencies of self-preservation and defence are so great that we are morally justified in throwing off the shackles of an obligation which ought in morals no longer to bind us. But is that this case? Has anything been done by the government of the Chinese Empire or by the people and inhabitants of that country in derogation of this treaty and in violation of our rights under it?

Now, I am not willing, Mr. President, by my voice and by my vote to bring upon this nation and country the reproach of covenant breakers. It may be that these people are pagans and heathens and outside of the circle of Christian sympathy, if, indeed, pagans and heathens are outside of that, which certainly is not in conformity with my idea of the area of human interests that is covered by the Christian principle of human brotherhood. These people are intelligent; they know the force and meaning of words, and they understand a good deal about the relation of things, and we can approach them with all the reasons and arguments necessary to convince an intelligent people of the propriety of amendments and modifications of this treaty; and when we have their final refusal, when we know the extent of the evil under which we suffer and that there is no other remedy, none to be obtained by and through negotiation and treaty stipulation with them, then, sir, and then only, for the first time will it be in order in the parliament of morals to commence the consideration of such a proposition as this,

We are told that these people are aliens to us, aliens in thought, aliens in religion, aliens in language, aliens in dress, aliens in race, aliens in every circumstance of civilization, and that their presence is a fatal poison in our body-politic. Ah, Mr. President, I thought American civilization was a robuster child than that. I thought from the descriptions which from boyhood I have read and heard in reference to the vigor of our character as a people and the adaptation to all possible human circumstances of our admirable and perfect institutions of freedom, that this was a land and a country which could safely welcome to its shores the outcasts of every other clime, that its powers of digestion and of assimilation were such that the very evils which afflicted mankind elsewhere would be taken up into the blood and circulation of this people and convey nutriment and health and strength to every limb and part of our economy. It is the boast, perhaps my friend the Senator from California who sits nearest to me [Newton Booth] may sarcastically say, of Fourth of July orators. Ah, Mr. President, has the oratory that is peculiar to the Fourth of July come to be a hissing and a by-word, a scorn and a reproach, and our flag ''a flaunting lie'' in this day and generation when we supposed that we had practically vindicated every abstract and elemental truth in the Declaration of our Independence? Is it enough to smother opposition and put down argument to say that that is merely the sentimentality of a Fourth of July oratory, and not the words of soberness and truth? Then by what token is it that we vaunt the superiority of our civilization and of our government and of our institutions over those of the effete monarchies and despotisms of the Old World? Is it or is it not true that the young democracy of this continent is still a lusty giant able to throttle all the serpents that attack him even in his cradle, and to outlive all the ordinary contingencies and vicissitudes which have sapped and undermined the foundations of other governments because they were not founded on the doctrines of human equality and human rights?

Is our religion so exotic, so merely professional, so merely sentimental that the joss in the temple of ''the heathen Chinee'' is likely to supplant in our affections and veneration the great ''I Am'' who called into being him as well as us, and made Himself the Father of us all? Or is it not a great conquering, overwhelming, and triumphant propaganda which going forth from its original seat in the land of Judea, known to us as the Holy Land, preached as the gospel ''to every creature'' and made the welcome tidings of ''peace on earth and good-will to men'' without respect to the color of their skin or any other of the accidents of race or birth? Are we compelled by voting for this bill not only to admit that our democracy is a piece of hypocrisy, but that our religion is a sham and superstition? Is there indeed a God above or righteousness on earth or any truth or reality in the unseen things which we are told are eternal when the seen things shall have passed away like a scroll?

And yet, if I understand the argument, it is because the freedom of our institutions and the purity of our religion are endangered by the huddling together of forty thousand Chinese in the city of San Francisco! And we are warned by the history of the ages and the experience of the world and our own observation that we should be very careful how we endanger the peace and security of our age by courting the essential conflict of antagonist races. The same cry made the Jew an exile for hundreds of years and crowded him into the Ghetto at Venice because he was an alien in race and had crucified our Saviour. The same thing made a chattel slave of the poor African that had been torn from his home and brought here against his will. And we are reminded of the dire and bloody conflicts which his presence inspired and carried on until our own land saw them expire in the blood of hundreds of thousands of patriotic men. Ah! Mr. President, was it the presence of the black man on this continent that brought in upon us all this woe, or was it his presence here as a slave? Was it not rather the presence of that invisible specter, the injustice with which we treated him, which came upon us with the retribution of a just Heaven and inflicted upon us the punishment for our joint and common sin?

Conflict of races? Sir, is the globe not big enough for us all? Who made it and those that dwell upon its face and made them all of one blood, with one immortality and the same destiny? Is there any gentleman here that thinks he is competent to improve upon the work of creation and make it better than it was made by Him that doeth all things well? If we can live upon the surface of the same earth, what hinders us from living together on the same continent? Are we to have no communication with them, no intercourse, commercial, political, personal? Why, Mr. President, the civilization of Europe thundered on the Asiatic coast with fleets armed with guns to open China to Christian civilization, to compel them to sell to us their tea and to buy our opium.

GEORGE F. EDMUNDS [Vt.].—And to admit our people to reside in their territory.

SENATOR MATTHEWS.—Undoubtedly, to reciprocal rights.

XI—16

You forced the treaty out of them; or, if the American did not do it, he stood by when others, bolder and more courageous, extorted theirs, and came in on the footing of "the most favored nation."

It is said that this conflict of races is inevitable and necessarily injurious, and that the difficulties which spring from it are insoluble. Mr. President, perhaps they are to the human heart in its natural and unregenerate state; but there has been a Divine prescription and remedy. There is no trouble—I say it in the presence of all the Senators—there need be no trouble to-day within the limits of these States between the white man and the black man whenever the reign of righteousness becomes as practically applied as we mouth it and profess it. Do right; treat every man, white or black, copper-colored or whatever, as you would be done by yourself in like circumstances; and then any evil you may suffer is greatly better to be borne than the evil which you inflict by not administering that rule. It is simply to apply in politics, in our social economy, in our personal intercourse, in the institutions of society, wherever human action is called into being, the Christian rule, the law of divine benevolence and of human brotherhood, and all the difficulties of caste and creed, and all the conflicts which spring up from the apparently irreconcilable and adverse interests of men disappear, vanish away like the mist and the morning dew in the presence of the warm and bright and health-giving influences of the rising sun.

But it is said that it is not so much a conflict of race, of religion, of color, of caste, as it is a degradation of labor. Mr. President, I trust and I believe that I take to heart the suffering condition of labor in this country and elsewhere as much as does any other Senator or any other man. If I cannot agree in any remedies that may be proposed for the evil of that condition, it is not because I do not recognize the fact of the evil or the necessity of the remedy, but because I believe there is a remedy and that it lies elsewhere and in another direction. I do not at all believe with my distinguished and respected friend the Senator from California who sits nearest to me [Mr. Booth] that the antagonism with labor and the sufferings in its condition, the privations and distress to which it is subjected, are problems that are insoluble. They are difficult, I admit; they are not solved, I know; but I think that if the time that is wasted by public men of all nations upon comparatively trivial and unimportant things were directed to the solution of the labor problem we should find some Edison to arise in the world of moral politics who would invent some principie or some scheme of political institution which would remedy their evils.

Why, Mr. President, the evil of our labor system is not the cheapness of production. On the contrary, the thing that we strive for, the thing to which we are directing our energies, the thing to which the inventive genius of our race is constantly applied, is to find out from day to day by what economics, by what contrivances, the product of labor can be furnished to the world at the least cost. Why is it that to-day the metallic treasures of Europe and the world, in addition to the flow from our own mines, are turning their currents into our treasury here? Why? Nothing more and nothing less than that owing to the cheapness of our productions we are sending the products of our labor into the markets of the world at prices less than they can be afforded there by any other people.

What, then, is the real difficulty? It lies not in the administration of the laws of production at all, but in the law of the distribution of wealth; and if every man had the due share which upon a just system would come to him by reason of his industry and his exertions there would be no starving man on this continent or elsewhere.

Why, Mr. President, they tell us that the presence of forty thousand Chinamen in San Francisco is beggaring the laboring population of this country. What is it that to-day beggars the operatives in Liverpool, in Glasgow, in the iron districts of Wales? What causes the suffering in Germany, in Austria, and here? Is it the forty thousand Chinamen that are working at under-wages in San Francisco, or is it not rather more at least attributable to the vile demagogism of another product of California politics, Dennis Kearney and his associates? If we have no other and greater evils here than exist across the Atlantic in Europe, why is it necessary to recount this idle tale about the misery and the injury of Chinese immigration? The Chinaman is a laborer wherever he is, in America or in his own country; and why should he whose sympathy runs out to labor as such, to necessity, because it is the God-given way to work out the destiny of men, because it is our destiny and our birthright and our way to improvement, stop short at the Chinaman, and not let it go out through the length and breadth of the whole world of labor and say that here, there, everywhere where there is a man and a laborer, there you are to sympathize with and help him?

The principle of competition, which it is said in some schools of social and political economy lies at the root of the unequal and unjust distribution of the world's goods, shows itself in this attack wherein the laboring man, delivered up only to the selfish consideration of merely an individual interest, turns and rends his brother laborer because the common Father of them all has dressed him in a different color and endowed him with a strange speech. Is that the way this heaven-high problem of labor is to be solved; or is it not in a different and more reverent spirit, recognizing the great fundamental, underlying principles of justice, of right, of equality, which, although abstract and invisible, are as real and as everlasting as the throne of God?

On February 14 James G. Blaine [Me.] supported the bill. He denied the statement of Senator Matthews that we had solicited the treaty with China, saying that it was that country which had done so. And the last clause of the treaty, which provided that immigration to either country should be voluntary, had been violated by the Six Companies, a Chinese commercial guild.

The Senator from Ohio asks what we should do if the other party to the treaty were Great Britain or Germany or France or any other power that was able to make war. I ask the honorable Senator what he would advise us to do if Great Britain or France or Germany should locate six commercial companies in New York, whose business it should be to bring hither to this country the worst class and the lowest class of the population of those three kingdoms?

SENATOR MATTHEWS.—Mr. President, I would say this, that instead of inaugurating an arbitrary and *ex parte* act of legislation on our own part, giving our own construction to the treaty and the conduct of the other party under it, I would, through the usual diplomatic representative of this country, make representations to that government making complaints of the alleged breach of the treaty, and ask what answer could be made to that; and only in the event of our receiving a contumacious refusal to obey the plain requisitions of the treaty obligation would I, as a last resort, repudiate our own obligations under the treaty.

SENATOR BLAINE.—Ah! but the Senator does not answer the question I asked him, what he would do in case they had themselves broken it, and we were the victims of the breach? He answers me that he would take hat in hand and bow politely before them, and ask them if they would not do better! What are we to do as a measure of self-defence when they have broken it, and taken the initiative? I say that this country and this Senate would not hesitate to defy any European power.

The Burlingame treaty is peculiar; it relates to a commercial and personal connection of emigration and of trade, but it does not say that it shall last ten years or twenty years, or any other period. It is interminable in its provisions. It does not provide that we shall give notice in a certain way, or that they shall give notice in a certain way. There is no provision in the world by which you can terminate it unless you take the initiative, as is proposed now.

Somebody must necessarily take the initiative. The Senator from Ohio says he would go to the Emperor and make certain representations. Then I ask the honorable Senator: Suppose the Emperor should refuse, what would he do then? Suppose the Emperor should say "you have entered into a treaty with us for all time; its very terms show that there was to be no limit to it." Now I ask the honorable Senator from Ohio what he would do then? Suppose we are unanimously of opinion here that the treaty ought not to continue, what would the honorable Senator do in case the Emperor should say, "I desire to stand by that treaty"? What then?

SENATOR MATTHEWS.—I should take it into consideration. [Laughter.]

SENATOR BLAINE.—That is a very exact, executive way of doing things. [Laughter.] That is just about what I supposed.

The Senator read us a lesson upon the great obligations that rested upon us as a nation of honorable people, as if we were about to do something in the way of terminating a treaty which would give us a bad name and fame among the nations of the earth.

Now, in answer to the honorable Senator, I say this, that it has been the usual habit of nations, and is laid down in the very *principia* of the law of nations, that, when a people find a treaty that is "pernicious to the nation," the very words of Vattel, it may terminate it, and we took advantage of a French authority on a very memorable occasion. The treaty that we made with France in 1778, which was considered the origin of the strength that gave us success in the Revolution, contained this article:

Neither of the two parties shall conclude either truce or peace with Great Britain without the formal consent of the other, first obtained.

And the French afterward said that the Americans, without giving them the slightest notice, "stealthily precipitated" a peace and left them open either to war or negotiation, and when we were accused of it we turned to their own author and said this was an absolute and essential thing to the life of our people; we were compelled to do it and we did do it. Self-preservation is the first law of nations as well as of nature, and we used it.

Proceeding to the second branch of the subject, I lay down this principle, that so far as my vote is concerned I will not admit a man to immigration to this country that I am not willing to place on the basis of a citizen. We ought not to admit in this country of universal suffrage the immigration of a great people, great in numbers, whom we ourselves declare are utterly unfit to become citizens.

What do we say on that point? In the Senate of the United States on the 4th day of July, 1870, a patriotic day, we were amending the naturalization laws. We had made all the negroes of the United States voters practically; at least we had said they should not be deprived of suffrage by reason of race or color. We had admitted them all, and we then amended the naturalization laws so that the gentleman from Africa himself could become a citizen of the United States; and an immigrant from Africa to-morrow, from the coast of Guinea or Senegambia, can be naturalized and made an American citizen. Then Senator Trumbull moved to add:

Or persons born in the Chinese Empire.

There was a vote of 31 against 9 in a Senate three-fourths Republican declaring that the Chinaman never ought to be made a citizen. I think that settles the whole question if that was a correct vote, because you cannot in our system of government as it is to-day, with safety to all, permit a large immigration of people who are not to be made citizens and take part in the Government. The Senator from California tells us that already the male adult Chinese in California are more numerous than the white voters. It seems to me that, if we adopt as a permanent policy the free immigration of those who by overwhelming votes in both branches of Congress we say shall forever remain political and social pariahs in a great free government, we have introduced an element that we cannot handle. You cannot stop where we are; you are compelled to do one of two things, either exclude the immigration of Chinese or include them in the great family of citizens.

The argument is often put forward that there is no particular danger of numbers coming here; that it is not a practical question; and, as the honorable Senator from Ohio is free to answer, I ask him if the number should mount up into the millions what would be his view then?

SENATOR MATTHEWS.—I would say that, when there was a reasonable apprehension by the United States of the immigration mounting up to such numbers, then I would take that into consideration.

SENATOR BLAINE.—Take that into consideration! The Senator is definite. That is practical legislation! That is legislating for an evil upon us to-day! The Senator's statesmanship is certainly of a considerate kind.

Well, what about the question of numbers? Did it ever occur to my honorable friend from Ohio that the incalculable hordes in China are much nearer to the Pacific coast of the United States, in point of expense of reaching it, than the people of Kansas?

Ought we to exclude them? The question lies in my mind thus: either the Anglo-Saxon race will possess the Pacific slope or the Mongolians will possess it. You give them the start to-day, with the keen thrust of necessity behind them, and with the ease of transportation before them, with the inducements to come, while we are filling up the other portions of the continent, and it is entirely inevitable if not demonstrable that they will occupy that great space of country between the Sierras and the Pacific coast. They are themselves to-day establishing steamship lines; they are themselves to-day providing the means of transportation; and, when gentlemen say that we admit from all other countries, where do you find the slightest parallel? And in a republic especially, in any government that maintains itself, the unit of order and of administration is in the family. The immigrants that come to us from all portions of the British Isles, from Germany, from Sweden, from Norway, from Denmark, from France, from Spain, from Italy, come here with the idea of the family as much engraven on their minds and in their customs and in their habits as we have it. The Asiatic cannot go on with our population and make a homogeneous element. The idea of comparing European immigration with an immigration that has no regard to family, that does not recognize the relation of husband and wife, that does not observe the tie of parent and child, that does not have in the slightest degree the ennobling and the civilizing influences of the hearthstone and the fireside! Why when gentlemen talk loosely about emigration from European states as contrasted with that, they certainly are forgetting history and forgetting themselves.

My honorable colleague [Hannibal Hamlin] and the Senator from Wisconsin [Timothy O. Howe] voted that the Chinaman ought not to be a citizen of this country, voted that he ought not to become a voter in this country. My honorable friend says *sotto voce* that he did not vote that he never should; but you are like the honorable Senator from Ohio; you voted "no," and then proceeded to take the question "into consideration" [laughter], which you have been doing for ten years. When the question was up, whether the Chinaman should be a subject of naturalization, you said "no." I think that vote largely precipitated the trouble. I think the Chinaman in California, if he is to be forced upon us in great numbers, would be safer as a voter, dangerous as that would be, than as a political pariah.

SENATOR HOWE.—Why not apply that remedy?

SENATOR BLAINE.—I am talking about a choice of evils. That is not the remedy. You do not remedy one evil by putting in another evil. I want to remove both. That is no remedy at all. You only present me another evil. I am opposed to the Chinese coming here; I am opposed to making them citizens; I am opposed to making them voters.

HENRY L. DAWES [Mass.].—I should like to be certain about this matter of the naturalization of Chinamen. They naturalize Chinamen in my State.

MR. BLAINE.—The United States laws are directly in the teeth of that.

SENATOR SARGENT.—The United States circuit court in San Francisco, on a test case and in a very able opinion delivered by Judge Sawyer, held that under the laws of the United States Chinamen cannot be naturalized.[1]

[1] This case was "In re Ah Yup," 5 Sawyer, 155. The date of the decision was April 29, 1878.

Section 2169 United States Revised Statutes reads: "The provisions of this title (the naturalization act) shall apply to aliens being free white persons, and to aliens of African nativity and to persons of African descent."

In this case the Court said: "This being the *first application* made by a native Chinaman for naturalization, members of the bar were requested by the Court to make such suggestions as *amici curiae* as occurred to them upon either side of the question. Question: Is a person of the Mongolian race a 'white person' within the meaning of the statute?' The Court cites effort of Senator Sumner in Congress at time of passage of Amendment of the naturalization act, 1870, to strike out the word "white" from naturalization laws, and debate by Senator Morton and others as reported in *Congressional Globe*, pt. 6, 1869-70, p. 5122.

"It was clear Congress retained the word 'white' in naturalization laws for sole purpose of excluding Chinese from the right of naturalization . . . . . .

SENATOR BLAINE.—I will repeat my question: Should we be justified sitting still here in the administration of this Government and permitting this treaty and the immigration which it allows to go forward until those three States should be over-ridden by that population?

SENATOR HAMLIN.—When the sky falls we shall catch larks. The statistics show that in the last thirty years the immigration hence from China has exceeded a little four thousand a year.

SENATOR BLAINE.—Still my honorable colleague is evading the question, not answering it.

SENATOR HAMLIN.—I am not going to evade it. I will come a little nearer my colleague than the Senator from Ohio; I will take it into consideration now. When the time shall come that I become satisfied that the population of China will over-run our country, and there shall be danger or imminent peril from that immigration, I will join with my colleague in abrogating all treaties with them. I will not meet the case by an attempt to abrogate a treaty upon a little point while we are the beneficiaries in the great and substantial points. I am indifferent to all the danger that shall come away down into the stillness of ages from the immigration of the Chinese. Treat them, I will not say like pagans, because Confucius would shame us if we go to his counsel—treat them like Christians, and they will become good American citizens. [Applause in the galleries.]

SENATOR BLAINE.—Still the wonder grows with me that if the aggregate immigration is so small and will remain so small, as my colleague states, he should still have thought that they ought not to be citizens, and could not be safely trusted with the elective franchise.

The Senator from Ohio [Mr. Matthews] made light of race trouble. I supposed if there was any part of the world where a man would not make light of race trouble it was here. I supposed if there was any people in the world that had a race trouble on hand it was ourselves. I supposed if the admonitions of our own history were anything to us we should regard the race trouble as the one thing to be dreaded and the one thing to be avoided. We are not through with it yet. It cost us a great many lives; it cost us a great many millions of treasure. Does any man feel that we are safely through with it now?

"I am therefore of the opinion that a native of China, of the Mongolian race, is not a white person within the meaning of the [said] act of Congress." . . . . "The petition must be denied, and it is so ordered."

Does any man here to-day assume that we have so entirely solved and satisfactorily settled on a permanent basis all the troubles growing out of the negro race trouble that we are prepared to invite another one? If so, he views history differently from myself. If any gentleman looking into the future of this country sees, for certain sections of it at least, peace and good order and absolute freedom from any trouble growing out of race, he sees with more sanguine eyes than mine. With this trouble upon us here, not by our fault, to deliberately sit down and invite another or permit another and far more serious trouble seems to be the very recklessness of statesmanship.

Treat them like Christians, my friend says, and yet I believe the Christian testimony from the Pacific coast is that the conversion of Chinese on that basis is a fearful failure; that the demoralization of the white is much more rapid by reason of the contact than the salvation of the Chinese race, and that up to this time there has been no progress whatever made. I think I heard the honorable Senator from California who sits on this side of the Chamber [Mr. Booth] say that there was not, as we understand it, in all the one hundred and twenty thousand Chinese, more or less (whether I state the number aright or not does not matter), there did not exist among the whole of them the relation of family. There is not a peasant's cottage inhabited by a Chinaman; there is not a hearth-stone, in the sense we understand it, of an American home, or an English home, or a German home, or a French home. There is not a domestic fireside in that sense, and yet you say that it is entirely safe to sit down here and permit that to grow up in our country. If it were a question of fifty years ago I admit with my colleague it would not be practicable. Means of communication, ease of access, cheapness of transportation have changed the issue and forced upon our attention a crisis in it. I undertake to believe at least that if the Congress of the United States should decide adversely, in effect confirming the treaty and the status of immigration as it now is, you cannot maintain law and order in California without the interposition of the military five years hence. Do I overstate that?

SENATOR SARGENT.—I am sorry to say that I think the Senator does not overstate it.

SENATOR BLAINE.—I do not justify the brutality of the treatment of those Chinese who are here; it is greatly to be regretted; it is greatly to be condemned, but you must deal with things as you find them. If you foresee a conflict upon that coast by reason of an immigration that calls for the interposition of the military, I think it is a good deal cheaper and more direct way to avoid the trouble by preventing the immigration.

I have heard a good deal about their cheap labor. I do not myself believe in cheap labor. I do not believe cheap labor should be an object of legislation, and it will not be in a republic. You cannot have the wealthy classes in a republic, where suffrage is universal, legislate for cheap labor. I undertake to repeat that. I say that you cannot have the wealthy classes in a republic where suffrage is universal legislate in what is called the interest of cheap labor. Labor should not be cheap and it should not be dear; it should have its share, and it will have its share. There is not a laborer on the Pacific coast to-day who does not feel wounded and grieved and crushed by the competition that comes from this source. Then the answer is, "Well, are not American laborers equal to Chinese laborers?" I answer that question by asking another. Were not free white laborers equal to African slaves in the South? When you tell me that the Chinaman driving out the free American laborer only proves the superiority of the Chinaman, I ask you, did the African slave labor driving out the free white labor from the South prove the superiority of slave labor? The conditions are not unlike; the parallel is not complete, and yet it is a parallel. It is servile labor; it is not free labor such as we intend to develop and encourage and build up in this country. It is labor that comes here under a mortgage. It is labor that comes here to subsist on what the American laborer cannot subsist on. You cannot work a man who must have beef and bread, and would prefer beer, alongside of a man who can live on rice. It cannot be done. In all such conflicts and in all such struggles the result is not to bring up the man who lives on rice to the beef and bread standard, but it is to bring down the beef and bread man to the rice standard. [Manifestations of applause in the galleries.] Slave labor degraded free labor; it took out its respectability; it put an odious caste upon it. It throttled the prosperity of a fine and fair portion of the United States, and a worse than slave labor will throttle and impair the prosperity of a still finer and fairer section of the United States. We can choose here to-day whether our legislation shall be in the interest of the American free laborer or for the servile laborer from China.

In conclusion, or, by summary, I maintain that this legislation is in the strictest accord with international obligation. We have given notice, and the Chinese Empire has itself violated the treaty. Whether you take it on the one ground or the other, we are entirely justified in the legislation proposed. They have never lived for one month on their side by the terms of the treaty. A treaty, I repeat, which is interminable, so far as its own language is involved, when one party or the other desires it to be terminated, must be terminated by just such action as this bill proposes. That question out, the only one we have to regard is whether on the whole we will devote that interesting and important section of the United States to be the home and the refuge of our own people and our own blood, or whether we will continue to leave it open, not to the competition of other nations like ourselves, but to those who, degraded themselves, will inevitably degrade us. We have this day to choose whether we will have for the Pacific coast the civilization of Christ or the civilization of Confucius. [Applause in the galleries.]

On February 15 Hannibal Hamlin [Me.] opposed the bill.

We negotiated a treaty with a friendly and a foreign power. We, in connection with other governments, forced that treaty upon that power. We battered down a wall of commercial restriction that had surrounded the Chinese government in the long ages of the past, almost as restrictive as that Chinese wall that preserved that empire from the Tartar hordes of the North. We secured the right of trial by jury of our own citizens in that empire, which opened up a given number of ports which should be accessible for the commerce of our country, and we granted in return the immigration of Chinese subjects to our own country. Why, sir, who does not remember with what welcome, with what rejoicing that treaty was hailed upon the Pacific coast. To say that they honored it is hardly adequate. That they did homage to the men who negotiated it is nearer the truth. Now, it is affirmed that that treaty is injurious to our friends on that coast, and from its effects they desire to be relieved.

Mr. President, if there is wrong, if there are evils to be corrected, if there is that which demands the interference of the American Congress to correct an existing condition of things, I am as ready as any member upon this floor to apply the proper remedy. I am not willing, however, to apply that remedy of might which subverts the remedy of right. What is, then, the true statement of the case practically as it is presented right here and now? Let us look at it as a practical question. We are asked to secure a modification of the treaty thus negotiated which allows an unlimited immigration from the Chinese Empire to this country. That is the precise question, and it is sought in direct contravention of the fifth article of the treaty to limit that immigration. Is it a desirable thing to do? I will not stop to consider that, but, conceding it to be a desirable thing to do, what is the mode in which it should be done? And that brings us directly to the division which we have here upon this question. I would proceed by the ordinary rules of negotiation; I would treat that empire as I would treat every civilized nation upon the earth, and I believe that there are few Senators on this floor who would be willing to treat a war-like power of Europe in the summary manner in which this bill proposes to treat the Empire of China. I would first make the distinct proposition to that empire to treat. On their failing to treat, after full and ample notice, I would say then that we might take the matter into our own consideration and apply the remedy which in our own judgment should be demanded.

What has been, Mr. President, the practice of our Government in matters very similar to this? Only a few years since, when the British government undertook to interpolate into the extradition treaty of 1842 words which should exonerate them from surrendering fugitives from this country to theirs, by insisting upon certain declarations on the part of our Government that the person claimed should not be tried for other offences than those for which the reclamation was demanded, we denied the right. What did Secretary Fish say? "The United States adheres to the position announced in my former instruction, that it will recognize no power to alter or attach conditions to an existing treaty without its previous consent," and he declares in the same dispatch the binding obligations of treaty provisions "upon all courts, both State and national," and, further, "while the treaty shall be in force the Government of the United States would be strangely forgetful of the dignity and rights of the country if a foreign state were permitted to exact stipulations or engagements pursuant to *her* law, but foreign to the treaty, as a condition of obtaining the performance of treaty stipulations."

Here is the proposition of our Government in a case parallel as nearly as may be with that which is presented to us for our consideration. I have stated that we have a power to abrogate a treaty. We may abrogate it in gross or we may abrogate it upon an immaterial point, but we may not suppose for a single moment that if we seek to annul and abrogate a single clause in that treaty it will remain binding upon the part of the government of the other party that negotiated it with us. So, if we shall abrogate that article which allows the free immigration of Chinese into this country, it is an annulment and an abrogation of that treaty in all its parts if the Emperor of China shall so think fit to regard it.

It has been said that this treaty has been violated on the part of China; that she has passed no law in conformity with the sixth article of the treaty, regulating the free emigration of her citizens to this country. I have only to say that that is simply a declaration. We have had no evidence of it here, none whatever. We have not been advised whether China has or has not passed the laws or ordinance or edicts of the empire required within the provisions of the treaty. I may say, then, that this was a simple declaration, a simple assumption upon which the argument is raised that we are released from our obligations under the treaty because China has not fulfilled her obligations.

Mr. President, all these general assumptions are erroneous, and I feel that I am authorized to state here and now that the Emperor of China did issue immediately, or very soon after the treaty was promulgated, his edict to the viceroyalties of the empire, enjoining against any and all forcible transportation of Chinese people to any foreign country or government.

JOHN H. MITCHELL [Ore.].—Has it been enforced?

SENATOR HAMLIN.—I will go further, and the penalty was made death whenever the laws should be violated. Not only this; the emperor has in some cases issued his edicts against transportation with the consent of the emigrants, when learning that misrepresentations of promised advantages led to the transportation of his people where they were badly treated; notably one case was against the transportation to Peru with their consent.

I have looked very carefully at the revised statutes of the United States, and I fail to find the first word of any law that we have passed to meet that obligation upon us which it is alleged the Chinese government have not complied with. Then we are the party derelict, and not the Chinese government.

It is alleged next that, the Emperor of China having violated this provision, we are at liberty to apply any remedy which in our judgment we shall deem right, or in other words we are at liberty to apply the precise remedy named in this bill.

The emperor of China has done his duty more fully than we have done ours. He has complied with every term and letter of the articles of the treaty. We have not.

Now, is it expedient? and that brings me to the question, is it right? It has been said that we can maintain no very considerable population in our midst who have not the right of suffrage. I am very sorry to say that I am inclined to concur very much in that proposition, and when I do so it is a reflection on our own Government which I am indeed sorry to make. I regret that every man of every creed and of every clime may not come here, and, obedient to the law and obeying it in all its parts, may not receive its protection.

But we do know from the condition of things in a certain portion of the country that such is not the fact. We cannot wink it out of sight. In this connection was read a record from the *Congressional Globe* of certain Senators who had voted upon a certain question. I suppose if it had any pertinency it was to show their inconsistency on this question. And it is affirmed that said vote referred to is a declaration that Chinese in this country are never to be allowed the rights of naturalization. Allow me to say, it means no such thing, it proves no such thing. Let us see.

The amendment striking "white" from the naturalization laws was adopted, myself voting for it. Subsequently at another stage I voted against the amendment, as did those who had previously voted with me for it. And why? It was upon a bill regulating elections. Then we were told in consultation that with that amendment attached the bill must fail. There was a greater good to be accomplished than this one thing, and to accomplish the greater good there were those of us who were willing to change our position, and we did change it. I myself moved to reconsider the vote by which that amendment was adopted, stating in just so many words that my opinion had not changed, but as a matter of consultation the wisest thing to do, the best thing to do (and in that I was sustained by the best men of the body), was to pass the bill without that amendment. We came to the conclusion that then and there upon that bill was not the appropriate time or place to put that amendment, and for those considerations we voted to reconsider our action.

We have four million colored population that had come to us from a state of servitude, and it was a question wisely to be considered whether we would add then and at that same time another element and another class who were to be assimilated to us, who were to be educated, who were to understand the rights, who were to learn the duties that belonged to American citizenship, and I thought we might postpone for a limited period when we would bring in the Chinaman and give to him the ballot. I know other Senators voted from the same considerations.

But, sir, I am a little inclined to think that I made a mistake in the vote to which attention has been drawn. I am a little inclined to think that if all the Chinamen in our land had the ballot in their hands to-day we should not have heard a word of this Chinese question here. I think that is a key to a solution of the whole question. I am willing to admit them to naturalization. I think all persons who come here to make their permanent home ought to participate in our Government, ought to be citizens, and ought to have the right of franchise conferred upon them. I voted for it once; I will vote for it again; and, I believe, Mr. President, that if you will treat these people upon the Pacific slope with common humanity they will assimilate, not, perhaps, as readily as other nationalities to our institutions, but within a reasonable time.

The Senator from California has drawn a graphic and a revolting picture of the social condition of some of these Chinamen, but there are other social evils still more revolting upon which the genius of my friend from California could give us pictures even more shocking than those he has already drawn. Nor is there a class of immigrants coming to us from any nationality among whom you cannot find men in whom you may discover in person, in morals, in all the attributes almost that belong to humanity, as much to revolt us as that which belongs to the lower orders of the Chinese.

I am not going to tire the patience of the Senate by a discussion of the labor question. I have very clear ideas about it. Very much of this talk against "cheap labor" would apply with equal force against every improvement in your machinery. They tell you the Chinese consume nothing and work cheap. Well, the lady's sewing-machine that she takes into her parlor and uses sometimes as a recreation and sometimes as a task supplants the necessity of the sewing-maid and thereby diminishes the compensation or the rate of wages of the sewing-maid. Your reapers that traverse the vast fields and savannas of California, all your labor-saving machinery, indirectly, not as directly, affect the laborer. But my opinion is that this is a thing temporary in its nature. Treat the incoming immigrant as he ought to be treated, give him the protection of law, and make his home sacred to him, and my judgment is that it will require a very limited period of time in which to solve the whole problem. A man comes from a distant country where labor is lower than here; he does not adopt the lower scale of labor if he is skilled to occupy the higher grade, nor does it diminish the compensation of labor unless the supply is beyond the demand. But I insist that this labor in California of Chinese has advanced that State a century beyond where she would now be had she been deprived of it. What say the best men? Public opinion is divided; when you count numbers I concede it is largely against the Chinese population, but when you take the intelligent, the cool, the deliberate, and the Christian portion of that population, there is a very respectable minority in that State who tell you that the Chinese have built their railroads, have reclaimed their tule lands, and that uncounted millions of wealth have been added to that State which without the labor of the Chinese would not be in existence to-day. There are some of the best men in that State who tell us that they are a people observant of law, that they are cleanly in their habits, and that they are a desirable class of population as laborers. With all this diversity of opinion, I am not to be drawn into a minute discussion of the effect of the labor question there, because it can be but temporary.

There is another view of the question, Mr. President, broad and national, which addresses itself to the man of Maine, to the citizen of Louisiana, of Virginia, of Georgia, or of New York alike. It is the commercial aspect of this question in which we have an undivided and a common interest. We have a great deal said in these days about reviving the commerce of our country. There is here a great question of commercial intercourse, and it affects every State in this Union; it addresses itself to every man who would aid in bringing back the commerce of our country to what it was a few years since. Our importations and our exportations to China but a few years ago were limited to two or three millions of dollars. What are they to-day? Twenty-four million dollars. And of what do our exportations consist? A particular quality of the cotton goods of the North is finding an open market in China, and we exported to Hong Kong during the last year very considerably exceeding two and a half million dollars in value of that fabric. We sent from the port of San Francisco alone more than a million dollars' worth of breadstuffs, showing that by commercial intercourse we are inducing the Chinese to take our flour in place of their rice.

XI—17

SENATOR EDMUNDS.—That flour is grown on the fields of California.

SENATOR HAMLIN.—And that flour is grown upon the Pacific coast, produced, more or less, by "Chinese cheap labor!"

Let me say here that Chinese labor averages more to-day than is paid to the laborer in my State. "Chinese cheap labor!" It is a canting cry, it is a cry addressed to the prejudices, not to the cool judgment of men. "Chinese cheap labor!" My colleague knows that I have been a manual laborer from my boyhood to this hour, and God knows that there can be no sympathy that man should possess that is not in my heart in favor of the productive labor of our country, but, while I am thus in favor of that labor, I will not violate a great and a fundamental principle of my Government. We will welcome within its borders the native of every clime and of every country, and be he pagan or be he Hottentot, be he of this or of that creed, let us receive him here within the arms of a Christian civilization, that civilization which we believe to be the best on earth, the civilization of Christ, and if we cannot overcome paganism or any other ism in all the broad earth when we send missionaries to convert them, if we cannot overcome their system of government, their system of prejudices or religion or the want of religion, then when that shall be demonstrated it will be time enough to tell me that they shall not come here, and when I see in the great productive industries of the country that this labor as a whole produces wealth that otherwise would not be produced, and that though an inequality exists it can be but brief in its existence, I have no fear of this talk about "cheap Chinese labor."

I see, Mr. President, a mighty country, an empire upon the Pacific; I look at its vast resources of soil, of forest, of mine, of water that rolls its way to its own vast ocean home unvexed by the utilizing hand of man. I want no vision to tell me what shall be that empire of commerce, of arts, and of agriculture that in the future shall arise upon that coast. I look beyond, and I see the mighty commerce that shall come from India to us if we are wise, if we do not do that which shall compel the Emperor of China to retaliate upon us and to make reprisals. Who believes that, if we to-day shall determine that but fifteen Chinamen shall come to this country in each vessel from the Empire of China, he will not say but fifteen barrels of that flour which goes in uncounted thousands from California shall be the limit that shall be taken upon any vessel that traverses the Pacific to China? Who does not believe that if we place unnecessary and harassing restrictions upon the Chinese government, if we violate our plighted faith and national honor to them, they will not feel exonerated and retaliate upon us? Oh, I cannot bear to see a stop put to the untold millions of commerce that shall roll to our shores; I cannot bear to see that uncounted commerce that shall go from us to them interfered with. I can see how it shall stimulate the industries of our land, how it shall benefit the operative and the manufacturer alike, how it shall benefit the Government and the citizens, and I can see too how it may be obliterated or retarded or prevented.

We to-day who are against this bill are not against redressing every grievance that needs or rightfully demands redress. We have passed and rightfully passed legislation very strict against coolie immigration. It does not exist to-day. No Chinaman can come here to-day without the clear certificate of the consul of Hong Kong, and nine hundred and ninety-nine out of every thousand that come here have come from the British port of Hong Kong.

I shall vote against the measure, and I leave that vote the last legacy to my children that they may esteem it the brightest act of my life.

The Senate passed the bill by a vote of 39 to 27.

President Hayes vetoed the bill on March 1. He gave the following reasons for his action:

A denunciation of a treaty by any government is confessedly justifiable only upon some reason both of the highest justice and of the highest necessity. The action of Congress in the matter of the French treaties in 1798, if it be regarded as an abrogation by this nation of a subsisting treaty, strongly illustrates the character and degree of justification which were then thought suitable to such a proceeding. The preamble of the act recites that "the treaties concluded between the United States and France have been repeatedly violated on the part of the French government, and the just claims of the United States for reparation of the injuries so committed have been refused, and their attempts to negotiate an amicable adjustment of all complaints between the two nations have been repelled with indignity," and that "under authority of the French government there is yet pursued against the United States a system of predatory violence, infracting the said treaties, and hostile to the rights of a free and independent nation.''

The history of the Government shows no other instance of an abrogation of a treaty by Congress.

Instances have sometimes occurred where the ordinary legislation of Congress has, by its conflict with some treaty obligation of the Government toward a foreign power, taken effect as an infraction of the treaty, and been judicially declared to be operative to that result. But neither such legislation nor such judicial sanction of the same has been regarded as an abrogation, even for the moment, of the treaty. On the contrary, the treaty in such case still subsists between the Governments, and the casual infraction is repaired by appropriate satisfaction in maintenance of the treaty.

The bill before me does not enjoin upon the President the abrogation of the entire Burlingame treaty, much less of the principal treaty of which it is made the supplement. As the power of modifying an existing treaty, whether by adding or striking out provisions, is a part of the treaty-making power under the Constitution, its exercise is not competent for Congress, nor would the assent of China to this partial abrogation of the treaty make the action of Congress, in thus procuring an amendment of a treaty, a competent exercise of authority under the Constitution. The importance, however, of this special consideration seems superseded by the principle that a denunciation of a part of a treaty, not made by the terms of the treaty itself separable from the rest, is a denunciation of the whole treaty. As the other high contracting party has entered into no treaty obligations except such as include the part denounced, the denunciation by one party of the part necessarily liberates the other party from the whole treaty.

I am convinced that, whatever urgency might in any quarter or by any interest be supposed to require an instant suppression of further immigration from China, no reasons can require the immediate withdrawal of our treaty protection of the Chinese already in this country, and no circumstances can tolerate an exposure of our citizens in China, merchants or missionaries, to the consequences of so sudden an abrogation of their treaty protections. Fortunately, however, the actual recession in the flow of the emigration from China to the Pacific coast, shown by trustworthy statistics, relieves us from any apprehension that the treatment of the subject in the proper course of diplomatic negotiations will introduce any new features of discontent or disturbance among the communities directly affected. Were such delay fraught with more inconveniences than have ever been suggested by the interests which are most earnest in promoting this legislation, I cannot but regard the summary disturbance of our existing treaties with China as greatly more inconvenient to much wider and more permanent interests of the country.

The vote in the House to pass the bill over the President's veto resulted: 110 yeas, 96 nays. James A. Gar-

WHAT MAY COME TO PASS

From a Cartoon in New York "Truth," during the Presidential Campaign of 1880

field [O.] was one of those voting in the negative.[1] The requisite two-thirds majority not having been secured, the bill did not become a law.

Early in the session of 1881-82 John F. Miller [Cal.] introduced in the Senate a bill "to execute certain treaty stipulations relating to Chinese." It was referred to the Committee on Foreign Relations, which, on January 26, 1882, reported a bill on the subject, with the following provisions:

1.   That the immigration of Chinese laborers shall be suspended for twenty years.

2.   That masters of vessels bringing such Chinese shall be fined not more than $500 for each Chinaman, and may be imprisoned not over one year.

3.   That the act do not apply to Chinese formerly in this country, nor to Chinese in transit to foreign ports, nor to vessels making an American port in distress.

4.   That Chinese leaving this country are to be readmitted upon certificates of residence here.

5.   That Chinese entitled to enter this country under the Burlingame treaty and this act are to have passports and identification papers from the Chinese government.

6.   That such Chinese shall be registered by the Treasury (Customs) Department.

7.   That certificates of such registration shall be given to the Chinese registered.

8.   That persons assisting in evasions or frauds connected with such registration shall be fined not over $1,000 and imprisoned not more than five years.

9.   That shipmasters shall make manifests of Chinese immigrants in forms, and under penalties for infraction, provided in case of manifests of cargoes.

10-14.   These sections related to details, penalties, etc., of preceding provisions.

15.   That officers of Chinese government and their servants shall be exempt from the act.

16.   That Chinese shall not be admitted to citizenship by State or United States courts.

17.   "Laborers" to be construed as skilled and unskilled laborers and miners.

[1] For the part which Chinese exclusion played in Garfield's campaign for President, see Garfield, James A., in Index of Proper Names, Vol. XIV.

After a thorough discussion, in which the familiar arguments for and against Chinese immigration were repeated, and the question was debated of whether or not the act violated in letter and in spirit our treaty obligations with China, the bill was passed by the Senate on March 9, 1882, by a vote of 29 to 15. After a similar debate in the House it was there passed on March 23 by a vote of 167 to 66. It was vetoed by President Arthur on April 4 because it repudiated our treaty obligations with China.

The Senate voted on passing the bill over the veto upon April 5: yeas 29, nays 21. As the affirmative vote was less than the two-thirds required to pass the measure, the veto was sustained.

The bill was then amended so as to remove the objections of the President, was passed by the House and the Senate, and signed by him on May 6, 1882.

On January 7, 1884, Barclay Henley [Cal.] introduced in the House a bill amending this act. It was referred to the Committee on Foreign Affairs. The majority reported it, and on May 3 it came up for discussion before the Committee of the Whole.

William W. Rice [Mass.] presented the minority report of the committee, and moved to amend the proposed bill by striking out the words "subjects of China or any other foreign power." His motion was voted down *viva voce*. The bill was passed by a vote of 184 to 13. The Senate passed it on July 3 by a vote of 43 to 12, and it was approved by President Arthur on July 7, 1884.

On July 11, 1888, Joseph N. Dolph [Ore.], from the Committee on Foreign Relations, announced in the Senate that a bill committed to the committee, relating to the execution of certain treaty stipulations with China, was reported adversely, and in its place he reported favorably a bill to prohibit the coming of Chinese laborers to this country. The second bill came forward for discussion on July 20.

After considerable debate, in which the speakers attempted to make party capital out of former action upon the question of Chinese exclusion, and all declared themselves in favor of the present bill, this was passed on August 8.

RECORD OF GENERAL HARRISON ON THE CHINESE QUESTION

HOUSE OF REPRESENTATIVES, AUGUST 18-20, 1888

On August 9 the House referred the bill to the Committee on Foreign Affairs, which reported it on August 18. The debate followed the same lines as that in the Senate. The Democratic speakers attempted to show, in particular, that Benjamin Harrison, the Republican candidate for President, had opposed the exclusion of Chinese laborers while a member of the Senate, referring to his vote against the bill for the suspension of Chinese immigration for twenty years, introduced in 1881 by Senator Miller [Cal.].

On this point William D. Bynum [Ind.] said:

In 1880 in the city of Indianapolis a number of Chinamen were induced by Republicans to declare their intentions of becoming citizens. Upon this declaration they were marched to the polls and voted the Republican ticket. That General Harrison was cognizant of the intentions of his party to vote these persons there can be no doubt. He was the candidate of his party for the United States Senate, active in politics, and the oaths were administered to them by his most intimate friend and loyal supporter. In addition to this it has been publicly charged in the Indianapolis *Sentinel,* and not denied by him, that during the agitation of this question he read a production before a literary club in that city advocating in strong terms the right of the Chinese to become citizens of the United States.

Why, Mr. Speaker, the Republican party had such a tender regard for the rights of the Chinese that it placed joss-sticks and joss-lights on the free-list while the Bible was made to bear a duty of 25 per cent. [Laughter and applause on Democratic side.]

I notice, however, that General Harrison and his friends offer another excuse for his position on this question. They say that he did not understand the question at the time, but that he has since learned all about it and is all right now. Of all the subterfuge that has been attempted this certainly is the shallowest. This question had engaged the serious attention of the American Congress, when he entered the Senate, for more than ten years.

It had agitated the minds of the people and especially the laboring classes for over twelve years. General Harrison's entire absence of association with and want of sympathy for the great masses of the people may have destroyed his intuition of this question, but, if he had never heard of the subject before he entered the Senate, he heard enough during the debate to have satisfied any person with one spark of sympathy for that class of our citizens who were compelled to earn their bread by the sweat of their brow. He may daily mount his platform during this campaign and declare "that the standard of American wages must be maintained," but I challenge any one to point out a single word or expression of sympathy by him for the wage-earners during this entire debate. From the beginning to the end he remained callous, heartless, and immovable to every appeal. [Applause.]

On August 20 Joseph McKenna [Cal.] replied to Mr. Bynum.

The attempt to make politics out of the Chinese question is ludicrous. It is ludicrous even in a Democratic Congress. [Laughter.] If there is any question that I had supposed was settled, that has passed from dispute to conviction, it is the Chinese question, and how thoroughly idle it is, how thoroughly nauseous it is to recur from the final and settled stages of a question to the first and disputable stages I need not emphasize. But, sir, it appears that the Democratic party is always doing this. It loves to delve among dead things, and is never so happy as when it is buzzing about a corpse. Why, sir, from the action of some of its members I should think that the only light that it cares to shine by is the light of decay and putrescence.

But I am surprised at the gentleman from Indiana. He has been an active member—his face to the front, and to the future. He has not heretofore appeared in the rôle of the antiquary or the grub. [Laughter.] This has been the office of the antique Congressmen who have been in so many Congresses that they have become fond of relics, and think the mummy of an issue better than a live issue.

But, Mr. Speaker, as the gentleman from Indiana has always been an active member and has always lived in the present, he ought to have known, and I have no doubt did know, that in the rawness of the first stages of the question opposition is excusable. Afterwards it may be reprehensible; afterwards the important inquiry is not whether one was reluctant to begin, but how strong one is now. Not when one began, but how long has he held out and will he hold out.

Judas Iscariot commenced very early, but he quit as early. Saul of Tarsus commenced later, and preceded his commencement with bitterness and persecution, but his conversion was thorough and constant afterwards, and his teaching and example marched down the ages, and will march down the ages forever and forever. [Applause.]

And, Mr. Speaker, as I can recall the time and movements of his magnificent mission and the glorious eloquence of his addresses to the Ephesians and Corinthians, the eager, entranced multitudes that followed him and loved him, I can also recall some pitiful, piddling Democratic Gentile from an ancient Indiana snapping and snarling and frantically squealing, "Look at his record!" "Look at his record!" [Laughter and applause.]

Mr. Speaker, what would have been the destiny of Christianity if that ancient Indiana Democrat could have been heard? [Laughter.] Look at records! The Democratic party should be the last to recall records. No party has claimed so much or has received so much from the charity which forgets and forgives as has the Democratic party. If we are willing to let bygones be bygones, you should be. Gentlemen, turn from the past. Hail with us the light of the new issue. Its sun has full high advanced and is advancing. Do not avoid or deny it. In the language of another you may raise a smoldering smoke that may obscure it from your own eyes, but you can not strike it from the heavens. But I do not blame you. In its light there is no gladness for you or hope. To you it is the "sun of Austerlitz."

The Democratic party has threatened the industries of the country, and it stands appalled at the doom that awaits it from the indignant workingmen of the country. It is trying to deflect the blow to General Harrison by a conjuration of the Chinese question, but, Mr. Speaker, the attempt will not succeed. The object and purpose of it is too evident. Besides, the principles of that party, if consistently carried out, lead directly to Chinese immigration. I do not mean to say that Democrats are not sincere in their position, but I say if they were consistent under the declaration of their principles they would favor cheap Chinese labor. It is a natural deduction from the economic doctrines they have announced. They declare that they are in favor of cheap goods. Why not be in favor of the cheap cause of cheap goods?

General Harrison opposes Chinese immigration. He has declared so, or he could not be the candidate of the Republican party at this time on its platform, because, sir, coincidently with clear declarations for the protective system is as clear a declaration for the absolute prohibition of Chinese immigration, and the declaration is consistent and just. The prohibition of Chinese immigration is the concretest form of protection to American labor. Under it all the evils of cheap foreign goods and cheap foreign labor are seen the distinctest and felt the bitterest. Through it and on account of it the country has been forced to the conviction that the time has at last come to consider, not to whom it can extend its civilization, but for whom it can preserve it; not to whom it may give liberty, but for whom it may lose liberty; not to whom it may give bread, but for whom it can save bread. These are the alternatives of free trade and protection, and from them, there is also forced this other consideration, that equality and freedom are not alone to be the radiance of the heights, heaven-kissed enough, of ease and wealth, but must illumine and adorn the slopes and levels where struggle is and where labor is, where the nation is and forever must be, and where grace and beauty and happiness must come to it if they come at all. And if they come at all they can only come and stay and grow from protection to American labor. The very essence of the protective system, the very essence of the principles of the Republican party, is exclusion to cheap goods and cheap men, and General Harrison is its chieftain, and will be its President. [Applause on the Republican side.]

Nelson Dingley [Me.] reinforced the last point of Mr. McKenna.

The logic of protection requires that it should be applied not only to the imported products of cheap labor, but also to imported labor under contract made abroad to work at foreign cheap wages. The sober, industrious, voluntary immigrant who comes here to improve his situation and become an American in every sense of the term, and who has entire freedom of choice after his arrival, demands and soon receives American wages, and their coming in such numbers as they are likely to voluntarily leave old homes will not reduce the wages of labor.

On the other hand, the logic of free trade in the products of foreign labor inevitably calls for free trade in imported labor, for, if the American producer is to be compelled to compete freely with the foreign producer, he must be given the privilege of getting his labor in the cheapest market. The latter is the correlative of the former, as Henry George has so clearly shown in an article pointing out that the Democratic leaders, in professing to desire to restrict the incoming of foreign labor, are simply convicting themselves of inconsistency. Every argument presented in the late tariff debate in favor of free trade, or removal of restrictions of importations, applies with equal force to the free importation of labor.

Indeed, the position taken by the gentleman from Indiana, and made the keystone of his argument by the gentleman from Texas [Roger Q. Mills], that our labor measured by results is the cheapest in the world, is as decisive an argument against restricting the importation of contract labor as it was claimed to be against restriction of importations of products.

It is evident, Mr. Speaker, that the appeal of gentlemen on the other side to the workingmen to vote to remove restrictions on the importation of the products of cheap labor, in order to punish a few men who, in defiance of law and largely because the Democratic Administration has not properly enforced the law, have imported cheap labor under contracts made abroad to work at foreign wages, is only a shrewd device of free-traders to obtain assistance in tearing down that system of protection which makes it possible to maintain more than 50 per cent. higher wages on the average in the United States than in Great Britain. Mr. Speaker, this transparent device will fail. [Prolonged applause on the Republican side.]

BENTON McMILLIN [Tenn.].—My distinguished friend from Maine [Mr. Dingley] says that Henry George has written a very true and logical article on the subject of the importation of the products of labor and the importation of the labor itself, and he has just announced gravely to the House that the same logic which asks for bringing in the products of labor free would also require bringing in of the laborer free.

If my distinguished friend from Maine will give me his attention I will suggest to him that if his proposition be true the converse of the proposition would also be true, and the logic is just as sound that those who proclaim in favor of allowing the importation of free labor must also favor the importation free of the articles produced by labor. According to his own reasoning I propose to convict the gentleman of having been a free-trader. Because, Mr. Speaker, as much as it will astound the House, when the question was up for consideration to restrict Chinese immigration in the past the gentleman from Maine on more than one occasion held the ground that it was wrong to do so and improper to keep out the Mongolian race, and voted to allow them to come in. [Applause on the Democratic side.]

MR. DINGLEY.—I declined to vote for a bill that I believed was in contravention of an existing treaty. I have three times voted for the exclusion of the Chinese.

MR. McMILLIN.—And the treaty remained the same all the time! How does the gentleman reconcile his logic? Why did he vote against the act restricting Chinese immigration at all?

MR. DINGLEY.—The act itself will tell.

MR. McMILLIN.—The gentleman has himself simply done what his candidate for the Presidency has done and is doing; he has heard from the people on that question. [Laughter and applause on the Democratic side.]

MR. DINGLEY.—The act itself was so modified as to conform to the treaty, and in my judgment the objections were removed.

MR. McMILLIN.—Now, I do not want this fought out on any improper line, nor shall it be if I can prevent it. We are to have the tariff fight fought over on this subject, it seems. The gentleman would have been deeply interested in getting up a tariff fight, or a chicken fight, or a bull fight, or any other fight that would obscure his own record from the public gaze. He was not content with voting it once, but he voted over and over again against bills to exclude Chinese for all time, and then voted against excluding them for even ten years! That is the consistency that has characterized him. If I am to be criticized and my party is to be hounded down, at least give us the delectable pleasure of being criticized and hounded down by those who have consistent records on the question themselves.

Joseph G. Cannon [Ill.] developed the suggestion of Mr. McKenna, saying that, in the days of the apostles,

"If misrepresentation and garbling the records of public men and of a great party had been a crime, as it was to keep money from the common treasury, and if the gentleman from Indiana had been there, Ananias would have had a surname, and it would have been Bynum." [Laughter.]

The bill was passed without division. It was approved by President Cleveland on September 18, 1888.

CHAPTER VI

RESTRICTION OF IMMIGRATION

Debate in Senate on House Bill Restricting Immigration: Varying Views by Henry Cabot Lodge [Mass.], George G. Vest [Mo.], William E. Chandler [N. H.], Gen. John M. Palmer [Ill.], George F. Hoar [Mass.], John T. Morgan [Ala.], Donelson Caffery [La.], Wilkinson Call [Fla.], Roger Q. Mills [Tex.]; Bill Is Amended and Passed; Conference Appointed; Its Report Adopted by House—Speech of Sen. Charles H. Gibson [Md.] in Opposition to the Amendment of Representative John B. Corliss [Mich.]; Senate Adopts Conference Report—President Vetoes Bill: His Reasons—House Repasses Bill; Senate Commits It.

ON December 9, 1896, a bill excluding illiterate immigrants over 14 years of age, which had been passed by the House during the previous session, was brought forward in the Senate by Henry Cabot Lodge [Mass.], from the Committee on Immigration, where it had been amended to ameliorate certain harsh cases of exclusion, such as that of an aged illiterate who is the parent or grandparent of an admissible immigrant, and to provide a specific and fair test for finding whether the immigrant could read and write in any language.

EXCLUSION OF ILLITERATE IMMIGRANTS

SENATE, DECEMBER 10-17, 1896

On December 10 George G. Vest [Mo.] opposed the provision relative to illiteracy.

Mr. President, it seems to me that this provision ought to be confined to male immigrants. The Senator from Massachusetts [Mr. Lodge] in making the report from the committee gives as the basis for this legislation that the admission of illiterate immigrants debases our citizenship and degrades our labor. Now, there are a large number of young women over the age

270

of 14 years who come to the United States and who are engaged as domestics by the people of this country. Under the laws of the United States in regard to national suffrage they can not vote, and I take it that really at the bottom of this whole question is illiterate suffrage. I do not see how the workmanship or the labor of a man who can not read or write debases the labor or workmanship of anybody else. If he is an industrious, temperate, and honest workman, how does his employment degrade any other labor in this country?

We might just as well be frank with each other in discussing this question. The great objection to illiterate immigration is that it corrupts our suffrage and endangers the basis of our Government, which is the virtue and intelligence of the people. The last report of the Commissioner of Immigration shows that the number of women who come into this country as immigrants is very inconsiderable compared with the men who come as immigrants. It shows, for instance, that from Italy—and I take that as the country which figures most conspicuously in this whole question, because it is from Italy that there comes the most objectionable and the largest immigration—in 1895-1896 there came into the United States 49,980 male immigrants, and in the same year there came 16,465 women immigrants from the same country. The number of women is very inconsiderable, and their coming into this country can neither debase our citizenship nor degrade our labor. I can conceive of no reason except an arbitrary one why this provision should be extended to women.

SENATOR LODGE.—Mr. President, I trust that the amendment to insert the word "male" will not prevail. It would create division of families. Of course it is perfectly true, as the Senator from Missouri says, that the women do not affect the suffrage. I think they affect very largely the quality of citizenship in a somewhat broader way. But the point which seems to me to overrule all others in this consideration is the great body of the unemployed in this country. Every immigrant who comes into the country is some of the unemployed of other lands coming in here.

I will confess that I am very radical upon this question. I should be glad to see immigration stop until every man and woman seeking work in this country have employment. Women certainly work for low wages, and the lines of work for which they compete are overcrowded. I think that that which makes it desirable to exclude the male immigrant makes it just as desirable to exclude the female immigrant. The illiteracy test

is simply an effort to adopt a test which shall restrict immigration, lower the number of immigrants coming to this country,
and do it by shutting out the most undesirable class. That all
persons who can not read and write are undesirable no one
will contend. No form of exclusion can be perfectly accurate,
but it comes as near to it as any test.

Senator Lodge presented petitions in favor of the bill
from a number of labor organizations.

Now, Mr. President, I have read these lists and resolutions
simply to show the Senate that the demand from the people
who feel in daily life this competition goes far beyond anything
the pending bill proposes. The people gathered in our great
cities without employment, who see a constant stream of the
unemployed of other nations pouring in, know that that is
one direct form of competition with them. They may differ
as to other policies in other respects, as to the tariff and the
currency questions, but there is no doubt that they are all united
to-day in feeling that this unrestricted competition of the unemployed of other lands should be prevented. That it affects them,
and affects them badly, no one can doubt. It is perfectly plain
that if there are unemployed here and you pour in additional
unemployed constantly, you add to the chance all the time that
our own unemployed will remain as they are. That, to me, is
the controlling reason for this legislation. That is why it makes
no difference in my mind whether it be the competition with
the labor of women or the competition with the labor of men.
I think at this period we ought to do something to check it.

William E. Chandler [N. H.] replied to Senator Vest.

The Senator has assumed that the principal object in requiring that immigrants shall read and write their own language
is in order that we may have intelligent voters in this Republic,
and he assumes that that rule does not apply to women. I
beg to call the Senator's attention to the fact that the cause
of female suffrage is rapidly growing in this country, and that
in the Western States at the recent election a vast number of
votes of women was cast. Therefore, the distinction which
the Senator is making, if it is a good one, is rapidly disappearing. If I were to have my choice as to requiring the absence
of illiteracy from only one class, I would insist upon it that
the women who come here, the girls of whom the Senator speaks,

shall be compelled to learn to read and write before they come, and would allow the male citizens to come without that qualification.

Mr. President, this is not a severe bill. I call the attention of the Senator from Missouri to the fact that it will not keep out anyone. Anybody can come who chooses, if he will only delay his coming until he learns to read and write his own language. It only requires persons of suitable age and physically capable to learn to read and write, and a man or a woman or a child who wants to come here can simply delay coming long enough to learn the rudiments of education. I ask the Senator from Missouri if that is a very severe qualification. It will not make a difference of over three months in the coming of any human being otherwise entitled to come. Why should not that be required of the females as well as of the males who come?

A man is not the tutor of his own children. It is the mother who teaches the children. The children of this country do not learn to read and write in the schools. They learn to read and write by the family fireside. And who is the teacher? The mother. Where is the greatest danger from illiteracy in the families of this country? Mr. President, it is in the illiteracy of the mother. If the father can read and write and the mother cannot the children will grow up in ignorance. But if the mother can read and write she teaches her children to read and write in the sanctity of her home. With this requirement as to the women who come here we may be sure that the little children who grow up in the families of the immigrants will learn to read and write, not because the laws of the country compel education, as the laws of many of the States do, but because through the pride and the love and affection of the alien mothers who come here their children will be taught the elements of education, which will make them good men and women, and which will make not the voters of this generation, perhaps, but the voters of the next generation, whether they be all males or whether they be males and females alike, intelligent and fit to exercise the suffrage in this Republic of ours.

On December 17 Senator Vest moved to advance the minimum age of exclusion to 16 years. John M. Palmer [Ill.] moved to advance it to 21 years. He said:

This bill as it now stands would present this remarkable state of facts, that the father himself being able to read and

XI—18

write, as required by the bill, his children under 14 years of age might be admitted, but his children over 14 years of age and under 21, members of his family, for whose care and maintenance he would be responsible by the laws of all civilized countries, could not be admitted, and he would be compelled either to return with the whole family or he would be compelled to permit the return of his children between those ages to the country from which they came. In the family relation of a man of fair intelligence the nurture and parental care of the father over his children, in my judgment, would be worth more than mere literary training.

I believe, where young men have sufficient enterprise and energy to emigrate from foreign countries to the United States, the mere spirit of adventure which dictates that migration furnishes an evidence that they are themselves good citizens, bad citizens being excluded by our existing laws.

SENATOR CHANDLER.—Does the Senator realize that this bill is no hardship upon his own statement of the case, because it can only exclude the children of this father and mother and delay them for a period of time sufficient to enable them to educate those children?

SENATOR PALMER.—Mr. President, the remark of the Senator from New Hampshire goes upon the assumption that the father and mother have the means of educating their children and that they have the opportunity of doing so. It means that they will know what the laws of the United States are in that respect; it means an indefinite delay in the matter of emigration. My own observation is that emigration very often is the result of necessity or the result of an ambitious and earnest spirit and desire for the well-being of the emigrant. I can see no reason, assuming that the law is already in force which excludes improper persons, for a regulation like this, aside from its injustice.

I believe in the right of expatriation. I believe in the right of emigration. I believe that this world was made by the Almighty, and that these attempts at controlling the movements of good people are wrong. I admit the right of any government to exclude from its borders persons of bad character, persons addicted to crime, dangerous persons of all classes, but I want to say that I have no idea in the world that the class of persons whom it is really desirable to exclude from the country will be affected by this bill. I understand the dangerous classes more generally read and write than the classes which are not so dangerous.

GEORGE F. HOAR [Mass.].—I should like to observe that this is not really so important a matter as it seems, for it is almost never that you would find two parents, father and mother, both able to read and write and their children unable to do so.

Senator Vest's amendment was agreed to.

In view of the fact that refugees from Cuba were coming to the United States, Senator John T. Morgan [Ala.] offered an amendment admitting them without restriction.

He said in support of his amendment:

My amendment has reference to a particular provision of our treaty with Spain; thousands of immigrants are here, and none of them have been extradited, nor has any demand for their extradition been made. We know perfectly well that there are men here to-day who would be extradited to Spain or to Cuba for trial there for their lives for offences alleged to have been committed against the Spanish Crown if extradition were possible.

Now, why is it not possible? It is because the treaty provides that there shall be no extradition for a political offence.

DONELSON CAFFERY [La.].—Is not the clause in the treaty with Spain that political offences are non-extraditable common to all treaties with foreign nations?

SENATOR MORGAN.—As a general proposition, what the Senator from Louisiana says is true. There is no extradition for political offences, although treaties vary very much in their language as to the definition of political offences.

We had serious trouble in regard to a treaty with Russia on that account. In the treaty which we negotiated and concluded with Russia that question arose as to the actual murder of a member of the royal family. It was concluded that that was not a political offence; that it need not necessarily be a political offence. It might be done through the purpose of a single anarchist. So that, while the general rule of course is as stated, there may be exceptions to it.

I have no disposition to make any particular discrimination in favor of the Cubans as exhibiting my sympathy with those people. My sympathy for Cuba rests upon very much higher ground than that. This is not an amendment which smacks of Cuban sympathy any more than it does of sympathy for any other oppressed people—the Armenians or any other. The right of expatriation is a right which we recognize distinctly. When a man expatriates himself for reasons which are satisfactory to him, whether dislike of his own government or a greater fondness for ours, or to escape some evil or peril in his own government, whatever his motive may be, our doors stand wide open to receive him upon the ground that he has a right to expatriate himself and apply his allegiance to this country.

SENATOR HOAR.—Does the Senator apply that principle to paupers and ignorant persons?

SENATOR MORGAN.—Paupers seem to have no rights except those which the public chooses to give them. They are excepted out of the general rules, because they are of no use in political circles. Paupers are considered as a peculiar condition of humanity that demands universal benevolence, and therefore, being thrown upon the pity of society, we say to the people abroad: "You must provide through your own charitable institutions for your own people needing charity." That is what we say when we send a pauper back. "You belong to a different beat, a different ward, a different jurisdiction. You are a charge upon the world, but you are a charge upon a particular part of it, because you happened to have been born there or live there, and you can not come and give us that guardianship by your own voluntary act."

They are excluded. They have no option in the matter. The criminal classes are excluded because they are dangerous to society. We exclude them upon the same grounds or very similar grounds to those upon which we exclude immoral publications and some species of deadly instrumentalities which are put under the ban. A criminal is considered as a man who has no right to the protection of any country at all in the choice of his domicile. He must stay in the country against which he committed the crime, and suffer his penalties there, and, if his own country has branded and stamped him as a criminal, then he has no appeal either to our mercy or to our sense of justice in welcoming him to this country.

I do not in my heart and mind and conscience place the illiterate upon the ground either of paupers or criminals. Illiteracy may be a misfortune, and is a misfortune in the general sense, although I have seen a great many people educated out of all ability to earn a living, out of all capacity for any usefulness in life. I have seen them educated in those arts and practices of crime which excel almost the imagination

of man as to their ingenuity and the persistence with which
they are pursued. It is not to be said that education in letters
is the reformer of the human heart. It is a higher power that
reforms the human heart. It is the law of morality that does it.
Politics does not do it. Education in the schools does not do it.
It requires some power of regeneration that is stronger and
better than either of those to take a bad man and make a good
man out of him.

WILKINSON CALL [Fla.].—Mr. President, I shall vote for
this bill with the amendment placed upon it by the Senator
from Alabama allowing the Cubans to come into the country
during the present disorder, but I can hardly see the justification of the principles upon which the bill is based. Intercourse
with foreign nations is either desirable or undesirable. If all
commercial intercourse by the coming or going of the inhabitants
of different countries is to be entirely prohibited, we return
to the condition of China. If it is to be limited intercourse
between the persons of different populations and different
countries, how is it to be limited? This bill proposes to limit
it by the ability to read and write, adding to it the exclusion
because of criminal conduct contained in the act of Congress
of which this is to be an amendment. Is that a test? Is a
country filled with people who can read and write of necessity
a country capable of advancing the arts of civilization? Does
the skilled laborer, the man of inventive genius, always have
this qualification accompanied by the capacity to read and
write?

That is not my observation of mankind. It is desirable that
the country should teach every citizen to read and write. That
it is a means of acquiring intelligence, that it expands thought,
that it is a necessity for higher civilization is beyond doubt,
but have we no need of the sturdy laborer in the intercontinental
railroad between this country and South America, which is soon
to be built? Do the great public works have no need of the
sturdy hand and the strong limb and the muscle of the laborer
who can not read and write? Is it true that we have in our
country a dearth of necessary employment—I do not mean from
transitory causes, but a permanent surplus of labor, more than
the necessities of this Western Hemisphere demand? I doubt
it, Mr. President. I question that when we consider the vast
area of desert land, with the as yet uncultivated land areas not
only in this country, but of the adjacent island of Cuba, capable
of sustaining a population of 10,000,000 or 12,000,000, now only
1,500,000, which population will be supplied from this country,

because it will not be six months after the recognition by this country of the independence of Cuba shall be made before there will be 100,000 Americans there, and their places will need to be supplied. So of Mexico. The overflow of our population will go into Mexico, it will go into the Central American republics, and it is a grave question whether or not we should exclude the honest, the laborious, the capable laboring man of other countries who is not able to read and write.

In the treaty-making power we have the means of suspending all intercourse with foreign countries, or of opening or continuing immigration or prohibiting it.

It seems to me that this is a serious defect, and that it will be wiser to establish some system of treaty stipulation by which we can exclude objectionable people from our shores, rather than by an act of Congress, which provides a restriction including all the sturdy laborers who may come from other countries, however good their character may be.

The question of suffrage or how far aliens should be admitted to the rights of suffrage and citizenship is an entirely different question. Residence and commerce rest on different grounds from citizenship and a participation in the government of a country.

Intercourse, commerce, and the advantages of it, or the disadvantages, are one thing and the participation in the government of a country is a different thing, and the reasons which demand the one and prohibit the other are entirely distinct.

ROGER Q. MILLS [Tex.].—I do not believe that the ability to read and write constitutes the whole sum of what it takes to make a good average citizen of the United States. This is a change of the policy of our Government adopted at its very foundation. We are losing sight of a fundamental truth that was at the bottom of our Government when it was formed, that we were erecting on this continent a government which was to be set free and the home of a free people, that it was to be the asylum of the downtrodden and the oppressed of other countries. We admitted all to come to our shores except paupers and criminals. The pauper who could do nothing to support the Government or to help build up the society which sustained him had no right to put himself upon our society to become a charge. The criminal is a violator of law, and we have a natural right to exclude all such from coming to our shores. That has been the policy of our Government from its foundation until the present time. Now, sir, it seems that the civil-service idea has taken such a hold upon the American people that we are extending it to the immigration of foreigners coming to this country; and we are, I imagine, to establish a civil-service commission to try these people so as to determine whether they can read and write, and whether they understand the Ten Commandments in the Bible or the ten commandments in the Constitution [the first ten amendments] which were referred to by the Senator from Alabama [Mr. Morgan].

I remember some years ago a distinguished citizen of the State of Ohio was telling me about some Irishmen who sought naturalization in one of the courts of Cincinnati. One of the judges told the leading Irishman who had his fellow countrymen in charge to take them out, to read to them the Constitution of the United States, to explain it to them, and see whether or not they understood it, and then to come back and report in court after he had performed this duty. He took them out and read the Constitution to them from beginning to end, and explained it to them, and brought them back into court. The judge said: "Pat, have you read the Constitution to them?" "Yes, sir." "Have you explained it to them?" "Yes, sir." "Do they understand it?" "Yes, your honor; they understand it and are delighted with it." [Laughter.]

I am opposed to making an educational test of citizenship for those who are coming to this country. I am willing to receive them if they are not paupers and criminals and give them an opportunity to be educated and become good citizens here. Some of the very best citizens we have in this country are men who have come to us from foreign countries. Our forefathers were foreigners; great numbers of them could not read and write; and yet they laid the foundation of the greatest republic of the earth.

This is a free country. We have hitherto invited the oppressed of the world to come and enjoy the blessings of liberty with ourselves, and now we say: "Because your government is a despotic government and has enslaved you and your children and it is impossible for you ever to educate them, you shall be proscribed from coming to this country and enjoying the blessings of free government."

This is the only really free country in the world. It is a peculiar government among the governments and nationalities of the world. This continent was dedicated to liberty when this Government was erected, to be the home of a free people, of a self-governing people, of a people who held their liberties in their own hands; and now we are told that the civil service must apply to the immigration of people coming from foreign countries, and a man or his children who cannot stand the test of a civil-service examination must be remanded back to despotism again because they have lived in a despotic government which cared not for them.

No, Mr. President, I am opposed to the educational test. The capacity to read and write is no evidence of virtue either in manhood or womanhood, and I have not a doubt but that the penitentiaries of every State in the Union are full of criminals who can read and write, and read and write well. I have not a doubt that the majority of the wretches whose necks have been broken on the gallows could read and write. The acquirement of the capacity to read and write does not dispel vice and wickedness from the heart. On the contrary, there are thousands and hundreds of thousands of good people in this country and in other countries who cannot read and write. I doubt very much if one in ten of the men or women who first came to this country could read and write; but yet see what a precious heritage they have created in this country and bequeathed to us.

These, sir, are the reasons which constrain me to vote against this bill, and to preserve and persevere and continue in the policy of our fathers to keep the test of pauperism and crime the only test to be applied to foreigners coming to enjoy this heritage of liberty with us.

Senator Morgan's amendment was agreed to by a vote of 47 to 6. The bill was passed by a vote of 52 to 10.

The House refused to concur in the Senate amendments, and a conference was appointed, which failed to come to an agreement. A second conference was appointed, which agreed virtually to the Senate amendments and added to the House bill the following provision known as the Corliss amendment from having been proposed by Representative John B. Corliss [Mich.]:

"Sec. 4. That it shall hereafter be unlawful for any male alien who has not in good faith made his declaration before the proper court of his intention to become a citizen of the United States to be employed on any public works of the United States, or to come regularly or habitually into the United States by land or water for the purpose of engaging in any mechanical trade or manual labor, for wages or salary, returning from time to time to a foreign country."

The report was adopted in the House by a vote of 217 to 36.

In the Senate, on February 17, Charles H. Gibson [Md.] vehemently opposed the Corliss amendment.

The immigration bill seeks, under what is known as the Corliss amendment—the fourth section—to make a crime of the privilege of going and coming when and where you please, in pursuance of that maxim of the civil law that you are permitted to use your own and to do as you please, so far as you interfere with no one else. A crime, Mr. President, is sought to be made out of the sacred right that belongs to individuals of earning their bread by the sweat of their brow.

Such legislation would bring dishonor and disgrace to us as a nation and blacken the fairest page of our country's history. The Corliss amendment, under the provision of the Senate bill, to which attention was called when it was first considered by the Senate in the speech of the distinguished Senator from Massachusetts, was intended to reach what he called birds of passage from Italy to the United States. Italians who came to this country and, under the system of labor by which higher wages were secured than elsewhere, had made a little money had gone home to spend it, and came back again the following season, going alternately backward and forward as they saw fit, were to be excluded under the Corliss feature, as the distinguished Senator from Massachusetts said. That feature of the Corliss amendment will not exclude Italian laborers alone. They are but few in this connection. They are not the "birds of passage" that are affected by the bill, but it is a class of citizens on our borders, in the States bordering on the Canadian and Mexican frontier, that are affected.

Senators Lodge and Chandler found themselves—

As the Philadelphia *Record* says—

unable to frame a statute to arrest railway engineers and firemen at the Canadian line and put native Americans in charge of the trains on this side of the border, and so they gave it up. But woe to the wight who should come over the line from Canada in the morning to work in Detroit, Toledo, Oswego, Plattsburg, or some other border town, and go back in the evening! The guilty wretch so offending habitually would be liable to punishment for misdemeanor by a fine of $500 or by imprisonment for a term not exceeding one year, or both.

What a rare jewel is consistency, Mr. President!

Massachusetts and slavery, the selling of slaves in the South and the horrors of separation of families and the "Fugitive Slave law"!

What iniquities more strongly denounced by Massachusetts than these? And yet to-day we have Massachusetts invoking in an immigration bill what it suited her purpose in times before to inveigh against.

The Fugitive Slave law, which was intended to further the carrying out of the Constitution with reference to the return of fugitive slaves in the South, is absolutely adopted in the conference report.

The Philadelphia *Record* proceeds to say—

We know of no legislation so despicable as this since the passage of the Fugitive Slave law. That law was designed to better enforce a provision of the Constitution requiring the delivery of fugitives from labor. But it was so mean and so atrocious in its premises, making crimes of acts innocent and humane in themselves, that the moral sense of the country revolted against it, and the Government was powerless to enforce it. This immigration bill attempts to make a crime out of the right of locomotion and of the equally sacred right of earning a living by the sweat of the brow. The Fugitive Slave law denounced heavy penalties against any person who, in obedience to the dictates of humanity, should give food to a fugitive or refuse to deliver him up to his owner. This immigration bill would subject to like fine and imprisonment any citizen of the United States who should employ a Canadian or Mexican crossing the border to and fro in pursuit of his daily vocation.

Meaner than the Fugitive Slave law this bill would violate the simplest rites of hospitality and the observance of good neighborhood.

Mr. President, I should like to ask the distinguished Senators composing the conference committee on the part of the Senate what earthly meaning, what earthly connection in the sense that it is germane, section 4 of this conference report has to the illiteracy test which is intended to be submitted to the immigrant?

It was an educational test which the Senate directed the conferees to report upon. It was an educational test to which the immigrant was to be subjected. You have done all that after repeated endeavors, and now, when the alien is "capable and qualified," you want to starve him to death!

Undemocratic, anti-American, cruel, such legislation! "What a shameful step in the nation's downward progress." Even if it does put a check upon the immediate immigration of "undesirable immigrants from southern Europe"; even if it does keep "out these birds of passage" across our Canadian and Mexican border, it brings a blush to the cheek of every American who has heretofore rejoiced that—

> His country's
> Free latch-string never was drawn in
> Against the poorest child of Adam's kin;

and who is humiliated to reflect that the United States is no longer—

> She of the open soul and open door,
> With room about her hearth for all mankind.

The alien who comes across the border in violation of this edict, and the citizen who gives him shelter, under circumstances where the good Samaritan might have bound up his wounds and given him meat and drink when he had fallen among thieves by the wayside, is to be punished under this law by imprisonment and a fine of $500 in the discretion of the courts of the United States. Find me in any of the provisions of the Fugitive Slave law, so vehemently inveighed against by that proud Commonwealth of Massachusetts, any language which presents features so repulsive to the sense of the American citizen and the American people as is proposed by this conference report, denying the alien upon whom the storm may beat the right to a roof over his head, denying a crust of bread to him who has appealed for relief, and subjecting those who furnish it to fine and imprisonment.

The Senate concurred in the conference report by a vote of 34 to 31.

The President vetoed the bill on March 2, 1897. He submitted the following reasons for his action:

A Radical Departure from Our National Policy

President Cleveland's Veto of the Immigration Bill

A radical departure from our national policy relating to immigration is here presented. Heretofore we have welcomed all who came to us from other lands, except those whose moral or physical condition or history threatened danger to our national welfare and safety. Relying upon the zealous watchfulness of our people to prevent injury to our political and social fabric, we have encouraged those coming from foreign countries to cast their lot with us and join in the development of our vast domain, securing in return a share in the blessings of American citizenship.

A century's stupendous growth, largely due to the assimilation and thrift of millions of sturdy and patriotic adopted citizens, attests the success of this generous and free-handed policy which, while guarding the people's interests, exacts from our immigrants only physical and moral soundness and a willingness and ability to work.

A contemplation of the grand results of this policy cannot fail to arouse a sentiment in its defence, for, however it might have been regarded as an original proposition and viewed as an experiment, its accomplishments are such that if it is to be uprooted at this late day its disadvantages should be plainly apparent and the substitute adopted should be just and adequate, free from uncertainties and guarded against difficult or oppressive administration.

It is not claimed, I believe, that the time has come for the further restriction of immigration on the ground that an excess of population overcrowds our land.

It is said, however, that the quality of recent immigration is undesirable. The time is quite within recent memory when the same thing was said of immigrants who with their descendants are now numbered among our best citizens.

It is said that too many immigrants settle in our cities, thus dangerously increasing their idle and vicious population. This is certainly a disadvantage. It cannot be shown, however, that it affects all our cities nor that it is permanent; nor does it appear that this condition where it exists demands as its remedy the reversal of our present immigration policy.

The claim is also made that the influx of foreign laborers deprives of the opportunity to work those who are better entitled than they to the privilege of earning their livelihood by daily toil.

An unfortunate condition is certainly presented when any persons who are willing to labor are unemployed. But, so far as this condition now exists among our people, it must be conceded to be a result of phenomenal business depression and the stagnation of all enterprises in which labor is a factor. With the advent of settled and wholesome financial and economic governmental policies and consequent encouragement to the activity of capital, the misfortunes of unemployed labor should, to a great extent at least, be remedied. If it continues its natural consequences must be to check the further immigration to our cities of foreign laborers and to deplete the ranks of those already there. In the meantime those most willing and best entitled ought to be able to secure the advantages of such work as there is to do.

It is proposed by the bill under consideration to meet the alleged difficulties of the situation by establishing an educational test, by which the right of a foreigner to make his home with us shall be determined. Its general scheme is to prohibit from admission to our country all immigrants "physically capable and over 16 years of age who cannot read and write the English language or some other language"; and it is provided that this test shall be applied by requiring immigrants seeking admission to read and afterward to write not less than twenty nor more than twenty-five words of the Constitution of the United States in some language, and that any immigrant failing in this shall not be admitted, but shall be returned to the country from whence he came at the expense of the steamship or railroad company which brought him.

The best reason that could be given for this radical restriction of immigration is the necessity of protecting our population against degeneration and saving our national peace and quiet from imported turbulence and disorder.

I cannot believe that we would be protected against these evils by limiting immigration to those who can read and write in any language twenty-five words of our Constitution. In my opinion it is infinitely more safe to admit a hundred thousand immigrants who, though unable to read and write, seek among us only a home and opportunity to work than to admit one of those unruly agitators and enemies of governmental control who can not only read and write, but delights in arousing by inflammatory speech the illiterate and peacefully inclined to discontent and tumult. Violence and disorder do not originate with illiterate laborers. They are rather the victims of the educated agitator. The ability to read and write, as required in this bill, in and of itself, affords, in my opinion, a misleading test of contented industry and supplies unsatisfactory evidence of desirable citizenship or a proper apprehension of the benefits of our institutions. If any particular element of our illiterate immigration is to be feared for other causes than illiteracy, these causes should be dealt with directly, instead of making illiteracy the pretext for exclusion to the detriment of other illiterate immigrants against whom the real cause of complaint cannot be alleged.

The provisions intended to rid that part of the proposed

legislation already referred to from obvious hardship appear to me to be indefinite and inadequate.

A parent, grandparent, wife, or minor child of a qualified immigrant, though unable to read and write, may accompany the immigrant or be sent for to join his family, provided the immigrant is capable of supporting such relative. These exceptions to the general rule of exclusion contained in the bill were made to prevent the separation of families; and yet neither brothers nor sisters are provided for. In order that relatives who are provided for may be reunited, those still in foreign lands must be sent for to join the immigrant here. What formality is necessary to constitute this prerequisite, and how are the facts of relationship and that the relative is sent for to be established? Are the illiterate relatives of immigrants who have come here under prior laws entitled to the advantage of these exceptions? A husband who can read and write and who determines to abandon his illiterate wife abroad will find here under this law an absolutely safe retreat. The illiterate relatives mentioned must not only be sent for, but such immigrant must be capable of supporting them when they arrive. This requirement proceeds upon the assumption that the foreign relatives coming here are in every case by reason of poverty liable to become a public charge unless the immigrant is capable of their support. The contrary is very often true. And yet, if unable to read and write, though quite able and willing to support themselves and their relatives here besides, they could not be admitted under the provisions of this bill if the immigrant was impoverished, though the aid of his fortunate but illiterate relative might be the means of saving him from pauperism.

The fourth section of this bill provides "that it shall be unlawful for any male alien who has not in good faith made his declaration before the proper court of his intention to become a citizen of the United States to be employed on any public works of the United States, or to come regularly or habitually into the United States by land or water for the purpose of engaging in any mechanical trade or manual labor for wages or salary, returning from time to time to a foreign country." The fifth section provides "that it shall be unlawful for any person, partnership, company, or corporation knowingly to employ any alien coming into the United States in violation of the next preceding section of this act."

The prohibition against the employment of aliens upon any public works of the United States is in line with other legislation of a like character. It is quite a different thing, however, to declare it a crime for an alien to come regularly and habitually into the United States for the purpose of obtaining work from private parties, if such alien returns from time to time to a foreign country, and to constitute any employment of such alien a criminal offence.

When we consider these provisions of the bill in connection with our long northern frontier and the boundaries of our States and Territories, often but an imaginary line separating them from the British Dominions, and recall the friendly intercourse between the people who are neighbors on either side, the provisions of this bill affecting them must be regarded as illiberal, narrow, and un-American.

The residents of these States and Territories have separate and especial interests which in many cases make an interchange of labor between their people and their alien neighbors most important, frequently with the advantage largely in favor of our citizens. This suggests the inexpediency of Federal interference with these conditions when not necessary to the correction of a substantial evil affecting the general welfare. Such unfriendly legislation as is proposed could hardly fail to provoke retaliatory measures to the injury of many of our citizens who now find employment on adjoining foreign soil.

The uncertainty of construction to which the language of these provisions is subject is a serious objection to a statute which describes a crime. An important element in the offence sought to be created by these sections is the coming "regularly or habitually into the United States." These words are impossible of definite and certain construction. The same may be said of the equally important words "returning from time to time to a foreign country."

A careful examination of this bill has convinced me that for the reasons given and others not specifically stated its provisions are unnecessarily harsh and oppressive, and that its defects in construction would cause vexation and its operation would result in harm to our citizens.

On March 3 the House passed the bill over the President's veto by a vote of 197 to 37 (more than two-thirds).

The Senate referred the bill to the Committee on Immigration, and it did not become a law.

CHAPTER VII

CHILD LABOR

President Roosevelt's Message on "Labor of Women and Children"—Bills Introduced on the Subject in the Senate by Albert J. Beveridge [Ind.], Henry Cabot Lodge [Mass.], and F. M. Simmons [N. C.], and in the House by Herbert Parsons [N. Y.]—The Senate Committee on the District of Columbia Reports the House Bill Prohibiting Child Labor in the District—Debate: In Favor, Jonathan P. Dolliver [Ia.], Sen. Lodge; Opposed, Nathan B. Scott [W. Va.], Joseph B. Foraker [O.], Redfield Proctor [Vt.], Samuel H. Piles [Wash.]; Sen. Beveridge Moves to Amend the Bill by Prohibiting Interstate Commerce in Child-Labor Products: Varying Views by Sen. Beveridge, Augustus O. Bacon [Ga.], Benjamin R. Tillman [S. C.], Jacob H. Gallinger [N. H.], Edward W. Carmack [Tenn.], John C. Spooner [Wis.], Charles W. Fulton [Ore.], Nelson W. Aldrich [R. I.]; Bill Is Supplanted by One Introduced by Sen. Gallinger, Which Is Amended by the House and Enacted—Edward L. Taylor [O.] Reports in the House from the District of Columbia Committee a Senate Bill to Incorporate National Child Labor Committee; It Is Opposed by Finis J. Garrett [Tenn.]; Enacted—Bill Is Enacted to Investigate Condition of Women and Child Laborers.

IN his annual message of December 4, 1906, President Roosevelt spoke as follows on the subject of labor of women and children:

The Congress at its last session wisely provided for a truant court for the District of Columbia; a marked step in advance on the path of properly caring for the children. Let me again urge that the Congress provide for a thorough investigation of the conditions of child labor and of the labor of women in the United States. More and more our people are growing to recognize the fact that the questions which are not merely of industrial but of social importance outweigh all others; and these two questions most emphatically come in the category of those which affect in the most far-reaching way the home life of the nation. The horrors incident to the employment of young children in factories or at work anywhere are a blot on our civilization. It is true that each State must ultimately settle the ques-

288

tion in its own way; but a thorough official investigation of the matter, with the results published broadcast, would greatly help toward arousing the public conscience and securing unity of State action in the matter. There is, however, one law on the subject which should be enacted immediately, because there is no need for an investigation in reference thereto, and the failure to enact it is discreditable to the national Government. A drastic and thoroughgoing child-labor law should be enacted for the District of Columbia and the Territories.

In response to the President's recommendations in regard to child labor, a number of bills and resolutions on the subject were introduced in the Senate and the House during the session.

On December 5, 1906, Albert J. Beveridge [Ind.] introduced in the Senate a bill to prevent the employment of children in factories and mines. It was referred to the Committee on Education and Labor.

On the same day Henry Cabot Lodge [Mass.] introduced in the Senate a bill to prohibit the employment of children in the manufacture or production of articles intended for interstate commerce. It was referred to the same committee.

On December 6 Herbert Parsons [N. Y.] introduced in the House a bill to prevent the employment of children in factories and mines. It was referred to the Committee on Interstate and Foreign Commerce.

On December 10, 1906, the Senate took up a bill which had been passed by the House during the previous session to prohibit child labor in the District of Columbia. The Committee on Education and Labor reported the bill with slight amendments. The committee said:

This bill is based upon a broad consideration of the social welfare of the community. It is modeled upon the State legislation which has proved most efficient and passed the scrutiny of the courts. It involves both a labor question and a problem of public morality. The intrusion of young children into breadwinning occupations is an injustice to the army of workers who are charged with the support of families. It is also an injustice to those whose taxes maintain the public school system. A community which expends the vast sum required for the main-

tenance of the public schools of Washington has a right to require that children of school age give their attention to the
studies which fit them for a useful life. Night schools for children who ought to be at home in bed are a barbarism, unfit for
the countenance of the capital of the United States.

More important, however, than the labor question and the
school question involved in the employment of children for
wages is the question of the moral ruin of hundreds and thousands of boys and girls who, in proper surroundings, might
grow up into useful members of society. What effect upon the
children themselves does this untimely bearing of the burdens of
life have? Dr. Henry J. Harris, secretary of the citizens' child
labor committee of the District of Columbia, stated before your
committee that in the last three months 300 children less than
16 years of age have graduated in this city from the care of
employers to the guardianship of the criminal courts. Such a
condition is intolerable anywhere, and least of all in the District
of Columbia, where Congress is sole legislative authority:

CHILD LABOR IN THE DISTRICT OF COLUMBIA

SENATE, DECEMBER 10, 1906

Nathan B. Scott [W. Va.] opposed the bill.

Mr. President, in anything that I may say in opposition to
this bill I do not want to have it construed that I am opposed
to the education of the children of this country. Many boys,
one of whom I happened to have been, have had to make their
living long before 16 years of age, and many a boy has had to
support his aged mother and, perhaps, younger children. Many
a boy has to receive an education at a night school.

Mr. President, as I understand the pending bill and its
operation, you are going to compel boys to desist from labor.
You are going to place them in a position where they will not
be allowed to earn anything for the support of themselves or
their families. You propose to say that they shall go to school.

I think if gentlemen will take the trouble to investigate they
will find that at the present time the schools in this city are in
no condition to take into the lower grades the boys and girls
who are classed in this bill as being compelled to attend school.
Many of the grades in many of the schools are so full now that
children are not able to attend even half a day, and they are
compelled to remain at home.

You may talk about the morals of the boys and girls under 16 being ruined. I ask the Senator from Idaho what possible legislation could be passed that would lead, I might say, to more direct immorality on the part of the girls and boys than being compelled by this law to remain idle and yet unable to attend school?

I say, Mr. President, that this bill, ironclad as it is, compelling children to remain idle, would do them the greatest injustice this Senate could possibly inflict. What will become of our pages here in front of you? You could not employ a boy as a page. You will have to get pages over 16 years of age in the Senate chamber. These boys are earning something for their mothers and fathers, perhaps, and at the same time they are acquiring an education in a way. You would debar them.

JONATHAN P. DOLLIVER [Ia.].—I desire to call the attention of the Senator from West Virginia to the fact that the bill is so amended as to be no longer applicable to the pages.

SENATOR SCOTT.—I would ask the Senator, why except these youths?

SENATOR DOLLIVER.—The advantages that are derived from our society are supposed to reimburse them.

SENATOR SCOTT.—Mr. President, there is a good deal of reform, moral preaching on honesty, and so forth, that appears to be abroad in the land. A gentleman by the name of Edwin Markham, writing a magazine article not long ago, said that he had visited the glasshouses and had seen children—boys and girls—with emaciated forms, with their eyes, as it were, protruding from their sockets, all due to overwork. He spoke of their little bodies being blistered by the hot furnaces, and a lot more of that kind of magazine stuff, for it is nothing but stuff.

I have been engaged in the manufacture of glass for thirty-five years and over, Mr. President, and if Mr. Markham had come to my factory to see the boys employed there he would have found an entirely different class from those he has described. He would have found an active, energetic set, ready to play leapfrog, catch, and hide and seek, and everything else; and in addition he would have found them singing songs in the factory, the latest production of some comic opera.

I am under the impression that he was not in a glass factory at all. If he was, he misrepresented the conditions prevailing there. The glasshouse boy of to-day becomes the glass manufacturer of to-morrow. There is scarcely a manufacturer of glass in the city of Pittsburgh, or in the Ohio Valley, so far as my knowledge goes—and I know the majority of them—who did not commence to learn his trade, as it were, starting from what we call "warming-in boys," "sticking-up" and "carrying-in" boys. They were boys who saved their money; boys who learned their trade well, and in the course of a few years became manufacturers.

If gentlemen are so anxious to have this bill become a law, I ask them to wait until we can provide the facilities in our schools for taking care of the boys and girls who will be thrown idle upon the streets by its passage. I am not opposed, as I said at the beginning of my remarks, to the education of the youth of the land. But I am opposed to the bill as it now stands. I will gladly vote for it if it is amended as proposed by the Senator from Washington [Samuel H. Piles]. With this amendment it would read, "who is not wholly dependent upon his own labor or who is not the sole support of a disabled father, or a widowed mother, or of a younger brother or sisters."

HENRY CABOT LODGE [Mass.].—Mr. President, the Senator from West Virginia [Mr. Scott] seems to me to prove too much. He argues that it would be a hardship to compel children to go to school because they might be used to support their families and themselves. If that is true, and that argument is sound, there ought to be no child-labor law on any statute book, and we should leave children unrestrained to earn their living and go without education.

There is nothing new, Mr. President, in these efforts to protect children. The laws limiting the hours of labor for women and children are of an old date in England, and go back to their factory acts passed in the forties and the fifties. Those factory acts or similar acts were brought forward in the early fifties in my State by my late colleague, Mr. Hoar. It is generally recognized in all civilized communities that there should be proper legislation protecting the children of the community, boys and girls who are growing up, and giving them that education on which, according to our American belief, the safety of the country and of the State rests.

While I want the children to have all the education the State can give them, I want them also to have all the chance that is possible to develop soundly and well physically. I believe that the Massachusetts plan is the sound way to treat the question— to exclude the child from the factory, the workshop, and the mines at any time of the day until he or she is 14 years of age; and after that, if they have a school certificate that they have been to school, then they can get employment. But up to that time I would exclude them absolutely. As to other employments out of doors, healthful employments in places which keep the children about and moving and out in the open air, I would give the same relaxation that the Massachusetts laws give. I would allow them to pursue those callings in the hours when the schools are not in session. I think it is the soundest policy, not only economically, but in the interest of humanity and of the future of the voters and citizens of the United States to have legislation of that kind.

SENATOR DOLLIVER.—It is obvious that the Government of the United States is face to face with a universal discussion of the child-labor question. There are good people, and wise people, too, who believe that the most important question now pending at the bar of American public opinion is the rescue of these children, in number amounting, it may be, to millions, from the heavy burdens and hardships of life in their tender years, that they may be left in the schoolhouses where they belong in the daytime and in their beds at night under the protection of their fathers and mothers.

Now, the District of Columbia is a favored spot on the map of this country. It constitutes a model for the States of the Union throughout the breadth of our national domain. It appears to me a strange negligence of Congress, which has the sole authority here, that not a line has been put upon the statute books of the United States in keeping with the philanthropic spirit of our States in respect to the employment of child labor in the District.

This proposed bill intends to correct that oversight.

I confess to you, Mr. President, that, when it was stated before our committee in cold blood that practically half of the children employed in the District under 14 years of age in the course of a single year make their way through the police court to the reform school, it filled my heart with a good deal of sadness and anxiety for the future of the District of Columbia. That state of things ought to be corrected, and it ought to be done now. It is not a sound public policy to maintain a system of public schools as costly as we have here in the District of Columbia and then send our children to night schools. Children who work in the daytime, according to the testimony of all teachers, cannot study at night in any proper sense of the word. The body is weary, the energies are overtaxed, and study at night schools is an addition to the burdens of these struggling young lives that ought to be avoided.

I have as much sympathy as anybody has with the gospel of hard work. I believe that the work which men do in this world is their salvation, physically, intellectually, and morally. I shall not say a word here to disparage that. And yet there is in the good providence of God a little respite from labor given to the very young and to the very old. It is given to the young in order that they may mature their bodies and train their minds to the labors of life, and that little respite we ought not to deny to the children who live under the shadow of the dome of the Capitol of the United States.

JOSEPH B. FORAKER [O.].—Does the testimony show how many of those about whom this testimony was given, who made a failure of life, so to speak, and drifted into the criminal court, would have drifted there anyhow if they had not been employed? That is to say, was it the employment that led to it? I do not think that result would follow employment in a dry goods store as a cash boy. In any employment of that kind it never occurred to me that there was any danger of a boy being destroyed there—not half as much as if he were out in an alley playing marbles for keeps with some other boy.

REDFIELD PROCTOR [Vt.].—I myself, like the Senator from Ohio, am a believer in the saving ordinance of work, and I know a great many boys who, I think, have been saved from harm by work, even at a comparatively early age. I believe many more are saved than are harmed, and in this city especially. It is one where there is a great official population, and there is employment for many boys as messengers, servants, etc. There are many families who I know would suffer seriously if this employment was cut off. If it is a question between the family starving and the child going to school, and at the same time having a chance to work outside in some decent employment, I should say give the child a chance to work.

SENATOR PILES.—I wish to say that I am in favor of a law which will prevent children from becoming public messengers, from working in mines, factories, and all other places deleterious to physical and intellectual development; also in all places which have a tendency to degrade or reduce the moral tone of the children of the country. But I believe, Mr. President, that every boy should have the right to fight his way in the world and an opportunity to make a name for himself in all employments which are not harmful to his physical, mental, and moral development; and when a boy to that end desires to engage in any such employment I do not think he should be restrained by law from so doing and forced to accept public charity in order to attend the public schools. You need not, Mr. President, worry about a boy with the spirit of success in him, for he will find both the way and the means to acquire an education which will be of real and lasting benefit to him and the country in which he lives.

SENATOR DOLLIVER.—I am, of course, impressed by what the Senator has said and by what is said by men of such practical wisdom in this world as the Senator from West Virginia [Mr. Scott] and the Senator from Vermont [Mr. Proctor], and I probably would be entirely persuaded by what they say if I did not find the same arguments as to child labor scattered freely through the entire controversy from the beginning of the agitation more than half a century ago.

There could be no more serious weakening of this proposed law than to amend it in such a way as to allow people to permit their children to work when they are under the pressure of poverty and necessity. It does seem a little hard to let them starve when they might be saved by the labor of a child, but that same hardship appears in the enforcement of our health laws and in the enforcement of many of the schemes that society has adopted for its own preservation.

I was so impressed by the argument that families living in poverty might be saved from distress, at least, by the labor of little children that I asked the good people who appeared before the Committee on Education and Labor how stood that case in the District of Columbia, and those who were familiar with the work of the Board of Charities in this District, being before our committee, upon their authority and responsibility in connection with the associated charities of Washington, said that that association had investigated in this District every case in which a child could properly be said to be working for the support of anybody, and there publicly, before our committee, they undertook that that association would relieve all the distress occasioned by the discharge from the army of workers of these little children of the District of Columbia.

INTERSTATE COMMERCE IN CHILD-MADE GOODS

SENATE, JANUARY 23-29, 1907

On January 25 F. M. Simmons [N. C.] introduced in the Senate a bill to prohibit interstate commerce in articles made in factories or produced in mines in violation of State child labor laws. It was referred to the Committee on Interstate Commerce.

Already (on January 23) Albert J. Beveridge [Ind.]

had moved to amend the District of Columbia bill by prohibiting interstate commerce in the products of mines and factories employing child labor.

In supporting his amendment Senator Beveridge said:

According to the census of 1900, there are not far from two million children in the United States under 16 years of age working in "gainful occupations."

Of these, according to the census of 1900, nearly *seven hundred thousand* are employed in industries other than agricultural.

This bill does not strike at the employment of children engaged in agriculture. I do not for a moment pretend that working children on the farm is bad for them.

I think it is the universal experience that where children are employed within their strength and in the open air there can be no better training. All educators have now come to an agreement that the technical schools and the manual training schools in our cities are by far the best features of our educational system.

And I am in favor of and look forward to the time when, as a part of the educational system of this country, children will be taught to work. For, I repeat, there is no training like labor.

But, Mr. President, the evil at which this bill strikes is not such labor. I may say, and truthfully say, that this bill does not strike at such labor at all. It strikes at child toil, and I will emphasize it still more in saying that it strikes at child *slavery* in the mines, the factories, and the sweat shops of the nation.

But the record of the census, bad as that is—terrible as it is—is totally inaccurate. Anybody who has studied this question knows why it is inaccurate.

False certificates, which are universal; the hiding of children when the factory inspector comes; the reliance of the census enumerator upon reports of interested parties; all these very naturally acted to give only a fraction of this terrible truth.

I quote John Spargo, who is perhaps as accurate an authority upon this subject as anyone. Says Mr. Spargo in his "Bitter Cry of the Children":

I am convinced that the number of children under 15 years of age who work is much larger than the official figures give, notwithstanding that these are supposed to give the number of all workers under 16 years of age.

It would, I think, be quite within the mark to say that the number of child workers under 15 is at least 2,250,000.

I suppose we may say, putting it upon a conservative basis, that as I speak to you there are now not less than 1,000,000 children under 16 years of age (and I shall show by sworn testimony that some of them are *five* and *six* and *seven* years of age) at work in the coal mines, in factories, and in the sweat shops of this nation.

These are figures, Mr. President; but *figures* give no idea of what this means. Of course no Senator here would permit *his* boy or girl under 16 to work in a coal breaker or in a sweatshop or a factory. But it is not the children of *Senators* who are involved; it is the children of the *people*.

Yet if I were merely to say that so many children were employed that would give no idea of what this evil is. Figures cannot, of course, describe it. Figures only give you an idea of its extent. I propose now to describe it. I propose to show to the Senate and the country precisely what it means, and I shall do this by the description of these children at work, of how their work is conducted, of its effect upon them, and in each instance by the sworn testimony of eyewitnesses who have personally investigated this matter.

Now, before I go on I want to say that the examples which I am giving are by no means the worst ones. I do not propose to refer to what can be referred to and proved unless the indifference of the Senate compels it—such, for example, as the pouring of cold water on little children to keep them awake after they have worked *standing on their feet ten hours*.

Furthermore, in reading what is sworn to in each one of these affidavits, I have carefully excluded everything that might be called the "excited sentimentality" of the writers; "excited" by the horrible things which they witnessed themselves. Also I shall confine the statements that I am going to read to the Senate to such as are typical—neither the worst nor the best, but such as are typical—and every one of these statements I will support by affidavits and further proof if anyone questions the statements.

Mr. Spargo gives the following example:

During the Philadelphia textile workers' strike in 1903 I saw at least a score of children ranging from *8 to 10 years* of age who had been working in the mills prior to the strike.

Here is another example. This is from Paterson, N. J.:

At 6 o'clock the whistles shrieked and the streets were suddenly filled with people, many of them mere children. Of all the crowd of tired, pallid, and languid looking children I could only get speech with one, a little girl, who claimed 13 years, though she was smaller than many a child of 10.

If my little Paterson friend was 13, perhaps the nature of her employment will explain her *puny, stunted body*. She works in the "steaming room" of the flax mill.

Senators seem to think this very funny. I do not think that you will find, as we go along, any particular materials for amusement. Mr. Spargo continues:

All day long, in a room filled with clouds of steam, she has to stand *barefooted* in pools of water, twisting coils of wet hemp. When I *saw* her she was *dripping wet*, though she said that she had worn a rubber apron all day. In the coldest evenings of winter little Marie and hundreds of other little girls must go out from the superheated steaming rooms *into the bitter cold in just that condition*.

Here is the description of the labor of children in a certain kind of glass factory.

It was a big wooden structure, so loosely built that it afforded little protection from drafts, and surrounded by a high fence with several rows of barbed wire stretched across the top. I went with the foreman of the factory and he explained to me the reason for the stockade-like fence.

"It keeps the young imps inside once we've got 'em *for the night shift*," he said.

The "young imps" were, of course, the boys employed, about forty in number, at least ten of whom were less than *12 years of age*.

It was a cheap bottle factory, and the proportion of boys to men was larger than is usual in the higher grades of manufacture. *Cheapness and child labor go together*—the cheaper the grade of manufacture, as a rule, the cheaper the labor employed.

Then he describes the labor of glass blowers:

The work of these "carrying-in boys," several of whom were *less than 12* years old, was by far the hardest of all. They were kept on a slow run *all the time* from the benches to the annealing oven and back again. The pay of these boys varies from 60 cents to a dollar for eight hours' work.

A continued uninterrupted "trot"—that is the term they use for it—without rest, without cessation, without relaxation of nerve or muscle in the superheated atmosphere of the factory.

I have given some figures about the work of children in the Pennsylvania mines. Here is what Mr. Spargo, who personally investigated this thing, says about that:

According to the census of 1900, there were 25,000 boys under 16 years of age employed in and around the mines and quarries of the United States.

In the State of Pennsylvania alone—the State which enslaves more children than any other—there are thousands of little "breaker boys" employed, many of them not more than 9 or 10 years old.

The law forbids the employment of children under 14, and the records of the mines generally show that the law is "obeyed."

Yet, in May, 1905, an investigation by the national child labor committee showed that in one small borough of 7,000 population among the boys employed in breakers 35 were 9 years old, 40 were 10, 45 were 11, and 45 were 12—over 150 boys illegally employed in one section of boy labor in one small town!

Work in the coal breakers is exceedingly hard and dangerous. Crouched over the chutes, the boys sit hour after hour, picking out the pieces of slate and other refuse from the coal as it rushes past to the washers. From the cramped position they have to assume most of them become *more or less deformed and bent backed, like old men.*

When a boy has been working for some time and begins to get round shouldered, his fellows say that "he's got his boy to carry round wherever he goes." The coal is hard, and accidents to the hands, such as cut, broken, or crushed fingers, are common among the boys. Sometimes there is a worse accident. A terrified shriek is heard, and a boy is mangled and torn in the machinery, or disappears in the chute, to be picked out later smothered and dead.

I tried to pick out the pieces of slate from the hurrying stream of coal, often missing them; my hands were bruised and cut in a few minutes. I was covered from head to foot with coal dust, and for many hours afterwards I was expectorating some of the small particles of anthracite I had swallowed. *I could not do that work and live;* but there were boys of *10 and 12 years* of age doing it for *50 and 60 cents a day.* Some of them had never been inside of a school; few of them could read a child's primer.

. . . .

From the breakers the boys graduate to the mine depth, where they become door tenders, switch boys, or mule drivers. Here, far below the surface, the work is still more dangerous.

Here is another example taken from another industry:

In New Jersey and Pennsylvania I have seen hundreds of children, boys and girls, between the ages of 10 and 12 years, at work in the factories belonging to the "cigar trust." Some of these factories are known as "kindergartens" on account of the large number of small children employed in them. It is by no means a rare occurrence for children in these factories to faint or to fall asleep over their work, and I have heard a foreman in one of them say that it was "enough for one man to do just to keep the kids awake."

In the domestic manufacture of cheap cigars many very young children are employed. Often the "factories" are poorly lighted, ill-ventilated tenements in which work, whether for children or adults, ought to be absolutely prohibited. Children work often as many as *fourteen or even sixteen hours* in these little "home factories," and in cities like Pittsburgh, Pa., it is not unusual for them, after attending school all day, to work from 4 P. M. to 12.30 A. M. making "tobies" or "stogies," for which they receive from 8 to 10 cents per hundred.

In York, Pa., children as young as 3 years of age are required to work nearly all day and at night until as late as 10 o'clock.

This is also a description, by Kellogg Durland in the *Outlook*, of the work of children in Pennsylvania:

Helen Sisscak, a wan mite of a girl not nine years of age, who spoke no English, told Judge George Gray, of the Coal Strike Commission (1902), that she cleaned bobbins at 3 cents an hour. She went to work at half-past

Suffer little children to come unto me and forbid them not, for of such is the kingdom of Heaven.
—*Christ.*

Suffer little children to come unto me and forbid them not, for they bring profit unto me.
—*Mammon*

SUFFER THE CHILDREN
By J. H. Morier in "The Comrade"

6 at night and worked till half-past 6 in the morning. It was when this child had finished her story that Judge Gray exclaimed, with much feeling: "Here we actually find the flesh and blood of little children coined into money"; and, shortly after, "This matter of night labor by young girls should be thoroughly investigated by those who will not shirk the work and the result made known in every part of Pennsylvania." This work has been done. Yet the indifferentism of legislators or the lack of public pressure has resulted in a continuance of the system, with never a strong hand raised in protest.

Senator Beveridge continued his speech on January 28.

Now Mr. Durland takes up the silk mills. He says:

Less kindly is the State toward the girls. They may work at 13 years. They may work at *twelve-hour shifts by day or by night*. Their work is often in a warm, moist atmosphere, out of which they pass into the chill dawn of winter mornings. They must *stand* at their work. They must be unceasingly diligent lest an unnoticed broken strand of silk entangle others and damage the work.

They are unprotected from moral dangers shocking almost beyond credence. The State has refused to protect these children because the abolition of child labor at night would necessitate the remodeling of certain industrial plants, and the citizens of the State bow to the wishes of the manufacturers in this matter as quietly as if it were a moot point, complicated by subtle technicalities. The moral phase of the matter is completely subjugated to the pecuniary.

"I deplore this business as much as you do," a silk-mill owner said to me one day, "but I am part of a great industrial system, and so long as the system exists I must run my mill as other mills are run." The gentleman had come to me to beg *that I keep silent* on what I had seen in his mill the previous night.

Now, let us see the conditions under which they are working. Of course these are not *our* children. They are the children of somebody else that are working *twelve hours a night*. If they were *our* children, we would forget lunch and not sit up nights contriving arguments to show that the Constitution won't let us rescue them.

Mr. Durland continues:

The perpetual click of the rattling looms, the whirr of belts, the crunch and rumble of wheels made a deafening din. The looms moved so regularly that I found my eyes easily tired watching them. It needed only a few moments of fixed gazing to appreciate the story told by one little girl, who had been transferred to the day shift:

"When I first went to work at night the long standing hurt me very much. My feet burned so that I cried. My knees hurt me worse than my feet, and my back pained all the time."

I stop here to remark that this is no occasional instance. It is typical and common.

"Mother cried when I told her how I suffered, and that made me feel so badly that I did not tell her any more. It does not hurt me so much now, but I feel tired all the time. I do not feel near as tired, though, as I did when I worked all night.

"My eyes hurt me, too, from watching the threads at night. The doctor said they would be ruined if I did not stop the night work. After watching the threads for a long time *I could see threads everywhere*. When I looked at other things there were threads running across them. *Sometimes I felt as though the threads were cutting my eyes*."

No wonder. She had been working twelve hours at night, looking at the ceaseless play of the threads; she was 9 years old; she had been standing on her feet; and this is going on in a country about which we make earnest and passionate Fourth-of-July orations.

But Mr. Durland says that—

Bad as this aspect is, there is another, a sadder and more terrible feature. The close atmosphere of the factory rooms in the dead of night tends to stupefy the children. To freshen them and drive the natural drowsiness away they are encouraged to spend their midnight half hour running in the open air.

Mark that humanity. The silk mills really give the children a half hour for luncheon at midnight. I hope American women will think of all these things when they put on their silks. Mr. Durland goes on:

The mills usually occupy isolated sites. They are often on the edge of a mining village, sometimes by the banks of the Susquehanna, or near the foot of the hills. Open fields and shadowy woods surround them.

And then occurs a statement which I prefer not to read, but which every Senator will quickly infer.

Thus far, Mr. President, these items, uninteresting perhaps to Senators, but of infinite consequence to this nation, have concerned foreign children more than American children.

But now, Mr. President, I come to a section of the country where this evil is greatest and most shameful and where it is practiced *upon the purest American strain that still exists in this country*—the children in the Southern cotton mills.

Miss Ashby went South as an investigator of the American Federation of Labor. She says:

I was prepared to find child labor, for wherever easily manipulated machinery takes the place of human muscles the child is inevitably drawn into the labor market, unless there are laws to protect it. But one could hardly be prepared to find in America to-day *white* children, *6 and 7* years of age, working for *twelve hours* a day—aroused before daybreak and toiling till long after sundown, in winter, with only *half an hour* for rest and refreshment.

Ladies told me of a common sight in the mill cottages—children lying *face downward on the bed sleeping with exhaustion, just as they had come in from the night shift, too utterly weary even to remove their clothes.*

Continues Miss Ashby:

Often the whole family, except the baby actually in the cradle, is in the mill. Two or three of 8 years or older might be on the pay roll, but the youngest paid worker can get through her "side"—

"Side" is the term by which they measure the pay.

At 10 cents a day—

At 10 cents a day! A child 6 years of age, working *twelve hours, standing on her feet,* at 10 cents a day!

at 10 cents a day—with more ease if she has her little brother of 6 to help her.

I have *seen* a boy *under 4* beginning his life of drudgery by pulling the yarn off bobbins to make bands.

I am familiar with the slums of two continents, but I can say I have never seen a more pitiful sight than the mill children, nor known little ones for whom the outlook was more hopeless.

It is not only that they are pale, shrunken, and bowed—they look as if their brains were hypnotized and their souls paralyzed. A friend of mine in Atlanta, thinking to give some of these little victims a treat, asked a number out to her place in the country and turned them into the woods to play. What were her distress and amazement to find that *they did not know what the word or the thing meant.*

I shall now read illustrations of what exists in the South, written in a remarkable series of articles in the *Saturday Evening Post,* of Philadelphia, from Mrs. Van Vorst's personal investigations.

Here is a description of one of the future "capitalists," which the New York *Sun* seems to think will develop from these children. This is the best description of the best child that Mrs. Van Vorst specifically describes:

This boy was 15 years of age, and had begun to work at 7. He could not read or write and insisted that next year he was going to school. He was helping to support his mother. He was a fine type of boy.

He had been for years up before dawn and plied in the *service of a machine for twelve hours a day;* he had spent his childhood as a laborer, a bread winner, who earned food and shelter not only for himself, but for another; he had lived without pleasure, without amusements, without hope—without hope, yes; but never without courage.

And when at last an opportunity presented itself, what form did it take? The chance to extenuate his remaining energies working night and day; to be drenched to the skin; to be too tired to eat when food was put before him, too exhausted to sleep when his head touched the pillow. This was his chance, and he met it fighting the good fight and bound to be victor. His lank and withered body gave evidence sufficient of what he was going through.

In Georgia, I think it was—the Senators from that State can tell me, if it was not—there was a "gentlemen's agreement" among mill owners in lieu of the law such as they have now.

AUGUSTUS O. BACON [Ga.].—There was.

MR. BEVERIDGE.—That took the place of the law. You have a law down there at present which, for the purpose of stopping child labor, is not worth the paper it is printed on.

SENATOR BACON.—Mr. President, I would not undertake to follow the Senator in his criticism at this time, but in order that I may not be misunderstood I will simply say to the Senator that the need for a law had been generally recognized in my State. One has been passed that is working well at the present time, and it is worth a little more than the paper it is written upon, and the question which is, I think, in the minds of Senators here is not as to whether there has been and is a great evil in regard to this matter, but really whether this is a matter for the attention of the States or a matter to be dealt with, as the Senator proposes, by Federal legislation.

SENATOR BEVERIDGE.—I do not think that in its broader aspects this is a State question at all. I do not intend now to get into the legal part of this argument; but I will say this—that I have so drawn this bill as to eliminate the question of "State's rights," because I myself profoundly respect those who sincerely hold to that political doctrine. I have so drawn the bill that every "State's rights" man can vote for it without violating his constitutional convictions. I think that the broader aspect of this evil is purely national. It is not only State citizens that you are ruining, it is the citizens of the Republic as well. It is not only Georgia children that are being murdered, it is American children as well.

BENJAMIN R. TILLMAN [S. C.].—I hope the Senator will not omit to get all well-authenticated facts into the *Record*, so that we may have ammunition with which to begin crusades at home to keep our legislatures from being influenced by *Northern* millionaires who have gone down there and built mills and made industrial slaves out of white children instead of the chattel black slaves of the old days. I will join the Senator if he can show me how to do it here constitutionally.

JACOB H. GALLINGER [N. H.].—There is Northern money in South Carolina; and God help South Carolina if there was not Northern money there. [Applause in the galleries.]

I want to add one further suggestion on that point.

I recall very distinctly that in one of Elbert Hubbard's articles he stated that the parents in the South demanded that the children should work in the mills, and that they were infinitely more to blame than the men who furnished the capital to run the mills.

SENATOR BEVERIDGE.—There is no doubt about that; but the infamy of the murder of children is not to be excused on account of the infamy of parents who are willing to see them work. The mill owner, however, ought not to satisfy his conscience by what he knows to be a perjured certificate.

SENATOR TILLMAN.—I know there are fathers and mothers in South Carolina as well as there are elsewhere who to my mind occupy the relation toward their children of cannibals, who force them to get up before day and go to work, while they, especially the father, sit around and loaf and live off their children's labor. But I do not see the force of the sneer of the Senator from New Hampshire in saying God help South Carolina if there was no Northern money there. I will say to that Senator that rather than have Northern money go there and exercise its lobbying influences through the instrumentalities of mill presidents and directors and others who go to the legislature and maneuver and manipulate and manage to keep proper child-labor laws from being enacted, I wish that he and all others who can keep Northern money away would keep it away from the State.

EDWARD W. CARMACK [Tenn.].—I want to state that so far as one State is concerned no Federal legislation is needed to bring about this reform.

SENATOR BEVERIDGE.—I will show the Senator that it is, and I will now tell him why.

SENATOR CARMACK.—Not so far as Tennessee is concerned.

SENATOR BEVERIDGE.—Yes; and I will show the Senator why when I come to the point. I want to say to the Senator and all Senators that I am only too delighted to give way at any time to any Senator for a question upon any point. I am as earnest about this matter, I think, as he can be, and if at any point I am wrong on a question of fact or a question of law I want to be interrupted.

JOHN C. SPOONER [Wis.].—Does the Senator think he is any more earnest in the discussion of child labor than the remainder of his colleagues?

SENATOR BEVERIDGE.—Yes; I think a good deal more earnest. I have been earnest enough to spend nights and days and weeks and months in accumulating testimony. I have been earnest enough to appeal to the American people all over this country during the last campaign, from as far west as Nebraska to as far east as Maine. Has the Senator done as much?

SENATOR TILLMAN.—The Senator mistakes zeal for earnestness. That he is very zealous we undoubtedly know, but I deny that he is more earnest than I am and than all other Senators are.

SENATOR BEVERIDGE.—I want to say to the Senator from Tennessee what I was going to say when the Senator from Wisconsin interrupted me. The manufacturers of the Senator's own State have by the very righteousness of your State laws been put at a commercial disadvantage with the manufacturers of Georgia, Alabama, South and North Carolina, because the manufacturers of your State cannot longer employ cheap labor. They cannot longer make the blood of children into gold, and that can be done by every manufacturer in these other States.

That is the trouble with the whole thing. I shall submit in a moment, when I come to present that particular question, the affidavit of a man who testifies to having been on a train that was carrying a "shipment" of *children* from Tennessee, where they cannot be worked, to the cotton mills of other Southern States, where they can be worked.

Mr. President, perhaps in the interest of the dividends which these mill owners earn—and I shall present a book here written by one of them, showing that the poorest cotton mill in the South does not earn less than 10 and from that up to 30 per cent., and even higher—we might waive consideration of the ruin of the children themselves, but we are confronted with a far graver consequence, and that consequence is this: It is the process of the deterioration of the race. It is the production of a degenerate class in this Republic.

The lowest estimate now is that we are pouring into American citizenship every year at least 200,000 "Hooligans," boys and girls, who are broken in body and stunted in mind and soul, and who *know* it, and who are living engines of hatred toward society—and I do not blame them—and who become the parents of still other degenerates. We all hear talk about the dangers of a certain "lower class." Had we not better do something to stop the production of that "lower class," that "dangerous class"? Anyhow, I shall try to stop it.

Great Britain is an example of precisely a condition such as I have detailed that has shocked the world. The world did not know about it. England herself did not know about it until the United Kingdom had to meet 28,000 Boer farmers in South Africa.

You will remember the newspaper accounts of the almost impossibility of getting soldiers for the English service. You will remember the descriptions of how small and feeble they were. You will remember the tales—true tales—of their being swept off like flies by enteric fever. It was the poorest army that that first of powers ever sent to the battlefield.

The director-general says that from 40 to 60 per cent. of all the soldiers that England recruited for South Africa in the Boer war were unfit for service. Over 30 per cent. of all attempted to be recruited were rejected, although the standard was purposely lowered by the British authorities.

The cause of these rejections were undersize, narrow chest, bad teeth, bad vision, flat feet, and other causes that showed physical and racial deterioration.

Now, then, when this was brought home to the attention of the British nation and of the world, it startled the British statesmen as nothing had startled them for a hundred years, because they were suddenly face to face with the fact that the United Kingdom, with over 40,000,000 people, found herself hard put to it to raise 320,000 British soldiers to meet 28,000 Boer farmers upon the field of battle.

They were suddenly face to face with the fact that, upon land, England has not the men to meet any first-class nation in the world.

They were suddenly confronted with the fact that, while they had become the mistress of the seas in commerce, they had sunk into a low place in manhood and stamina, which is the foundation of all commerce and of all greatness of every kind.

And so a commission was appointed to examine into and report upon the causes of this physical deterioration of the British people, and here it is in my hand [exhibiting].

It was found that a general physical deterioration of the people did exist. It was found that its immediate and present causes were poverty, overcrowding, living in towns, insufficient nourishment, and inherited tendencies. Now anyone who has studied the question knows what the cause of that is.

It began in England one hundred and fifty years ago with the invention of the spinning machines, and precisely the same process is going on in Pennsylvania, in South Carolina, and other States of the American Republic to-day.

As soon as the factories started up in England in the eighteenth century the mill owners found themselves in precisely the condition that the Southern mill owners find their factories to-day. They *used precisely the same arguments to get the children into the mills.* They soon found that the nimble fingers of the children could do the work of attending the machines better than those of old people. Also they soon found that children were more "tractable," more easily "managed," and they found, above all other things, that *they were cheaper*.

And so, first—all Senators are familiar with that, of course —the orphanages were emptied into the mils, and then the country was invaded by the mill owners, just as to-day in the Southern States the hill people are being drawn from their farms to the factories.

The strongest people from the country were induced to go to the factory towns. They left the inferior country people on the farms to run the farms and raise up the future yeomanry of the empire.

And these stronger young men and young women coming into the factories soon degenerated in health, and they produced children who were weaker still than they were, and so the process went on from bad to worse until seventy-five years later, nearly all the population of England in the meantime having become an urban population, a mill-working population, the great irresistible causes of degeneration had done their work, and when the Boer war came England was hard put to it to raise from among 40,000,000 people 320,000 able soldiers to meet the Boers on the field of battle.

There gradually grew up in England a hundred years ago an agitation such as there is growing up in America now. It was resisted. It was resisted by the factory owners just exactly as the agitation is now being resisted by the factory owners. Sir Robert Peel began the reform of it in 1802. He did not succeed very well; but finally he got the Peel bill passed.

Then it was succeeded by the agitation which resulted in the Sadler bill, which limited the hours of work to ten hours. A very singular thing occurred, and I cannot help referring to it now, we are so precisely paralleling the experience of England. The manufacturers resisted the Sadler bill in every way they could. Finally they said: "This bill is being passed upon '*vague*' representations; it is being passed at the clamor of working people; let us '*investigate*' it; let the whole subject be '*investigated*.' "

Of course they knew it would take a year or two in which to "investigate," and in the meantime their enormous profits would go on. Many great fortunes in England to-day are founded upon that system. No wonder England, having thus sowed the wind, is now reaping the whirlwind.

So they asked that the thing might be "investigated," and

they carried their point. But so terrible were the conditions, and the report of that investigation committee had so terribly alarmed them, that they aligned themselves for the purpose of delaying and, if possible, defeating action on that report; for the report showed conditions even worse than they were represented, just as the report of the "investigation" of this crime here in America and in the twentieth century will show—if the investigation is honest.

Finally the cause of those English children was taken up by a man whom everybody who reads the English language and knows anything about English history or human industrialism knows and loves and applauds—John Ashley, Earl of Shaftesbury. He gave his whole life to it. He gave up his official place; society turned against him; his rich associates reviled him. He was of the noblest nobility of England itself, but they all deserted him. "Shaftesbury," said England's "better classes"—England's "best people," to repeat the favorite phrase of the Senator from Georgia [Mr. Bacon]—"Shaftesbury," said they, "has joined the 'lower class.'"

Nevertheless he gave his life to the curing of this infamy, and to-day John Ashley, Earl of Shaftesbury, is one of the proudest names in English history. When the name of Marlborough is forgotten and when the name of Wellington shall have become a memory the name of John Ashley, Earl of Shaftesbury, will glow, with ever-increasing radiance, in the permanent heaven of mankind's regard.

They did not succeed in stopping that evil for seventy-five years—these English "reformers," these English sympathizers with the despised "common people," these English lovers of humanity—and it was not until perhaps twenty-five years ago that the evil was entirely ended.

Does any man think that England pursued a wise policy? I hold in my hand here the original notes of the statements of some of the mill owners in the Senator's State of North Carolina, where they resisted the passage of a law for the compulsory education of children and improvements over North Carolina's wretched child-labor bill, all of which the manufacturers of North Carolina defeated.

One of them goes on to say: "We want more mills. It is all right to work the children. They say that England is building more mills, and she has become the money center of the world and the commercial mistress of the seas."

Well, Mr. President, that is what England has done. She has become "the money center of the world," and she has become "the commercial mistress of the seas." But does anybody think that she has not paid too high a price? Does anybody think that the proud eminence upon which she stands in commerce and trade has not been bought too dearly when it has been bought at the sacrifice of men and women?

The Boer war can teach us a lesson as well as it taught England a lesson. England cannot meet *on land* a single first-class power to-day. That is the price she paid for becoming "the commercial mistress of the seas." Gone is that splendid yeomanry which under the Iron Duke overwhelmed the veterans of Austerlitz and bowed to the dust the forehead of the greatest captain of the world. Gone is that splendid stock that produced a Shakespeare and a Milton, and a Thackeray and a Dickens; that produced an Arkwright; that produced the great statesmen of the past. There is not to-day a single English soldier, statesman, or writer who comes even up to the arms of the great Englishmen of yesterday. The English people paid too high a price when they gave their children to make the English mill owners the greatest capitalists in the world.

I respect capital as much as anyone. I respect property as much as any man. I like to see wealth grow and expand, both individually and nationally, but I tell you we are thinking too much about money *as money*. We are thinking too much about prosperity *as prosperity*. The chief use of prosperity is not to put food in your stomachs or clothes on your backs or a roof over your heads. That is an important use; but the great use of prosperity is that it gives you time and strength to think on righteousness and write conscience into laws without ruining the people.

Now, Mr. President, there is the consequence not only of the labor of children to-day, not only the ruin of their lives, but the certain deterioration and the establishment of an ever-increasing degenerate class in America.

Mr. President, it has got to stop. I infer from what I have heard here in the interruptions that everybody agrees it has got to stop. As a matter of fact, I have never seen any human reform proposed in this Senate that everybody was not "for" it, but most were against any effective *means* of accomplishing it. We are confronted now with a proposition. I have heard it whispered about the corridors, and so have other Senators, that we must not go "too fast"; that we are bound to have an "investigation."

Oh, no; let us not go "too fast." The evidence is before the Senate of the slow murder of these children, not by tens or hundreds, but by the thousands. But let us not "hasten" to their relief "too fast." Let us "investigate," just as the manufacturers of England asked when they were confronted with the same kind of a reform.

Now, Mr. President, it has got to be stopped and *stopped now*. We all agree upon that—anyhow, everybody says that he agrees it must be stopped; "only," say some, "let us be careful about the Constitution." The Constitution, it appears, is a very mysterious instrument. But never mind; child labor has got to be stopped. How? The States cannot stop it.

I hear that "State's rights" is to be used as the excuse for killing this bill. I say there are no "State's rights" involved in this bill. I see the junior Senator from South Carolina [Asbury C. Latimer] making a remark to another Senator upon that statement. If the Senator thinks there are some "State's rights" in this bill which prohibit the transportation in interstate commerce of the products of child labor, why did not the Senator think there were some "State's rights" in his bill for prohibiting the transportation in interstate commerce of the boll weevil and the gypsy moth?

Mr. President, something has been said more or less all along about "State's rights." But suppose State's rights were involved a little bit. Last year we passed the quarantine law. For a hundred years the subject of quarantine has been universally recognized to be exclusively within the province of the States. The effect of the law last year was to make it a national quarantine system. There was not a bit of resistance to it. The people were not willing to quibble; the people were not willing to make a strained construction of the Constitution when yellow fever was knocking at the gates. There was no resistance in the Senate. There was some resistance in the House, made purely upon the "State's rights" proposition that it was the province of the State, and that the national Government was taking the right to quarantine from the States. I was very greatly struck by a speech made in the House by Robert C. Davey [La.]. He said:

If gentlemen who have taken part in this debate had gone through a yellow fever epidemic, as I have, they would not stand here upon technicalities.

That is the spirit of a humane man; but, if we could speak thus for a bill to kill yellow fever, how much more should we speak for a bill to kill child labor?

SENATOR TILLMAN.—I think that the good sense and the

love of humanity in any State, where it is pointed to properly, will redress this wrong and cure the evil, or kill it, if the facts are ever presented to the people.

SENATOR BEVERIDGE.—But the Senator would not object to having the nation do it if the Senator believed that it was entirely within the province of the nation to do it?

SENATOR TILLMAN.—If the Senator can convert me on that point, I will be ready to go with him, but I want to call the Senator's attention to another phase of it. We have in the South a very large number of children from 6 years up who help pick cotton in the fall. Would the Senator have the cotton crop stopped from entering into interstate commerce because little children are engaged in helping to gather it?

SENATOR BEVERIDGE.—So far as this measure is concerned, it lets them pick cotton.

CHARLES W. FULTON [Ore.].—The Senator from South Carolina suggests that the children of South Carolina engage in picking cotton. The Senator from Indiana says he does not purpose by this bill to prohibit the shipment of cotton as an article of interstate commerce. But I ask the Senator if the principle is not exactly the same?

SENATOR BEVERIDGE.—I know exactly what the Senator is going to ask. He is going to ask, if we can exclude the products of the factory, can we not exclude the products of the farm? Certainly we can, as a matter of *power;* but we never will as a matter of *policy*.

SENATOR FULTON.—Let me ask the Senator if Congress can prohibit cotton from being shipped from one State to another because it was picked by children—

SENATOR BEVERIDGE.—Yes; or a red-headed girl.

SENATOR FULTON.—Can it not prohibit wheat from being shipped from one State to another because a person was employed more than eight hours?

SENATOR BEVERIDGE.—Why, undoubtedly; as a matter of *power;* though that has nothing to do with this bill. This bill rests on much narrower foundations.

SENATOR FULTON.—Then there is nothing that Congress cannot regulate in our internal affairs.

SENATOR BEVERIDGE.—I am glad the Senator has brought that question up. Let us meet the questions of human industry face to face and vote on them. As long as I am in public life I am prepared to vote on any question that arises, and I never shall shield myself and excuse myself from voting upon them with any strained constitutional construction.

SENATOR FULTON.—I assume the Senator does not mean to say that he believes if Congress is without constitutional power to enact certain legislation he will nevertheless insist on voting on it.

SENATOR BEVERIDGE.—Mr. President, most certainly I do not.

Now that the Senator has asked that question, I would not be surprised that a good deal of anxiety about the constitutionality of this bill is wrapped up in that very eight-hour question. It may be that many people hope that this is unconstitutional, so that they will not have to vote on it and the whole group of questions associated with it.

Mr. President, the next reason why the States cannot adequately handle this question is because neither in this nor in any other important question have the States ever succeeded in having uniform laws; and it is clear that this evil cannot be remedied unless there *are uniform laws upon it.*

Suppose, for example, that Ohio passes an excellent child-labor law and my State repeals ours, instantly every manufacturing establishment in my State would drain the child labor from Ohio to us, because it is cheaper and more profitable, and the manufacturers of Ohio would be at a disadvantage with the manufacturers of Indiana.

Not only that, but if every single State in the Union but one were to enact a good law and execute it, nevertheless the one State that did not and that continued to permit the infamy would be ruining citizens not of that State only, but citizens of the nation also.

A child that grows up in New York and becomes a citizen is not alone a citizen of New York. He is a citizen of the Republic as well, and when any system of labor or of lack of education ruins him for citizenship in the State he is ruined for citizenship in the nation.

So not only, Mr. President, is there inequality of business opportunities, but by that inequality the ruin of citizens in any one State, the murder of the innocents in any one commonwealth, affects the entire Republic as much as it affects that State.

If there is any person on this floor, including the Senators from the South, who has a greater affection than I for that section of the country, from which I draw my own blood, I do not know it. And now I want to give a solemn warning to my brothers of the South.

We have had much of this session taken up with a discussion of the race question [the Brownsville case]. We have had the assertion of the superiority of the white race made time and time again; that the white race would never yield to the black race.

Yet the children who are at work in the Southern cotton mills are from the white working class of the South; and this terrible situation stares the South in the face that, *whereas the children of the white working people of the South are going to the mill and to decay, the negro children are going to school and improvement.*

I am glad to see the negro children going to school, but it is enough to wring the heart to think that day by day you are permitting a system to go on which is steadily weakening the white race for the future and steadily strengthening the black race for the future.

It is not in the power of any man to keep ''superior'' by *asserting* superiority. The truth of it is the South is face to face with the situation of their white children in the mills and their black children in the schools.

There is another thing which we on this side—the Republican side—might as well take into account. I have here the present tariff law. I was reading before I came up to the Capitol, after I got into the office, the tariff on cotton, the tariff on glass, the tariff on coal. I ask Senators who, like myself, are protectionists, With what grace can we go to the country asking that the tariff be continued on these things when the industries in these lines are supported by cheap child labor?

And now I wish to speak right here another warning to labor, and I will ask to put into my remarks numerous statements made under oath to prove it. I want the laboring men and women of this country to understand what every labor leader knows—and if he does not know it he is not fit to be a labor leader or any other kind of a leader—that *child labor tends to bring down manhood wages and womanhood wages to the child-wage level.* You are not only killing your children, laboring men, but you are reducing your own manhood wages.

Mr. President, I come now to the constitutionality of this proposed law.

The power of the States over commerce was *absolutely sovereign* under the Articles of Confederation. Of course no Senator will deny that.

But *all* such power which the States had under the Articles of Confederation was by the Constitution *given to Congress.* The States parted with that power absolutely, and the power given to Congress, so far as interstate traffic is concerned, is *as complete and absolute as the power of the State over State commerce.*

There were in existence at the time the Constitution was adopted some twenty-seven acts of the English Parliament in which the phrase "to regulate commerce" occurs. In each one of them those words mean in those laws "prohibition" of commerce in some form or other or in some article of commerce.

So when the Fathers lifted out of the English statutes and put into the Constitution the phrase "to regulate commerce," they lifted out words that had a definite meaning in the acts of the British Parliament which were directly before them.

It was not very long after the Constitution was adopted until there arose the very question which we have here raised, the question as to whether under the commerce clause Congress had the power, in regulating commerce, to *"prohibit"* commerce in any article, and that was decided in the affirmative in the case which every lawyer has had by heart since he went to law school—in Gibbons *v.* Ogden, in the great opinion by Chief Justice Marshall.

SENATOR BACON.—Even if we concede the power of Congress to prohibit the introduction of an article, does the Senator recognize no difference between the power to prohibit the introduction of an article vicious in itself or objectionable for any reason, as most of these decisions pass upon questions of that kind, and an article not objectionable in itself, not vicious, or in any manner detrimental to the public good—

SENATOR BEVERIDGE.—I understand the Senator's question.

SENATOR BACON.—An article thus not objectionable, but where the point of the objection simply is as to the manner in which it has been produced in the State?

SENATOR BEVERIDGE.—As a question of *power,* no; none in the world; but, yes; as a question of *policy.* We have the power. It is a power which we can abuse. But if we do abuse that power, which in us is unlimited, the remedy is at the ballot box, as was pointed out by Chief Justice Marshall in Gibbons *v.* Ogden, where the very question was raised.

SENATOR FULTON.—Would not that, followed to its logical conclusion, mean that Congress could absolutely prohibit commerce among the States?

SENATOR BEVERIDGE.—Certainly. That question was raised in Gibbons *v.* Ogden. There was a definition of the *power* to pass an embargo law. An embargo was an absolute *prohibition* of commerce, and the argument was made against it that we had no such power under the Constitution, because, they said, it meant the *annihilation* of commerce. Here is what Chief Justice Marshall said:

> The power to regulate—that is, *to prescribe the rule by which commerce is to be governed*—like all others vested in Congress, is complete in itself, may be exercised to its utmost extent, and *acknowledges no limitations* other than are prescribed in the Constitution.
>
> If, as has always been understood, the sovereignty of Congress, though limited to specified objects, is *plenary as to those objects*, the power over commerce with foreign nations, *and among the several States*, is vested in Congress *as absolutely as it would be in a single government*, having in its constitution the same restrictions on the exercise of the power as are found in the Constitution of the United States.

The debate was resumed on January 29. Nelson W. Aldrich [R. I.] asked Senator Beveridge if he were not aware that the power of Congress does not depend entirely upon one clause in the Constitution, the so-called "commerce clause," but upon the taxing clause as well.

Senator Beveridge granted this.

But let me call the Senator's attention to this. The Senator is a great tariff expert, but, *constitutionally*, you have the right to lay taxes, to put on tariffs, under the taxing power, *only for the purpose of revenue*.

When you lay a tariff for *protection* it comes within the *commerce clause* of the Constitution.

That question came up early in our constitutional history. They said a protective tariff was unconstitutional, and the Supreme Court admitted that it is unconstitutional *under the taxing power alone*. Under that Congress has power to lay taxes, impose imposts, etc., and nothing else.

But, when it comes to *protection*, your power is derived from the *interstate and foreign commerce clause* of the Constitution, and *from that alone*. The Senator will find one entire chapter of very interesting reading, demonstrating that fact, in Story on the Constitution. Perhaps the ablest piece of work Mr. Justice Story ever did was to demonstrate that that power existed *under the interstate and foreign commerce clause*.

Now, Mr. President, *if, then, the power of Congress over foreign commerce and interstate commerce is the same*, and by virtue of the former we have *prohibited* convict-made goods, we may also *prohibit* the transportation of convict-made goods in interstate commerce. But, if *convict*-made goods may be prohibited in interstate commerce, then why can we not also prohibit *child*-made goods?

If we have the power to *prohibit* the transportation in interstate commerce of cattle *without a certificate, well or ill;* if we have the power to *prohibit* the transportation of certain *insects;* if we have the power to *prohibit* the transportation of loose *hay* in vessels; if we have the power to *prohibit* the transportation of gold and silver goods merely because they have two words on them, and all *under the interstate commerce clause;* if we have the power to *prohibit* convict-made goods, why have we not the power to *prohibit* the transportation in interstate commerce of child-labor-made goods?

So far as the question of *power* is concerned, in none of these cases that I have shown did the *power* come, *in a single instance,* from the evil of the article prohibited. As a matter of *policy* we enacted those laws because they were good for the "interests of the nation." But if it is good for the "interests of the nation" to *prohibit* the transportation of *insects* from State to State; if it is good for the "interests of the nation" to *prohibit* the importation of convict-made goods; if the *power* over *interstate* commerce equals the power over *foreign* commerce, as the Supreme Court has said, unless it is overruled by a sub-committee of the Senate; if we have the *power* to *prohibit* convict-made goods in interstate commerce, as we have; if we have actually *prohibited* the transportation of gold and silver merely because they had two words which inconvenienced the business of certain men in New York and New Jersey, all upon the theory that it affected the "interests of the nation," to use again Chief Justice Marshall's famous phrase, how much more have we got the *power* to *prohibit* the transportation in interstate commerce of child-made goods which affect the "interests ___tion," aye, and the perpetuity of the nation?

___ grow excited about refinements. I ask them to ___ *that are on the statute books. Why* did we ___ any "danger of the extension of the Federal ___ were enacting those statutes? Why is it ___pt to stop the murder of children and ___and the ruin of our citizens by ___ goods in interstate ___ of an artificial

___tional fight ___een made ___ *only*

sometimes wonder what is the purpose of these "free institutions" about which we talk so much. Why was it that this Republic was established? What does the flag stand for?

Mr. President, what do all these things mean? They mean that the people shall be free to correct human abuses.

They mean that men and women and children shall day by day grow stronger and nobler.

They mean that we shall have the power to make this America of ours each day a lovelier place to live in.

They mean the realities of liberty, and not the academics of theory.

They mean the *actual* progress of the race in the tangible items of real existence, and not the theoretics of disputation.

If they do not mean these things, Mr. President, then our institutions, this Republic, our flag, have no meaning and no reason for existence.

Mr. President, to see this Republic of free and equal men and women grow increasingly, with each day and year, as the mightiest power for righteousness in the world has been, and is, and always will be, I pray God, the passion of my life—a nation of strong, pure human beings; a nation of wholesome homes, true to the holiest ideals of man; a nation whose power is glorified by its justice, and whose justice is the conscience of scores of millions of free, strong, brave people.

It is to make this people such a nation that all our wars have been fought, all our heroes have died, all our permanent laws have been written, all our statesmen have planned, and our people themselves have striven.

It was to make such a nation as this that the old Articl[es] of Confederation were thrown away and the Constitution [of the] United States, about which we debate so much, wa[s]

Mr. President, it is to make this nation[...] holy destiny that I have presented this bil[l] of American children and the ruin of [...] zens. [Applause in the galleries.]

The bill was [...] of other chil[...] labor in th[...] the follo[...] in the [...]

sometimes wonder what is the purpose of these "free institutions" about which we talk so much. Why was it that this Republic was established? What does the flag stand for?

Mr. President, what do all these things mean? They mean that the people shall be free to correct human abuses.

They mean that men and women and children shall day by day grow stronger and nobler.

They mean that we shall have the power to make this America of ours each day a lovelier place to live in.

They mean the realities of liberty, and not the academics of theory.

They mean the *actual* progress of the race in the tangible items of real existence, and not the theoretics of disputation.

If they do not mean these things, Mr. President, then our institutions, this Republic, our flag, have no meaning and no reason for existence.

Mr. President, to see this Republic of free and equal men and women grow increasingly, with each day and year, as the mightiest power for righteousness in the world has been, and is, and always will be, I pray God, the passion of my life—a nation of strong, pure human beings; a nation of wholesome homes, true to the holiest ideals of man; a nation whose power is glorified by its justice, and whose justice is the conscience of scores of millions of free, strong, brave people.

It is to make this people such a nation that all our wars have been fought, all our heroes have died, all our permanent laws have been written, all our statesmen have planned, and our people themselves have striven.

It was to make such a nation as this that the old Articles of Confederation were thrown away and the Constitution of the United States, about which we debate so much, was adopted.

Mr. President, it is to make this nation still surer of this holy destiny that I have presented this bill to stop the murder of American children and the ruin of future American citizens. [Applause in the galleries.]

The bill was passed over during this session in favor of other child labor legislation. Restriction of child labor in the District of Columbia came up again during the following session in the form of a new bill presented in the Senate on February 3, 1908, by Jacob H. Gallinger [N. H.]. It was referred to the Committee on Education and Labor, which reported it on February 25. It was

If we have the power to *prohibit* the transportation in inter-state commerce of cattle *without a certificate, well or ill;* if we have the power to *prohibit* the transportation of certain *insects;* if we have the power to *prohibit* the transportation of loose *hay* in vessels; if we have the power to *prohibit* the transportation of gold and silver goods merely because they have two words on them, and all *under the interstate commerce clause;* if we have the power to *prohibit* convict-made goods, why have we not the power to *prohibit* the transportation in interstate commerce of child-labor-made goods?

So far as the question of *power* is concerned, in none of these cases that I have shown did the *power* come, *in a single instance,* from the evil of the article prohibited. As a matter of *policy* we enacted those laws because they were good for the "interests of the nation." But if it is good for the "interests of the nation" to *prohibit* the transportation of *insects* from State to State; if it is good for the "interests of the nation" to *prohibit* the importation of convict-made goods; if the *power* over *interstate* commerce equals the power over *foreign* commerce, as the Supreme Court has said, unless it is overruled by a sub-committee of the Senate; if we have the *power* to *prohibit* convict-made goods in interstate commerce, as we have; if we have actually *prohibited* the transportation of gold and silver merely because they had two words which inconvenienced the business of certain men in New York and New Jersey, all upon the theory that it affected the "interests of the nation," to use again Chief Justice Marshall's famous phrase, how much more have we got the *power* to *prohibit* the transportation in inter-state commerce of child-made goods which affect the "interests of the nation," aye, and the perpetuity of the nation?

Gentlemen grow excited about refinements. I ask them to explain the laws *that are on the statute books. Why* did we never hear before of any "danger of the extension of the Federal power" when you were enacting those statutes? Why is it that only when we attempt to stop the murder of children and the debasement of our race and the ruin of our citizens by *prohibiting* the transportation of child-made goods in interstate commerce that Senators are aroused in defence of an artificial liberty?

It is a curious thing to me that every constitutional fight that has been made in the Supreme Court has *always* been made against laws prohibiting something in interstate commerce *only* when some business interest was affected by it.

Why, Mr. President, when I think about these things I

less drastic than the former bill, in that means were provided for children working (under proper regulations) when they contributed to the expenses of a needy family, and the interstate commerce feature introduced by Senator Beveridge was eliminated for future separate consideration. It was passed on May 6, 1908, without division.

The House amended the bill, making it still less drastic, and passed it on May 9 by a vote of 200 to 0, 187 Representatives not voting. The Senate disagreed to the House amendment. A conference was appointed, which reported on May 21 that the Senate recede from its disagreement, and the bill was passed on May 25. President Roosevelt approved it on May 28, 1908.

OTHER CHILD LABOR ACTS

On December 18, 1906, a bill was reported in the Senate, from the Committee on Education and Labor, authorizing the Secretary of Commerce and Labor to investigate and report upon the industrial, social, moral, educational, and physical condition of women and child workers in the United States. It was passed on the same day. The House committed the bill.

On January 21, 1897, Richard Bartholdt [Mo.] moved to take the bill from committee and pass it. After some debate the bill was passed. President Roosevelt approved it on January 31.

On December 14, 1906, Edward L. Taylor, Jr. [O.], from the Committee on the District of Columbia, reported in the House a bill, originating in the Senate, to incorporate the National Child Labor Committee. This committee had been formed in Carnegie Hall, New York City, in 1904, and had a membership of 1,500 scattered through 16 States.

The bill came up for discussion on January 14, 1907.

Finis J. Garrett [Tenn.] opposed the bill:

One purpose of the committee that is set forth in the bill is to bring about legislation. Now, why, Mr. Speaker, should the Congress of the United States incorporate a lobby? I do not use the word lobby as applied to it in any offensive sense. I do not mean to imply that legislation against child labor is improper legislation. In fact, I think it is within the States. But why should Congress organize any association or incorporate any association whose avowed purpose is to bring about certain legislation?

The bill was passed with an amendment reserving the right to alter or repeal the act.

The Senate objected to this amendment on January 25, and a conference was ordered. The conference committee reported on February 16 that the Senate accept the House amendment. This was agreed to by the Senate. President Roosevelt approved the act on February 21, 1907.

CHAPTER VIII

Injunctions in Labor Disputes

Robert L. Henry [Tex.], Sereno E. Payne [N. Y.] and Others Introduce Bills in the House to Regulate Grants by Federal Courts of Restraining Orders—Debate: In Favor, Mr. Henry, Henry D. Clayton [Ala.]; Opposed, Charles E. Littlefield [Me.].

ON December 2, 1907, Robert L. Henry [Tex.] introduced two bills in the House: (1) to regulate the granting by the Federal courts of restraining orders and injunctions; and (2) to define contempts of court and fix their punishment. The bills were referred to the Committee on the Judiciary.

Curbing the Power of Federal Judges

House of Representatives, January 28, 1908

On January 28, 1908, Mr. Henry supported the principle of his bills:

The first question I propose to discuss this morning is that of limiting the power of Federal judges in the issuance of temporary restraining orders and injunctions. For years the laboring people have appealed to Congress, and particularly to the Judiciary Committee. Their demands have been just and reasonable. I discuss them not because this is class legislation, but because it is just legislation that should be enacted in the interest of the whole people. Session after session bills have been introduced and referred to that committee and other committees, but they have been silently pigeonholed and never reported back to the House.

Is this legislation just? Is it something that is reasonable? Mr. Chairman, it is legislation that should be passed, and I only take the floor this morning because these bills have been introduced from time to time and no attention has been paid to

321

them by this body. Let me call attention to the provisions contained in my bill.

Be it enacted, etc., That no writ of injunction or temporary restraining order shall be granted in any case without reasonable previous notice to the adverse party, or his attorney, of the time and place of moving for the same: *Provided,* That nothing herein contained shall be held to authorize the issuance of any injunction or restraining order not now authorized by law.

Mr. Chairman, substantially that language was the law of the country for seventy-nine years. In the act of 1791 it was provided that notice should be given by Federal judges before the issuance of temporary restraining orders and injunctions. In 1872 Congress passed an act which eliminated the provision requiring notice in injunction proceedings, and since that time Federal judges have held their star chamber sessions and have issued their temporary restraining orders and injunctions without any sort of notice to the adverse party or his attorney. This manifest defect should be remedied by an act of Congress. Are you ready and are you willing to pass legislation, not only for the benefit of the laboring people who have demanded it, who have been tyrannized over by injunction suits, who have felt the sting of unjust government by injunction, but are you ready to give it to the American people?

Secretary Taft, seeing the impending storm, has sought cover, and now tries to face about and win back those he unjustly oppressed while he was Federal judge. He says in a letter to the Ohio labor organizations:

"Second. You ask me what I think of a provision that no restraining order or injunction shall issue except after notice to the defendant and a hearing is had. This was the rule under the Federal statutes for many years, but it was subsequently repealed. In the classes of cases to which you refer I do not see any objection to the reënactment of that Federal statute. Indeed, I have taken occasion to say in public speeches that the power to issue injunctions *ex parte* has given rise to certain abuses and injustices to the laborers engaged in a peaceful strike. Men leave employment on a strike, counsel for the employer applies to a judge, and presents an affidavit averring fear of threatened violence and making such a case of the *ex parte* statement that the judge feels called upon to issue a temporary restraining order. The temporary restraining order is served upon all the strikers; they are not lawyers; their fears are aroused by the process with which they are not acquainted, and, although their purpose may have been entirely lawful, their common determination to carry through the strike is weakened by an order which they have never had an opportunity to question, and which is calculated to discourage their proceeding in their original purpose. To avoid this injustice I believe, as I have already said, that the Federal statute might well be made what it was originally, requiring notice and a hearing before an injunction issues.

"Third. In answer to your third question, it would seem that it is unnecessary to impose any limitation as to the time for a final hearing if before an injunction can issue at all notice and hearing must be given. The third question is relevant and proper only should the power of issuing *ex parte* injunctions be retained in the court. In such cases I should think it eminently proper that the statute should require the court issuing an *ex parte* injunction to give the person against whom the injunction was issued an opportunity to have a hearing thereof within a very short space of time, not to exceed, I should say, three or four days."

Gentlemen, will you heed the voice of the people? If not, the time will come when they will be accorded this relief. I don't know whether it will be at the hands of a Republican Administration or at the hands of a Democratic Administration, but as certain as we live such legislation will be enacted.

JOHN W. GAINES [Tenn.].—Why was the law changed?

MR. HENRY.—I have investigated, and find that when the statutes were recodified it was left out, as it has been since stated, inadvertently, and that it was not done intentionally. Yet during all this time the omission has remained upon the statutes, although session after session bills have been introduced and Representatives have come before the Judiciary Committee and have asked for relief.

There is no demand for radical legislation, nor are the people who have come before the Judiciary Committee asking for that kind. They would be satisfied with a reënactment of the statute that was law for seventy-nine years, which requires notice by a Federal judge before an injunction issues.

The bill provides only for previous reasonable notice. Letters from a number of Federal judges have come to me approving this bill, stating that it is reasonable and manifestly just and ought to be passed; that star-chamber proceedings ought to be stopped, and blanket injunctions without notice ought to cease; that traps for trying, convicting, and imprisoning men should no longer be set. [Applause on the Democratic side.]

I have no attack to make upon the judiciary of this country, either the Federal or State judiciary. But legislation of this kind ought to be given the American people. Before anyone is enjoined in his property rights or his personal rights he ought at least to have notice from Federal tyrants. He ought to have the poor privilege of appearing, filing answer, and being heard. Equity rule 55 provides for and requires notice in all such cases, but for years Federal tyrants have ignored it, flagrantly violated it, and spat upon it. They utterly disregard this plain provision of our equity rule. Let us pass a simple mandatory statute requiring previous reasonable notice before these blanket injunctions, or any other kind, can be issued by a Federal judge. Let us as Representatives of the people rob them of the power of imprisoning good and innocent men with their midnight orders and injunctions without hearing the other side, which often has a complete defence. But your Speaker and his Committee on Rules will stand with their eyes shut and as firmly as the walls of this Capitol spurn this just demand for relief. I freely make that prediction. [Applause on the Democratic side.]

MR. GAINES.—Are not cases reported where parties have been punished for contempt of court who had no real notice of the injunction and who disobeyed it unwittingly?

MR. HENRY.—Yes; there have been such cases, where they have been hauled up before a Federal judge without any notice that they were even charged with an offence, and Federal judges have denied them the poor privilege of trial by jury and placed them in prison and outraged them in many ways. Such judicial outrages ought to cease in this country, regardless of whether the man is a laboring man or any other citizen of the Republic. [Applause on the Democratic side.]

I have introduced another bill, one that passed the United States Senate a few years ago by unanimous vote, with the exception of Senator Hoar, of Massachusetts. He did not vote against the measure, but refrained from voting for it because he had not investigated it. I refer to the bill which passed that body providing for a trial by jury in cases of indirect contempt —that is, in cases of contempt committed out of the presence of the court. It passed the Senate and came to this body, and session after session, year after year, it has been reintroduced, and those entitled to the relief have been demanding its enactment; and yet it has never found its way out of the Judiciary Committee, and, in my humble judgment, will never do so until the American people command the Speaker of this House and that committee to take favorable action. [Applause on the Democratic side.] Substantially the same bill has been introduced by me at several sessions of Congress. It is now pending before the Judiciary Committee, of which I have the honor to be a member. It divides contempts into two classes—direct contempts and indirect contempts. Where the contempt is committed in the presence of the judge there should be no trial by jury, but the judge himself should have the power to punish summarily such offences. But where it is committed out of the presence of a court, where the offender does not know whether or not he has committed a contempt, he ought to have the privilege of calling for a jury. Aye, more. We ought to transfer the case from the jurisdiction of the Federal judge that issued the injunction, and let some other judge, without prejudice, try the offence.

Are you ready to enact such legislation as that? Is the Republican Speaker ready to give ear to the demands of the people who have called for this legislation year after year? You will give hearings this session, but no relief. Year after year they have come in a body and have demanded it of the Speaker, and he has frowned upon them. They will come again and make the same demands. I serve notice now that as long as I am in Congress this matter will be pressed until you act. These people would be satisfied with reasonable legislation if we would enact it. True, some of them want to go further. This House should not enact any law that is unreasonable, that is too radical, but we could certainly afford to reënact this old statute, and we agree that an offender in cases where an injunction has been issued without notice shall be entitled to the constitutional right of trial by jury. Jefferson said, and truly, that the Federal judges are "the sappers and miners, gradually undermining the foundation of this Government"; and he never stated a truer proposition.

Mr. Chairman, we have seen year after year one right after another taken from the American people, from the respective States of this Union by the Federal judiciary. When a power is conferred upon them they clamor for more. I know that in some quarters it is not fashionable to talk about State's rights. I know that it is not fashionable to denounce tyrannical Federal judges. And I do not criticize the just ones. The Constitution does not commend itself to some gentlemen. But we observe that only a few days ago the Supreme Court again decided a measure which passed through this House was unconstitutional. This reminded us that we still have a Constitution to govern us in our actions, and may go only so far in our legislative actions.

There is another bill introduced by me touching this subject—that no Federal judge shall issue an injunction or restraining order against a State officer or enjoin a State statute. That is to say that, whenever a State like Virginia, or North Carolina, or Alabama, or Missouri, or Pennsylvania, or any other State has enacted a solemn statute, there shall be some presumption in favor of the justice and validity of the statute, and Federal judges shall cease to enjoin them, at least "before final judgment on the merits of the case."

Now, gentlemen, we can afford to go that far. I would even go further, if I had my way. I would provide that where a corporation or an individual attacks the validity of a State statute they should raise that defence in the courts of the State, and if they have a Federal question involved in their litigation the case should go by writ of error from the court of last resort of the State to the Supreme Court of the United States. Let us not deprive any citizen or any corporation in this broad land of the privilege of going into the Federal courts and adjudicating their rights. Let us not take from them any right that is guaranteed by the Constitution and the statutes. Throw wide the doors of the Federal courts and the State courts as well to every citizen and corporation who has a right to assert. But, Mr. Chairman, when a Federal judge can enjoin a solemn act of a State acting within its inherent sovereignty the time has come when we should have legislation preventing such exercise of Federal power. Not many months ago when a railroad corporation in Missouri applied to Judge Smith McPherson to enjoin the 2-cent passenger-fare law of the State of Missouri he said:

"Gentlemen, the solemn enactments of the State of Missouri are entitled to some consideration, and I will not enjoin the enforcement of this State law, restraining the officers of the sovereign State of Missouri. I will allow it to be in operation for some time and see if it confiscates your property, as you say."

[Loud applause.]

Such is the true doctrine that should actuate a Federal judge. But it finds lodgment in the breasts of very few.

THOMAS HACKNEY [Mo.].—I wish to make the suggestion that such order was made against the railroad companies a year ago, and they have made no application to have the injunction issue.

MR. HENRY.—I am glad the gentleman has made that statement, and desire to say that I understand the railroads have found remunerative business in carrying passengers at the rate of 2 cents per mile, although they swore in their *ex parte* affidavit that their property was being confiscated. [Applause.] Mr. Chairman, give the other side a hearing, give them an opportunity, and, whenever a State in this Union passes a law, the presumption should be that it is acting within the scope of its constitutional authority and in accordance with the Constitution of the United States. [Applause.] For the just Federal judge who respects his oath and the Constitution, who recognizes the rights of the States have not been surrendered to any other power, who believes that the people of the States have retained some powers, I have a wholesome respect. But I fail to see the goodness and patriotism of those who would spit upon State statutes, as has been done in Virginia, North Carolina, Alabama, and other States. [Applause.]

Let me call your attention to another fact. In many instances where corporations have taken their cases to the Supreme Court of the United States, that court has held that the State statutes are constitutional and that they should not have been enjoined.

Such legislation as I propose will come. We will all live to see the time when it will be law. There will be jury trial in contempt cases. The American people will have it, and, though justice may be tardy, it is certain. The power of Federal judges will be curbed. The period is rapidly approaching when those whom you choose to call the laboring people will come into their rights. They are asking for nothing more than that which should be accorded to every honest and patriotic American citizen.

Let me warn the Republican side of this House that, while these people have patiently waited while demanding relief from you, they have done so for the last time. They will do so no longer. The party which I represent is ready to heed their just demands. We are ready to join hands with you and be just. Help us to command the Speaker in his high place, surrounded by his arbitrary Committee on Rules, and these just measures will be speedily presented to the American people as solemn statutory enactments. [Loud applause.]

On April 20, 1908, Sereno E. Payne [N. Y.] introduced in the House the following bill:

Be it enacted, etc., That hereafter no preliminary injunction nor restraining order shall be granted by any judge or court without notice to the party sought to be enjoined or restrained, unless it shall appear to the satisfaction of the court . . . that the immediate issue of such injunction or restraining order is necessary to prevent irreparable injury.

Sec. 2. That any such injunction or restraining order granted shall contain a rule on the opposite party to show cause within five days why (it) shall not be continued.

This bill, as well as others on the subject, was referred to the Judiciary Committee. The general discussion came up in the House on May 26, 1908.

INJUNCTIONS BY FEDERAL COURTS

HOUSE OF REPRESENTATIVES, MAY 26-30, 1908

MR. HENRY.—The President, many Senators of the United States, and a multitude of Representatives believe that inferior Federal judges should be curbed in relation to issuing restraining orders and injunctions. There is a widespread sentiment throughout the country that such legislation is necessary, and there has been and is now a strong popular demand for a law governing the issuance of restraining orders and injunctions. On the 10th day of April, 1906, it was my proud privilege to introduce the first bill amending the statutes in relation to granting restraining orders and injunctions by Federal courts. Since then many Representatives of both parties have introduced measures substantially like the one presented by me. At each session of Congress since that time it has been my privilege to reintroduce the same bill.

On April 3, 1893, Circuit Judge William H. Taft, now Secretary of War and probable nominee for the Presidency, rendered the following opinion in what is known as the "Ann Arbor case":

DECISION OF JUDGE TAFT

The Toledo, Ann Arbor and North Michigan Railway Company, complainant, *v.* The Pennsylvania Company *et al.*, defendants.

This is a motion by the complainant for a temporary injunction—to remain in force pending this action—against P. M. Arthur, the chief executive of the Brotherhood of Locomotive Engineers and a defendant herein, to restrain him from issuing, promulgating, or continuing in force any rule or order of said Brotherhood which shall require or command any employees of any of defendant railway companies herein to refuse to handle and deliver any cars of freight in course of transportation from one State to another, to the complainant, or from refusing to receive and handle cars of such freight which have been hauled over complainant's road, and also from in any way, directly or indirectly, endeavoring to persuade or induce any of the employees of the defendant railway companies, whose lines connect with the railroad of complainant, not to extend to said company the same facilities for interchange of interstate traffic as are extended by said companies to other railway companies. A temporary restraining order to this effect was issued by me against Arthur *ex parte*. A hearing has since been had, and the question now is whether, on the evidence produced, the order shall be continued in force until the final decision of the case.

Judge Taft continued the temporary injunction.

On July 13, 1894, Circuit Judge Taft rendered the following opinion in the case of Thomas *v.* Cincinnati, N. O. & T. P. Ry. Co., which discusses at great length the proposition involved in the above bill and one hereinafter to be set out:

Samuel M. Felton is receiver of the Cincinnati, New Orleans and Texas Pacific Railway Company, which is more commonly known as the "Cincinnati Southern Railroad." On Monday, July 2, 1894, he filed an intervening petition in the original action, in which he stated that during the previous week and at the time of filing the petition he was greatly impeded in the operation of the road by a strike of his employees and of the employees of other railroads in the city of Cincinnati, who were prevented from receiving from him and delivering to him freight carried or to be carried over his road; that said strike was the result of a conspiracy between one F. W. Phelan, now of Cincinnati, and one Eugene V. Debs and others, to tie up the road operated, as the said conspirators well knew, by the petitioner as receiver, and other roads in the Western States of the United States, until certain demands or alleged grievance of certain persons not in the employ of the receiver or of any other railroad of the United States were acceded to by persons in no manner connected with the management of any railroad of the United States; that the demand of the employees of one George M. Pullman, or of the Pullman Palace Car Company, at Pullman, Ill., for higher wages was refused, whereupon said Debs, Phelan, and others, members of an organization known as the "American Railway Union," combined and conspired with each other and with sundry persons, who became members of the organization for the purpose to compel the Pullman Company to comply with the demands of its employees, and that for the purpose of injuring the Pullman Company, and of thereby forcing from it the concession demanded, Debs, Phelan, and the others named had maliciously conspired and undertaken to prevent the receiver of this court and the owners of other railroads from using Pullman cars in operating their roads, though they are under contract to do so; that, in pursuance of said conspiracy, Phelan, a resident of Oregon, came to Cincinnati a week before the filing of the petition and set on foot and incited a strike among the employees of the receiver and of other railroad companies whose lines run into Cincinnati; that on June 27th and at other times and places Phelan made inflammatory speeches to such employees, well knowing many of them to be employees of the receiver, in which he urged them all to quit the service of the receiver and the other railroads of the city, and to tie them all up, and to prevent others from taking their places, by persuasion, if possible, by clubbing, if necessary; that said Phelan was still in the city, directing and continuing the strike and interfering with the receiver in the operation of the road; that as a result of the conspiracy and strike the receiver has been obliged at great expense to secure and maintain the protection of armed men for his employees, and that all of the foregoing constituted a contempt of this court and a ground both for committing Phelan and for enjoining him from a continuance of said acts.

Upon the filing of the petition an attachment was issued for Phelan, the contemner, and on the morning of the 3d of July he was arrested and brought before the court. He was admitted to bail, and at the same time was enjoined by the order of the court from, either as an individual or in combination with others, inciting, encouraging, ordering, or in any other manner causing the employees of the receiver to leave his employ with intent to obstruct the operation of his road, and thereby to compel him not to fulfill his contract and carry Pullman cars. On Thursday, July 5, the motion of the receiver for Phelan's commitment came on to be heard.

The substance of Judge Taft's decision was as follows:

Any willful attempt, with knowledge that a railroad is in the hands of the court, to prevent or impede the receiver thereof appointed by the court from complying with the order of the court in running the road, which is unlawful, and which, as between private individuals, would give a right of action for damages, is a contempt of the order of the court.

Maliciously inciting employees of a receiver, who is operating a railroad under order of the court, to leave his employ, in pursuance of an unlawful combination to prevent the operations of the road, thereby inflicting injuries on its business, for which damages would be recoverable if it were operated by a private corporation, is a contempt of court.

Such inciting to carry out an unlawful conspiracy is not protected by constitutional guaranties of the right of assembly and free speech, and is not less a contempt because effected by words only, if the obstruction to the operation of the road by the receiver is unlawful and malicious.

A combination to inflict pecuniary injury on the owner of cars, operated by railway companies under contracts with him, by compelling them to give up using his cars, in violation of their contracts, and, on their refusal, to inflict pecuniary injury on them by inciting their employees to quit their services, and thus paralyze their business, the existence of the contracts being known to the parties so combining, is an unlawful conspiracy.

A combination by employees of railway companies to injure in his business the owner of cars operated by the companies, by compelling them to cease using his cars by threats of quitting and by actually quitting their service, thereby inflicting on them great injury, where the relation between him and the companies is mutually profitable and has no effect whatever on the character or reward of the services of the employees so combining, is a boycott and unlawful conspiracy at common law.

A combination to incite the employees of all the railways of the country to suddenly quit their service without any dissatisfaction with the terms of their employment, thus paralyzing utterly all railway traffic, in order to starve the railroad companies and the public into compelling an owner of cars used in operating the roads to pay his employees more wages, they having no lawful right so to compel him, is an unlawful conspiracy by reason of its purpose, whether such purpose is effected by means usually lawful or otherwise.

Such combination, its purpose being to paralyze the interstate commerce of the country, is an unlawful conspiracy within the act of July 2, 1890, declaring illegal every contract, combination, or conspiracy in restraint of trade or commerce among the several States. (U. S. v. Patterson, 55 Fed. 605, disapproved.)

Such combination, where the members intend to stop all mail trains as well as other trains, and do delay many, in violation of Revised Statutes, Section 3,995, punishing anyone willfully and knowingly obstructing or retarding the passage of the mails, is unlawful conspiracy, although the obstruction is effected by merely quitting employment.

It follows that the contemner is guilty as charged and it only remains to impose the sentence of the court. This is in the discretion of the court to be exercised on any information in reference to the convicted person which the court believes to be reliable. The court would be much more disposed to leniency in this case if the contemner, after his arrest, had shown the slightest regard for the order of the court which the receiver was attempting to comply with in the operation of the road. Even if he did not fully realize his position in this respect, his arrest, and the service of the intervening petition, together with the restraining order, should have quickened his conscience and his perception of his duty in this regard. What did he do? Instead of ceasing to incite the receiver's employees to leave his employ in pursuance of his unlawful conspiracy, there has been no change whatever in his course from that pursued by him before his arrest. By speeches every night since the arrest he has aggravated his contempt. On the night of July 4, 1894, in a speech to railroad employees of this city, it is in evidence that the contemner said, referring to this trial:

"I don't care if I am violating injunctions. No matter what the result may be to-morrow, if I go to jail for sixteen generations, I want you to do as you have done. Stand pat to a man. No man go back unless all go, and all stay out unless Phelan says go back."

The punishment for a contempt is the most disagreeable duty a court has to perform, but it is one from which the court can not shrink. If orders of the court are not obeyed, the next step is unto anarchy. It is absolutely essential to the administration of justice that courts should have the power to punish contempts and that they should use it when the enforcement of their orders is flagrantly defied. But it is only to secure present and future compliance with its orders that the power is given, and not to impose punishment commensurate with the crimes or misdemeanors committed in the course of contempt, which are cognizable in a different tribunal or in this court by indictment and trial by jury. I have no right, and do not wish, to punish the contemner for the havoc which he and his associates have wrought to the business of this country and the injuries they have done to labor and capital alike, or for the privations and suffering to which they have subjected innocent people, even if they may not be amenable to the criminal laws therefor. I can only inflict a penalty which may have some effect to secure future compliance with the orders of this court and to prevent willful and unlawful obstructions thereof.

After much consideration, I do not think I should be doing my duty as a judicial officer of the United States without imposing upon the contemner the penalty of imprisonment. The sentence of the court is that Frank W. Phelan be confined in the county jail of Warren County, Ohio, for a term of six months. The marshal will take the prisoner into custody and safely convey him to the place of imprisonment.

Mr. Henry continued:

The Democrats in the House of Representatives have frequently insisted on the passage of this bill and have challenged the Republican party to aid in its enactment. On many occasions Democrats in the House of Representatives have appealed to the Republican party and to the Speaker to permit the consideration of such a measure, and have met only with constant denial and scorn.

On May 30, Charles E. Littlefield [Me.] made an exhaustive speech on the general subject of injunctions.

In the matter of the use and abuse of injunctions in labor controversies so much is repeatedly and insistently said, and so vigorously have the courts been denounced, that I think it may be safely said that the impression generally prevails that there has been and still is more or less abuse of judicial discretion in controversies of that character. I am free to admit that, in a general way, I entertained that impression myself, until I made the investigation to which I shall now refer.

The assertions have hitherto been general and indefinite in character. It seemed to me that at this time it was both wise and proper that the parties making these assertions and engaged in wholesale denunciations of the courts should be required to specify the instances of abuse and call attention to the circumstances under which they claim judicial discretion has been abused and the power of granting injunctions in labor controversies has been oppressively or improperly exercised.

With that in view, on the 5th of February, 1908, when Mr. T. C. Spelling, the attorney representing the American Federation of Labor, appeared before the Judiciary Committee to urge the enactment of the Pearre bill, I took occasion to ask Mr. Spelling if he would be kind enough to specify the cases of injunctions where instances of abuse had occurred, and point out the circumstances connected therewith, also to give a list of cases where injunctions have been unlawfully ordered. Mr. Spelling replied that there were a great many such cases, and that he would furnish the required information or have it done.

This was on the 5th of February, 1908. It is proper to remark that up to to-day Mr. Spelling has not filed a single one of "the great many cases" he claimed existed.

Samuel Gompers, who appeared before the committee on the 24th of February, was requested to file everything he had in that line, but nothing was filed with the committee until about the 6th or 7th of May, when a mass of material, some of it relating to State injunctions, some of it having no connection with injunctions, some of it being injunction orders and opinions relating thereto, was filed. No criticism of any injunction order or decree was filed with this material, and, although I specifically requested the gentlemen representing this body to file with the other data such criticism as they had to make of these injunctions or orders, they absolutely declined to file any criticism whatever.

I shall introduce as an appendix an abstract of the material thus filed, so far as it relates to injunctions and decrees and the action of the courts thereon. This abstract was made by Mr. J. A. Emery, a lawyer of ability and experience, and I rely on the results of his work in my discussion thereof.

The papers thus filed show only twenty-three Federal decisions, orders, or complaints, beginning with an injunction issued December 19, 1893, by Judge Jenkins in the case of The Farmers' Loan and Trust Company *v.* The Northern Pacific Railroad (60 F. R., 803), being the celebrated Jenkins case, involving the Order of Railway Trainmen.

Of these twenty-three decisions, two are of the supreme court of the District of Columbia—Bender *v.* Union and the Bucks Stove and Range Company *v.* the American Federation of Labor.

In the Bucks Stove and Range case, on the motion to make the injunction permanent, the defendants did not contest the decree, which was made final without argument or criticism, and it is still uncertain whether or not their appeal from the final order will be perfected.

In the Bender case, after notice and full argument, the court declined to issue a preliminary injunction. The matter was then carried forward and heard on the pleadings and proofs, on motion for a permanent injunction, which motion the court granted. After full argument the court took the matter under advisement, and then ordered a final writ of injunction to issue. From this decree the respondents entered an appeal. This appeal has since been withdrawn. Such withdrawal operates as a confession by respondents that their case upon the facts was hopeless and unworthy of further contention. If these two cases are characteristic of the twenty-three, they are all above criticism.

In the celebrated Jenkins case the judge has been vigorously assailed for his action, and in connection therewith was threatened with impeachment proceedings before the Judiciary Committee. In this case the Northern Pacific Railroad Company, having gone into the hands of receivers, two days after their appointment a reduction of from 10 to 20 per cent. was ordered in the salaries of employees. The employees threatened to strike to prevent the carrying out of this order, and the receivers applied to the court to restrain the men from executing their threat.   Judge Jenkins issued a preliminary injunction containing the following clause:

And from ordering, recommending, approving, or advising others to quit the service of the receivers of the Northern Pacific Railroad on January 1, 1894, or at any other time.

Judge Jenkins subsequently modified the preliminary injunction by striking out this clause.   This case was carried on appeal from his refusal to further modify his injunction to the circuit court of appeals.   The opinion of the court of appeals was drawn by Mr. Justice Harlan, of the Supreme Court of the United States.

Mr. Justice Harlan discussed the issues in an elaborate and exhaustive opinion.   It appears that it was contended on appeal that the circuit court exceeded its powers when it enjoined the employees of the receivers "from combining and conspiring to quit with or without notice the service of said receivers, with the object and intent of crippling the property in their custody or embarrassing the operation of said railroad, *and from so quitting the service of said receivers with or without notice as to cripple the property or prevent or hinder the operation of said railroad.*"

The court held that this clause embodied two distinct propositions—one relating to combinations and conspiracies to quit the service of the receivers, "with the object and intent of crippling the property . . . or embarrassing the operation of the railroads in their charge"; the other having no reference to combinations and conspiracies to quit, or to the object and intent of quitting, but only to employees "so quitting" as to "cripple the property or prevent or hinder the operation of the railroad."

The court held that the court below (Judge Jenkins) should have eliminated from the writ of injunction the words:

And from so quitting the service of said receivers with or without notice as to cripple the property or prevent or hinder the operation of said railroad—

but upheld the injunction in all other respects.

On the other question of the distinction between the two propositions the court said, after having called attention to the fact that the employees as a body had a right to demand given rates as a condition for their remaining in service and to withdraw from service if these were not granted to them, without reference to the effect upon the property or upon the operation of the road:

> But that is a very different matter from a *combination and conspiracy* among employees, with the *object and intent*, not simply of quitting the service of the receivers because of the reduction of wages, but of *crippling the property* in their hands, and *embarrassing the operation* of the railroad.

In his order modifying the injunction and the reasons given therefor Mr. Justice Harlan simply emphasizes the familiar and well-established distinction between acts done or strikes inaugurated in pursuance of and for the purpose of carrying out a conspiracy and such acts entirely disconnected with such conspiracy.

Judge George Gray, in his celebrated decision in the anthracite coal strike case, concurred in by every other member of the commission, which included Carroll D. Wright, John M. Wilson, John L. Spalding, Edgar E. Clark, Thomas H. Watkins, and Edward W. Parker, one of whom, Mr. Clark, was a specific representative on the commission of organized labor, said:

> Our language is the language of a free people and fails to furnish any form of speech by which the right of a citizen to work when he pleases, for whom he pleases, and on what terms he pleases can be successfully denied. The common sense of our people, as well as the common law, forbids that this right should be assailed with impunity. . . . The right thus to work can not be made to depend upon the approval or disapproval of the personal character and conduct of those who claim to exercise this right. If this were otherwise, then those who remain at work might, if they were in the majority, have both the right and power to prevent others who choose to cease work from so doing.
>
> This all seems too plain for argument. Common sense and common law alike denounce the conduct of those who interfere with this fundamental right of the citizen. The assertion of the right seems trite and commonplace, but that land is blessed where the maxims of liberty are commonplaces.

The right to work and the right to employ are very obviously correlative rights. And this right to employ, it may be said, has been distinctly sustained by the Supreme Court of the United States in the Adair case.

In the case of Hitchman Coal and Coke Company *vs.* Mitchell *et al.* employees, who were to be displaced by union labor, were under specific and express contracts. It has always been held that a conspiracy to induce the violation of such contracts is restrainable as an infringement of a clear legal right. The authorities are innumerable in sustaining this proposition and no authority can be found that denies it, and it should be remembered that Judge Dayton's order in this particular case was expressly predicated upon the knowledge of the defendants of the existence of such contracts and their deliberate purpose to induce their violation.

This was one of the grounds upon which the court proceeded in the case of Thomas *v.* Cincinnati, New Orleans, and Texas Pacific Company (62 F. R., 803), in which the able opinion was drawn by Hon. William H. Taft; and the action of Judge Taft in this case is a specific precedent on all fours justifying the action of Judge Dayton in issuing this injunction. He said: "The breach of a contract is unlawful. A combination with that as its purpose is unlawful and is a conspiracy."

The contemplation of these salient and uncontrovertible facts must tend to a feeling of humiliating chagrin on the part of those zealous and earnest gentlemen who in season and out of season have been boiling their vicarious and baseless indignation over the action of Judge Dayton in this case.

HAS CONGRESS POWER TO LIMIT OR CONTROL THE JUDICIAL POWER OF A COURT OF EQUITY

I premise the legal discussion of this question by the statement, which must be obvious, that I can not expect to exhaustively discuss any of the propositions involved. The most that I can attempt to do is to lay down, so far as I can, the foundation principles—legal and constitutional—involved in this question.

The question goes to the very foundation of our whole constitutional system. As I understand our form of government, it involves the exercise of three great coördinate, independent powers—the executive, legislative, and judicial. Each of these powers within its own constitutional sphere is absolutely supreme and independent and can not be controlled or interfered with by any of the other powers.

DISTINCTION BETWEEN JURISDICTION AND JUDICIAL POWER

The Constitution of the United States, section 1, Article III, says:

The judicial power of the United States shall be vested in one Supreme Court and in such inferior courts as the Congress may from time to time ordain and establish.

While it is true that Congress may ordain and establish inferior courts, and in a sense create them and in the same sense can destroy them, when once ordained and established and their jurisdiction is defined, the source from which they derive their judicial power is the same.

Section 2 provides that the judicial power shall "extend to all cases in law and equity arising under this Constitution," etc. The jurisdiction once defined, my belief is that within the limits of the jurisdiction, the court having the jurisdiction of the subject-matter and the parties, the judicial power to be exercised by it is beyond the power of the legislature to either impair, modify, or control.

I submit that while jurisdiction may be defined by the legislature the judicial power is conferred by the Constitution itself. The legislature may limit the jurisdiction of the court to the parties and the subject-matter, but within those limitations it can not impair the exercise of the judicial power.

There are those who seem to entertain the view that there is in some way a distinction in this respect between inferior courts that Congress may from time to time ordain and establish and the Supreme Court, on the ground that the Supreme Court is by name mentioned in the Constitution and that the inferior courts are to be created by the Congress. And it is contended that inasmuch as Congress has the power to create a court it has the power to destroy it, and if it can destroy in whole it can destroy in part, and if it can destroy in part it can impair or modify the judicial power of an inferior court, because that is not a court created by the Constitution.

In my judgment this distinction has no warrant either in reason or authority.

While Congress does "ordain and establish inferior courts" by the express provision of the Constitution, it is also true that, as an effective instrumentality for the administration of justice, the Congress ordains and establishes the Supreme Court itself. The Constitution does not provide of how many judges that court shall consist, nor does it provide when or where it shall sit, or how its decrees shall be enforced, or how its procedure shall be regulated. It is a practical impossibility for the Supreme Court, *ex proprio vigore,* without the necessary machinery provided by the legislature, to perform effectively any of its judicial functions. Therefore the constitutional distinction that is said to exist between it and the inferior courts as to "judicial power," because of the power of Congress to "ordain and establish inferior courts" and because of its assumed lack of power over ordaining and establishing the Supreme Court as an effective judicial instrumentality, has no substantial, logical, or constitutional basis upon which to rest.

XI—22

THE COURT CAN NOT BE DEPRIVED OF THE RIGHT TO PUNISH FOR CONTEMPT

In the message of President Roosevelt, under date of April 27, 1908, he says:

In contempt cases, save where immediate action is imperative, the trial should be before another judge.

In Secretary Taft's reply to the president of the Mine Workers' Association some two or three months since he suggested not only that there should be notice and hearing before any injunction was issued in labor controversies, but that the hearing upon the question of contempt should be before another judge; and the recommendation of the President in his message of April 27 is precisely in line with the reply of Secretary Taft to the president of the Mine Workers' Union. And the first question I wish to call attention to is whether or not it would be competent for the Congress to deprive the judge, while sitting as a court where a contempt is committed, of the power of protecting his own court by his own decree and determining the facts himself, by transferring that right to another judge, or, as suggested in some of the remedies proposed, to a jury for determination.

The opinions of the court upon this question are not open to misconstruction. In the case of Little *vs.* The State (90 Ind. 339) the court said:

Among the *inherent powers* of a court of superior jurisdiction is that of maintaining its dignity, securing obedience to its process and rules, protecting its officers and jurors from indignity and wrong, rebuking interference with the conduct of business, and punishing unseemly behavior. *This power is essential to the existence of the court.* Without the power to punish for contempt, no others could, as decided in United States *v.* Hudson, *be effectively exercised.* There is no doubt that the power to punish for contempt is an *inherent one, for, independent of legislation, it exists and has always existed in the courts of England and America.* It is, in truth, *impossible to conceive of a superior court as existing without such a power.*

The legislature may regulate the exercise of this power—may prescribe rules of practice and procedure, but it can neither take it away nor *materially impair it.*

It is also to be observed that, while a violation of an order of the court in connection with labor controversies may result in the commission of a crime, it is at the same time a violation of the order, and it is for the violation of the order and not for the commission of a crime that the respondent, under such circumstances, is punished by the court. While the respondent in such a case in violating the order of the court may have by the same act committed a crime, either against the State or against the Federal jurisdiction, he can be punished for that and also punished by the court for the violation of its order, the two being entirely distinct and independent legal proceedings, and having, so far as the remedy or the offence is concerned, no connection whatever with each other.

This whole subject of contempt, and the power of the court relative thereto, and the distinction to which I have just adverted are thoroughly gone over by the court in its opinion in the case of *In re* Debs (158 U. S., 594), the opinion being drawn by Mr. Justice Brewer, speaking for a unanimous court. In the course of the opinion, in discussing the power of the court to protect itself by punishing disobedience of its orders as a contempt, the court said:

But the power of a court to make an order carries with it the equal power to punish for a disobedience of that order, and the inquiry as to the question of disobedience has been, from time immemorial, the *special function of the court.* And this is no technical rule. In order that a court may compel obedience to its orders it must have the right to inquire whether there has been any disobedience thereof. To submit the question of disobedience *to another tribunal, be it a jury or another court, would operate to deprive the proceeding of half its efficiency.* In the case of Yates (4 Johns., 314, 369) Chancellor Kent, then Chief-Justice of the Supreme Court of the State of New York, said:
"In the case of the Earl of Shaftesbury (2 St. Trials, 615; S. C. 1 Mod., 144), who was imprisoned by the House of Lords for 'high contempts committed against it,' and brought into the king's bench, the court held that they had no authority to judge of the contempt, and remanded the prisoner. The court in that case seems to have laid down a principle from which they never have departed, and which is essential to the due administration of justice.

I feel bound to say that I must part company with the President and the Secretary and stay with the court and its solemn determination, and under no circumstances will I consent to the enactment of any legislation that will be thus in violation of what I believe to be profound, inherent, essential, fundamental principles.

The legislature has no power to deprive the court of the inherent right to protect itself, and, if it had, I could not agree to legislation that would *"be a disgrace to the legislation and a stigma upon the age which invented it."*

It can not be necessary, in general, for me to further elaborate the proposition that the basis of the charge of the labor organizations against the courts proceeds entirely and absolutely from an incorrect hypothesis. The contempt proceedings of which they complain always arise where specific orders of the court have been violated. The parties are punished by the court, not because they have committed crimes, not because the act itself may have been the commission of a crime, but because the act is a violation of the specific order of the court, and it is to maintain its dignity and enforce its decrees that the parties, under such circumstances, are held for contempt.

THE CONSTITUTIONAL RIGHT OF EQUITABLE PROCEDURE

Thus far the discussion has involved the inviolability of the judicial power in general and the constitutional right of the citizen to its full, unlimited, and unhampered exercise. I think it is equally well settled that the Constitution as clearly guarantees to each citizen the right to the exercise by the chancellor of the full equity power of the court.

In the case of Callaman *vs.* Judd *et al.* (23 Wisc., 350) the court said:

When the Constitution vested in certain courts judicial power as to matters in equity, it clothed them with this power, as one of the established elements of judicial power in equity, so that the legislature can not withdraw it and confer it upon juries.

RELIEF BY INJUNCTION IS AN INHERENT EQUITY POWER

What, then, is the equity power so far as the right to injunctive relief is concerned?

In the case of State of Pennsylvania *vs.* The Wheeling, etc., Bridge Co. *et al.* (13 Howard, 563) the Supreme Court of the United States held:

In exercising this jurisdiction the courts of the Union are not limited by the chancery system adopted by any State, and they exercise their functions in a State where no court of chancery has been established. *The usages of the high court of chancery in England,* whenever the jurisdiction is exercised, govern the proceedings. This may be said to be the common law of chancery, and since the organization of the Government it has been observed.

A reference to Eden on Injunctions (1821), an English work, discloses the universal and immemorial practice of issuing restraining orders without notice and without hearing where the chancellor is confronted with threatened irreparable harm with an inadequate remedy at law.

The obvious purpose of a restraining order is to maintain the *status quo* until a hearing can be had upon the merits.

Under the Constitution the citizen can not be deprived of life, liberty, or property without due process of law. When the citizen presents to the court in equity a state of facts showing threatened irreparable harm with an inadequate remedy at law, "due process of law" in "controversies dealt with by equitable methods" entitles him to the issuance without notice and hearing of a temporary restraining order, to preserve his property until a hearing can be had upon the merits. If the order is issued, his property is preserved. The denial of this "due process of law" may, and probably would, result in the destruction of his property. Here the legislature steps in and by its arbitrary act declares that under no circumstances shall the suitor have his constitutional right to "due process of law" accorded to him until a notice shall have been given and a hearing had, which will precipitate the destruction of his property, leaving him without an adequate remedy at law, and depriving "due process of law" of all of its value. What answer is there to the proposition that such legislation deprives the citizen of his property "without due process of law" in violation of the fifth amendment to the Constitution?

I do not believe that the legislature has the power to thus impair the equitable methods of procedure which, under the authorities cited, are guaranteed to the citizen as inviolably as is the right of trial by jury in actions at law.

THE ACT OF 1793

There is apparently some misconception of the circumstances under which this old statute of 1793 ceased to be a part of the statute law. The gentleman from Texas [Mr. Henry] expressed what is no doubt the prevailing misconception in relation thereto.

The statement of the gentleman from Texas is erroneous in three particulars: First, the original statute did not apply to a temporary restraining order, but applied only to the writ of injunction; second, the alleged change was not the result of an inadvertence; and, third, it was not made when the statutes were recodified.

The alleged change in the law was by no means an inadvertence, but was deliberate and premeditated. The debate that occurred in the Senate shows that at that time at least the practice was universal for the courts of equity to grant temporary restraining orders without notice and hearing when they were confronted with threatened irreparable harm.

It is very clear that Congress understood that, in making this section a part of a general statute, they were putting into statutory form the existing law.

There is another phase of this subject which shows that a requirement of notice and hearing would deprive the writ of injunction of all of its value in labor controversies. It is perfectly competent, and it is the usual practice, for the court, in issuing an injunction to restrain the carrying out of a conspiracy, to make the injunctive order to run not only against the respondents named, but against all other persons conspiring, combining, and confederating with them. It not only restrains the individuals named, but it prevents the enlarging and spreading of the conspiracy by preventing others, not named and not known when the order is applied for and issued, from joining and making general such a conspiracy. The necessity for this in a labor controversy is too apparent for discussion. Without the power to issue such an order in the vast majority of instances, the writ would be for all practical purposes a nullity. Such an order, however, could under no circumstances be issued under the legislation proposed, as each person to be affected by the order must have notice and hearing before the order is made.

There can be no question under the provisions of the fourteenth amendment—which provides that no State shall deprive "any person of life, liberty, or property without due process of law, nor deny to any person within its jurisdiction the equal protection of the laws"—that legislation of this character would be clearly unconstitutional if enacted by a State.

If a State legislature undertook to control the judicial power of a court of equity so that it could exercise its protecting power to conserve the safety of persons and property in all cases except labor controversies, it would be clearly the exercise of class legislation, partial in its character. It would deny to the plaintiff, whose property was threatened by a labor conspiracy, the protection of the law guaranteed by the Constitution, while giving to every other litigant in connection with every other controversy that protection. The State courts, as well as the courts of the United States, when confronted with such an attempt to deprive the citizen of the equal protection of the law, would wipe such a law from the statute book as quickly as hoar frost vanishes before the morning sun.

For both of these reasons, then, Mr. Speaker—because the

legislature has no power to restrain the court in its right to issue a temporary restraining order and because it has no right to pass any legislation discriminating between classes, in addition to the practical difficulty of the substantial destruction of the equity power as a remedial process, I am unalterably opposed to legislation of this character.

The issues tendered by the leaders of the labor organizations are, shall the boycott and black-list be legalized or penalized, and shall the right to do business be outlawed, or shall it be maintained. On these issues I am unalterably against the boycott and black-list, and I stand unqualifiedly for the maintenance of the right to do business and its protection by the law. These issues transcend in their vital importance all the issues that now divide the two great political parties. Any candidate, from the Presidency down, that either truckles, or panders, to such a propaganda in either the Democratic or Republican party deserves to go down in overwhelming defeat.

With reference to this legislation and the action that should be taken thereon, I know not what course others may take, and I think I may be pardoned for going so far as to say I care not what course others may take, but, as for me, I propose to base my action upon considerations which I believe to be elemental and fundamental. So far as I have the power to control or shape legislation, the legislation shall be upon the principles of the equality of all before the law—the high and the low, the rich and the poor, the weak and the strong, the oppressor and the oppressed, the wage-earner and the wage-payer, friend and foe shall receive from me the application of the same universally operating principles of fundamental eternal justice. Whenever I fail to be actuated by these principles, which I believe to be essential to the perpetuation of the constitutional government of a free people, may "my tongue cleave to the roof of my mouth, my right hand forget its cunning," and may I be "anathema maranatha."

On the same day (May 30, 1908) Henry D. Clayton [Ala.] gave a consensus of the recommendations on the question presented by President Roosevelt in his messages, the best of which, claimed Representative Clayton, had been "borrowed from Democratic platforms and other Democratic sources."

It may not be amiss for me now to invite attention to the failure of the Republican party, which is in control of both branches of Congress, to enact the legislation recommended by the President.

On December 3, 1906, in his message to Congress the President said:

In my last message I suggested the enactment of a law in connection with the issuance of injunctions, attention having been sharply drawn to the matter by the demand that the right of applying injunctions in labor cases should be wholly abolished. It is at least doubtful whether a law abolishing altogether the use of injunctions in such cases would stand the test of the courts; in which case of course the legislation would be ineffective. Moreover, I believe it would be wrong altogether to prohibit the use of injunctions. It is criminal to permit sympathy for criminals to weaken our hands in upholding the law; and if men seek to destroy life or property by mob violence there should be no impairment of the power of the courts to deal with them in the most summary and effective way possible. But so far as possible the abuse of the power should be provided against by some such law as I advocated last year.

In this matter of injunctions there is lodged in the hands of the judiciary a necessary power which is nevertheless subject to the possibility of grave abuse. It is a power that should be exercised with extreme care and should be subject to the jealous scrutiny of all men, and condemnation should be meted out as much to the judge who fails to use it boldly when necessary as to the judge who uses it wantonly or oppressively. Of course a judge strong enough to be fit for his office will enjoin any resort to violence or intimidation, especially by conspiracy, no matter what his opinion may be of the rights of the original quarrel. There must be no hesitation in dealing with disorder. But there must likewise be no such abuse of the injunctive power as is implied in forbidding laboring men to strive for their own betterment in peaceful and lawful ways; nor must the injunction be used merely to aid some big corporation in carrying out schemes for its own aggrandizement. It must be remembered that a preliminary injunction in a labor case, if granted without adequate proof (even when authority can be found to support the conclusions of law on which it is founded), may often settle the dispute between the parties; and therefore if improperly granted may do irreparable wrong. Yet there are many judges who assume a matter-of-course granting of a preliminary injunction to be the ordinary and proper judicial disposition of such cases; and there have undoubtedly been flagrant wrongs committed by judges in connection with labor disputes even within the last few years, although I think much less often than in former years. Such judges by their unwise action immensely strengthen the hands of those who are striving entirely to do away with the power of injunction; and therefore such careless use of the injunctive process tends to threaten its very existence, for if the American people ever become convinced that this process is habitually abused, whether in matters affecting labor or in matters affecting corporations, it will be well-nigh impossible to prevent its abolition.

On December 3, 1907, the President said, in his message to Congress:

This question is becoming more and more one of prime importance, and, unless the courts will themselves deal with it in effective manner, it is certain ultimately to demand some form of legislative action. It would be most unfortunate for our social welfare if we should permit many honest and law-abiding citizens to feel that they had just cause for regarding our courts with hostility. Moreover, discontent is often expressed with the use of the process of injunction by the courts, not only in labor disputes, but where State laws are concerned. I refrain from discussion of this question as I am informed that it will soon receive the consideration of the Supreme Court.

The Federal courts must of course decide ultimately what are the respective spheres of State and nation in connection with any law, State or national, and they must decide definitely and finally in matters affecting individual citizens, not only as to the rights and wrongs of labor but as to the rights and wrongs of capital; and the National Government must always see that the decision of the court is put into effect. The process of injunction is an essential adjunct of the court's doing its work well; and, as preventive measures are always better than remedial, the wise use of this process is from every standpoint commendable. But where it is recklessly or unnecessarily used the abuse should be censured, above all by the very men who are properly anxious to prevent any effort to shear the courts of this necessary power. The court's decision must be final; the protest is only against the conduct of individual judges in needlessly anticipating such final decision, or in the tyrannical use of what is nominally a temporary injunction to accomplish what is in fact a permanent decision.

On January 31, 1908, in a special message to Congress the President said:

I again call your attention to the need of some action in connection with the abuse of injunctions in labor cases. As regards the rights and wrongs of labor and capital, from blacklisting to boycotting, the whole subject is covered in admirable fashion by the report of the Anthracite Coal Strike Commission (of 1902), which report should serve as a chart for the guidance of both legislative and executive officers.

It is all wrong to use the injunction to prevent the entirely proper and legitimate actions of labor organizations in their struggle for industrial betterment, or under the guise of protecting property rights unwarrantably to invade the fundamental rights of the individual. It is futile to concede, as we all do, the right and the necessity of organized effort on the part of wage-earners and yet by injunctive process to forbid peaceable action to accomplish the lawful objects for which they are organized and upon which their success depends. The fact that the punishment for the violation of an injunction must, to make the order effective, necessarily be summary and without the intervention of a jury makes its issuance in doubtful cases a dangerous practice, and in itself furnishes a reason why the process should be surrounded with safeguards to protect individuals against being enjoined from exercising their proper rights. Reasonable notice should be given the adverse party.

If some way of remedying the abuses is not found the feeling of indignation against them among large numbers of our citizens will tend to grow so extreme as to produce a revolt against the whole use of the process of injunction. The ultra-conservatives who object to cutting out the abuses will do well to remember that if the popular feeling does become strong many of those upon whom they rely to defend them will be the first to turn against them. Men of property can not afford to trust to anything save the spirit of justice and fair play; for those very public men who, while it is to their interest, defend all the abuses committed by capital and pose as the champions of conservatism will, the moment they think their interest changes, take the lead in just such a matter as this and pander to what they esteem popular feeling by endeavoring, for instance, effectively to destroy the power of the courts in matters of injunctions; and will even seek to render nugatory the power to punish for contempt, upon which power the very existence of the orderly administration of justice depends.

In a special message to Congress March 25, 1908, the President said:

I urge that action be taken along the line of the recommendations I have already made concerning injunctions in labor disputes. No temporary restraining order should be issued by any court without notice; and the petition for a permanent injunction upon which such temporary restraining order has been issued should be heard by the court issuing the same within a reasonable time—say, not to exceed a week or thereabouts from the date when the order was issued. It is worth considering whether it would not give greater popular confidence in the impartiality of sentences for contempt if it was required that the issue should be decided by another judge than the one issuing the injunction, except where the contempt is committed in the presence of the court, or in other case of urgency.

On April 27, 1908, in a special message to Congress the President said:

First, as to the power of injunction and of punishment for contempt. In contempt cases, save where immediate action is imperative, the trial should be before another judge. As regards injunctions, I ask that the power to grant them be limited in some such way as that I have already pointed out in my previous messages, for the very reason that I do not wish to see an embittered effort made to destroy it. In a democracy like ours it is idle to expect permanently to thwart the determination of the great body of our citizens. It may be, and often is, the highest duty of a court, a legislature, or an executive, to resist and defy a gust of popular passion; and most certainly no public servant, whatever may be the consequences to himself, should yield to what he thinks wrong. But in a question which is emphatically one of public policy, the policy which the public demands is sure in the end to be adopted; and a persistent refusal to grant to a large portion of our people what is right is only too apt in the end to result in causing such irritation that when the right is obtained it is obtained in the course of a movement so ill considered and violent as to be accompanied by much that is wrong. The process of injunction in labor disputes, as well as where State laws are involved, should be used sparingly, and only when there is the clearest necessity for it; but it is one so necessary to the efficient performance of duty by the court on behalf of the nation that it is in the highest degree to be regretted that it should be liable to reckless use; for this reckless use tends to make honest men desire so to hamper its execution as to destroy its usefulness.

Mr. Clayton then put on record the two bills of Mr. Henry.

Many of the laboring people of the country believe that these two measures, or either one of them, would largely lessen or prevent the injury sometimes done them by the injudicious and improper use of restraining orders and injunctions issued by United States courts and judges.

Mr. Clayton then put on record the bill of Mr. Payne.

Mr. Speaker, this last bill is, of course, only a pretence, and intended to muddy the waters.

Mr. Henry then placed on record the other bills upon the subject.

Mr. Speaker, none of these bills which I have inserted in the *Record* suggests anything very novel in the legislative and judicial history of the United States. The act of March 2, 1793, provided:

That writs of *ne exeat* and of injunction may be granted by any judge of the Supreme Court in cases where they might be granted by the Supreme or a circuit court; but no writ of *ne exeat* shall be granted unless a suit in equity be commenced, and satisfactory proof shall be made to the court or judge granting the same that the defendant designs quickly to depart from the United States; nor shall a writ of injunction be granted to stay proceedings in any court of a State; nor shall such writ be granted in any case without reasonable previous notice to the adverse party, or his attorney, of the time and place of moving for the same.

Note the part of this good and sound, if old, law about "staying proceedings in a State court" and about "reasonable previous notice" in all cases. Under this law our courts worked for seventy-odd years.

The old law of 1793 was repealed by omission by codifiers in revising the statutes, and never openly, bravely, or expressly. Yet we are charged as "revolutionists" because we wish virtually to reënact it.

Even Secretary Taft has acknowledged that such legislation ought to be had. He said in a letter to Ohio labor organizations not very long ago that he favored such legislation. I quote what he said [see page 322].

Mr. Speaker, from this record we may be justified in concluding that some in high official places have been attempting to play politics with the laboring people.

CHAPTER IX

SOCIALISM

Sketch of Socialism and Its Growth in America—Speech of Victor L. Berger [Wis.], Socialist, in the House, on "The Necessity of a Workingman's Party": Questions, Objections and Remarks by John L. Garner [Tex.], Carl C. Anderson [O.], John J. Fitzgerald [N. Y.], Richmond P. Hobson [Ala.], Frank Buchanan [Ill.], Cyrus Cline [Ind.], James R. Mann [Ill.]—The Socialist Platform.

SOCIALISM may be generally defined as a movement for the realization of an economic system in which industry is directed by society for the common benefit and industrial competition between individuals is eliminated. In a more particular sense socialism is the movement to attain this end by political action, the term communism being reserved for those voluntary withdrawals from society as at present organized, and the establishment of coöperative commonwealths.

Communism was the first movement developed in this country, as in the world-at-large. A number of coöperative colonies were organized in the United States during the first half of the eighteenth century, modeled on the plans of the Frenchmen, Etienne Cabet, Count Henri de Saint-Simon, and Charles Fourier, and one (at Harmony, Ind.) was founded by Robert Owen, a British communist.

Louis Blanc [1811-1882] and Ferdinand Lassalle [1825-1864] were the connecting link between these early Communists and the present Socialists, in that they advocated political action in order to secure aid from the State for coöperative communities.

The founder of Socialism proper was Karl Marx [1818-1883], who, in his book, "Capital" [1867], denounced the entire system of our present politico-social

348

organization as founded on the capitalistic principle, and therefore as unfit to be used as an instrumentality for the attainment of the coöperative commonwealth (or the social democracy, as it had come to be called) until this principle was eliminated.

Accordingly, the program of the Marxian Socialists in this country, as well as abroad, is, first, the capture, through the ballot, of the Government by the wage-earners, and then the establishment of public ownership and operation of all the means of production. In this term are included land (which Marx regarded as a form of capital) and capital in its orthodox acceptance: that is, labor products used for the production of wealth, such as machinery, factories, and (combined with land) railroads, and all forms of what are now called "public services."

A considerable number of Socialists in Great Britain and America, including many men and women of note in literature and art, while accepting in the main the economic theory of Marx, do not follow the program of the so-called "Marxians," but are "opportunists"—that is, they coöperate with existing political movements for reforms which tend toward socialism, such as the public ownership of social services, transportation, illumination, communication, etc. The center of this circle in Great Britain is the "Fabian Society," whence these "opportunists" there, as well as occasionally in America, are known as "Fabians."

The Socialists are often confounded with the Anarchists. This is a mistake, although a natural one, since both are striving for the same end, the coöperative commonwealth. But the Socialist would use all the powers of the State to this end, and, indeed, augment them, while the Anarchists (more properly the Anarchist-Communists) would abolish the present State, with its essential principle of legal compulsion, believing that there would arise in its place a voluntary association of men for mutual aid. Those who would use non-forcible means, such as education and the ballot, for such an end are called "philosophical Anarchists"; those who justify and exercise force in bringing about this result are revolutionary Anarchists.

Because of their common principle of voluntary association, all Anarchists are pure individualists. This principle was first enunciated by Pierre Joseph Proudhon [1809-1865] in his book, "What Is Property?" published in 1840. Proudhon enunciated the dictum, "All property is theft," claiming that property was the creation of human and not of natural law.

Mikhail Bakunin [1814-1876] developed Proudhon's theory into that of the coöperative commonwealth. Indeed, for a time he worked with Marx for its realization, but, differing diametrically in their theories, as we have seen, they parted company, and now their respective schools, while agreeing in opposition to the established order of society, are openly antagonistic. In the contest in this country Socialism has almost obliterated Anarchism as a practical force.

As the careful reader will have noted [see Vol. X, chapter II], the Single Tax philosophy stands midway between Socialism and Anarchism. With Socialism it holds that rent is a social product, and therefore should be used for public purposes. Unlike Socialism, however, it maintains that rent is the *only* social product, and upholds the absolute right of individuals to labor products. Like Anarchism, the Single Tax philosophy maintains that the Government should not concern itself with those economic matters which by nature are private affairs. But Anarchists hold that *all* economic matters are by nature private affairs, while the Single Taxers contend that, by the natural law which distributes product to producer, the rent, or "unearned increment" of land, should go to the public which created it, and therefore a government must exist in order to take it from the individuals in whose hands it necessarily accrues.

Socialism, having primary regard for the wage-earners, has been closely connected with the trades union movement in advocacy of measures such as legal limitation of the hours of labor and state regulations of its conditions.

Laying aside the early communistic experiments, such as Brook Farm, the Oneida Community, etc., Socialism proper may be considered to have been introduced into America from Germany in about 1848, when the revolutionary disturbances in that country caused many radicals to emigrate to the United States. Among these were formed gymnastic societies, or *"Turnvereine,"* which were, in the early days, avowedly Socialistic. The first of these was founded in New York City in 1850, and so rapidly did they spring up that, before the close of the year, there were a number formed in other places, all belonging to the Socialistic Gymnastic Union (*Socialistische Turner Bund*).

In 1868 the followers of Lassalle organized in New York City a Social Democratic party, which, in the following year, affiliated with the International Workingmen's Association founded in Europe in 1864 on the principles of Marx.

From the trades unionist in the United States a labor reform party was founded in 1868, and this was supported by Socialists. This soon passed out of existence.

In 1874 the Socialists formed a Social Democratic Workingmen's party at a convention held in Philadelphia in 1874. At a convention in New Jersey in 1877 the name was changed to Socialist Labor party, which is still retained by a branch of the movement.

In 1884 a great impetus was given to socialism in America by the publication of "The Coöperative Commonwealth," by Laurence Gronlund, an American citizen of Danish birth [1846-1899].

In 1886 the Socialists joined in with the United Labor Party which nominated Henry George for Mayor of New York City. The following year, however, when the party in convention at Syracuse, N. Y., nominated George for Secretary of State, it repudiated Socialism. This caused the Socialists to decide, in 1888, not to affiliate with any other party.

Thus far Socialism in America had been distinctly of a foreign cast, its leading exponents, such as Wilhelm Weitling [1808-1871], Daniel DeLeon [b. 1852], and

Gronlund, being of foreign birth. In 1888 the movement received powerful aid in the propagation among native Americans of its general spirit, although not of its special program, by the publication of a Socialistic novel, entitled "Looking Backward," by Edward Bellamy [1850-1898], a man of a long line of New England ancestors. From Bellamy's book, as well as a subsequent treatise, "Equality" [1897], sprang up a movement called nationalism, which, however, was more educational than partisan in its nature, and soon ceased to be a factor in American politics, its disciples affiliating themselves, when it came to political action, with the Socialists and the Populists.

In 1893 Julius A. Wayland [1854-1913] established a periodical called *The Coming Nation* at Greensburg, Ind. He was at first a "Utopian" Socialist—one who desires, by the establishment of an ideal Socialistic community to demonstrate to the rest of this country the advantages of coöperative over competitive industry. Wayland promoted such a colony at Ruskin, Tenn., but it was short-lived. Opponents of Socialism have held up its failure, as, indeed, that of a number of other similar colonies, as a demonstration of the impracticability of Socialistic theories, while Socialists, especially of the party of political action, have declared that the failure showed only the malignity of the universal competitive system in the country, which choked out every beginning, necessarily a feeble one, of coöperative organization. Accordingly, of late, they have frowned upon proposals to establish such communities, and have concentrated their energies upon capturing the national, State and municipal governments by the ballot. This accomplished, they intend to reorganize all public business on the coöperative principle, limiting competition to the purely private field and letting it strive there as best it can against voluntary coöperation.

Mr. Wayland was converted to this way of thinking, and, moving to Kansas, published at Girard a paper, *The Appeal to Reason,* which virtually has become the national organ of political Socialism.

The establishment of the 'American Railway Union in 1893, and the Pullman strike in the following year, says the writer of the article on Socialism in the "International Encyclopædia," are epoch-making in the history of American Socialism. Early in 1897 Eugene V. Debs, president of the Union, announced his conversion to Socialism, and he and Victor L. Berger, of Milwaukee, were largely instrumental in establishing the Social Democratic party.

After 1899 there were dissensions in the Socialist Labor Party, terminating in a complete split, one faction, and that rapidly becoming the larger, joining with the Social Democratic party, which thereupon adopted the name of the Socialist party.

This party has obtained some success at the polls. It has repeatedly nominated Mr. Debs for President, with successive increments of ballots, until, in 1912, he polled nearly a million votes.

In industrial States, such as Massachusetts, Connecticut, and New York, the Socialists, beginning in 1898, have elected members of the legislature, mayors of minor cities, etc. Western cities, such as the mining town of Anaconda, Mont., have also been carried at elections by the Socialists.

Milwaukee, Wis., having been largely settled by Germans, beginning with the revolutionary exiles of 1848, has been a center of Socialism, and in 1910 the Socialists elected Emil Seidel mayor of the city, and sent Victor L. Berger to Congress, the first of his party to enter the national legislature.

On July 18, 1912, Mr. Berger spoke in the House on the theme, "The Working Class Must Have Its Own Party to Give Expression to Its Own Class Interests."

THE NECESSITY OF A WORKINGMAN'S PARTY

VICTOR L. BERGER, M. C.

Fourth of July orators tell us that there are no classes in America, that in this country "men are born free and equal."

And there are still some persons in this country who believe that this being a Republic there are no classes.

It is true that interesting historical document, the Declaration of Independence, says that "all men are born free and equal." But that was not so, even at the time when the sentence was written. It is less so now.

Men are not born equal. They do not live as equals. They do not die as equals.

The child of the rich is surrounded by comforts and luxury even before it is born. It is raised with tender care. Danger and sickness are kept away from it. It has every advantage that our civilization affords. Unless killed by an accident or by yielding to the temptations which wealth affords, these children of fortune grow up to a ripe old age, honored and respected by everybody and especially by their children, who expect to inherit their wealth and their privileges.

How about the child of the poor? It is born in want and misery which had their beginning long before the child was born. More than half of the poor die before they are a year old. The child that survives and grows up to manhood or womanhood leads a life of toil and misery, filled with temptations of all kinds, which often lead to crime and prostitution. Old age means beggary or the poorhouse—at best, the aged poor are a great burden to their children. Many prefer an early grave.

Now, where is the equality of birth? Or during life, or even at the deathbed?

We are told, however, that equality in the Declaration of Independence means equality before the law.

I fail to see it there, either.

There is equality before the law when both parties are rich or both parties are poor. There is no equality in the case of a poor person against a rich person or against a wealthy corporation. Rich people will have the best lawyers, while a poor man may, if he has a good case, get a pettifogger on a half share.

Let us watch a common police court on any day. Two men— one looking prosperous, the other looking poor—are arrested for a similar offence. Each is fined $10 and costs. The prosperous man will put down his $10 and walk out smilingly. The other man can not pay and is sent up to the house of correction. Now, it is clear to any observer that the poor fellow is deprived of his liberty, not on account of his misdemeanor, but because he did not have $10.

Do we have classes in America?

Supposing a man out of work is picked up in some alley or under some bridge. He is trying to spend the night there because he does not have the money for a night's lodging. The next morning he is fined and deprived of his liberty as a vagrant, because he did not have any money to pay for a lodging. In other words, in our country it is a crime to be without money.

We not only have classes, but most all of our legislation is class legislation—by the ruling class or its agents.

We have a plutocracy—we are ruled by the wealthy class.

The existence of classes is nothing new. The class struggle began with civilization. It is therefore foolish to accuse the Socialists that they are trying to "create classes"—that we incite class antagonism and class hatred.

We want to abolish classes, class antagonism, and class hatred.

If in former centuries, however, when the working class meekly submitted to oppression and deprivation, there was some reason for it. There were not enough of the world's goods to go around. Naturally, therefore, the stronger took the first choice for themselves and their kin, and the people got the leavings, if there were any.

The economic basis has changed.

We have secured control over the forces of nature to such a degree as to bring the possibilities of comfort and well-doing within the reach of everybody, at least in civilized countries. With the present machinery of production it is within the power of society to supply all the reasonable wants of every man, woman, and child living.

And if there should not be enough of any product we could easily multiply it infinitely, provided every man would do his reasonable share of work; and provided, also, that society would apply all the machinery at its disposal.

Then we could all have plenty. And the work time of every worker could be shortened considerably. In all probability it need not be half of what it is now.

In order to accomplish this, however, the working class must have its own representation. The proletarians of America must have a political party of their own to give expression to their own needs and wants, just as the working class of every other civilized country has its own political party.

The working class has nothing to hope for from either the Republican party or the Democratic party. The representatives of these parties may be, and very often are, very cultured and accomplished gentlemen. Most of them are personally honest. However, they represent the capitalist system, and the more honest and consistent they are the more loyal they are to their class.

And the two parties may fight about the spoils of this system, but neither of them is willing to change the economic basis of the present society.

It is, therefore, only natural that every law passed by the Republican or Democratic parties benefits the capitalist class, or some group of it, in some manner—even laws that obviously seem to favor the workers, like the workmen's compensation act.

Political parties are simply the expressions of economic interests.

The Republican party is the favorite organization of the big capitalists. Why? Because it stood for a great deal of "business" during the late Civil War, and because, by its high tariff proclivities and its banking laws, it has given a strong impetus to the profits of the manufacturers and bankers. [Applause on the Democratic side.]

For a generation it was considered the conservative business man's party of the country.

The Democratic party, in its great majority, stood for the economic and political interests of the slave owners before the Civil War. After the war it naturally has become the dominant party of the South, where the former slave owner is slowly getting to be a manufacturer, a banker, or a capitalist. Up North the Democratic party, not having any great economic interests to express, soon fell into the hands of corrupt machines, at least in the large cities. Thus we have Tammany in New York, the Cook County Democracy in Chicago, the Rose Democracy in Milwaukee, and other benevolent graft institutions. It naturally also became the favorite organization of the liquor interests in the Northern States. [Applause on the Republican side.]

The capitalist class, therefore, is just as willing to deal with the Democratic party as with the Republican party. While the latter is conservative, the Democratic party is, to all intents and purposes, reactionary, especially on the industrial field; it would like to go back to the days before the war. Being behind the time in most things, it is especially ignorant and brutal in regard to the labor question, as the laws of many Southern States prove.

However, the workingmen of this country have votes, and

MAKING COMMON CAUSE

"When it comes to putting down Socialism we have to join hands"

By Ryan Walker in "The Comrade"

that is the reason why the Democrats have in recent years discovered that they "dearly love the workingman." [Laughter on the Republican side.]

That is the reason why we have passed a few labor laws in this House. Of course, these laws have not passed the Senate nor the scrutiny of the Supreme Court; however, they will do in that form as campaign food on the eve of a presidential election.

Of course none of these laws will add a single sandwich to the daily fare of the many millions of workingmen and working women. None of these laws will take care of the old invalids of industry or help along the young. Every civilized country on the globe has done a great deal in that direction of late.

Not we. Nowhere is human life as cheap as in America.

That most of this waste of human life is wholly unnecessary is shown by Dr. John Randolph Haynes, special commissioner on mining accidents of the State of California, in a paper which was originally read before a joint session of the American Association for Labor Legislation and the American Economic Association on December 30, 1911, and is now printed as a Senate document.

Dr. Haynes says that 35,000 workmen are annually slain in the United States while engaged in their daily occupations, and that, if the wounded and crippled in industry are added, Mr. Mercer, of the Minnesota Employers' Compensation Commission, was not far wrong when he claimed that industry in our country now kills and cripples more each year than did bullet and shrapnel in any year of the Civil War.

Coal mining, according to Dr. Haynes, is the most hazardous of all American industries, killing outright from 3,000 to 5,000 and killing and seriously injuring from 8,000 to 10,000 each year. The United States kill more coal miners than all the rest of the world combined.

The following table shows the casualties of employees on American railroads in comparison with those of other countries. The figures are for yearly accidents, based on five-year averages, from 1905 to 1909, inclusive. The table is taken from a statement made by the gentleman from Maryland [David J. Lewis] and appears in Senate Document No. 90 of the Sixty-second Congress:

	Number of employees to 1 killed.	Number of employees to 1 injured.
1. United States	421	19
2. Germany	1,016	431
3. France	1,068	517
4. Switzerland	1,071	26
5. United Kingdom	1,351	134
6. Norway	2,125	340
7. Austria	2,205	160

A DIVIDEND OF TEN PER CENT. FOR CAPITAL. A MORTALITY OF TEN
PER CENT. FOR LABOR

By R. Battle in "The Comrade"

359

However, as long as cheap trades for votes can be made with so-called "union labor leaders"—giving the working class nothing, and promising twice as much for next year—both the Democratic and the Republican parties believe themselves safe.

The only trouble just now is to make the workmen believe that the Democrats are different from the Republicans.

JOHN N. GARNER [Tex.].—How about the "bull moose" party?[1]

MR. BERGER.—I shall make a few remarks about that species also, if the gentleman will give me time. [Laughter.]

Of course there is still that old stand-by—the tariff—God be thanked. And Mr. Woodrow Wilson, being a profound man—a man of the type of that other profound gentleman, Grover Cleveland—has declared that the tariff is to be the issue.

But how is it to be done this time?

The Republicans declared themselves to be in favor of a "downward revision." The Democrats are in favor of a "tariff for revenue," but they cautiously add in their platform that they do not want to harm any industry.

Now what does that mean?

If it means anything at all it means that the Democrats do not want to harm any owners of factories, because the South is waking up industrially. The South is beginning to have numberless "infant industries" that want protection. The Democratic party must take care of these infants.

Since this is the case, how is the good professor expecting to make good on the tariff as an issue in the coming election? Is he to have a platform of his own—other than that adopted in Baltimore, for which the "peerless leader" stood sponsor?

Mr. Wilson will have to do so if he wants a demarcation of some kind between the old parties. As it is, the names of the two parties could be exchanged in both platforms and nobody would notice the difference.

Nothing is left in the Democratic platform of the great anti-capitalist war cry for which Bryan was so well known in 1896. One can readily see that Mr. Bryan of 1912 is a different man—he got to be quite a capitalist himself, and that fact unconsciously changed his point of view.

It may be that he expected to be a candidate himself and wanted all votes in sight, including the dissatisfied conservatives.

One might say, however, the platforms of the old parties

---

[1] A popular term applied to the Progressive party from a remark made by its leader, Theodore Roosevelt, comparing his good spirits to those of the animal in question.

are seldom read and even more seldom carried out. The main thing, then, is the personnel of the candidates.

But just at that point there is really no difference if one is to vote an old-party ticket. One might just as well shut his eyes and vote. The result would be absolutely the same.

All of the candidates are honest men, personally, as the term is understood in business and society nowadays. None of the candidates has ever been accused of any wrong other than "stealing convention delegates"—willing and ready to be stolen.

Mr. Roosevelt, who wants to start a party on the issue "Thou shalt not steal," and on business principles, should know that political graft is the very application of business principles to politics.

Furthermore, he also has openly been accused in the Senate of trying to buy delegates both this year and in 1904.

Moreover, the three candidates of the two old parties all enjoy the support of the trusts, the bosses, and the political machines.

Mr. Wilson, the Democratic candidate, has probably more support of that kind than any of the rest. Although a so-called progressive, he has with him Boss Murphy, of Tammany; Boss Smith, of New Jersey; Boss Sullivan, of Illinois; and Boss Taggart, of Indiana; their machines, and what they stand for. He was also jubilantly hailed by the reactionary capitalist element of both parties as a "second Grover Cleveland," and was warmly indorsed by every reactionary paper. Belmont and Ryan are his warmest supporters. Wilson's election will not only perpetuate the power of the bosses and their machines, but also inaugurate another era of reaction and "high finance" as we had under Grover Cleveland.

Mr. Wilson is very much handicapped by his past. Mr. Wilson has written books, and, being a recent convert to the cause of progressivism, his works stand out against him. Mr. Wilson has not only attacked the south European and Slavonic immigration, but he has also denounced organized labor.

He once declared that he preferred a Chinese coolie to an American trades-union man, because the former were more law-abiding and more industrious and worked cheaper—or words to that effect. As recently as 1909 he denounced union labor as "unprofitable labor." Mr. Wilson may have changed his mind, but he will have to explain, and the candidate that must explain is in a very poor position. His behavior during the late strikes in New Jersey will also require explanation.

It is unnecessary to tell where Mr. Taft stands. It is as natural for a man of his type to be allied with men like Root, Crane, Guggenheim, and Hammond as it is for a duck to take to the water. Until Mr. Taft ran for the office of President he had never gone to the common people for any indorsement. He was appointed assistant prosecuting attorney of Cincinnati, appointed a Federal judge, appointed a commissioner to the Philippine Islands, appointed a Secretary of War, and finally appointed the "heir of my policies" by Theodore Roosevelt.

Mr. Taft knows the history of the Republican party as the favorite organization of the big capitalists. And he wants that party to remain the favorite.

Moreover, the Republican party has no other reason for existence than to serve capitalism. It has accomplished one great historical fact—it has freed the negro. That was done, not for humanitarian reasons, but because chattel slavery was incompatible with modern capitalism.

Modern capitalism rests upon wage labor. The Democratic party of 1860 failed to understand this simple fact—and that is the reason why the Republican party was founded and grew up to be just what it is now.

It was the party of William Lloyd Garrison, Wendell Phillips, and Abraham Lincoln. And it became just as naturally the party of John Sherman, Nelson W. Aldrich, and Richard Ballinger.

That Mr. Taft has the support of many big political bosses and capitalist exploiters goes without further explanation.

The opposition in the Republican party is represented by the ex-President, Theodore Roosevelt. Where Mr. Roosevelt stands on all the great questions of the day nobody seems to know. I doubt whether Mr. Roosevelt knows himself, because, with his brilliant, but very erratic, mind, Mr. Roosevelt may revise and change all of his principles and convictions by to-morrow afternoon. [Laughter and applause.]

At this time it does not appear that he will play much of a part if he does, unless he is satisfied to be the pathfinder of a new organization which is on its way to nowhere in particular.

But a glance at some of the "honest progressives" who are now setting out to purify politics will at once demonstrate that Robin Hood's famous assemblages of outlaws had nothing on the company that are now rallying around Theodore Roosevelt.

There is, for instance, little Tim Woodruff, veteran of the famous "Old Guard" of Albany in bygone days, and such a doubtful asset generally that two years ago Mr. Roosevelt ousted

him from the position of State chairman of New York.
Then there is Boss Flinn, of Pittsburgh, a reactionary from
head to heel, soaked and saturated in the municipal corruption
of that smoky inferno.

"HE'S GOOD ENOUGH FOR ME!"

[Parody on Homer Davenport's famous cartoon, depicting Uncle Sam
saying this of Roosevelt, which was used as a Republican campaign document in the Presidential campaign of 1904]

By F. Opper in the Hearst paper

And Lucius Littauer, of Gloversville, N. Y., a reactionary to the backbone, mixed up in a post-office scandal several years back.

And George W. Perkins, of Morgan and the Steel Trust.

Furthermore, Medill McCormick, of the Harvester Trust and the Chicago *Tribune*. Comment is really superfluous. [Applause.]

In short, all three candidates are well supported by the organization of their class.

As to the tariff issue as such, this issue is to the working class exactly what every other capitalist issue is. The working-men are interested in the tariff—as the tariff is now—as consumers only.

The tariff does not protect labor; at the same time any sudden change would be disastrous. It is mainly a manufacturer's issue—until labor really gets its share of the protection.

The tariff is not responsible for the trusts; there are trusts in England, where they have free trade. Moreover, the trusts are now in favor of free trade.

With us the great issue is the difference between what a workingman in this country produces on the average and what he gets.

It is a class issue; it is the great issue of the working class.

In 1909, in the 268,000 factories of this nation, 6,600,000 wage earners added $1,290 apiece for every worker employed.

Did those workers receive the value they put into the product? Not at all. They received $518 apiece.

The other $772 went to the employers and landowners. This surplus value went to the capitalist class as such—to the landowners, the bankers, and employers, and the holders of special privileges of some sort or another.

Wherever this surplus value goes it goes to some individuals or groups of the capitalist class in some form—either as profit, rent, interest, insurance, and so forth.

In 1909 the number of factory wage-earners was 6,615,046, an increase of 21 per cent. in 5 years and of 40.4 per cent. in 10 years. Women have constituted exactly 19.5 per cent. of the factory population in each of the three last censuses. Children constituted 2.5 per cent.

Wage-earners do not increase relatively in anything like the proportion that salaried employees do. The gain of the former in 10 years has been 40.4 per cent.; of the latter 117 per cent.

It is true of all highly developed countries that the number of persons employed to handle, sell, and promote the sale of commodities increases far more rapidly than the number of persons who make things. This will help to explain the rise in the cost of living.

The number of wage-earners does not increase proportionately with the increase of capital.

Capital has increased 45.4 per cent. in 5 years and 105.3 per cent. in 10 years. Big capital now controls industry, and the figures are truly amazing.

In 1904 nine-tenths of 1 per cent. of the establishments turned out 38 per cent. of the product, and in 1909 1.1 per cent. turned out 43.8 per cent. of the product. Each of these establishments produced values in excess of $1,000,000, and there were 1,900 of them in 1904 and 4,061 in 1909.

Counting the establishments producing more than $100,000 in values annually, it is shown that in 1904 11.2 per cent. of the total of 216,180 establishments turned out 79.3 per cent. of the total product, and that in 1909 11.5 per cent. of the total of 268,491 establishments turned out 82.2 per cent. of the total.

The other 88.5 per cent. of the establishments had to be satisfied with the leavings of 17.8 per cent. of the product.

The average salary drawn in 1899 was $1,046; in 1909, $1,187. These salaries are not classified in this report, as similar salaries are classified in the report of the Interstate Commerce Commission. It is therefore impossible to tell just what rank of employees drew the increase. There is plenty of evidence, however, from common observation that the average poorly paid clerk or accountant has had no raise in the last 10 years.

Wage-earners received more money in 1909 than they did in 1904. Their average in the former year was $477, in the latter year $518, a difference of $41 or about 79 cents a week. The figures of wages are not yet classified for men, women, and children, and so we can not tell where the greater rate of increase has gone, though the probability is that it has gone to the men.

The value added to production (that is, the value of the product less the cost of materials) averaged $1,150 for each wage-earner in 1904. It now averages $1,290. But the relative share of the worker in the value of his product is less than it was in either 1899 or 1904.

One of the particularly brutal elements of capitalism is shown by the figures for the seasonal variations in the amount of employment in the various great industries. Capital can not keep its workers employed.

When it wants them it wants them bad, and when it does not want them they may go and starve. In some of the industries the variation in the state of employment is only moderate.

In printing and publishing, for instance, the lowest number of wage-earners employed at any time constituted 93.3 per cent. of the largest number employed.

But in brick and tile making the minimum represented only 36.5 per cent. of the maximum, and in canning and preserving only 12.9 per cent.

Even in the great steel and iron industry the number employed in March was 25 per cent. less than that employed in December. Throughout the whole industrial scheme seasonal unemployment is a necessity under capitalism.

Moreover, another fact must be taken into consideration. The capitalist class numbers only about 4 per cent. of the population, the middle class 24 per cent., and the working class 72 per cent.

Under these circumstances, is it surprising that we look upon the agitation for a low tariff or for a high tariff as a shameless humbug when we compare its importance with the question of the exploitation of labor?

Is it surprising that we look upon the return of the tariff issue as simply a sham battle to divert the attention of the workingmen from the main issue?

And the real issue is this:

Under the present system, which we call in political economy the capitalist system, the workingman's labor has become a mere ware in the market.

And since the man's labor can not be separated from the man, the workingman himself has become a commodity, whose time is bought and sold. The workingman, or rather his labor power, is subject to the same conditions as every other ware, especially to the conditions of supply and demand and to competition.

The workingman's labor—that is, his time—is bought now in the open market by the highest bidder on the one hand, from the lowest seller on the other.

And the employers—who are really the master class—care only to buy the workingman's time when he is young, strong, and healthy. When he is sick, or when he gets old, the employer has no use for him.

The employer is not in business for the sake of charity. He is in business in order to make profits—to make money.

And, because of this, we can see that our so-called free workers are sometimes worse off—from the purely economic point of view—than the blacks were under slavery before the war.

The negro was property and represented about a thousand dollars in value—sometimes more, sometimes less—he was prop-

WAGE SLAVERY

1903: "I thought I should find Freedom on the Earth when I came."
Father Time: "No, my son—I've only changed the style of the chains,— and the color of the slaves."

By Ryan Walker in "The Comrade"

erty which the master owned. Therefore, the master, if he had any sense, took good care of his human chattel. The master was eager to have the slave as long and in as good condition as possible. When he became sick, or when he died, the master lost money.

The case is entirely different with the white workingman, the so-called free workingman. When the white man is sick, or when he dies, the employers usually lose nothing.

And high tariff, or tariff for revenue only, or free trade, "have nothing to do with the case."

The fact is that the capitalist, the average employer of to-day, is more concerned about a valuable horse, about a fine dog, about a good automobile, than he is about his employee, or about his employee's family.

In most cases, the employment is absolutely impersonal. The employer does not know his employee by name, or even by number. This is invariably the case with a stock company where the shareholders are scattered all over a city, a State, or all over the country, sometimes over Europe.

Nor can any individual capitalist or employer, no matter how charitably inclined he may be, change anything in these conditions. A business or corporation that should try to run its plant on a charity basis would not last long.

As a matter of fact, under the present system it is usually the worst employer who sets the pace. The employer who can fleece and skin his workingmen best is best equipped for the fight in the open market. He can produce his goods the cheapest.

Thus competition has come to have a fearful meaning to the working class.

On the one hand it compels the employers to get their labor as cheaply as possible; on the other hand it compels the workingmen to compete with one another for jobs. Competition among the workers has become, therefore, a cut-throat competition. It is a question as to who is to live and who is to starve. It is often a question as to whether a man is to stay with his family or to become a tramp.

And the tariff has nothing to do with that question, either.

There is always free trade in labor.

In many cases now the laborer is compelled to disrupt his family and to send his wife and his children to the shop or the factory.

For this is the great curse of machinery—or rather of the individual monopoly of machinery—that capital can be coined out of women, and even out of infancy. Thus not alone are men turned into wares, governed by demand and supply, but they are also made to scramble for a precarious living with the wives, sisters, and children.

The evil of child labor is especially glaring down South, where my Democratic friends rule absolutely.

Lewis W. Hine, while taking photographs of the employees of the Gulf coast canneries for the National Child Labor Committee, says that he personally interviewed 13 children from 3 to 5 years old, 25 from 6 to 8, and 15 from 9 to 11, and that he counted in all 125 boys and girls whom he judged to be from 3 to 11 years of age.

No human being knows how many children under 10 are employed in the canning industry in the United States or in the numberless industries carried on in tenement houses in our great cities. But everyone at all familiar with the subject knows that there are thousands.

In six Southern States nearly 1,000 children from 7 to 11 years old were found at work in cotton factories by agents of the United States Labor Bureau, whose investigation covered only about one-fourth of the cotton industry of these States.

It is conservative therefore to estimate that 5,000 children from 7 to 11 years old are prolonging their infancy in the cotton mills of the South.

And yet this is the economic basis of the wage system.

Therefore we say the wage system was a step in the evolution of freedom, but only a step. Without trade-unionism and labor associations, the wage system would produce a social state lower than that of feudalism.

Social freedom, complete justice, can be accomplished only by the collective ownership and democratic management of the social means of production and distribution.

We realize that all this can not be brought about by a single stroke—by a one day's revolution. But we know that all legislation, in order to be really progressive and wholesome, must move in that direction—must be in accordance with the modern economic progress.

And the only party that is in accordance with the trend of the time is the Socialist party. That is the reason why all the "progressives" are simply trying to appropriate some of our minor planks.

With the Socialists political issues are of minor consequence; economic issues are of paramount importance.

We refuse to be diverted or led astray by mere political reforms like the initiative, referendum, and recall. Each in itself is a good enough reform. Each of them has been agitated for a long time by the Socialists and forms a part of our program to-day.

XI—24

Mere changes in the mechanism of expressing the will of the people are, however, of secondary importance when compared with any change in the economic conditions of the people.

We want the initiative. But we want much more to secure an old-age pension for every workingman and workingwoman of 60 and over.

We stand for the referendum. But insurance against being out of work is of much more value.

We agitate for the recall. But State help for orphans—at least for those who have no father—and assistance for working women during the period of child bearing is infinitely more useful to the race than the right to recall a judge.

The bourgeois reformer, even when well meaning, does not understand us. He lacks our class consciousness.

Of the political reforms a new Constitution is most important. As long as we have the old Constitution, thorough social reforms are almost impossible.

No matter how good and beneficial a law may be, it will, as a rule, be declared unconstitutional by the Supreme Court. Our Constitution was framed at a time entirely different from ours, and for entirely different conditions—and good laws suited to the present conditions are really unconstitutional.

When our Constitution was framed this was a nation of frontier farmers and hunters, with a few merchants in the seaports.

There was no machinery used. There was no manufacturing to speak of. There were no railroads; no telegraphs.

There were no millionaires and no proletarians. There were no corporations in the present sense—a corporation in those days meant a city.

And there were no trusts, of course.

If Washington, Jefferson, Madison, and Hamilton could get up from their graves to-day they would not know the country. We live in a different world.

And yet we have to wear the same political cloak. We must live under the same Constitution.

In other words, a grown-up nation has to wear its baby cloak. It does not fit anywhere, and has been torn and patched in the most ridiculous way by "decisions of the Supreme Court" in order to make it do, yet anybody who dares to suggest a new suit is considered a traitor by the "interests."

But we must have a new Constitution or we shall have a bloody revolution. Yet, though political reforms are necessary, they are of little account when compared with the necessity of changes in order to keep step with the development of economic conditions.

The economic changes are upon us.

We see the trusts not only doing away with competition, but also asking for Government interference and for Government regulation of prices.

THE PILL

UNCLE SAM: I'VE HAD A GOOD MANY DOSES OF THAT STUFF ALREADY, BUT IT DONT CURE"

By Ryan Walker in "The Comrade"

In other words, we have the spectacle of the trusts surrendering part of their ownership and practically offering that part of the ownership to the people.

Thus the trusts, or at least some of the trusts, are willing to part with their ownership because they feel that their business has ceased to be a private concern. Because the trusts feel that their business has become a public utility of the most public and utilitarian sort.

But the change is also coming from the other side.

The great majority of the people have no interest in keeping up the present system. And especially the working class is bound to become revolutionary as a class.

Our workingmen to-day build a few palaces and many hovels. The workingmen live in the hovels and the few capitalists in the palaces.

Our workingmen in the woolen mills make a small amount of fine clothes and millions of yards of shoddy. The working-men wear the shoddy and the rich idlers wear the fine clothes.

Workingmen and their children have to go down into the mines, workingmen and workingwomen and their children have to go into dingy, ill-ventilated factories and workshops and toil from 8 to 12 hours a day. They must ruin their health by over-work, so that a few people who have the money may ruin their health by too much leisure.

The majority now degenerates through poverty so that the small minority shall be able to degenerate through luxury.

Again, I say, the great majority have no interest in keeping up the present system.

There is this also: In former epochs the ruling class was by far the abler and stronger—physically and mentally.

In former years a few nobles, clad in iron—and trained and accustomed to warfare—could hold in subjection 20 times their number of common people.

The ruling class only was at that time in the possession of the wisdom of the world—whatever wisdom the world had then.

The ruling class at that time also had in its favor the belief that this system was God-ordained, and that anybody rebelling against it was a rebel to God.

Things are different nowadays.

The working class not only builds the houses, ships, and machines, but the working class also teaches in the public schools and colleges, and writes and prints our literature. Not only the man who sets up the type for the papers and the books, but also the man or woman who writes them usually belongs to our class.

The capitalist class depends upon us for a living, for information, and for defence.

The ruling class surely has no better fighting qualifications than we. It is our class that has to furnish most of the men in case of war, although the capitalists may start the war and buy the bonds. Even in order to hold the working class in subjugation, the capitalists have to hire such workingmen as are for sale to do the fighting for the rulers.

We deny that the capitalist class is our superior in any way.

And as long as the public schools exist, and men and women are learning how to read and write, no priest or clergyman will ever be able to make us believe again that this system is God-ordained. We will never believe that it is God-ordained that a trust magnate shall have fifty or sixty million dollars a year, or more, and that his employees should earn $1.75 a day on the average.

Moreover, we have the ballot. No subjected class in history ever had the same political basis as the ruling class. The modern proletariat is the first.

On election day my vote is as good as Rockefeller's. And we are many and the capitalists are few.

In short, the future belongs to the working class. Nothing can stop us. All we have to do is to organize our forces. There is no other party that has grown like ours during the last four years.

And, I want it understood, the Socialist party, while it is revolutionary in its final aim, is none the less distinctly evolutionary and constructive in its method. We welcome all kinds of reforms that are real reforms—not political baits.

Social reforms of all kinds are welcomed by the Socialist for many reasons.

In the first place, by reforms we can stop the increasing pauperization and consequently also the enervation of the masses of the people. If real reforms are seriously taken up and carried out with determination they uplift the masses to a considerable extent.

But the main reason for our favoring social reforms is that such reforms, if logically carried out, offer the possibility of a peaceful, lawful, and orderly transformation of society.

The Socialist party, therefore, is the only true reform party in existence. We agitate for the organization of the masses. And organization everywhere means order.

We educate, we enlighten, we reason, we discipline.

Besides order we bring also law, reason, discipline, and progress to men and women who have been torn from their old conditions by capitalism—and who would otherwise become Apaches.

It is, therefore, absolutely false to represent our Socialist party as destructive, as intending to overthrow and annihilate society, as an appeal to the brute passions of the masses.

Just the opposite is true.

Our Socialist party wants to maintain culture and education and carry them to the homes of every worker of the land.

Our party wants to guard this nation from destruction and bring it to a level hitherto unknown in history.

We appeal to the best in every man, to the public spirit of the citizen, to his love of wife and children. [Applause.]

CARL C. ANDERSON [O.].—I think the gentleman will admit that the Democratic party has passed more bills in the interest of labor than have been passed by this House in the last 20 years.

MR. BERGER.—I do not admit that. I said the Democratic party has voted for some so-called labor bills, but so did the Republican party, and so did the only representative of the Socialist party in Congress.

MR. ANDERSON.—Then he admits that this is good legislation?

MR. BERGER.—I admit that some bills that have been passed in this session are fair bills as far as they go. Otherwise I should not have voted for them. They do not, however, add to the standard of living of the American working class. They are of ridiculously small importance, considering the magnitude of the labor question.

MR. ANDERSON.—If the House had been Socialistic it would undoubtedly have voted for the same bills.

MR. BERGER.—If the House had been Socialistic it would not have wasted time with insignificant palliatives of that kind, because it would have taken up legislation of a million times greater importance.

MR. ANDERSON.—If the House had been Socialistic, would it have passed the Sherwood pension bill?

MR. BERGER.—No; because we would have pensioned not alone the old soldiers, but everybody who——

MR. ANDERSON.—The gentleman said that if the Socialistic party had been in power they would have pensioned everybody. Where would the gentleman get the money to pension everybody?

MR. BERGER.—Mr. Speaker, I wanted to say that by pensioning everybody who did some useful work in their earlier manhood or womanhood it would be needless to pension the old soldiers. The old soldiers have done some useful work besides being soldiers in a war. I honor every man who went to the war to free the black man and to save the Union, but I honor just as much the men and women who are fighting for civilization every day—the men and women who are making our civilization possible.

Official figures show that 35,000 are annually slain in the industries of the country, not counting the hundreds of thousands that are the victims of occupational diseases.

Do you not think that a man who works for the welfare of the nation on the battlefield industry is taking as many chances as the man going to war? And that the worker is doing more necessary work than the soldier?

Moreover, the old working people who will get the pensions will have paid for them during the time they worked. In fact, they will have paid for the pensions many times over before they get them.

As I stated before, in 1909 every workingman and working-woman added about $1,290 worth to the nation's wealth and received on the average only $512 in wages.

The pensions should be paid from the surplus value the capitalist class is getting.

JOHN J. FITZGERALD [N. Y.].—Does not the gentleman from Wisconsin know that until the Democrats got control of the House of Representatives neither the Republicans nor the Democrats nor the Socialists could get a chance to vote for an eight-hour bill?

MR. BERGER.—I do not know anything of the kind.

MR. FITZGERALD.—If the gentleman will permit me to inform him, I have served in the House 14 years, and until the Democrats got control of it an eight-hour bill could not be reported into a Republican House from the committee.

MR. BERGER.—And I want to inform the gentleman from New York, if I may, that the first eight-hour bill was passed in 1868 by a Republican House. [Applause on the Republican side.] As a Socialist and trades-union man I have, of course, no more love for one capitalist party than for the other, but I want to be fair.

MR. FITZGERALD.—And the Republican Attorney-General so construed the law as to make it absolutely valueless. [Applause on the Democratic side.]

MR. BERGER.—Well, we do not know how this bill may be construed by a Democratic Attorney-General and by the Supreme Court. [Applause on the Republican side.]

MR. FITZGERALD.—If there is a Democratic Administration, there will be no fault found with it.

MR. BERGER.—Then the gentleman thinks the Supreme Court decides questions of law according to politics?

RICHMOND P. HOBSON [Ala.].—The gentleman stated that the South was coming to stand for the principle of protection in order to protect their infant industries against competition. I will ask him what effect can the tariff have in protecting the South when we already have the giant industries of the North in direct competition with them?

MR. BERGER.—I can only answer the gentleman from Alabama from my point of view, which is the point of view of modern economics. As I see it, the South still has the advantages of position for certain industries.

For instance, cotton is raised right there, and the cotton factory of the South saves the freight, of course. Furthermore, the South has cheap labor, unorganized labor, colored labor; it also has longer hours than the North. Then, you have woman and child labor—in some cases children from 3 to 11 years old are at work. ["Oh, no!"]

Well, in many Southern States that is the case in the cotton and in the canning industries. I do not mean to say that there is child labor in every industry in the South. For some work women and children are not strong enough.

MR. HOBSON.—The things the gentleman enumerates would tend to relieve the South from the need of protection instead of explaining its alleged desire for protection. There is no such desire, and there is no logical foundation of the oft-repeated allegation that the South has come to advocate high protection.

MR. BERGER.—I will say to the gentleman from Alabama that if it were not for the elements mentioned even a high tariff could not protect the South, but with those elements in existence the South may try, for a while at least, to successfully compete with the giant trusts. Of course it is a fight at the expense of humanity—at the expense of the race. Moreover, very soon the war will be found unprofitable and the combatants will unite.

As a confirmation of my statement that the South is beginning to ask for protection, the gentleman need only read over some of the discussions on the various tariff bills introduced by the Democrats themselves.

FRANK BUCHANAN [Ill.].—Does the gentleman define the working class as being composed of those who work for wages alone? In my locality we have a man who is running a grocery store. His wife and daughter work in that grocery store. He also works long hours, early and late. He is in fact a workingman. Does the gentleman agree that a man who operates a business of that sort is a workingman or a capitalist?

MR. BERGER.—Mr. Speaker, of course our present society does not only divide into two classes; there are three classes. We have the working class, the middle class, and the capitalist class. The lines are not very closely drawn in our century and our country. In some cases the workingman may have a little business on the side, or a capitalist may draw his income in the form of a salary, but as a whole it is safe to describe the division between classes as originating from the way a person derives his or her income.

The workingman or workingwoman derives his or her income through work for daily, weekly, or monthly wages, or, when working in schools and offices, through working for an annual salary. It is always work for pay—either work with hands or with brains, or with both, that gives the wage-worker his status in society.

The middle class derives its income from rents and profits, either by buying and selling, or by employing a small number of men, women and children.

The capitalist class derives its income in the same way on a large scale, besides controlling the means of transportation and the means of communication, most of the natural resources, and the banks.

Of course different men have made different demarcations. But all agree that the smallest class in number but greatest in power is the capitalist class which controls the capital of the country—that part of the surplus value which is now used to create more surplus value instead of being used to give comfort to the people.

MR. BUCHANAN.—Does the Socialist party confine its membership to the working class? Is it not a fact that it has some wealthy men in it?

MR. BERGER.—Oh, every honest man, even a capitalist, may become a member of the political party of the working class if he agrees to aid us in the emancipation of the working class. We must be satisfied, however, that the man is honest in his intentions to help us to bring about a complete change of the present system by sane and legal methods. [Applause.]

MR. BUCHANAN.—I want to ask if the gentleman does not believe that Abraham Lincoln, who was the leader of the Republican party during the war at the time the slaves were freed, would also exercise his influence if living to strike the shackles from the industrial slaves of to-day?

Mr. Berger.—He would, if he lived to-day. Lincoln would, in my opinion, be a Socialist, if he lived to-day.

Mr. Buchanan.—Then, after all, it is not so much in the party as the men who control the party.

Mr. Berger.—No. Men are the second consideration, principles are paramount. Good men are necessary, of course, to carry out these principles. But good men are useless or dangerous in the wrong party.

Mr. Buchanan.—Is it not a fact in this country, where the workingmen have the ballot, their troubles are largely due to their own inactivity in politics, and if they would exercise their united influence in politics it would put them in the position of controlling any party for themselves?

Mr. Berger.—Mr. Speaker, the party must be worth controlling. It must stand for what a certain class or a certain group wants that party to stand, and must be made up accordingly.

Mr. Buchanan.—And would not any party serve their purpose if the working people would control them?

Mr. Berger.—No! No! No! If you want to ride horseback, you will not take a donkey. [Laughter.] The two old parties represent certain groups and certain interests of the capitalist class. Both of these parties are made up accordingly. They can never represent the working class.

The Democratic party and the Republican party have certain principles, certain ideas for which they stand. Their aim, their platform is capitalistic. They could not abolish the present system of exploitation without abolishing themselves. You can not expect a tiger to eat grass nor a gray wolf to live on berries. [Laughter.]

The more honest the leaders of the old parties are, the more they will try to abide by the principles of their platform; the more loyal will they be to the capitalistic interest, which they represent.

Cyrus Cline [Ind.].—I understood the gentleman to say in his address that the Socialist party was in favor of common ownership of most of the agencies of production and distribution.

Mr. Berger.—For the collective ownership and the democratic management of the social means of production and distribution.

Mr. Cline.—I want to understand to what extent you carry that doctrine, Who are the beneficiaries and how they are to derive the profits of it?

MR. BERGER.—Well, the Socialist party stands for the collective ownership of the social means of production and distribution.

MR. CLINE.—How are you going to evolve the system?

MR. BERGER.—We believe that everything that is necessary for the life of the nation, for the enjoyment of everybody within the nation, the nation is to own and manage. Therefore we shall take over the trusts, railroads, mines, telegraphs, and other monopolies of national scope. Everything that is necessary for the life and development of the State the State is to own and manage. There are certain business functions that the State will have to take care of, like interurban lines, for instance. Everything that is necessary for the life and development of a city the city is to own and manage, like, for instance, not only street cars and light and heating plants, but also abattoirs, public bake shops, the distribution of pure milk, and so forth. Everything that the individual can own and manage best the individual is to own and manage. That is simple enough.

In other words, the trust as a business has reached a stage where it is unsafe in private hands. It is a menace to the nation as long as it is in private hands. It can only be managed by the nation for the profit of everybody. The same holds good for certain private monopolies in cities, as far as the cities are concerned.

MR. CLINE.—How are you going to change the present economic basis? Give us a concrete statement of that proposition.

MR. BERGER.—That is easy enough. We could surely get the trust properties in the same way as the trusts got them. The trusts paid for their properties almost entirely in watered stock, preferred and common. We can give the best security in existence to-day—United States bonds.

MR. CLINE.—Have the Government buy them?

MR. BERGER.—Have the Government buy the trust properties. Why not? But pay only for the actual value. That will be paid for out of the profits of these trusts in a very short time.

MR. ANDERSON.—Speaking of the eight-hour bill, the gentleman claimed that he voted for all labor measures. Now, the bill went to the Senate and was amended, and when it came back was the gentleman present and did he vote for that bill, or was not he in Indianapolis?

MR. BERGER.—Supposing I did go to the national convention of the Socialist party. I was surely doing as good work in Indianapolis for the welfare of the country as I do here. It was fully as important that I should attend a convention of the Socialist party as to vote for some of the demagogical and insincere bills put up here by the party of the gentleman from Ohio [Mr. Anderson] in order to catch the labor vote for capitalism and the Democratic party. In fact, it was more important for me to be in Indianapolis.

MR. ANDERSON.—That does not answer the question.

JAMES R. MANN [Ill.].—The gentleman from Wisconsin may not have been here, but the gentleman from Ohio certainly was not. [Applause and laughter.]

THE SPEAKER.—The time of the gentleman has expired.

MR. BERGER.—I thank you one and all, gentlemen. [Loud applause.]

At the National Socialist Convention, held on May 12-18, 1912, at Indianapolis, the following platform was adopted:

THE SOCIALIST PLATFORM

The Socialist party of the United States declare that the capitalist system has outgrown its historical function, and has become utterly incapable of meeting the problems now confronting society. We denounce this outgrown system as incompetent and corrupt and the source of unspeakable misery and suffering to the whole working class.

Under this system the industrial equipment of the nation has passed into the absolute control of a plutocracy which exacts an annual tribute of billions of dollars from the producers. Unafraid of any organized resistance, it stretches out its greedy hands over the still undeveloped resources of the nation—the land, the mines, the forests, and the water powers of every State in the Union.

In spite of the multiplication of labor-saving machines and improved methods in industry which cheapen the cost of production, the share of the producers grows ever less, and the prices of all the necessities of life steadily increase. The boasted prosperity of this nation is for the owning class alone. To the rest it means only greater hardship and misery. The high cost of living is felt in every home. Millions of wage workers have seen the purchasing power of their wages decrease until life has become a desperate battle for mere existence.

Multitudes of unemployed walk the streets of our cities or

A GARLAND FOR MAY DAY

[The Many Arguments for Socialism]

By Walter Crane

trudge from State to State awaiting the will of the masters to move the wheels of industry.

The farmers in every State are plundered by the increasing price exacted for tools and machinery and by extortionate rents, freight rates, and storage charges.

Capitalist concentration is mercilessly crushing the class of small business men and driving its members into the ranks of propertyless wage workers. The overwhelming majority of the people of America are being forced under a yoke of bondage by this soulless industrial despotism.

It is this capitalist system that is responsible for the increasing burden of armaments, the poverty, slums, child labor, most of the insanity, crime, and prostitution, and much of the disease that afflicts mankind.

Under this system the working class is exposed to poisonous conditions, to frightful and needless perils to life and limb, is walled around with court decisions, injunctions, and unjust laws, and is preyed upon incessantly for the benefit of the controlling oligarchy of wealth. Under it also the children of the working class are doomed to ignorance, drudging toil, and darkened lives.

In the face of these evils, so manifest that all thoughtful observers are appalled at them, the legislative representatives of the Republican and Democratic parties remain the faithful servants of the oppressors. Measures designed to secure to the wage earners of this nation as humane and just treatment as is already enjoyed by the wage earners of all other civilized nations have been smothered in committee without debate, and laws ostensibly designed to bring relief to the farmers and general consumers are juggled and transformed into instruments for the exaction of further tribute.

The growing unrest under oppression has driven these two old parties to the enactment of a variety of regulative measures, none of which has limited in any appreciable degree the power of the plutocracy, and some of which have been perverted into means for increasing that power. Anti-trust laws, railroad restrictions and regulations, with the prosecutions, indictments, and investigations based upon such legislation, have proved to be utterly futile and ridiculous.

Nor has this plutocracy been seriously restrained or even threatened by any Republican or Democratic executive. It has continued to grow in power and insolence alike under the administrations of Cleveland, McKinley, Roosevelt, and Taft.

In addition to this legislative juggling and this executive connivance, the courts of America have sanctioned and strengthened the hold of this plutocracy as the Dred Scott and other decisions strengthened the slave power before the Civil War. They have constantly been used as instruments for the oppression of the working class and for the suppression of free speech and free assemblage.

We declare, therefore, that the longer sufferance of these conditions is impossible, and we purpose to end them all. We declare them to be the product of the present system in which industry is carried on for private greed instead of for the welfare of society. We declare, furthermore, that for these evils there will be and can be no remedy and no substantial relief except through Socialism, under which industry will be carried on for the common good and every worker receive the full social value of the wealth he creates.

Society is divided into warring groups and classes, based upon material interests. Fundamentally this struggle is a conflict between the two main classes, one of which, the capitalist class, owns the means of production, and the other, the working class, must use these means of production on terms dictated by the owners.

The capitalist class, though few in numbers, absolutely controls the Government—legislative, executive, and judicial. This class owns the machinery of gathering and disseminating news through its organized press. It subsidizes seats of learning— the colleges and schools—and even religious and moral agencies. It has also the added prestige which established customs give to any order of society, right or wrong.

The working class, which includes all those who are forced to work for a living, whether by hand or brain, in shop, mine, or on the soil, vastly outnumbers the capitalist class. Lacking effective organization and class solidarity, this class is unable to enforce its will. Given such class solidarity and effective organization, the workers will have the power to make all laws and control all industry in their own interest.

All political parties are the expression of economic class interests. All other parties than the Socialist party represent one or another group of the ruling capitalist class. Their political conflicts reflect merely superficial rivalries between competing capitalist groups. However they result, these conflicts have no issue of real value to the workers. Whether the Democrats or Republicans win politically, it is the capitalist class that is victorious economically.

The Socialist party is the political expression of the economic interests of the workers. Its defeats have been their defeats and its victories their victories. It is a party founded on the science and laws of social development. It proposes that, since all social necessities to-day are socially produced, the means of their production and distribution shall be socially owned and democratically controlled.

In the face of the economic and political aggressions of the capitalist class the only reliance left the workers is that of their economic organizations and their political power. By the intelligent and class-conscious use of these, they may resist successfully the capitalist class, break the fetters of wage slavery, and fit themselves for the future society which is to displace the capitalist system. The Socialist party appreciates the full significance of class organization and urges the wage earners, the working farmers, and all other useful workers everywhere to organize for economic and political action, and we pledge ourselves to support the toilers of the fields as well as those in the shops, factories, and mines of the nation in their struggle for economical justice.

In the defeat or victory of the working class party in this new struggle for freedom lies the defeat or triumph of the common people of all economic groups, as well as the failure or the triumph of popular government. Thus the Socialist party is the party of the present-day revolution, which marks the transition from economic individualism to Socialism, from wage slavery to free coöperation, from capitalist oligarchy to industrial democracy.

As measures calculated to strengthen the working class in its fight for the realization of its ultimate aim, the coöperative commonwealth, and to increase its power of resistance against capitalist oppression, we advocate and pledge ourselves and our elected officers to the following program:

COLLECTIVE OWNERSHIP

1. The collective ownership and the democratic management of railroads, wire and wireless telegraphs and telephones, express services, steamboat lines, and all other social means of transportation and communication and of all large-scale industries.

2. The immediate acquirement by the municipalities, the States, or the Federal Government of all grain elevators, stockyards, storage warehouses, and other distributing agencies, in order to reduce the present extortionate cost of living.

3. The extension of the public domain to include mines, quarries, oil wells, forests, and water power.

4. The further conservation and development of natural resources for the use and benefit of all the people:

(a) By scientific forestation and timber protection.

(b) By the reclamation of arid and swamp tracts.

Legislator Judge Soldier

PUPPETS OF CAPITALISM

By J. H. Morier in "The Comrade"

385

(c) By the storage of flood waters and the utilization of water power.

(d) By the stoppage of the present extravagant waste of the soil and of the products of mines and oil wells.

(e) By the development of highway and waterway systems.

5. The collective ownership of land wherever practicable, and, in cases where such ownership is impracticable, the appropriation by taxation of the annual rental value of all land held for speculation or exploitation.

6. The collective ownership and democratic management of the banking and currency system.

7. The abolition of the monopoly ownership of patents and the substitution of collective ownership, with direct rewards to inventors by premiums or royalties.

UNEMPLOYMENT

The immediate Government relief of the unemployed by the extension of all useful public works. All persons employed on such works to be engaged directly by the Government under a work day of not more than eight hours and at not less than the prevailing union wages. The Government also to establish employment bureaus, to lend money to States and municipalities without interest for the purpose of carrying on public works, and to take such other measures within its power as will lessen the widespread misery of the workers caused by the misrule of the capitalist class.

INDUSTRIAL DEMANDS

The conservation of human resources, particularly of the lives and well-being of the workers and their families:

1. By shortening the work day in keeping with the increased productiveness of machinery.

2. By securing to every worker a restperiod of not less than a day and a half in each week.

3. By securing a more effective inspection of workshops, factories, and mines.

4. By forbidding the employment of children under 16 years of age.

5. By abolishing the brutal exploitation of convicts under the contract system and substituting the coöperative organization of industries in penitentiaries and workshops, for the benefit of convicts and their dependents.

6. By forbidding the interstate transportation of the products of child labor, of convict labor, and of all uninspected factories and mines.

7. By abolishing the profit system in government work, and substituting either the direct hire of labor or the awarding of contracts to coöperative groups of workers.

8. By establishing minimum wage scales.

9. By abolishing official charity and substituting a non-contributory system of old-age pensions, a general system of insurance by the State of all its members against unemployment, illness, and invalidism, and a system of compulsory insurance by employers of their workers, without cost to the latter, against industrial diseases, accidents, and death.

POLITICAL DEMANDS

1. The absolute freedom of press, speech, and assemblage.

2. The adoption of a graduated income tax, the increase of the rates of the present corporation tax, and the extension of inheritance taxes, graduated in proportion to the value of the estate and to nearness of kin—the proceeds of these taxes to be employed in the socialization of industry.

3. Unrestricted and equal suffrage for men and women.

4. The adoption of the initiative, referendum, and recall, and of proportional representation, nationally as well as locally.

5. The abolition of the Senate and of the veto-power of the President.

6. The election of the President and the Vice-President by direct vote of the people.

7. The abolition of the power usurped by the Supreme Court of the United States to pass upon the constitutionality of the legislation enacted by the Congress. National laws to be repealed only by act of Congress or by a referendum vote of the whole people.

8. The abolition of the present restrictions upon the amendment of the Constitution, so that that instrument may be made amendable by a majority of the voters in a majority of the States.

9. The granting of the right of suffrage in the District of Columbia with representation in Congress and a democratic form of municipal government for purely local affairs.

10. The extension of democratic government to all United States territory.

11. The enactment of further measures for general educa-

tion and particularly for vocational education in useful pursuits. The Bureau of Education to be made a department.

12. The enactment of further measures for the conservation of health. The creation of an independent bureau of health, with such restrictions as will secure the full liberty of all schools of practice.

13. The separation of the present Bureau of Labor from the Department of Commerce and Labor and its elevation to the rank of a department.

14. Abolition of all Federal district courts and the United States circuit courts of appeals. State courts to have jurisdiction in all cases arising between citizens of the several States and foreign corporations. The election of all judges for short terms.

15. The immediate curbing of the power of the courts to issue injunctions.

16. The free administration of justice.

17. The calling of a convention for the revision of the Constitution of the United States.

Such measures of relief as we may be able to force from capitalism are but a preparation of the workers to seize the whole powers of government, in order that they may thereby lay hold of the whole system of socialized industry and thus come to their rightful inheritance.

CHAPTER X

NATIONAL MORALITY AND THE LIQUOR TRAFFIC

Bill to Tax Spirits in Warehouses: Debate in the House in Connection with the Bill on Moral Considerations in Taxation: George W. Ray [N. Y.], William P. Hepburn [Ia.], John D. Long [Mass.], Martin A. Foran [O.], William T. Price [Wis.], John W. McCormick [O.], Joseph D. Taylor [O.], Abram S. Hewitt [N. Y.], Seth L. Milliken [Me.]; Bill Is Enacted.

THE subject of national prohibition of alcoholic beverages was injected during the session of 1883-4 in discussion of a bill to extend the time for the payment of the tax on distilled spirits in warehouses. The bill was finally rejected.

TAXATION WITH INCIDENTAL MORALITY

HOUSE OF REPRESENTATIVES, MARCH 22-27, 1884

On March 22, 1884, George W. Ray [N. Y.] spoke.

If the continuation of this tax shall result in the destruction of the rum traffic, so much the better for the people, for civilization, for education, for religion, for progress among the nations. The men engaged in its manufacture will seek and find other fields of labor; the capital invested in the manufacture of distilled spirits will find other paying business, and the corn and grain of all kinds used in the business will be perhaps cheapened for the laboring people. The farming interests would not suffer, for the grain would go to the increase of animal production, and the decrease in price if any would be more than made up in the saving of taxes now paid for the support of the almshouse, the lunatic asylum, the jails, and State prisons. Remove the curse of intemperance, and the court expenses of this country would be reduced one-half, and peace, plenty, happiness, and contentment would reign supreme in the homes now made desolate by this great evil.

But we shall be told that this is idle, sentimental talk; that it is not practicable, and that we are to deal with the question of distilled spirits as a purely business question. That we must look at it in the light of profit and loss, and ignore the moral aspects of the case.

With the sober-minded, thinking people of this country the question of temperance has already become a practical question, and to some extent a political one. It reaches to their homes and firesides, to their pockets, to the peace of communities, and to the stability of the Government itself.

I am looking at the question in the light of profit and loss to the whole people, and not to a single State or community, nor the manufacturers and dealers in alcoholic spirits.

I shall never give my vote to aid or encourage the manufacture or sale of distilled spirits or alcoholic liquors of any kind for other than medicinal or mechanical purposes. With my last breath will I protest against any action by this Congress that shall lend the aid of this Government to the protection of the liquor trade.

There is no business in this country so rich and powerful, so grasping and aggressive, as the liquor interest. Its combinations are alarming and its influence beyond comprehension. What we gain in taxes for the support of the general Government we lose in the wealth of individuals, in the moral degradation of the people, in the increase of pauperism and crime, and in the direct tax upon the people in the several States for the support of the almshouses, inebriate, and lunatic asylums, jails, and State prisons. Gentlemen may figure out the profit and loss at their leisure, but they will find that the simple rules of arithmetic substantiate every statement that I have made.

WILLIAM P. HEPBURN [Ia.].—Gentlemen have told us that this great "industry" controlled the markets for corn and fixed the price of that staple. This sounds very strange to my ears. They tell us, too, that unless this bill passes there will be a falling off in the consumption of corn next year of ten millions of bushels, and the consequence will be ruin to the agricultural interests. Why, Mr. Chairman, did you ever recall the utter insignificance of the relation this industry bears to the corn production of the country? Two counties in the district I have the honor to represent have in a given year produced more than 18,000,000 bushels, the equivalent of the whole quantity consumed by all of the distilleries in the United States in the manufacture of spirits in the year 1883. The stoppage of every one of the 844 distilleries would have no more effect upon the price of corn than the passing summer shower would have on the back of a duck.

Mr. Chairman, we are told that, unless we pass this bill and give the holders of whisky now in bond and on which they have been granted a period of three years in which to pay the tax of 90 cents a gallon two additional years, the entire "industry" will be ruined; that the distillers will be bankrupted, and that in their fall they will pull down banks, capitalists, and all manufacturers, thus involving the country in a period of panic and financial chaos such as we have seldom, if ever, witnessed.

There are almost as many laborers engaged in the two "industries" of making pickles and preparing patent medicines as are employed in the great "industry" of making distilled spirits, and the sum paid them as wages is very nearly the same. Surely, in the labor aspect of the case, no one would contend that irretrievable ruin would come upon us if the compounding of patent medicines and the preparation of pickles should be numbered speedily among the lost arts.

Mr. Chairman, ever since this debate began, and by every speaker supporting this bill, we have heard over and over and again repeated that the manufacture of whisky was a "legitimate industry," a "legitimate business." No one has attacked its legitimacy up to this time. Gentlemen have seemed to fear that such attack might be made, and have hastened to parry before a blow was aimed. In the sense that by the Federal law it is not proscribed I am willing to concede its legitimacy, and to the extent of the 18,000,000 gallons of alcohol and spirits that are used in the arts and medicines I am willing to concede legitimacy; but, sir, I am not willing to go further.

Legitimate industries are those that bring blessings to mankind; that lift the burdens from toiling men and women; that bring comforts; that feed, clothe, warm, and enlighten them; that brighten their lives and remove the shadows of care. They clear the forests and subdue the prairies; they build our cities; they bridge our rivers, carry railways across continents, work our mines, fill the air with the hum of spindles and the music of anvils; they mark out paths for commerce across oceans, and light the skies with the eager fire of countless forges. They make man better, happier, and give him gradual approach to the perfect standard of his Maker.

I have yet to learn, Mr. Chairman, that measured by these standards the manufacture of whisky could be classed with "legitimate industries."

One member has said that this class of manufactures during the Civil War kept our armies in the field, preserved the national credit, and enabled the Government to put down rebellion. Another has said that they erected the splendid public buildings that adorn this city. Up to the close of the war the total revenue raised from distilled spirits was but little in excess of $46,000,000; not enough to meet the expenses of the Government for fifteen days of war. This "industry kept our armies in the field!" Oh! no, sir; not the armies of patriotism. It was powerless to do that. But it did recruit some of our armies. It has ever been most efficient in recruiting the armies of crime, the armies of pauperism, the army of drunkards, unfortunate children of its thrift, that every year, many thousands strong, fall into dishonored graves.

"This industry erected our splendid public edifices!" Yes, Mr. Chairman, unfortunately it has. But not our capitols, not our seminaries of learning, nor yet our schools of art. It has erected our jails and poorhouses, our insane hospitals, and our penitentiaries; and here and there a gibbet is seen in the land that it, too, has erected. Whatever there are of the sad sights that may be seen in this otherwise bright land of ours, these are the fruits of this "industry." Is it a broken and dismantled home; a wicked life of wife or husband; a group of hungry-eyed, ragged children; a crowd of youths, neglected, drifting in idleness and ignorance crimeward; the ignorant criminal classes, withholding their quota of labor from the aggregate that produces the wealth of the State, who increase the expenses of him who bears his full share of the burdens of government; the classes who retard progress and make doubtful our civilization—if these sights are seen, or any of them, we may point with almost unerring certainty to this "legitimate industry" as the agency that has made possible scenes like these in every hamlet and town and city of this otherwise blessed country of ours. Except for the 18,000,000 of gallons used in the arts the "industry" might cease to be and no man would be the worse for its disappearance. But all men in every strata of society would have added prosperity, added blessing, additional hope. We are so knit together that every man is made to feel the woe it is laden with. In some way or other it comes home to each of us, and always with a curse. No day ever dawned upon nation or people brighter or more fraught with blessing than that good day coming when the evil flowing from this "industry" shall by wise prohibitory laws, backed by a more perfect civilization, be driven from the land.

On March 25 John D. Long [Mass.] spoke.

The gentleman from Maryland [John V. L. Findlay] waxed eloquent, and called this commodity a very "hell-broth" of woe, and asked if we were prepared to pour it broadcast over the land, instead of confining it in the receptacle of the warehouses of the nation. He knows better. He is not deluded with the notion that our warehouses are built and stored with whisky for the pleasure of its accumulation or with the benevolent purpose of keeping it from public use and public consumption. He knows that to pass this bill will indeed pile it up in those warehouses, but will pile it up only to be poured out a few years later—and the longer delay the more abundantly—in a deluge of ruin and madness over the land.

I, too, like him, find my guide not in any noisy clamor, not in any false outcry of the popular voice, but in my own conscience and judgment. And these tell me, as a matter of sound public policy, of recent historical experience, of present justice, of the true interest even of the parties appellant, of honest fulfillment of obligation and law, of statesmanlike prevention of greater impending evils, and of arresting, even at some possible cost to a few, a disease which, by delay, will only grow worse in its general calamity—these unite and tell me that it is my duty, even aside from all questions of domestic good morals, to vote against this bill. [Great applause.]

MARTIN A. FORAN [O.].—The gentleman from New York [Mr. Ray] is mistaken if he believes that the production of distilled spirits is productive of poverty. The proposition that poverty is caused by intemperance is true only in isolated instances. As a general rule intemperance is merely an incident to poverty, which is to a very large extent the result of an unequal, an iniquitous distribution of wealth. If the gentleman can devise, and make operative by appropriate legislation, any plan by which the working classes can secure a just and equitable proportion of the wealth they produce, it will not be necessary for Government to buy grain to feed the poor and hungry.

Intemperance of every kind is an evil. But restrictive measures will not cure it. Human perfection can be attained only through education and intelligence, and the only way to advance the cause of true temperance is to improve the material conditions—intellectual, moral, and religious status of humanity. If you are determined to refuse these men relief simply because they deal in whisky, do so; but I submit it is neither fair nor manly to abuse them for furnishing the public with an article which the public demands and insists upon having. If it is wrong to drink intoxicants as a beverage, convince the drinkers of that fact, and the production of the article for that purpose will quickly cease.

WILLIAM T. PRICE [Wis.].—This petted, pampered pirate [the liquor business] comes asking alms, when in all its nefarious history it was never known to confer a blessing on a man, a State, or a nation. It asks to be selected from the whole multitude of business enterprises and placed above and beyond all the others as a recipient of public favor, in the face of the fact that it has been the deadliest and direst foe that the public has ever had to deal with.

Its advocates claim this remarkable concession because it pays annually a tax of near $100,000,000, but they would have us forget that it destroys grain enough to feed all the starving sons of earth; that it lowers the standard of public virtue, debases the public conscience, lowers the standard of citizenship, slimes its wicked way up to the seat of political power, destroys the high standard of intelligence and the nice sense of virtue so essential among a people every one of whom is a voter and thereby a ruler. They would have us forget that wherever its sway is recognized it has desolated homes, beggared its votaries, and physically, mentally, and morally dragged down and degraded its victims. They would have us forget that to-day, while we talk, all over this fair land its victims are suffering, starving, dying. They would have us forget that for every dollar which it pays to support government the legitimate industries and wealth of the country are taxed tenfold the sum thus realized to overcome or correct the costs of its destructive influences upon our people. They would have us forget that, financially considered, this branch of commerce has always been and must always and inevitably be a failure. They would have us forget that this business has always been a lawbreaker when it has been unable to buy such laws or lawmakers as suited its purposes.

The gentleman from Kentucky [Philip B. Thompson] said he never knew one of these temperance cranks but would "go behind the door and take a drink." I cannot dispute him; my only regret is that it has been his misfortune to have only associated with or made the acquaintance of the insincere and the unworthy, and I will do my unfortunate friend the kindness to inform him that there are heights he has not climbed, realms of moral excellence he has not explored, and that, if he will abandon the attitude of standing as the apologist of a trade that degrades, debauches, demoralizes, and damns everything it touches, he may thereby lift himself to the right of association with men whose patriotism would lead them to legislate for the "greatest good to the greatest number," whose philanthropy would impel them to reach down to the gutter and lift their weaker brother from the degradation to which he has been brought by commerce in whisky, and place him on the broader, purer platform of an independent manhood; men the purity of whose lives and conduct and their lifelong devotion to principle enable them to regard pityingly the men who charge them with insincerity.

This monster for which they plead was conceived in sin, born in corruption, and reared in iniquity. Its lullaby has been the sigh of the suffering, the yell of the maniac, the groan of the murdered; and its requiem shall be the clearly expressed and indignant protest of all respectable people against its longer existence.

On March 26 John W. McCormick [O.] spoke.

The question involved in this discussion seems to me to be one of policy against principle, of expediency against right. Policy asks what is easiest, what will pay best? while principle asks the question, What is right? and, knowing the right, performs it.

What ought to be done in regard to the liquor traffic is to members of this House in their official capacity a question of momentous importance. It is a question not to be dealt with rashly, or decided hastily, or without regard for the rights of the citizen; and by the citizen we mean the great body of our people of all classes and conditions in life. Statistics give the whole cost of liquors in the year 1873 at $700,000,000. A recent statement in an editorial of the New York *Tribune* gives the amount of $800,000,000 spent in this country yearly for drink; an amount exceeding by $100,000,000 the entire sum raised by taxes of all kinds, national, State, county, city, town, and school district, as stated upon the authority of the Census Bureau. America pays whisky dealers more than she pays the laboring classes. Drink costs more than three times as much as we pay for clothes, fourteen times as much as we pay for public schools, and eighteen times as much as we give to the poor.

A traffic that costs in actual payment and in loss of productive labor more than half the national debt every year is not an insignificant matter to the true political economist, leaving out of the question the class who oppose the traffic from moral convictions. The cost of pauperism, of crime from intemperance, the waste of grain, and loss of productive industry in their effects upon the country cannot be evaded by the loyal statesman who has his country's good in view and seeks the perpetuity of our free institutions. Such a drain as these make on a nation's resources affords grounds for alarm that cannot fail to claim his thoughtful consideration, and against which he fails in duty if he does not lift a warning voice. But there is another phase of this question that necessarily presents itself for our contemplation; other things besides the pecuniary affairs of the nation affect its welfare.

Secretary Seward in his lifetime said:

No republican government can stand that has not for its support the morality and virtue of the people.

In the same connection he goes on to say:

But what a fearful decay of public virtue attends the liquor traffic, degrading and destroying to those who should become the pillars and strength of our Government.

It has been well said that "government emanates from the moral attributes of mankind. It is a thing of moral necessity, and its power and obligation are of a moral kind." It is the duty of the Government to make it difficult to do wrong and easy to do right, to throw around the citizen such safeguards and such wholesome protection as will secure him against the impure and vicious and stimulate within him the desire for the pure and the good. But the effect of the liquor traffic, direct and indirect, view it as he may, upon the individual and upon society, is paralyzing to the physical, intellectual, social, moral, and political well-being of the community and State.

Burke has defined law as beneficence acting by rule; but who, in looking at the immeasurable evils, can plead in behalf of the beneficence of the liquor traffic? The thousands of millions of revenue to the Government would soon fly upward in the balance as weighed against the burdens and griefs and anguish and death it entails upon society.

In its hold upon the country this traffic is aggressive in its character and is becoming more and more exorbitant in its demands. What other business or traffic comes into the council chambers of this nation seeking such help and such special priv-

ileges as are demanded by this bill? By what right or precedent does it come here seeking to be freed from its obligations,
when no other business would for a moment indulge the thought
even that it had any right to make such a claim? But this
traffic, in all its boldness and effrontery, according to its accustomed habit of seeking to dictate and control the policy of
States, does so assert itself and presents its claims for recognition here. The question that confronts us, then, is this: Is it
right that this bill pass? Looking at that question in the length
and breadth and full scope of its pecuniary significance, is it
for the welfare of our citizens, the comfort of our free homes,
and the prosperity of our country? Can we honestly, sincerely,
and conscientiously answer that question in the affirmative by
our votes in favor of this bill? Are we to give this commerce of
death a stronger hold upon us, or is it not a wiser, safer, truer,
nobler policy to seek rather to loosen its hold on the vitals of
this nation than to suffer it to bind us more strongly in its fatal
coils?

JOSEPH D. TAYLOR [O.].—We have been asked to ignore the
moral aspect of this question. When we are asked to pass over
all the great realm of productions and select one as the object
of special legislation, cannot we inquire as to the effect of the
only use to which this commodity is applied? It is impossible
to avoid doing this, as is evidenced by the fact that the friends
of this bill were the first to discuss the moral phase of the question and have kept it up all the way through this discussion.
They felt the necessity of this and began to defend before they
were attacked, and from the first speech to the last thus far they
have felt the necessity of meeting this phase. They have steadily sought to divert attention from the moral phase of the question by the statement that it is a purely business measure, connected with a branch of industry that is adding constantly to
the national resources.

It has been said, and truly, that this is a great business, involving millions of dollars, but I deny that it is any source of
wealth to this country. You cannot separate a business from
its legitimate results, and the legitimate results of the whisky
business, trace it where you will, are poverty, suffering, degradation, disease, and death. Every dollar it brings into the
coffers of its vendors is reeking with blood and tears. The
modicum of value it may have as a mechanical and medicinal
agency is overborne and buried out of sight under the untold
burdens it binds upon humanity. Beneath its touch the strongest arm falls paralyzed and the clearest eye grows dim. Youth,

strong ambitions, glorious youth, becomes feeble and palsied as with age at the blighting touch of this monster; keen intellects lose their godlike powers and grovel in the dust. Kind hearts are turned into demons, and blight and blast, without a throb of remorse, their own most cherished ones. Home and friends and peace and honor all go down in one surging sea of horror, and the starless night of a drunkard's eternity closes over more than 60,000 souls in our own country every year. And yet gentlemen can stand here and make a jest of intemperance, and wreathe their lips with sarcastic smiles at the idea of there being any question of temperance in a whisky-extension bill. The financial ruin so touchingly depicted here as consequent upon the failure of this bill will, if it should follow, not be the first financial ruin that has dated back to whisky. The country is full of the scarred and blackened ruins of homes and fortunes and the darker ruins of noble lives, the wrecks of manhood and womanhood, the foul and festering things cast up from the mire and filth of intemperance, which but for this "legitimate business" might have been radiant with the attributes of Heaven.

There is no turning away or ignoring these considerations or casting them aside with a flippant jest. They confront us on the floor of this House hidden in the provisions of this bill; and, disguise it as you may, it is the increasing and awakening conscience of this nation that is making it more and more difficult for the whisky power to succeed in its arrogant demands. It is the gleam of light on the horizon of the future, the one bow of promise against the dark background of the present, that men are coming to understand more fully and appreciate more correctly the animus of this business. And the time is coming when our children will blush for us that we should ever have temporized with this deadliest foe to human progress and human happiness.

ABRAM S. HEWITT [N. Y.]—Revenue taxation has nothing to do with morality or charity. The Constitution under which I have been brought up and have sworn to obey declares that taxation is for revenue and for revenue only. [Applause on the Democratic side.]

But we have had a school in this country which has been dominant, the members of which believe in taxation for protection; and we have had taxation for protection until the people of this country have been differentiated into two classes, the very rich and the very poor. Now that this system is breaking down, aye, when the light is penetrating into the State of Massachusetts, which has been the home of protection, but from which we now get the strongest advocacy of the doctrine of free raw material, it is necessary that the members of that school who have exhausted all the possibilities of taxation for protection shall invent a new gospel. And it was announced here yes-

"ALCOHOL IN THE ARTS"

How "protection" is to be taken. Open your mouth and shut your eyes

Cartoon by Thomas Nast

terday—taxation for morality. I suppose the gentleman would prefer me to say taxation for revenue with incidental morality. [Laughter.]

That idea is worthy of the party of great moral ideas. If you can support this Government or any government upon the vices of its people, if you can devise a revenue system which will compel those who depart from the ways of virtue to pay the expenses of the Government, then you will produce a new development truly admirable and worthy to be welcomed as the beginning of the millennium. Instead of dividing this country into the very rich and the very poor, you will divide it into the very good and the very bad, and the bad men will be made to pay all the expenses of the good men. Then, having founded your Government on the great basis of human depravity, you may economize to your heart's content, for you will want no more churches and no more colleges, but taxation for morality will be the panacea for all our woes. [Laughter.]

I have said that taxation has nothing to do with moral questions. It is just as legitimate to produce whisky, so far as taxation is concerned, as it is to produce pig iron. In the eye of the law both industries are equally reputable and equally valuable to the community. As a pig-iron maker, knowing its vast uses, I am at a loss to-day to say whether the production of iron, so the production of alcohol, is more useful to the human race. Yet if any man to-day were to propose to impose a tax upon the manufacture of pig iron he would be hooted out of this House, as he ought to be.

This is either a legitimate industry or it is not. If it is not a legitimate business, then it ought to be stopped; there can be no compromise. But, if it ought to be stopped on moral grounds, it does not belong to the national Federal Government to prohibit it. That is a matter of police regulation which is reserved to the States. Let them deal with moral questions; we here have nothing to do with them. Having nothing to do with the moral question, and having, as I believe, satisfied you, or at least satisfied myself, that no tax ought to be imposed upon production in any lawful industry, then there is but one logical conclusion; that is, that this tax ought to be abolished altogether, because such a tax violates a fundamental economic principle.

I vote for this bill on the broad proposition that it will be the first honest step toward the doctrine of free raw material, which in my judgment is the vital question of this age and this generation in the industrial development of this country.

Now gentlemen may be under some misapprehension as to the nature of the production of alcohol and its uses. I observe that alcohol has been dealt with here mostly on the ground of being a beverage, and a bad beverage at that. No gentleman here has brought to the attention of the House and the country the vast uses of this commodity in the arts. I myself have been profoundly astonished at the investigations I have had to make;

and you will be, Mr. Chairman, when I tell you that I am satisfied that one-half of the entire alcohol which is produced in this country is to-day, notwithstanding the drawback of an enormous excise duty, used in the arts, and not more than half is consumed as a beverage.

The varied uses of alcohol are beyond any estimate. I find it in the household, in the surgery; I find it in the photographer's shop and among the artists; I find it in every kind of manufacture with which I have anything to do or of which I have any knowledge. I find it to be the universal solvent by which all substances are transferred from one form to another; and I find this vehicle taxed as if it were on a turnpike road with a toll-gate every half mile. Yet we are expected to make progress in the innumerable arts dependent upon the use of alcohol as a vehicle.

Mr. Chairman, I announce now that from this time out, with my voice and my vote, I shall support every bill that proposes to free alcohol; and I shall not cease to work in that direction until the total abolition of this tax is accomplished.

SETH L. MILLIKEN [Me.].—It needs not that a man should be what gentlemen are pleased to style a temperance crank, it needs not that he should be a teetotaler or a prohibitionist, it needs only that he should be an intelligent man, observant of what is transacting in every community, to know that the whisky traffic inflicts upon our people one of the greatest of all their misfortunes, and it needs only that one should be a patriotic man and a lover of his race that he should most deeply deplore it. And, when the gentleman from Kentucky [Mr. Thompson] was depicting in colors so vivid the tears and sorrows of the wives and children of the whisky dealers to be made bankrupt by payment of their taxes, I could not but think how much broader a field he might have had for his eloquent description had he attempted a recital of but a small fraction of the pains and sorrows, misery, degradation, and crime of which whisky has been the prolific parent.

Whisky pleading for sympathy is like the boy who, having murdered his father and mother, when convicted of the crime and asked why sentence of death should not be pronounced upon him, appealed with tearful eyes to the court to have mercy upon a poor orphan!

CHAPTER XI

The Original Package [Liquor] Decision

James F. Wilson [Ia.] Introduces in the Senate Bill Subjecting Liquors Imported into a State to Laws of the State—Debate: George F. Hoar [Mass.], George G. Vest [Mo.], Matthew C. Butler [S. C.], James L. Pugh [Ala.], George Gray [Del.], George F. Edmunds [Vt.], John R. McPherson [N. J.], Henry L. Dawes [Mass.], Frank Hiscock [N. Y.], John H. Reagan [Tex.], William M. Evarts [N. Y.], Sen. Wilson—Sen. Gray Offers a Substitute Measure; It Is Passed by Senate; Conference; New Bill Is Enacted.

ON December 4, 1889, James F. Wilson [Ia.] introduced in the Senate a bill subjecting liquors imported into a State to the provisions of the laws of that State. It was referred to the Judiciary Committee. The committee reported a bill on the subject on May 14, 1890.

Original Package Bill

Senate, May 14-28, 1890

George F. Hoar [Mass.], of the committee, explained the occasion of the bill.

This bill is rendered necessary, in the opinion of the committee, by the late decision of the Supreme Court of the United States (Leisy & Co. *vs.* Hardin), which holds that intoxicating liquor manufactured in one State, conveyed into another, and there sold by the manufacturer or his agent, is protected by the Constitution of the United States from any regulation or prohibition of that sale by the State law on the ground that such prohibition or regulation is an interference with the regulation of commerce between the States. The Court, in their opinion, say that the States cannot pass such prohibitory or regulating statutes without the permission of Congress, which is understood to imply an opinion on the part of the Court that

402

Congress may give that permission, and that with that permission the States may pass the regulation or prohibitory enactment which they see fit.

I wholly concur in the propriety of this bill, but I suppose the principle of the opinion of the Supreme Court applies as well to gunpowder that a State may deem insecure and may desire to regulate the sale of as dangerous to safety, or to opium, a deadly drug, and poisons of all kinds. I should have preferred, myself, that the bill should apply to all articles the prohibition or regulation of the sale of which a State thinks necessary for its health, morals, or safety; but, as so large a number of State laws in regard to the sale of intoxicating liquors are affected by this proposed legislation, it is quite important that it should not be delayed, and therefore I agree with the rest of the committee in this bill.

George C. Vest [Mo.], of the minority of the committee, spoke against the bill.

I do not believe the Supreme Court of the United States ever intended to assert that Congress could permit a State to invade the exclusive interstate-commerce power of the national Congress. This bill, although it comes in a different shape from the other, does the same thing, and if we now can pass this measure giving to the State of Iowa the power to declare what is a subject of interstate commerce, as is done by this bill, the same power can be given under similar circumstances as to any other article of interstate commerce to Missouri and every other State.

Senator Wilson said:

While I may not believe that the decision of the Supreme Court is a sound interpretation of the Constitution of the United States, I recognize the suggestion and regard it as a possible method of removing from the way of the States that obstacle which prevents the enforcement of their just police powers.

I may say that under that decision, without some such legislation as this, no State in this Union can ever apply prohibition, license, local option, or any other form of control to the subject of the traffic in intoxicating liquors.

On May 20 Senator Wilson explained the effect of the bill.

The effect of the bill, if it shall become a law, will be to leave every State in the Union free to determine for itself what its policy shall be in respect of the traffic in intoxicating liquors. If a State shall desire prohibition it can adopt it and exercise it and enforce it under the provisions of this bill. If it shall desire license, high or low, the same conditions will attend that policy so far as this bill is concerned. If it shall prefer to adopt the policy denominated local option, it may do that, so that the traffic may be allowed in such counties or cities as desire it and prohibited in others.

Unless this bill or something which shall be its equivalent shall be enacted by Congress, then the several States are at the mercy of the citizens of other of the several States, and not only that, but the subjects of all foreign governments will have in the States of this Union greater rights and privileges than the citizens of the States have themselves.

Mr. President, that State which I in part represent in this body elected as its policy the prohibition of the manufacture and sale of intoxicating liquors. The people of the State are satisfied with it; they desire the enforcement of their law; but, since the decision from which I have read an extract was announced, agents of distilleries and breweries in other States of the Union are already traversing Iowa and organizing "the original-package saloon" within the State, and there is no limitation as to what "the original package" may be. It may be a pint or a half-pint bottle of whisky; it may be a bottle or a keg of beer; it may be in any quantity and whatsoever form of package agreed upon between the manufacturer of another State and the agent that he may send to transact his business in Iowa.

The State of Iowa wants her present policy; and she should have an opportunity to administer it until her people determine to adopt something else in its place.

MATTHEW C. BUTLER [S. C.].—Does the Senator hold that under the decision of the Supreme Court the State of Iowa would have the right, after the package gets into that State, to prevent the sale or take control of it in any way after it crosses the line?

SENATOR WILSON.—Undoubtedly the decision of the Supreme Court protects every package that may be transported into that State from abroad, from foreign countries or from other States, until it shall have passed from the hands of the importer and thereby become mingled with the common property of the State.

SENATOR BUTLER.—Then the State has the right to interpose by its laws and prevent the sale or any disposition of the article imported?

SENATOR WILSON.—After it shall have passed from the hands of the importer or his agent. But under this decision, whatever package may be introduced there—for instance, the brewer in Illinois, the distiller in Illinois or any other State may arrange to send his package in there, even in the shape of a vial containing a single drink, and organize his saloon on that basis, the importer holding possession, protected by the decision of the Supreme Court, until that package shall pass from his possession into the hands of his customer and that customer may drink a single drink of whisky in that original-package saloon in the good State of Iowa, and in spite of her laws.

SENATOR VEST.—The Senator from Iowa [Mr. Wilson] says that under the decision of the Supreme Court as it stands the citizens of any foreign country would have more rights than the citizens of any other State which may have adopted the prohibitory system.

Mr. President, the same argument would apply to any article of interstate commerce under the decision of the Supreme Court of the United States, and the argument of the Senator from Iowa, if worth anything, would sweep away the exclusive jurisdiction of the Congress of the United States over interstate commerce.

What has the Supreme Court decided? The Supreme Court has decided emphatically by a majority of its justices that alcoholic stimulants are an article of interstate commerce. They have decided, in the second place, that the power to regulate commerce among the States and with foreign nations and with the Indian tribes is an exclusive power vested by the Constitution in the Congress of the United States.

In the celebrated license cases, where Chief-Justice Taney and three of his associates rendered a dissenting opinion, five of the justices rendered an opinion that the interstate-commerce power of Congress was exclusive of any power within the States, and the other judges, some of them emphatically and some by indirection, held to the opinion that the power to regulate commerce was a concurrent power vested by the Constitution of the United States in certain cases in the States themselves.

The Supreme Court of the United States, in the case to which the Senator has referred, and which has called forth this proposed legislation, reaffirmed the doctrine of Gibbons *vs.* Ogden and the doctrine of the five judges, comprising the majority of the Supreme Court of the United States in the license cases, and upon one single expression which was *obiter dictum*—as I think I will show beyond a question—upon one single *dictum* of the chief justice who delivered this opinion is based the bill now pending in the Senate.

Let us in the first place understand, in the language of the court itself, what it has decided. Chief Justice Fuller says:

> The authority of Peirce *vs.* New Hampshire, in so far as it rests on the view that the law of New Hampshire was valid because Congress had made no regulation on the subject, must be regarded as having been distinctly overthrown by the numerous cases hereinafter referred to.
>
> The doctrine now firmly established is, as stated by Mr. Justice Field in Bowman *vs.* Chicago, etc., Railway Co., 125 U. S., 507, ''that where the subject upon which Congress can act under its commercial power is local in its nature or sphere of operation, such as harbor pilotage, etc., which can be properly regulated only by special provisions adapted to their localities, the State can act until Congress interferes and supersedes its authority; but where the subject is national in its character, and admits and requires uniformity of regulation, affecting alike all the States, such as—

Now mark it—

> transportation between the States, including the importation of goods from one State into another, Congress can alone act upon it and provide the needed regulations. The absence of any law of Congress on the subject is equivalent to its declaration that commerce in that matter shall be free. Thus the absence of regulations as to interstate commerce with reference to any particular subject is taken as a declaration that the importation of that article into the States shall be unrestricted. It is only after the importation is completed, and the property imported is mingled with and becomes a part of the general property of the State, that its regulations can act upon it, except so far as may be necessary to insure safety in the disposition of the import until thus mingled.

Now, says Chief Justice Fuller, commenting upon this decision of Mr. Justice Field in the case of Bowman *vs.* Chicago and Northwestern Railway Company:

> The conclusion follows that, as the grant of the power to regulate commerce among the States, so far as one system is required, is exclusive, the States can not exercise that power without the assent of Congress—

Upon these words, a simple *dictum*, is based the bill that is now pending before the Senate—

> and, in the absence of legislation, it is left for the courts to determine when State action does or does not amount to such exercise, or, in other

words, what is or is not a regulation of such commerce. When that is determined, controversy is at an end.

Now, Mr. President, I repeat that upon those simple words, a manifest *dictum* interpolated into this opinion, not necessary to the decision of the question pending before the Supreme Court, which intimates that Congress can give its permission to a State to regulate interstate commerce, is based the legislation that is now proposed.

When the Supreme Court declares that alcoholic stimulants are a subject of interstate commerce, can the Congress, when it is vested by the Constitution with exclusive power (and the Supreme Court has so decided in regard to the importation of alcoholic stimulants from one State to another), delegate that power to a State? That is all there is of it. It is not a question of the police power of the State; it is a question of delegation.

If that power can be delegated in regard to an article of merchandise, which alcoholic stimulants are admitted to be, it can be delegated, if sufficient political influence can be brought to bear in these halls, as to wheat, or corn, or oats, or oleomargarine, or any other article which is the subject of interstate commerce.

Are we to make this new departure? Are we upon the *dictum* of the Supreme Court to tear down the barriers of the Constitution? Are we to uproot the settled doctrine based upon the highest motives of policy to prevent confusion between the States and create uniformity?

In the Fiftieth Congress a bill was offered by the Senator from Iowa which had the same effect as the bill now pending, but differently constructed. That was referred to the Judiciary Committee. Five of us voted that the bill was unconstitutional and made a report against it, which was drawn by the Senator from Mississippi [James Z. George].

The Senator from Mississippi now substantially agrees with the majority of the committee. He comes to the conclusion that the Supreme Court of the United States has decided that Congress can give permission to a State to interfere in interstate commerce. That is his opinion, but it is not my opinion.

JAMES L. PUGH [Ala.].—It is perfectly manifest that the bill could not pass if it were not for the suggestion in the opinion of the Supreme Court that Congress can grant permission to a State to exercise the power of prohibiting the importation of intoxicants into her limits in the original package. Can that question of the power of Congress to give its consent, its permission, ever be raised and decided by the Supreme Court if this bill is not passed by Congress? How can we ever get the question decided if we do not pass this bill?

SENATOR VEST.—Mr. President, if I were requested courteously to frame a case for a moot court in a law university, I might be then willing to do what the Senator from Alabama intimates we ought to do; but I still have an old-fashioned idea that I have sworn to support the Constitution, and that I cannot vote for a bill which I think violates it.

GEORGE GRAY [Del.].—I observe in the opinion of the Supreme Court upon this case there is this language:

Whatever our individual views may be as to the deleterious or dangerous qualities of particular articles, we can not hold that any articles which Congress recognizes as subjects of interstate commerce are not such or that whatever are thus recognized can be controlled by State laws amounting to regulations, while they retain that character.

Now, without going into the matter of fact whether Congress has affirmatively recognized any particular article, such as intoxicating liquors, as a subject of interstate commerce, as it decided in the case of Brown *vs*. The State of Maryland that Congress had recognized that the articles there were the subjects of foreign commerce by imposing a duty upon them and including them in the schedule of dutiable articles, I ask the Senator whether it is not competent, within the meaning of the language of the Supreme Court just quoted, for Congress to decide by the passage of a bill that its jurisdiction under the commerce clause of the Constitution shall be confined to certain subjects-matter of commerce, or the converse of that proposition, that certain subjects-matter, or things that might be considered subjects-matter of commerce, shall be excluded from the jurisdiction under the commerce clause of the Constitution. Is it not true that Congress may limit the scope of the exercise of the power conferred upon it by the commerce clause of the Constitution?

SENATOR VEST.—I do not think so, because that is liable to the very objection which I have urged and which is at the bottom of this whole discussion. That clause of the Constitution gives an exclusive power to Congress, and the reason it was given to Congress was to prevent the very thing which would happen if the contingency arose contemplated by the Senator from Delaware; and what the framers of the Constitution meant was that there should be an impartial tribunal, the Congress of the United States, which should dispose for itself and in and of itself of all questions of interstate commerce, and which was intended to do away with the evil that was a giant one under the Articles of Confederation, when every State undertook to regulate that matter for itself.

If the Congress of the United States should do what the Senator from Delaware says, then it would only change the form of this action, and the same evils would come eventually. In other words, when they had said certain articles are articles of commerce, at the expense of one State, another State would come and add certain other articles, and if it had the power to carry Congress that would be the result.

GEORGE F. EDMUNDS [Vt.].—We are now on purely a question of constitutional law. I suppose that the Senator will agree that the traffic in passengers, the movement of persons from foreign countries to the United States and from State to State, is commerce, as the Supreme Court has decided.

SENATOR VEST.—Not all of it.

SENATOR EDMUNDS.—Where is the exception?

SENATOR VEST.—It goes further than the actual transit from one State to another or from a foreign country to this.

SENATOR EDMUNDS.—No, it is not all commerce, but it is a part of commerce.

SENATOR VEST.—Unquestionably.

SENATOR EDMUNDS.—Now, then, Congress has not chosen to pass any law on the subject of preventing the introduction of lepers into the United States, and the State says by law "that no person afflicted with leprosy shall come within the borders of this State at all, either from a foreign country or from another State." The movement of a leper, as a physical fact and as a mercantile fact, the paying transportation and all that, is just as much commerce as the movement of a healthy man is. Now, can Congress allow, or take its hands off, or whatever phrase you like to employ, and permit a State to say that no leper shall come into this State at all from anywhere?

SENATOR VEST.—Mr. President, we come back to the same question, no matter which road we travel; and that is whether this is not an exclusive power in the Congress of the United States and whether they can delegate it to the States in one form or another. The proposition made by the Senator from Vermont as to a leper does not touch this case at all, because the Supreme Court has decided that the commerce clause of the Constitution never was intended and never could have been intended to take away from the States the reserve police power to protect the life and health of their own citizens, and it has decided over and over and over again, as my friend from Vermont knows, that an article which is diseased and deleterious to human life and health can not be an article of commerce.

SENATOR EDMUNDS.—Where is the right to decide whether the article is diseased or not? Is it in the States or is it in the United States?

SENATOR VEST.—The power at last would be a judicial one; that is a question of construction, and it would rest with the Supreme Court. That brings us to the very point of this whole matter. No State has the right to say what shall be an article of commerce, and the Supreme Court has decided over and over again that that is a question for the national Congress to determine.

JOHN R. McPHERSON [N. J.].—I should like to ask the Senator whether in his opinion the right to import an article implies the right to sell it and the unrestricted use of all the channels of importation, whatever they may be, to the consumer. For instance, take the right to import a package of liquor into a State, which I understand Congress has not interdicted in any way, it being interstate commerce, where there were prohibition laws, where does the power of the State begin and where does the power that you get under the right to import cease?

SENATOR VEST.—The Supreme Court of the United States decided that in the case of Ward vs. Maryland, and the authority has been unbroken. It is decided in the case which is now before the Senate in regard to which this proposed legislation is asked. The broad doctrine is this: The power to import carries with it the power to sell, because the Supreme Court has said without the power to sell the other grant of power is nugatory and void. The interstate commerce clause of the Constitution attaches so long as the merchandise remains in an unbroken package in the hands of the importer. When it is sold, when the package is broken and the goods are mingled with the other goods of the citizens of the State, the merchandise ceases to be interstate commerce merchandise and becomes subject to the police power of the State. That is the decision of the Supreme Court of the United States simply repeated in the case which has been read here.

SENATOR McPHERSON.—Then the regulation of the State begins when the package is broken?

SENATOR VEST.—The regulation of the State begins just so soon as the original package goes out of the hands of the importer and the goods become mingled with the other goods of the State.

SENATOR EDMUNDS.—If I may ask the Senator a question, how can that be so on the logic of what my friend is saying? The Supreme Court, he says, has held that anything that a State does which tends to restrain interstate or external commerce is a regulation of commerce, indirect, but still effectual. If a man imports a ton of dynamite into the city of New York for use in the State of Missouri, to blow up St. Louis, etc., as his motive may be, but nobody knows that, upon what principle is it that Congress or the Supreme Court can say (Congress may say it, the Supreme Court can not) that that is secure in the hands of the man who imported it, while it is not secure in the hands of the man to whom he has agreed to sell it, because the effect of the repression is just as great when the property comes into the hands of the second owner as it is in the hands of the first, as everybody knows. The line is in another place when the Supreme Court comes to find it out.

SENATOR VEST.—The Supreme Court of the United States has always held that so far as the health and life of the citizens of a State were concerned the State had the power, it has it now, and always has had it by its police power, its reserved power, to protect that life and that health. If it is dynamite or gunpowder every Commonwealth in the Union has the power, whether it is the Government of the United States or the government of the State of Missouri or Vermont, to protect the health and life of its citizens. That is a power which always exists. It is an attribute of sovereignty. It is something the State can not divest itself of, for the Supreme Court has said that no State would have the right to divest itself of the power to protect the health and life of its own people. That shows how great and sovereign is their power and how absolute is the necessity of its exercise.

A remarkable spectacle is presented here in that extreme State-rights men defend the decision of the Supreme Court of the United States. It is the highest assertion of State rights to declare that the general Government has exclusive jurisdiction of certain questions and that the general Government alone can exercise that jurisdiction. If you once break down that barrier you destroy the doctrine of State rights. I therefore, a State-rights man beyond question, stand here to-day to defend this decision of the Supreme Court, and to declare that with Congress alone rests the exclusive power to declare what shall be a subject of interstate commerce and to regulate it.

SENATOR HOAR.—Mr. President, if this bill be not within the constitutional power of Congress, I think we must all agree that the condition of the American people in regard to this particular subject is more miserable than that of any other civilized nation on the face of the earth. I suppose there does not exist a community where men live together under law where the danger of permitting the unrestricted sale of intoxicating liquor is not recognized and guarded against by public authority.

Unless what we propose or its equivalent can be done, what is the result? The law, as I understand it, in the United States is this for the present and for all future time (unless we have a new Constitution in this respect), that any person, a dweller in another State or in a foreign country, may, through his own agencies, send intoxicating liquor into any of the States of this Union, and, having selected the kind of package in which he chooses to put it, he may, by those agencies, deliver it for use to any citizen of the State or dweller therein, and that it shall not be competent for any State authority to prohibit that delivery to a drunken man who has just come from a frenzy in which he has threatened the life or safety of his wife or children, to a criminal who desires it to fortify his courage for the commission of a crime, to a maniac or idiot whose slender intellect overcome by it will be simply the moving force to some arson or murder or assault by which the life and health and safety of innocent persons are threatened.

It is declared by the honorable Senator from Missouri [Mr. Vest] that, as he understands the law expounded by the supreme legal tribunal in this country, that is the condition of things to which we are to be hereafter exposed, with the supposable and practically impossible alternative that Congress itself shall enter upon the regulation of the traffic in intoxicating liquor so far as it is carried on by the agents of citizens of other States or citizens of other countries than the place where the liquor is to be sold and delivered.

Mr. President, one thing I think no man will question who knows anything of the history and character of the people of this country, and that is that if it had been supposed that the adoption of our fundamental law would have led to any such constitutional result there would not have been a State of the Union that would have given its assent to the adoption of the Constitution. It was hard enough as it was, and required the utmost exertion of the authority of the weightiest, and wisest, and best citizenship of that day, to induce nearly all the States to give their assent to the adoption of the Constitution, but if it had been said, "You are proposing an instrument to take from you the right to control your own beer shops or the sale of intoxicating drinks within your borders when it is attempted to be exercised and accomplished by the agency of persons living without your borders," I do not believe there would have been a hundredth part of the citizens of any State existing at that day who would have given their votes for the adoption of the Federal Constitution.

My honorable friend from Missouri spoke of this as a question of State rights. It is not a question of State rights. It is the question of the right being lodged anywhere to control crime.

When certain classes of our citizens or certain classes of political opinions are found now denying to the State, now denying to the United States, the power to exercise this, that, or the other function of legislation, it is not because they want to save the right, however they may deceive themselves, to do the thing to the place where the Constitution has lodged it; it is because they do not desire the legislative control over that thing to be exercised anywhere. As a rule, you will find that that class of citizens who are in favor of the most ample, thorough, and beneficent exercise of the constitutional and national rights of this Government are also in favor of the most ample, thorough, and constitutional exercise of the legislative powers and rights of the States for the public good, and they are also, as a rule, equally in favor of the most ample, thorough, and constitutional exercise of the right of the citizen to govern himself in regard to the matters where the human will goes astray, unless it is submitted to its own moral government. You will find in those sections of the country where the advocates of the powers of the nation dwell State vitality, State life, individual vitality, individual life, individual enterprise, all in the fullest and most benignant and most complete play.

Now, the Supreme Court of the United States, both majority and minority, in the decision which has been under discussion, have declared their opinion. Of course it is an *obiter dictum*, as the Senator from Missouri has said, but the concurrent opinion of these nine great lawyers on a grave constitutional question before them which they are considering in all its relations, even if not essential to the judgment which they are about to render, is entitled, I suppose, to the highest respect, a respect only surpassed by that which we owe to the constitutional judgment of the court itself.

What is it they have said Congress may do to remedy this difficulty? They have not declared that we may delegate power to the States of this Union. They have not declared that the reserved power which the Constitution leaves to the States or to the people thereof respectively can be enlarged or abridged one whit by act of Congress. They have not undertaken to say that there can be any legislative action of a State of this Union (unless, perhaps, it relates to some matter of national property which we may cede to them) which can derive the least vitality from any denial of our own power or affirmation of theirs by legislation. What they have undertaken to say is this—and it is what was suggested during the remarks of the Senator from Missouri by the honorable Senator from Delaware —they have undertaken to say that, recognizing the complete and exclusive control of Congress over interstate and international commerce, Congress may also by legislation declare that certain subjects shall not be for legislative purposes treated as subjects of interstate commerce, and that the question whether a particular contract is a contract of interstate or international commerce within the legislative power is not to be determined by the Supreme Court as a question of absolute fact of which they take judicial notice, but may be determined by the Congress of the United States in declaring that for all legislative purposes this shall not be considered as within the domain of interstate commerce.

Whatever Congress ought to do or might properly do in respect to the District of Columbia or the Territories, I suppose no Senator who differs from me on this question believes that Congress is likely to enact uniform laws for the entire country for the regulation of the traffic in intoxicating liquors which are conveyed from State to State or from foreign countries into any State.

HENRY L. DAWES [Mass.].—I should like to ask my colleague what would be the condition of things in a State if Congress should undertake to do that thing? As Congress can not regulate it among the citizens of the same State, there would be one rule for the foreigner and another rule for the inhabitant of the State.

SENATOR HOAR.—That suggestion of my colleague, as well as many others which might be added to it, would of course make it unlikely that we shall enter upon that field of legislation just now.

FRANK HISCOCK [N. Y.].—I ask, as a constitutional question, if, in the Senator's judgment, it is within the power of Congress to delegate to a State the right to prohibit the introduction into that State of any article of manufacture such as wool.

SENATOR HOAR.—I do not think I should go quite as far as that, but I would say that of course to do that in regard to the manufacture of wool would be a plain and gross violation of the sworn public duty of all of us.

SENATOR HISCOCK.—I suggest it purely as a constitutional question.

SENATOR HOAR.—But this is a question of the boundary line between two conflicting powers, one the police power, clearly reserved to the States, and one the power to regulate commerce, exclusively confided to the Government of the United States. Either that boundary is to be determined as a question of fact, if we may speak of this as a question of fact, a judicial question, to take judicial notice of it by reason of the nature of the subject-matter, which is practically impossible or difficult of attainment, or it is to be treated as a matter of law.

If it be a matter of law, it is a matter which the law-making power of the country may declare and determine and define. I hold, just as the Supreme Court said in the Louisiana case (to take that single illustration, which is better than any other, because it is one which the court itself has affirmed), that, it being clearly a reserved power and a duty of the people of the State of Louisiana to protect the city of New Orleans from infection or pestilence as a police power, the power of preserving and looking after the safety of their citizens, it being also a power of Congress to regulate interstate commerce, and in the course of that regulation to prohibit, if it see fit, the introduction of diseased and unhealthy persons or things, as the case of the leper put by the Senator from Vermont, there comes a domain which, as a matter of fact, could clearly be within one of these powers if the other did not exist. Suppose there were nothing but the United States as a Government where you come to these conflicting and overlapping domains. The Supreme Court of the United States say, as I understand the entire current of their decisions and as I understand the affirmation both of the minority and the majority in this last case, Congress may determine, as a question of law, as a matter of legislative enactment, the boundaries and limitations of those two jurisdictions, and as Chief Justice Fuller said in the course of his opinion in the case which has given rise to this bill:

Undoubtedly there is difficulty in drawing the line between the municipal powers of the one government and the commercial powers of the other, but when that line is determined, in the particular instance, accommodation to it, without serious inconvenience, may readily be found, to use the language of Mr. Justice Johnson in Gibbons *vs.* Ogden, 9. Wheat., 1, 238, in "a frank and candid coöperation for the general good."

SENATOR HISCOCK.—The other suggestion that I desire to make to the Senator is this: In respect we will say to the quarantine laws and in respect to navigable waters, they are entirely within the jurisdiction of the State for certain purposes and the State has the jurisdiction to legislate in respect to them until Congress takes that jurisdiction itself, absorbs it, takes the domain of it, because it in its wisdom thinks it wise to exercise certain powers or pass certain laws. Now, my mind is rather bent on inquiry than otherwise in respect to this provision. The State has no power primarily to regulate or to interfere with the goods against which this prohibition is aimed. It has no jurisdiction of the subject whatever. That has been decided. Now, having no jurisdiction originally, and that jurisdiction being absolutely vested in the Federal authority, can Congress delegate it? Is there not a wide difference between that class of cases and the class which the Senator has suggested, where the State has the power, until Congress has taken jurisdiction of the subject, to pass such laws and regulations as it chooses? It seems to me that there is a wide distinction.

SENATOR HOAR.—I differ with the Senator from New York in the premises.

SENATOR HISCOCK.—In one case the court holds that while the State has jurisdiction of the subject it can pass its regulating laws until Congress steps in and says, "No, you can not; we take jurisdiction of the subject, and your jurisdiction must yield to ours. It must yield to the Federal jurisdiction; you can not override it." In this case, I suggest to the Senator whether it is not a change in which the State has no jurisdiction whatever. The State can not touch it or legislate in reference to it, and the Supreme Court has so decided, until that power is given to it by Congress. The question is whether Congress can grant that power.

SENATOR HOAR.—Mr. President, I have endeavored in what I have said to express my own idea. On the question of delegating the right I certainly agree with the Senator from New York and with the Senator from Missouri, and I can designate it as strongly as I can make the statement. I think the State has an original and primary power to protect a child of ten years of age within its limits against danger to its morals, and the State has an original and primary power to say that nobody shall sell intoxicating liquor or opium to a baby of that age. It being the power of the State to do that thing, Congress has authority to say that the right to engage in interstate or international commerce shall not be understood to allow an Englishman or a citizen of another country to sell by himself or his agent his intoxicating liquor or opium to a child ten years old. That is clear. There are a primary power of the State and a power of Congress to restrain that.

Now, if it may do that, Congress may go further and it may say the power to engage in interstate or international commerce shall not be understood as permitting anybody to sell opium or intoxicating liquors to anybody else, and that they shall be excluded altogether from the domain of interstate commerce. That Congress has a right to say. If Congress, according to my interpretation of these decisions, has the right to say no person dwelling in another country or in another State shall sell opium or intoxicating liquors to children ten years old or under, if the State where they dwell has prohibited that act, and if it has a right to say that no citizen of another State or another nation shall sell or deliver intoxicating liquors or opium to any citizen of the State whose legislature has prohibited that act, then this bill is clearly within our power. That is not a question of delegated power. It is not a question of permission to the State. It is a question of the right of Congress to prescribe what shall be the limit of interstate commerce, and it may bar it out by a definition of its own, or it may say interstate commerce shall be kept within the limits in regard to a particular subject-matter where the police power of the State comes in, which the legislature of the particular State has defined.

JOHN H. REAGAN [Tex.].—The Congress authorizes the importation of alcoholic liquors. It levies a tax upon alcoholic liquors; it taxes and collects revenue from them. The action of Congress makes alcoholic liquors commerce. Some of the States prohibit the use of alcoholic liquors; a majority of them do not prohibit the use of alcoholic liquors. So the current opinion among the States would make alcoholic liquors an article of commerce.

If the Constitution of the United States were amended so as to declare that alcoholic liquors were injurious to the public morals and the public health and to repeal the laws which recognize them as commerce by recognizing their importation and levying duties upon them, that would be an act of outlawry

which might place them and would place them under the control
and power of the State legislatures. It would then cease to
be an article of commerce—that is, it would cease to be an
article of commerce if the States took the same view of it and
outlawed it as the Government would under such a change.

If this condition of things existed—that is, the outlawry
of alcoholic liquors by the Federal Government and by the
States—the States then, of course, could exclude intoxicating
liquor under their police power, as they may exclude anything
that they hold to be injurious to health and public morals or
dangerous to life.

The Senator from Massachusetts [Mr. Hoar] called attention
to a number of things to illustrate his view that the Congress
might confer the power upon the States or at least might
consent that the States should tax alcoholic liquors because of
certain other things that they could do. There is a number of
things in which the power of Congress and the power of the
States are concurrent. Attention was called to those things by
the Senator from Missouri [Mr. Vest], and I call attention to
them again, as they are recited by Mr. Justice Field in the Bowman case.

Here the speaker repeated Justice Field's opinions.

Now, that meets all the suggestions on that subject made
by the Senator from Massachusetts, except those which relate
to quarantine. That is a matter which relates to the security
of life and health, and the police powers of the State have
at all times been held to authorize the State to protect its
people against epidemic disease and those things which may
endanger the lives and the health of the people. That is not a
regulation of commerce in the sense in which the Constitution
speaks of the regulation of commerce, as we now have it under
consideration. The regulation of commerce as we now have
it under consideration means the regulation of trade and transportation between the States.

But it is assumed that Congress may permit the States to
take its place to a limited extent in the regulation of commerce. I understand, Mr. President, that jurisdiction even
in the courts is not a matter of consent, but a matter of law.
It is certainly true, I think, that where the Constitution has
conferred a power upon Congress the consent of Congress and
the States can not take from Congress its jurisdiction, nor can
the consent of Congress and the States confer upon the States

a jurisdiction which by the Constitution is conferred upon Congress. If that were true, it would conclude this portion of the argument.

While there is some inconvenience growing out of the Federal power to regulate interstate commerce, it is not a barrier to the power of the State to protect its people against the improper use or abuse of these liquors when they are taken within the State. That power remains with it.

Mr. President, it often happens in the discussion of questions that our desire to do good, that our desire to promote the public welfare, that our desire to accomplish some beneficent purpose leads us away from the consideration of our power to accomplish that end and causes us to forget that we are acting under a government of delegated and limited power. Whether that be convenient or inconvenient, it is the Government which our fathers made for us and adopted, and which has existed in all its beneficence as the grandest monument of human wisdom for more than a hundred years. If inconveniences arise they are but those inconveniences which may arise under any possible form of government.

If we forget on this subject, as we have on some others, that we have a Constitution which we have taken an oath to support, and if we undertake to do whatever interest, believing that we are doing right, or passion may tempt us to do, we cut loose from our anchorage, from our security, from the safety of the people and of the Government.

Mr. President, strong as my view may be that the use of intoxicating liquors is injurious to the public health and public morals, I am not willing to lay my hands upon the Constitution and tear it down in order to furnish a better remedy than the one which now exists.

SENATOR EDMUNDS.—Mr. President, it is a very curious circumstance that we have reached a condition of things where, according to the debate here and the judgments of the Supreme Court of the United States, under the Constitution of the United States there is an inherent, individual, civil, personal right in every man in one State to carry whatever another State considers to be injurious to its safety and life and welfare into it and sell it, and where Congress can not stop it and the States can not stop it, unless Congress does something, and Congress can not do that something.

Is not that a perfectly absurd result to come to in the Government and country, unless among the innate human rights which the Declaration of Independence intended to include when it said that every man had a right to pursue the avocations of peace, happiness, and prosperity is the right to carry dynamite, smallpox, rum, deleterious drugs, adulterated foods, and obscene literature from one State to another.

Now, let us begin with the Supreme Court. The court is an independent and coördinate branch of the Government. Its mission is to decide causes between parties, and its decision of causes between parties all good order and government require shall be carried out and respected as between parties. But, as it regards the Congress of the United States, its opinions are of no more value to us than ours are to it.

Suppose we think that this court has gone wrong and has made a mistake in deciding a given case between A and B that involves the safety and happiness of all the people of the United States in their respective States covering a continent, where an internal policy may be good for the Pacific coast and bad for the State on the Atlantic coast, are we to stop and say that the decision is the end of the mission of civilization in the United States? I take it not. It may be that when the next case comes up on a further and wider consideration the very gentlemen who now compose the court, differing as some of them did with the majority, may come to the conclusion that they had been led into an error. So I do not feel deeply embarrassed by the fact that the Supreme Court has taken the largest step that in the whole hundred years of the Republic has ever been taken toward the centralization of power somewhere in this case, either in the Supreme Court or in Congress.

I do not believe, for one, in the centralization of power. I believe in its segregation and separation in every respect that concerns the internal affairs of the body of the people in every one of the States, leaving out of the question those universal human rights that everybody agrees are intrinsic in man and citizen.

So I am not greatly disturbed in respect of what the Supreme Court have said and done, except so far as it makes it now the mission of Congress to exert its power upon the subjects according to the light that it thought it had shone upon it, in order to preserve the internal policy and police of every State for itself, whether you call it an independent right or the execution of a national power under agencies that Congress provides.

Mr. President, the Constitution of the United States has not said that Congress may regulate commerce in the States, but among the States. Has anybody until now undertaken to say that that implied an authority in the United States to declare that because a fabric, wool, if you please, to which my friend from New York [Senator Hiscock] referred, was made in one State and sent to another, whatever became of that wool in the other State was beyond the power of the State to which it went? I take it not. The Constitution has not given to Congress the power to say what shall be done with that wool after it has gone there. Would my friend from New York maintain that the State of New York can not say that no manufacturer of woolen goods should put in more than 75 per cent. of shoddy when he made up the wool and thus to cheat every laboring and other man who wishes to buy a pair of trousers?

The action of the State in repressing shoddy is practically just as effectual when it comes into the second hand as it is when it is in the first hand. If the Supreme Court of the United States follow out the logical sequence of what they have said there is no power in any State to regulate the sales and dealings in any commodity whatever which may be brought from one State into another State.

Now, where is the line? The line, which the Supreme Court of the United States appears to have gone over, is that when your act of transportation, your act of commerce among the States or from foreign nations, has become complete, and the word "among" no longer applies, and the commodity is in the State where its transportation is ended, and it is in the hands of its owner there—whether that owner be a citizen of one State or another makes no difference—it is then just like the commodity of the same nature, all the laws being equal, in the hands of the citizen of the State who made it there himself the subject of the State law, and that is what the Supreme Court of the United States within the next twenty years will come to.

You may say that that may interfere with the income of the United States on the importation of silks, if you please, or liquors, or whatever you please to call it. Very good. The power of the United States to regulate commerce and to levy taxes is no greater within its sphere than the power of the State is to deal with commodities and the conduct of people in that State over every one of the objects that the United States may choose to tax or allow the importation of. Both powers are supreme, and each must be exercised in its own order.

The Constitution provided that Congress shall not make any regulations of commerce in favor of one port of a State as against another; that the external operations of the United States as regards the ports should be equal everywhere. So as to taxes. When it comes to the regulations of commerce as distinguished from the taxing power, no such limitation or reservation or proviso was imposed upon it. So Congress for a hundred years, from time to time, with the assent and acquiescence of everybody as sound and just constitutional action, has prohibited the introduction of one article, allowed the introduction of another, and has authorized some agency or another that it chose to employ to declare whether given objects under given circumstances should be admitted into the United States at all. For example, it has employed an agency to exclude diseased cattle.

Now, on this aspect, if Congress has the power to regulate this commerce among the several States, it has the power to limit it, and it has the power to declare that no intoxicating liquor shall go from one State to another. If it has the power to say that no intoxicating liquor, under the decisions of the Supreme Court, shall come into the United States from abroad, under the same right it has the power to say that nothing of that kind shall pass from one State to another. The court itself puts this entirely upon the ground, and rightly in that respect, that there is no distinction in respect of constitutional power between foreign commerce and interstate commerce. All are within the regulation of Congress.

Congress prohibits obscene literature. I wish it went a great way further and included diseased meats, fraudulent teas, dishonest drugs, and so on. Has it not the power, if this decision of the Supreme Court is right, even in its narrowest application of the construction, to say that it shall not be lawful to transport from one State to another intoxicating liquors? If it has, has it not the right to affix, as it has on foreign commerce from time immemorial, the agencies and conditions and inspections and regulations that it thinks in its wisdom are right and just?

The objection that has been made to this bill is that we are delegating it to a State. I deny the proposition. I say that by this bill Congress is undertaking to regulate the traffic among the States of this thing by saying, "We employ the agency of the people through its legislative authority, of the State of Iowa, for instance, to say whether it is wise or not to admit this thing in the community from the State of Illinois."

It does not appear to me, therefore, that in any aspect of

the case there ought to be any difficulty in our relieving the people of the United States in each State according to its own local needs and necessities. If it be free liquor in Missouri, free liquor it is, Congress says; and if it be prohibition in Kansas, prohibition it is—equal everywhere, according to the adjustments that the needs of the societies in the various States require.

SENATOR VEST.—Mr. President, the position of the Senator from Vermont [Mr. Edmunds] simply amounts to this—and all his ability is not able even to disguise it—that the legislatures of the States shall regulate commerce among the States, and not Congress. What is the use of talking about instrumentalities when you adopt what the instrumentalities may do? Where is the discretion if Congress says, "Gentlemen of the States, go on and exclude what you please and we indorse it in advance; we give you a complete and absolute *carte blanche* to shut out of your respective States whatever you please"?

Why, sir, it is impossible to contemplate a case of more absolute abnegation of a constitutional power than that. It absolutely gives away the constitutional grant and says to every State in the Union, "Do as you please."

Mr. President, the Senator from Vermont repeatedly in this debate has injected here the idea of diseased commodities, diseased meats, and dynamite, and he has even invoked leprosy, the most horrible of all human diseases. I will answer him in the language of the Supreme Court:

> Articles in such a condition as tend to spread disease are not legitimate subjects of trade and commerce, and the self-protecting power of each State, therefore, may be rightfully exerted against their introduction, and such exercise of power can not be considered a regulation of commerce, prohibited by the Constitution; and the observations of Mr. Justice Catron, in the License Cases (5 How., 504, 599), are quoted to the effect that what does not belong to commerce is within the jurisdiction of the police power of the State, but that which does belong to commerce is within the jurisdiction of the United States.

SENATOR EDMUNDS.—Mr. President, if my friend will permit me, that amounts to saying that the power to regulate commerce with foreign nations and among the several States had been committed by the Constitution to the Supreme Court, and not to Congress.

SENATOR VEST.—It amounts to this, that a diseased article is not an article of commerce, and that the power to exclude a leper, a smallpox patient, diseased clothes, or articles of food is a police power which inures in every commonwealth, whether it be a national or a State government under our form of government. It is the power of self-preservation, and the Supreme Court says in another case that the State could not give it away if it tried to do so.

SENATOR EDMUNDS.—Then the State says that the unlimited sale of intoxicating liquors is just as injurious to the health and welfare of the State as the sale of diseased meat is, for only one ox out of a thousand probably will be diseased, while every bottle of whisky is diseased, and the Supreme Court is to be the determining power as to what it is good for a State to have.

SENATOR VEST.—Mr. President, the Supreme Court of the United States has declared in so many words that under the pretence of exercising the police power no State has the right to declare what is the subject of commerce and what is not. That is a question to be decided by the Congress of the United States, and the law of Congress is afterwards to be construed by the Supreme Court of the United States. The Supreme Court of the United States and Congress have both declared that alcoholic stimulants are a legitimate subject of interstate commerce, and that question is settled and eliminated from this debate and no longer open to discussion. A barrel of whisky is as much an article of commerce as a bushel of wheat or a bushel of corn, and it is begging this question entirely for the Senator to claim that a State has the right to declare that a bottle of whisky is injurious to its citizens and therefore can be excluded. The Supreme Court of the United States says the State can do no such thing. We collect taxes off whisky brought in from foreign countries, and we have an internal revenue tax upon it, and so long as we do this it is a legitimate subject of commerce and no State can come in and with its assumption of superior intellect and superior morality declare that it is to be interdicted and to be under the ban of that State and of the other States.

SENATOR EDMUNDS.—And yet, if the Senator will pardon me, when the Congress of the United States imposed its internal revenue tax upon the manufacture of alcoholic drinks it carefully provided, supposing then, erroneously perhaps, that it had some power over the subject, that that should not interfere with what was then regarded as the power of the State to prohibit the sale or disposition or movement a single foot after it left the distillery of any of the things that Congress taxed, and thereby by the same implication of an impost tax on an importation that it should not prevent the State from dealing with it, and nobody now for twenty-five years (even the Supreme Court of the United States, which is going pretty fast just now) has ever yet thought, and no liquor manufacturer in any State that I know of has ever yet thought, of undertaking to stand in the face of the law and say that Congress exerted the power—call it delegated or call it administrative or whatever—declaring that its action in that respect should not interfere in any way with the police power of the State to prohibit the traffic or the disposition of the property that had thus been once taxed.

SENATOR VEST.—Is there any contention here by the opponents of this measure that, after alcoholic stimulants go out of the original package and come under the territorial jurisdiction of a State and become mingled with the balance of the goods of the people of that State, that State has not the police power to regulate that subject?

SENATOR EDMUNDS.—What do you mean by mingled with the other property? Is it any more mingled after it has gone out of the hands of the producer?

SENATOR VEST.—I do not propose to go into the question of mixing drinks. *De gustibus non est disputandum.*[1] That is for every gentleman to determine for himself. I do not take it myself in either form, but that is my own business. The Supreme Court of the United States made this question very clear in its decision.

I repeat, sir, that, if the position of the Senator from Vermont be correct, you tear out of the Constitution the grant of the power to regulate by Congress interstate commerce, and you leave the State authorities, their respective legislatures, upon the broad sea of caprice, prejudice, interest, or whatever you please to term it, to do as they choose.

The very object of this clause in the Constitution was to create uniformity, and yet the position taken by the Senator from Vermont would destroy all uniformity.

As Justice Matthews said, suppose Missouri thinks it wise to taboo or to ostracize an article produced in Illinois; suppose it says, "We do this under the police power, and we will not have any Illinois corn because you make whisky out of corn and whisky produces crime and crime fills the penitentiary," and suppose Illinois says, "You can not bring Missouri wheat into Illinois and we exercise our police power to prevent it. Wheat is not a good article of food; it produces dyspepsia,

[1] "There's no disputing about tastes."

and dyspepsia in turn produces bad temper, and bad temper
produces crime''—*quod erat demonstrandum*—each one taking
care according to its own ideas of every article that comes under
the interstate commerce clause of the Constitution, and yet the
Senator from Vermont says this is the political millennium
which the authors of the Constitution contemplated! I do not
so understand it.

William M. Evarts [N. Y.] spoke on May 21 in support of the bill.

The root, Mr. President, of this contention between the
commercial power of importation, to carry thereby and by
that contract or transaction into the domestic control of taxation
in the State—the root of the whole matter is found, is expounded, and laid down in the case of Brown *vs.* Maryland, in
Twelfth Wheaton. It will be noticed, and it may be very briefly
so accepted, that the whole question there was this: The State
of Maryland had undertaken to impose a license tax upon the
sale of dry goods in their packages and also imported liquors
in their packages as a means of revenue to the State of Maryland.

The law in itself was discriminating and exclusive, and applied only to an item of this revenue to be gathered from the
sale in the hands of the importer of the packages as they
arrived and were then first to be put into commerce in the
traffic within the States. Obviously that was a question of
revenue measure of the State, that sought to find accessible to
taxation in itself the imported goods in the original condition
in which they had been introduced.

Briefly, I think I may say that the conclusions of the
court, John Marshall being chief justice, were that, by our
tariff, imposing or making free, as might be, this or that article
of foreign commerce, the Government itself had come into that
relation to the importation that entitled the importer and entitled the articles of importation to sale in this country, and
that any interception of the primary transaction of introduction and thence in sale, by taxation by a State, was a burden
on foreign commerce.

In that discussion there was a considerable, though not very
extensive, suggestion as to how far this claim of control by
the Government of the United States might impinge upon and
might interfere with what it was conceded in all quarters belonged to the States in regard to internal traffic, and then, by

illustration and cognate considerations, to police regulation of the State. No one can pretend, I think, that under the discussion of that case, whenever a matter was really within the province of the police regulation of the State, necessarily a commercial arrangement that was competent for the United States overrode the police regulation. No discussion, no illustration, no definition, no limitation has ever undertaken to say that the Federal Government possesses any regulation of the police province. If the power in any regard can be reduced and overridden within the State, it is not a province that can be taken up and executed by the Government of the United States.

In my judgment, in the accepted constitutional view and in the habit and universal estimate, both at the time of the formation of the Constitution and ever since, the regulation of the liquor traffic is in the very vital, central position of the police regulation and care of peace and morality and protection of the every-day interests of the affairs within each State. It is not peculiar to any one State; it is not local; it is not casual; it is not fugitive; it is not variable. The essential duty and the essential function remain, and it never entered into the head of any framer of our Constitution that the Federal Government did not and would not recognize that as a State occasion and a State necessity within it, as much as criminal legislation or any of the ordinary regulations of civil contracts within the States.

Now, the situation arises thus: I had supposed that in the License-Tax Cases, reported in 5th Howard, the conclusions of the judges of the court as well as the decision of the court— for there were no dissents to that decision—had substantially recognized the fact that the general commerce clause regarding intercourse between the States and with foreign countries had not assumed that police regulations must recede before the authority of the commercial power. I suppose that it was understood that whenever the question came up as to whether what might be a paramount authority of commercial regulation in the Government where it was brought in comparison with any efforts within a State to interfere with commercial regulations and revenue therefrom, whenever the great question came up whether the repugnance or the qualifications that were asserted within the State of its police regulations against mere general and common commercial interest and control, the court was precisely *ad idem* to look at the very case before it, and say whether this was or was not within one of those essential conditions of police control that could not be expected to recede before general qualifications of commercial action by the general Government. Much less, Mr. President, have I ever supposed that, in the absence of positive action by the Federal Government in respect to commerce between the States, the mere presence of that clause, never put forth and directed as bearing upon any question within the State of its police regulation, was to be treated as by its own force and presence in the clauses of the Constitution to be a paralysis of the police regulations of the State.

Now, I understand, Mr. President, and am instructed by the late opinion and decision of the Supreme Court bearing on this very matter in the case in 125th United States Reports, and in the recent decision, that there are an embarrassment and paralysis and, for aught I can see, a very unlimited and very vague pervasion of the subject and purpose of domestic control without any direction having been taken by Congress to that end and in preservation or protection of commercial intercourse.

That being the case, it seems to me of the greatest importance that Congress, having the power to do whatever it may see fit in regard to the vigor and reach and searching operation of this commercial clause when it is brought in the face of so vast, so essential, so universal an interest in the society of every one of the States of the Union, should relieve the situation as a judicial question from having Congress treat it and construe it as having suppressed this, what belongs on its face to domestic authority; and, therefore, I have concluded that it is my duty, and I should hope that it would be felt the duty of the Senate, to pass this bill in the shape it is now presented as reported from the Judiciary Committee.

No such pressure in support of the liquor traffic had ever been dreamed of as is now intended to be perpetrated in regard to the regulation of traffic within a State. The pretension is, under this clause of intercourse among the States and with foreign countries, that the original package is to be in a shape and in a modicum that permits no interception between it and the gullet of the consumer. This is an enormous fraud upon the whole system of importation and the whole scheme of original packages, and, for myself, I am not ready for one moment to rest under any such system as it may be possible to inflict upon the people within a State.

I hope, therefore, that this bill may be accepted, which is limited wholly to the proposition that the mere introduction into a community of a commodity from abroad or from other States does not liberate it from being under the control of the vital regulation of morals and duty and peace.

SENATOR WILSON.—As a practical fact in connection with this measure, I wish to read a telegram that appears in the New York *Tribune* of to-day which is as follows:

BRISK "ORIGINAL PACKAGE" TRADE IN IOWA

CHICAGO, *May* 20 (Special).—A dispatch from Des Moines, Iowa, says: "The 'original package' business is increasing daily. Scores of delivery wagons are running in the streets of this city, loaded with beer kegs and cases, and bottles of stronger liquids, without interference. The 'original package' has apparently come to stay. The next step will be to adapt matters to the new condition. It is evident that this can not be done under existing statutes."

On May 27 Senator Wilson, from the Judiciary Committee, presented a substitute for its original bill.

That when any intoxicating liquors or liquids shall be transported from one State or Territory into another State or Territory . . . (including District of Columbia) or from any foreign country to any State or Territory, such liquors and liquids so transported shall, when the actual and continuous transportation of the same shall have terminated, be considered to have ceased to be the subjects of commerce with foreign nations and among the several States and be a part of the common mass of property within such State or Territory, and subject to the respective powers of such State and Territory, in respect of all police regulations of prohibition, regulation, or taxation, equally and in common with other like property subject to the police powers of any such State or Territory.

On May 28 Senator Gray offered a substitute for the substitute. It was adopted by a vote of 25 to 20. Later it was amended to read:

That all fermented, distilled, or other intoxicating liquors or liquids transported into any State or Territory, or remaining therein, for use, consumption, sale, or storage therein, shall, upon arrival in such State or Territory, be subject to the operation and effect of the laws of such State or Territory, enacted in the exercise of its police powers, to the same extent and in the same manner as though such liquors or liquids had been produced in such State or Territory, and shall not be exempt therefrom by reason of being introduced therein in original packages or otherwise.

The bill was then passed by a vote of 34 to 10.

It was amended and passed by the House (yeas 117, nays 38) on July 22. The Senate refused to concur in the House amendment, and a conference was appointed. The Representatives on the committee receded from the amendment, and the bill was passed by the House by a vote of 119 to 93. President Harrison approved it on August 8, 1890.

CHAPTER XII

LIQUOR TRAFFIC IN THE ARMY

[THE CANTEEN BILL]

Debate in the House on Reëstablishment of Sale of Wine and Beer in the Army Post Exchanges: In Favor, Richard Bartholdt [Mo.]; Opposed, Charles E. Littlefield [Me.]; Lost.

O WING to the opposition of the temperance people, expressed through such organizations as the Women's Christian Temperance Union, the sale of alcoholic liquors in the "canteens," or exchanges connected with army posts had been forbidden in 1901.

On April 25, 1904, the subject of reëstablishing this sale came up for discussion in the House in connection with an army appropriation bill.

LIQUOR SELLING IN THE CANTEEN

HOUSE OF REPRESENTATIVES, APRIL 25, 1904

Charles E. Littlefield [Me.] opposed the reëstablishment, quoting an article which he had written for the *North American Review*, April and May, 1904.

On the 2d day of February, 1901, the following provision became the law of the land:

> The sale of or dealing in beer, wine, or any intoxicating liquor by any person in any post exchange or canteen or army transport, or upon any premises used for military purposes by the United States, is hereby prohibited. The Secretary of War is hereby directed to carry the provision of this section into full force and effect.

This is what has come to be popularly, though inaccurately, known as the "anti-canteen law." It is obviously not aimed against the canteen, but against the sale of prohibited beverages in the canteen or post exchange.

It was drawn and introduced by me as an amendment, in the House, on December 6, 1900.

431

This legislation will stand, I have no doubt, until a full opportunity shall have been given, under proper conditions, by practical operation, to demonstrate its wisdom or unwisdom. A vigorous effort is being made to satisfy the public that this test has been made and that the legislation has proved a failure. A candid examination of the facts will show that this effort must meet with failure.

Among the most pretentious contributions to this discussion are articles by Major Louis Livingston Seaman and Col. William Conant Church in the numbers for January and December, 1903, respectively, of the *North American Review.*

What purpose does the canteen seek to accomplish, and how does it propose to effect it from the standpoint of its advocates? Its purposes are twofold:

First, it furnished, it is claimed, a counter attraction to the saloon that is maintained near the post, where all kinds of liquor are sold, and, by satisfying by the milder and so-called "less harmless" drinks of beer and light wines the craving for vicious stimulants, becomes the lesser of two evils, as "its advocates frankly admit that the total abolition of intoxicants in the army is a desideratum devoutly to be wished."

Its primary purpose was to furnish to the troops, at reasonable price, such articles, the articles of ordinary use, wear, and consumption, not supplied by the Government, and to afford them means of rational recreation and amusement suitable to their station in life, which, if denied, they would seek outside the limits of the camp. (Seaman.)

A place, then, of amusement, recreation, and entertainment, where articles necessary to the comfort and convenience of the soldier can be purchased, is the dominant, salient, and *"primary purpose"* of the post exchange. The sale of beer and light wines is the incident only, the lesser evil, to be eliminated if possible. This "incident," however, is the chief among the "resources" of the canteen, as appears from the following official advice:

APRIL 27, 1903.

HON. CHARLES E. LITTLEFIELD, M. C.:

Of the several hundred post exchanges in the United States and the Philippines at the time of the passage of the act, February 2, 1901, but very few remain, and in the majority of cases it has been found difficult and *impracticable* to operate the post exchange *without the profits received from the sale of beer and light wines.*

Very respectfully,
HENRY P. McCAIN,
Acting Adjutant-General.

This, I have no doubt, fairly states the importance of the profits ensuing from the sale of beer and light wines as the main "resource" of the canteen, and it appears that without this "resource" it is practically impossible to maintain the primary features of the canteen, such as recreation, amusement, and entertainment.

It follows, then, that where there is no drinking of beer there is no recreation, amusement, or entertainment, and the more drinking of beer the most recreation, amusement, and entertainment, and the more variety for the mess.

Under the régime heretofore existing, as "every enlisted man is a stockholder in it" and participates equally in the advantages resulting therefrom, the men are naturally expected to contribute their share at least to the producing cause. Emerson truly said: "That is the one base thing in the universe, to receive benefits and render none." The total abstainer, while participating in the benefits derived from these profits, as he necessarily must, would be reaping where he had not sown, and this itself would furnish a powerful and insidious incentive to universal beer-drinking by the soldiers. In fact, the total abstainer was not infrequently taunted with his failure thus to contribute.

It will be seen that all of the considerations involved in this scheme—appetite, financial needs, pleasure, etc.—tend inevitably to the universal and increasing consumption of beer and light wines.

The inquiry at once arises, Why can not the "primary purpose" of the canteen be accomplished by supplying the funds necessary therefor from sources other than the deprecated profits from the sale of beer, and thus eliminate the lesser evil?

The possibility of there being such an alternative does not appear to have occurred to either Major Seaman or Colonel Church, surcharged as these writers are with information on this question.

Yet it is a fact that at the time when the Colonel, who is disturbed "by the studious ignoring of facts" by anti-canteen advocates, wrote his article, $1,000,000 ($500,000 available for the fiscal year 1902-3 and $500,000 for the fiscal year 1903-4) had been appropriated for that express purpose.

The American Public Health Association in September, 1901, by resolution invited "the intelligent coöperation of a very large element of good citizens . . . in taking successive steps toward the betterment of existing conditions, and thus

XI—28

assist in controlling and largely curtailing an evil which it is powerless at present to prevent.''

And its committee urged that—

The sale of soft drinks, warm lunches, coffee, tea, cocoa, bouillon, and soups should be encouraged as substitutes for alcoholic beverages.

This has the approval of Colonel Church, and is precisely what this appropriation is intended to accomplish.

These appropriations will take the place of the profits from the sale of beer, and it is the expectation that they will accomplish that purpose and contribute to the ''desideratum devoutly to be wished . . . the total abolition of intoxicants in the army.'' This is the laudable purpose that has led the distinguished chairman of the Military Affairs Committee in the House, the Hon. J. A. T. Hull, of Iowa, to work earnestly and successfully for these appropriations that are indispensable if the measure is to prove a success.

It is only proper to add that Senator Proctor, the acting chairman of the Military Affairs Committee in the Senate, has been an earnest advocate of these appropriations, and the membership of both committees, both of the majority and minority parties, laudably sustained their efforts.

These are the first appropriations of the kind that have ever been made. They were introduced in the Senate and successfully urged by Senator Hansbrough, a loyal and effective supporter of this policy. It necessarily follows that, until they shall have been generally uitilized throughout the army, as generally, at least, as was the canteen, we can have no condition or period with which the canteen period can be compared with any propriety or intelligence.

In addition to this appropriation, another should be made for a company fund, in order to insure the most complete success. The company fund enables the men to vary the monotony of the mess, and contributes greatly to their comfort. Prior to 1880 there was no post exchange with or without the sale of beer. Up to 1889, it was operated in comparatively few instances. Then the canteen became general, and continued until February 2, 1901, so that the canteen period is from 1889 to 1900, inclusive.

Prior and subsequent thereto we have no period—by reason of the lack of the place of recreation, amusement, entertainment, and lunch room, and a company fund to relieve the monotony of the mess—with which a statistical comparison of the canteen period will be of any value for the purpose of demonstrating the wisdom of the anti-canteen legislation. While this is true, it is to be observed that the facts, fairly analyzed, hardly justify the sweeping generalizations which have been made by the canteen advocates. The theory is that the establishment of the canteen drives the contiguous saloons out of business, and, conversely, that its discontinuance at once increases the number. This is the only theory that can justify the canteen. For instance, of Fort Myer, Major Seaman says:

> Before the introduction of the canteen there were between ten and twenty low groggeries between the terminus of the street railway and the entrance to Arlington, largely depending upon the patronage of the troops. . . . And that after ten years of the canteen at the post only two of these were left.

On the contrary, in that locality, instead of "between ten and twenty low groggeries," the commissioner of revenue of Alexandria County, Va., Mr. H. L. Holmes, informs me from his own actual knowledge that there were from three to four saloons open from 1880 to 1891, and instead of "only two of these being left" the records show that in 1900, the end of the canteen period, there were five in healthy working order. If all of the Major's assertions of facts are equally open to criticism, it may not be entirely safe to rely without any hesitation upon his conclusions.

Major Seaman asserts that "the liquor sellers and the W. C. T. U. are the strongest advocates of the law as it now stands," and Colonel Church says: "As no whisky or other strong drinks were sold, the stories of the influence exerted by whisky dealers to restore the canteen are obviously untrue." Whether the "whisky dealers" are for or against the canteen goes a very little way toward establishing the facts involved, but the obvious anxiety of the canteen advocates to separate themselves from the "liquor sellers" is certainly commendable.

Whether they succeed in stating the facts in that particular, it may be well to let the organs of the "liquor sellers" show:

> The *American Brewer* says that the members of the last Congress "allowed themselves to be influenced by a band of bigoted and narrow-minded prohibitionists in abolishing a most sensible institution which was very beneficial to the army."

> The *Liquor Trades' and Hotel Review* says: "It is almost certain that at the next session of Congress the anti-canteen law will be repealed. Almost every officer who is responsible for the maintenance of discipline in the army and solicitous for the higher standard of morality among the men has agreed to sign the petition to reëstablish the canteen. This bill

when presented will have the sympathy and support of every friend of the
'boys in blue' and of the cause of temperance.''

Believing with the most experienced military authorities that the canteen is conducive to the highest standard of sobriety and discipline, the
retail dealers, through their national organization, *aside from all selfish
considerations*, give their unqualified approval to this necessary adjunct of
the military department, and commend the firm and manly attitude of the
President in its defence and maintenance. (Resolution of the retail liquor
dealers at their national convention at Baltimore, in October, 1900.)

We don't consider this action taken by General Miles a deathblow to
the army canteen by any means. The fact that Mr. Miles has come out in
favor of the present anti-canteen law will not seriously affect the opponents
to this *unjust, fanatical measure.*

*The editor of the ''Sentinel'' will appear against the anti-canteeners
before the Congressional Committee in the coming session of Congress, and
we are glad to say in this connection that we, as a member of the Congressional Committee of the National Retail Liquor Dealers' Association,
are able to break down one of the obstacles which had great influence upon
the committee and the various members of Congress in the last fight.*
(Washington *Sentinel*, national organ of the Brewers' Association, Nov. 11,
1901; Lewis Schade, editor.)

In addition to the quotations given above, similar extracts
could be made from the resolutions of the conventions of brewers
and liquor dealers, and from the trade journals of the brewing,
distilling, and retail liquor interests.

It is interesting to note how Colonel Church gains courage
and tends gradually to convince himself as he gets into the full
swing of his argument. He has been thinking over the important matter of desertions, which, he says, have greatly increased; and this leads him to suggest that it ''is, in the opinion
of a majority of our army officers, the result, *in part at least,*
of the stimulus given to the drinking of vile liquors by the
abolition of the canteen.'' Note the commendable caution, ''a
majority of our army officers . . . the result, *in part* at
least.'' He continues to discuss this phase for a few paragraphs,
and the more he discusses it the more the peculiar infamy
of this anti-canteen legislation is borne in upon him, and getting
an accretion of courage he confidently asserts, as to this discontent, that ''if the *almost unanimous* opinion of officers *and
men* is to be accepted as *conclusive,* it is *very largely* due to
civilian interference with army administration.'' In twenty-
nine lines ''a majority'' becomes ''almost unanimous''; ''*men*''
are added to the officers, so as to include everybody, and ''*in
part* at least'' becomes ''*very largely.*''

There are 474 commissioned officers reporting. During this
time there were 3,820 such officers in the army, so that we have
reporting about 12 per cent. of the whole—rather an inadequate

representation upon which to base the assertion that "the almost *unanimous* opinion of the officers and men" sustains the canteen. What the "testimony" of the remaining 88 per cent. would be, uninfluenced by authority, we are not advised. We do not know, however, that the officers testifying against the canteen are among the most distinguished and eminent in their profession. They are such as Lieut.-Gen. Nelson A. Miles, Generals Ludlow and Henry, of sacred memory, Generals Howard, Shafter, Wheeler, Daggett, etc.

House Document No. 252 gives an itemized tab'e from the "reports." In referring to this document, Colonel Church says:

Of all the posts expressing positive opinion one way or the other, 90 per cent. reported that drunkenness, desertion, absence without leave, and trials by court-martial had increased.

I know nothing about the verity of these tables and take them as I find them. They cover the United States, Porto Rico, Cuba, and the Philippines. The following facts are taken from the table. In answer to the question, "Has drunkenness increased?" 120 answered "yes," 55 "no," 17 were uncertain; 175 expressed a positive opinion; only 69 per cent. thought it had increased. To the question, "Have courts-martial for offences caused by drunkenness increased?" 114 answered "yes," 55 "no," 18 were uncertain; 169 expressed a positive opinion one way or the other; only 67 per cent. say that they "had increased." To the question, "Has the number of cases of desertion and absence without leave increased?" 87 answered "yes," 84 "no," 15 were uncertain; 171 expressed a positive opinion one way or the other; 51 per cent. only say that they "had increased."

Colonel Church says "95 per cent. stated that the conditions of health had deteriorated, and all agree that morality and discipline had been injuriously affected." To the question, "Is the effect on health of command bad?" 108 answered "yes," 68 answered "no," 15 were uncertain; 176 expressed positive opinion one way or the other; 62 per cent. only say that the effect is bad.

To the question, "Is the effect on morality and the discipline of the command bad?" 129 answered "yes," 45 "no," 17 were uncertain; 174 expressed positive opinion one way or the other; 74 per cent. only stating that the effect was bad. These statements made by a critic who charges the friends of the anti-canteen legislation with "having reached certain dogmatic conclusions by the *studious ignoring of facts,"* require no comment. The inference is too obvious. Let us hope that this is not a sample of what we would get if "one rose from the dead to bear testimony to the truth." It is to be observed that these questions, instead of being framed so as to draw out a disinterested reply, are all leading, and intimate that an answer adverse to the legislation is expected.

The Hon. Elihu Root, late Secretary of War, opposed the anti-canteen legislation and expressed before the Senate Committee on Military Affairs the apprehension that it would discourage enlistments, saying on that point—

If you pass the provision which the House has put in, prohibiting the sale of beer and light wines in the canteen, you break that up, and the result is going to be, as soon as it gets round, it will stop our enlistments. That is a matter of serious, practical consequence. The men are not going to enlist when they understand that they are going to be confined in a reform school.

It must gratify Mr. Root to know that this doleful apprehension was unfounded, as this official table shows:

The two whole years 1901-2 show an average of 2,837 as against an average of 715 per year for the nine years prior to the war, and under normal canteen conditions, or four times as many per year when the "reform school" was staring the recruit in the face.

The "reform school" does not appear to have been a very vigorous deterrent. During the latter period, moreover, the Government has been exercising greater care in the selection of its men. Where 30,622 were enlisted in the year ending June 30, 1901, 86,407 applications were rejected. During the year 1903, 18,961 were enlisted and 74,256 rejected, showing that now where they enlist one they reject about three or four. The instructions for recruiting issued September 23, 1901, no doubt account for these rejections and also show the unfavorable conditions under which enlistments have largely increased. The first requirement was that "applicants for first enlistment must be between the ages of 18 and 35 years, *of good character and temperate habits,* able-bodied, free from disease, and must be able to speak, read and write the English language." Inasmuch as, under the War Department's theory of the canteen, the recruit is to be at once introduced to the official sale of beer in the canteen, and the maximum of sale is essential to the maximum of prosperity of the canteen, this regulation should read "of good character and temperate habits, *vigorous and efficient consumers of beer, of approved capacity preferred, etc."*

While the considerations heretofore suggested certainly at least tend to destroy the value of statistics, comparing the canteen period with the years preceding and succeeding it, so far as the anti-canteen law is concerned, there are other reasons which are also potent to show that these statistics do not justify the conclusions sought to be drawn therefrom. I can not state them more effectively than they have been stated by a practical soldier, who has won his rank by brave, gallant, and heroic conduct in battle, on the firing line, in every war in which the army has been engaged since 1861, including the expedition to China in 1900, Brigadier-General Daggett, United States army. He says:

Captain Munson, assistant surgeon, United States Army, has published statistics which seem to favor the canteen. The army has been constantly improving since its reorganization in 1866.

The barracks were poor, dirty, forbidding buildings, poorly lighted and heated. Candles were used, and a small allowance of them at that. Bunks were of rough boards and three stories high. A bed sack, filled with straw, and a blanket or two furnished the soldier's bed. A tin plate, an iron knife, fork, and spoon, were his table utensils. The principal ration was bacon or pork, occasionally beef, and bread, coffee, sugar, and beans.

Improvement in these things began in the seventies. Now the barracks are warm, cheerful, and well lighted. The beds and mess are much better than most recruits enjoyed at their homes. Then the recruiting officer could enlist whomsoever he pleased. Since then he has been held responsible for the utmost care in selecting men, morally and physically, on penalty of having to pay the expenses of clothing, feeding, and transporting the recruit to his station, should he be rejected after arriving, and should it be shown that the recruiting officer had been negligent.

Benevolent societies also began to furnish the soldiers with reading matter, etc. Many other things were done for the betterment of the soldiers. The army of new officers of 1866, after fifteen or twenty years of experience, had learned how to command and care for men. Too much importance can not be attached to this consideration. The fruits of all these things must necessarily have been a great reduction in desertions, admissions to hospital for alcoholism, and convictions by court-martial.

Now, Mr. Munson comes in and gives the canteen credit largely for these improvements. He makes 1889, the date of formal establishment of the canteen by the War Department, the central period of reckoning. The canteen had existed to some extent for four years before that time, but leave that out of consideration. The number of desertions from 1867 to 1874 was equal to 20.5 per cent.; from 1876 to 1880 they were equal to 8.4 per cent. President Hayes prohibited the sale of intoxicants to post traders during this period. From 1881 to 1889 the number of desertions was equal to 12 per cent.; from 1890 to 1897, 5 per cent.; from 1898 to 1900, 4.4 per cent.; from 1900 to 1901, only 1.9 per cent. This latter period is not for the whole year, but up to a recent date; but there has been no canteen since February 2.

The number of admissions to hospital for alcoholism during the canteen period (from 1891 to 1897), decreased 12.2 per thousand, while during the preceding period (from 1882 to 1890) the number decreased 27.3 per thousand.

These statistics show that a decrease in desertions and admissions to hospital for alcoholism began long before the canteen was thought of, and has been going on up to the present time, and that it was more rapid before than since the canteen was established.

General Daggett makes the following suggestions:

(1) Establish ample and attractive reading rooms, which may be the general places of resort, and where games and facilities for all sorts of proper social enjoyments can be found.

(2) Establish ample and attractive gymnasiums.

(3) Encourage and give facilities for all proper kinds of manly sports.

(4) Require the Commissary Department to supply many of the luxuries now furnished by means of the company fund.

These are covered by the appropriations made and proposed.

Major Elijah W. Halford's statement of conditions in the Philippines emphasizes this idea. He says:

A temperance canteen has been tried in at least four posts here in the islands, with good measure of success. At one post sales amounted to $500 per month; profits averaged $135 monthly during the eighty days it had been operated when report was made. It had very limited facilities, no capital, poor room, no sympathy from the officers, no soda fountain, hard to get ice, and other obstacles. With good facilities, with the sympathy of officers, and eliminating the poorly disguised devil of profit as in the old canteen, this is the practical solution of the canteen question for all soldiers except the chronic drinkers; who will have whisky anyway, beer canteen or no beer canteen. These begin their drunks in the beer canteen, but end them outside in the whisky shops.

Mr. Francis A. Buzzacott, a member of the Third Illinois, during the Spanish war operated a post exchange in connection with that regiment. The records show that during several months of its existence its profits cleared its original cost and amounted in all to $5,000, all of which was turned over to the regiment and distributed and used by its various companies during its campaign in the Tropics. It was operated in a tent, mammoth in size, capable of holding fifteen hundred, and benches for 300 troops. It had a restaurant and lunch counter, magazines and moral literature, and sold everything a soldier needed, except liquor, which was not allowed to be either sold or used on the premises. It had an organ, and musical entertainments were given. The regiment marched in a body to divine service therein on Sunday.

It closed up two beer canteens in its vicinity, and the soldiers boycotted their own canteens for the temperance canteen.

In the light of all these facts, how much foundation is there for Colonel Church's assertion that "the advocates of total abstinence say, in effect, that if there is any man in the army who refuses to accept theories that are rejected by the vast majority of men in this and every other civilized country, and who will drink, he should be permitted to go to the devil, and the shorter the road and the faster the pace the better?"

If we may be permitted to use the Colonel's choice and delicate language, we may ask, Who is it, in the light of the foregoing facts, that is keeping the obstructions out of the soldier's way "to the devil," shortening the road and accelerating the pace? The Colonel seems gratified to feel that he is with the "vast majority," laboring under the impression, evidently, that facts are settled that way. This is calculated to discontent the "Big Four" and other railroads, to make them realize that when, in order to secure keen, alert, clear-minded, and efficient men, they promulgate an order that their employees must not drink intoxicating liquors at all, whether on or off duty, they are in the minority in a "civilized country." If such a course will secure better men for railroading, it may be worthy of consideration whether it would not work as well in other cases. Do we need, especially in time of war, as good men for officers and men, from the standpoint of efficiency, as the railroads find they need in their business? If so, should we not make reasonable efforts to get them? King Edward evidently did not realize how lonesome he would be when, in a recent letter to an officer of the navy, this sentence was inserted: "His Majestiy would be glad if it is circulated privately that he considers his health is as much honored by those who drink it in water as by those who drink it in wine," an insidious and really reprehensible incentive to that vulgar and degrading and rather uncommon habit of total abstinence.

Let us hope that the adverse sentiment of our noble army, voiced so mildly by Colonel Church, may be broken to His Majesty gently and by degrees. Notwithstanding the Colonel's fervor, temperance is now being officially taught in the French and British, and encouraged in the German and Russian armies. A temperance society is one of the established institutions of the British army. His Royal Highness the Duke of Cambridge was its patron-general; His Royal Highness the Duke of Connaught is its president, and Field Marshal Lord Wolseley is its first vice-president. The flower of the officers of that army take pride in identifying themselves with it, and the Government contributes handsomely for its financial support. We in the United States are either not far enough or too far advanced for such an institution in our army. We think this legislation is in line with the most advanced thought, even if it may be in the minority.

That a post exchange, with proper provisions for recreation, amusement, and entertainment, and supplies for the men, and a company fund are essential to the success of this legislation is, we think, clear. Its friends, and especially the Rev. E. C. Dinwiddie and Mrs. Margaret Dye Ellis, the able, faithful, efficient, and untiring legislative representatives, respectively, of the American Anti-Saloon League and the Woman's Christian Temperance Union, at Washington, have been doing their best to procure and have utilized the necessary appropriations therefor. Instead of compelling the soldier to rely upon the profits of a beer saloon, whose sole customer he is, for furnishing him with the things essential to his welfare, we think he has a right to look to the people by whom he has been placed in a condition where these things have become essential.

For the beer saloon we substitute the treasury of the United States. In the effort to make this substitution, we believe we have the sympathy and support of all right-thinking citizens, and that we ought to have the hearty coöperation of the War Department and the officers of the army. We sincerely believe and earnestly hope that the substitution will prove a perfect success, but when it shall have been made, and shall have had a fair trial under such favorable conditions as are herein mentioned, if it shall prove to affect injuriously the condition of our soldiers, we will cheerfully join in a movement to reëstablish the beer saloon. There is practically an agreement that the sale of beer is at least the lesser of two evils. Every report that has been made, every opinion that has been expressed, every resolution that has been adopted, has been made, expressed, and adopted in the absence of conditions that all believe desirable, and that we believe essential. Should not judgment be suspended until these conditions have been created, and until they have had time to demonstrate their utility and wisdom? Would not a reversal of this legislation before that time be ill-considered, ill-advised, and unwarranted?

Richard Bartholdt [Mo.] supported reëstablishment.

No question but what the recent controversy between officers of the army and a member of Congress in a New York review, which now finds its way into the pages of the *Congressional Record*, has clearly developed the fact that the preponderance of evidence and of authority seems to be upon the side of the canteen as a method of promoting temperance among the soldiers of our army and keeping them apart and away from the worse temptations which lurk in their darkest form near to the military camps of all countries. The immediate cause of the passage of the provision of the law which resulted in the practical abandonment of several hundred canteens at the various army posts in the United States and at foreign stations appears to have been an agitation carried on against the sale of any kind of beverage except tea, coffee, and water to the soldiers by a class of people who, like the poor, are always with us and who seem not to be wise enough to look into the future and observe results so long as they are able to secure the passage of laws looking toward—as they believe—the prevention of the selling of intoxicating liquors to anyone. With them the end seems always to justify the means.

The logic of the man who maintains that no man has a right to drink liquor containing alcohol because he is liable to partake to excess would be about on a par with the crank who desires legislation to forbid all men drinking coffee or tea or any other beverage which, taken to excess, would cause physical and mental wrecks among their devotees. The only safety to the army as well as to the country at large is to organize as they do and to prepare tons of literature in the same manner as the Prohibitionists do, which will bring out the facts in reply to thousands of specious arguments and half truths. This misleading literature of the Prohibitionists is franked all over the country by the agitators against the canteen in ton lots, in many cases contrary to the postal laws of the country, to work up a hothouse public sentiment against the army canteen and against all who believe in the personal liberty of the individual to eat and drink in moderation.

Fortunately in this free and enlightened country, when the light is properly turned on so that the people are able to see the exact facts as they exist, there can be little danger as to final results.

It is not a light matter to trifle with the personnel and morals and social pursuits of the great body of men in the American army. No set of men in civil life, no matter who they are, have the moral right in the face of the opinions of

a majority of their officers and themselves to pass sumptuary
laws compelling them to do thus and so, or to remove from
them comforts or pastimes that they are justly entitled to.
Of course, the legal right rests on Congress to pass laws to
govern the army, but the personal rights of the individual, his
inalienable right to secure from life as much happiness as
possible consistent with his duty to the army and the Government, ought to have given the Congress pause before it proceeded to take away the humblest of the private soldier's
amusement without the most careful consideration and investigation, if need be, by Congressional committees empowered to
take sworn testimony and make a personal investigation into
the moral surroundings of each military post in this country
as well as abroad.

The moral aspects of the "canteen as related to the Federal
Government" have always seemed to cause the tender consciences of the civilian organizations and their supporters,
which oppose the sale of beer and light wines to soldiers, the
most severe twinges. The idea of the Government running a
"groggery," as these persons are pleased to term it, has been
known to cause a Congressman, whose district is largely afflicted
with Prohibitionists, the serious loss of sleep, and to bring upon
him to a considerable extent the *cacoëthes scribendi* [1] of the
ancients.

The Government is not selling "grog," nor is it selling soap,
or delicatessen, or any other article of wear or food which the
canteen supplies the soldier at cost. The Government never
went any further in the transaction than to prescribe certain
rules governing canteens. Of course, an argument of epithets
such as "groggery," or "saloon," or "gin mill," used by certain
reviewers, may appeal to a class of society that believes in
"sumptuary laws," so long as they do not apply directly to
themselves. Some of them would go so far as to advocate
that no civilian or soldier should be allowed by law to drink
a glass of beer if he wants to do so. This class is usually
beyond legitimate argument which may run contrary to their
prejudices. They can not possibly understand how men can
be constituted differently from themselves, or that the moderate
drinker should not be compelled to forego his beer because others
make hogs of themselves. In other words, the highest ideal
of their ethical system seems to be that laws should be enacted
to oppress the virtues and the pleasures of the many to reach
the vices of the few. To them "sumptuary laws" are the

[1] "The itch of writing."

"cure all" for all the foibles and follies of the human heart, and the blessings of him who has fought his battles against temptation and won are to them a sealed book.

It is useless to argue with this class. Neither the sanctity of truth, the restrictions of the franking privileges of the postal service, nor the sin of private gain will deter them from pursuing the poor soldier, or anyone else who can be reached by "sumptuary legislation." It is to be hoped that time will cure this trend of thought and that the light will some day break in upon their benighted philosophy. It has been urged time and again that the Government should appropriate money for the purpose of providing club-rooms for the soldiers at their various posts, and an appropriation of $500,000 and subsequently one of a million dollars were set apart for this purpose. Well and good. No one has objections to "Uncle Sam" devoting this amount and much more to the purpose, if he wants to, but that does not help the evil in anywise.

The soldier who wants beer or even whisky is bound to get it, and unfortunately the facilities are usually provided by saloons and "cheap groggeries" close to almost every military post in the country, where he can get it to satiety and bestial drunkenness. There is there no regulation to stop him when he gets too much. On the contrary, it is to the interest of the proprietor of the place to sell as much as he can to every customer. In addition to this, these saloons are frequently close to houses of other and worse vices, and the two money-making enterprises work together for drunkenness and vice. Shall the soldier, who naturally regards himself outside of all regulations except those which pertain to his military training, direction, and welfare, as a freeman, be subjected to firm regulations as to drink under military jurisdiction, with such surroundings as shall not make it a hardship, or shall he be allowed to go forth as a prey to the evil companions, both male and female, to be found in the purlieus and saloon districts of military camps almost everywhere in this country?

Even in the prohibition States are to be found the "bootleggers" and the "blind tigers" and the "walking dram shops" ready to sell any quantity of the vilest quality of whisky to the soldier as soon as he gets beyond the military reservation of his station. We must take the soldier as we find him, recognizing that he is not by any means a perfect being, and that among other defective traits he is apt to have a fondness for strong drink. If, then, by offering him the opportunity of procuring in moderate quantities comparatively harmless beverages, such as light wines and beer, we prevent him from indulging in or diminish his temptation to partake to excess of whisky, brandy, rum, gin, or other "strong waters," the too frequent use of which makes drunkards, or even worse, of men, who can deny that good is accomplished such as could not be brought about by any "sumptuary law," be it ever so strong?

Men are not prone to embrace the rod that smites them, nor do they like to obey a law passed to deprive them of their accustomed pleasures through agitations provoked and kept before the public by a lot of people whose experience with the military seldom goes beyond admiring the "khaki" from a distance and making collections of soldiers' brass buttons in time of war scares.

At posts without traders' stores, the canteen, as the co-operative store of the command, when managed by a reliable canteen steward and one or more detailed assistants of approved character, and working under the supervision of a board of officers and a carefully devised system of checks, can be made an efficient instrument for good. Its purpose is, or should be, to supply the enlisted men at moderate prices with plain lunches, light wine, beer, and other articles, to the absolute exclusion of spirits or strong intoxicants; to provide a library or a room in which they may read or write, besides furnishing them, whenever practicable, with the facilities of engaging in gymnastic exercises and manly sports. The sale of beer or wine should be restricted or interdicted in the discretion of the commanding officer, and is to be authorized only as a means to prevent excesses outside and to promote temperance.

Treating, gambling, and the playing of any games for money should be prohibited. The credit system, if allowed at all, should be carried on with great discretion. Under a plan of this kind it is believed that all classes of Americans would be willing to admit that canteens would improve the mental, moral, and physical condition of the average soldier, make him better satisfied with his lot, remove a part of the temptation to desert, and thus enhance greatly his value to the Government. It was of this kind of a canteen that Archibald Forbes, the great English war correspondent, spoke when he said that "it was the most important boon to the soldier of modern times."

To put in operation a canteen on this broad plan has been the aim of every post in the United States, but owing to a law passed by Congress, in response to a public opinion worked up apparently from outside sources, all canteens, amounting at one time to several hundred, were forbidden to sell even light wines and beer to the men in the ranks, by resolution appended to the army bill. The object of promoting temperance and governing the appetites of the men, under the immediate eyes of their officers, was thus defeated at one stroke. The men, or rather such of them as were addicted to ardent spirits to excess and consequent indulgence in still baser passions and appetites, were now thrown upon the tender mercies of the saloons to be found in the vicinity of all military posts, the walking "dramshops" and "bootleggers," and the wider temptations of the cities at large, when upon leave.

The members of Congress instrumental in securing this restrictive legislation, as well as the accredited representatives in Washington of the Prohibitionists and various temperance societies who urged it, have steadily repudiated the idea that they intended to deny to the soldiers their personal rights of forming and operating "cold-water clubs" with temperance drinks, etc., but it has been found by practical experience that when the sale of beer and light wines is cut out from the canteen by legal prohibition it is impossible to carry on the club in its various ramifications, on account of lack of both interest in its pursuits and profits in its investments.

The American Public Health Association, consisting of physicians and health officers of long experience in many cities upon the American continent, prepared a report upon the subject of the American army canteen, through a subcommittee, whose ability will be recognized all over the world, and when the same was submitted, at their annual convention in January, 1904, in Washington, D. C., it was unanimously adopted. The report is the most complete and unanswerable ever submitted, clearly setting forth the effect of the canteen upon the *morale* of troops from every conceivable standpoint. It passed the following resolutions:

"*Resolved*, That this body deplores the action of Congress in curtailing the operation of the army canteen or post exchange, and in the interest of general and military sanitation recommends its establishment on its former basis at the earliest possible date.

"*Resolved*, That this body, in the interest of temperance and humanity, cordially invites the intelligent coöperation of a very large element of good citizens who have been active in securing legislation against the sale in the military service of alcoholics of any character, in taking successive steps toward the betterment of existing conditions, and thus assist in controlling and largely curtailing an evil which it is powerless at present to prevent."

2. Your committee is aware of the fact that beverages containing

alcohol are an accessory food of value only when it becomes necessary to increase temporarily the elasticity of mind and body and a desire and capacity for work, and that the subsequent depressing effect and a baneful influence of their misuse require great care in their employment, especially when rest, proper food, and some of the alkaloidal beverages like coffee, tea, cocoa, and stimulants like meat broths and soups may accomplish the same purpose, and their sale as a substitute should be encouraged.

3. In spite of the fact that "beer drinking viewed in the abstract is unproductive of good," your committee believes that its sale in canteens under rational and comprehensive regulations, rather than its total prohibition, will subserve the best interest of scientific temperance, because so long as human nature is weak and the masses are not properly educated, the substitution of a lesser evil under military control appears not only justifiable, but will in the future, as it has in the past, prevent excesses which are fatal to the soldier, soul and body. At present every effort toward total abstinence at military posts merely opposes theory to facts and sentiment to statistics, and compels recourse to saloons of the lowest character, whose proprietors care nothing for the efficiency of the army or the ruin of a good soldier.

4. Every precaution should be observed to conduct post exchanges and the salt of light wine and beer along the lines recommended by Munson in his "Theory and Practice of Military Hygiene," pages 820-822, and your committee begs to emphasize the fact that the bar feature should be entirely abolished and that the exchange should in fact be a "soldiers' club," with ample facilities for reading rooms, legitimate amusements, and athletic sports, where the soldier as a self-respecting individual may satisfy in an orderly manner his craving for diversion from the routine duties of a military life without undue prominence of the refreshment feature.

5. The sale of soft drinks, coffee, tea, cocoa, bouillon, soups, and warm lunches should be encouraged as substitutes for alcoholic beverages, and medical and line officers should be directed to educate by precept and example the rank and file of the army that for persons in health alcohol in any form presents no advantages not found in other foodstuffs or stimulants, and which are, moreover, free from the dangers attending its use. In this connection it should be remembered that good food, well prepared, and properly cooked and served, is one of the most effective prophylactic measures against the "drink habit" in civil as well as military life, and no effort should be spared to bring the culinary department in the army to the highest state of perfection.

6. Military officers should point out the grave and far-reaching consequences of the effects of venereal diseases, so intimately connected with the drink habit, and make a strong plea in favor of continence. This may be done by telling these young men that while the sexual passion is strong it can be accelerated or delayed, excited or lowered, by the influence of the will. The soldier can be assured that by the cultivation of pure thoughts, removal of temptation, normal mental, and especially by vigorous physical, exercise, continence is not only possible, but easy.

7. A strong effort should be made to improve the social conditions of the soldier. There are times and occasions when the friendly advice of a company commander or attending surgeon, a personal interest in the physical and moral welfare of the young soldier, will prove of greater benefit to the service and to humanity than the cold verdict of a summary court-martial. Such personal efforts on the part of the officers, dictated by the spirit of a universal brotherhood of man, appear to us perfectly com-

patible with proper military discipline. It is also believed that the habit of making savings deposits with the army paymasters may be greatly stimulated by personal efforts.

One of the clearest and most forcible statements yet made on the subject of the canteen of the army is presented by Lieut.-Gen. S. B. M. Young, chief of staff of the United States army, in his report to the Secretary of War for the year ending June 30, 1903 (p. 143), in which he said:

Special attention is invited to the incisive comments of department commanders upon the demoralizing effect of the operation of Section 38 of the act of February 2, 1901, which prohibits the sale of beer and light wines in post exchanges. This law has now been in operation for over two years and a half and has been fairly tested. Reports received from officers of all grades throughout the army who have had practical experience in supervising and observing post exchanges under present conditions exhibit practical unanimity of opinion as to the evil effects of this restriction.

These evil effects show themselves in increased drunkenness; in loathsome diseases, contracted while men are under the influence of a bad or drugged liquor; in increased desertion resulting from the same cause, the men while in a drugged condition being robbed by depraved associates of both sexes, and for this reason reluctant to return to their posts; and, generally, in increased insubordination.

In addition to these considerations of morality, discipline, and health, there is a further one advanced by the commanding general, Department of Texas, that the soldier's rights and privileges should not be curtailed simply because he is a soldier; that he should be considered as a citizen in the community in which he is serving, and, where no impairment of his military efficiency would result therefrom, should have a citizen's rights and privileges.

Since the original establishment of the canteen feature of the post exchange there has never been a time when the dominant sentiment of the army did not approve that feature as tending strongly to promote morality, sobriety, and discipline among the troops.

The highest military and technical authority, the highest church dignitaries, and the selected experts of the highest medical authority on public health upon this continent have all declared in favor of the canteen as a benefit wherever operated in military posts under the strict military rules laid down in the United States Army Regulations. They declare that the canteen contributes to the health, happiness, contentment, and especially to the temperance of the soldier. They have said and have shown by statistics and incontrovertible facts that the canteen is an aid in keeping the enlisted man away from bad company and resorts which would lead to moral depravity and degradation. They have shown that there is no mode of life known which, in time of peace and the humdrum existence in the backwoods army posts, as well as in those situated near the temptations of cities, makes the social features of club life more essentially necessary than that of the common soldiers.

Men with leisure upon their hands and nothing to do during many hours each day, most of whom in all probability have led a gay and gregarious life before entering the army, cannot be confined in some "pent-up Utica" with accessories of "cold water" and hard-tack and without amusement or good cheer, if they are to keep contented and not be tempted to desert.

The restraint of strict military discipline is usually onerous to most Americans in time of peace, and the life should have all the attractions consistent with duty, temperance, and healthful conditions as an offset to the necessities of army discipline.

As against all this testimony of men best qualified to judge of the merits of the canteen in army life, its opponents, who have succeeded in causing its abandonment by enactment of law, have produced an agitation among church, temperance, and religious societies who have overwhelmed Congressmen and Senators with petitions against the army canteen, signed by people who would probably have to look in the dictionary to ascertain the difference between a canteen and a haversack.

The temperance and prohibition societies, knowing very little about army conditions and caring less, through their paid Washington agents have sent out tons of tracts containing a lot of irresponsible statements against the canteen, under congressional frank, contrary to law, in order to work up church and temperance society indignation against the canteen. It would appear to them a great victory of the cause to deprive the soldier of his drink of light wine or beer and to break up all his social life, so as to throw him upon the vices of outside resorts. To them the abolition of the canteen is a part and parcel of their crusade in favor of prohibition, which is based on the absurd dictum that the man who drinks moderately has no rights that any temperance organization is bound to respect.

Which should the people believe in this controversy—men who know whereof they speak or professional agitators who are bent on foisting a pet "ism" upon us by threat of the ballot against timorous occupants of seats in Congress? The army, at least, ought not to be subject to vagaries of theorists.

Let there be a halt right here and now to the tinkering with army regulations by temperance or any other so-called "moral or eleemosynary societies" with an axe to grind, and let the army canteen be reëstablished at once.

Liquor selling in the canteen was not reëstablished.

CHAPTER XIII

Pure Food

ON December 10, 1902, William P. Hepburn [Ia.], of the Interstate Commerce Committee, presented a pure food bill which had been reported to previous Congresses. In this Congress it had been proposed by Emmett Tompkins [O.].

Pure Food Bill

HOUSE OF REPRESENTATIVES, DECEMBER 18, 1902

Mr. Tompkins explained the measure on December 18.

Mr. Chairman, very few subjects have attracted more general and deep interest than the consideration of ways and means by which the people of the country may obtain pure food and unadulterated drugs. Nearly fourteen years ago the subject was first introduced into Congress by a Senator from Nebraska, and since then it has continually engrossed the attention of this body. Various societies throughout the country have taken action upon the question and made certain and emphatic recommendations. A large congress has been organized, known as the pure-food congress, and at its last meeting in this city there were present more than 400 delegates representing all classes, occupations, and all branches of industry and human pursuits.

451

As a result of the deliberations of the convention last mentioned, there was practically a unanimous recommendation to Congress that such a measure as the one now pending be enacted into a statute.

The purpose of this bill is not to prohibit the manufacture or sale of anything that is not deleterious, but it is to prohibit the manufacture of any sort of food that is deleterious, and to provide that any food or drug which is adulterated shall bear upon its face the badge of what it is, so that the purchaser may know what he is to get and he will secure that for which he pays.

The bill provides that the Secretary of Agriculture shall, from the chemical branch or bureau of the department, create a special bureau of chemists who shall examine food products and drugs which are placed upon the market. The authority of this bureau when constituted will not be permitted to go into any State and interfere with any such product manufactured within that State, but it shall have supervision over such products as are shipped from one State into another, into the Territories, or into the District of Columbia, and it will forbid the manufacture of any deleterious food product and sale of any adulterated product under false representation.

Now, this bureau of chemistry shall have authority to prescribe certain standards of excellence in food and of purity in drugs. When anyone ships an article from one State to another which is forbidden by this statute, or any impure drug, upon information delivered by an agent of this bureau upon inspection of any suspected article, the district attorney for the district in which the offending article is found shall institute proceedings in the proper court to inflict the prescribed punishment.

The bill defines what a "drug" is, and includes all medicines and preparations recognized in the United States Pharmacopœia for internal and external use. Defining the word "food": It includes all articles used for food, drink, confectionery, or condiment by man or domestic animals, whether simple, mixed, or compound. The term "misbranded" shall apply to all drugs or articles of food, or articles which enter into the composition of food, the package or label of which shall bear any statement regarding the ingredients or substances contained in such article, which statement shall be false or misleading in any particular, and to any food or drug product which is falsely branded as to the State, Territory, or country in which it is manufactured or produced.

There is no disposition on the part of the advocates of this

bill to invade any State and undertake to usurp the police powers of that State or to substitute its courts for the State courts in reference to any manufacture or any dealing in articles of commerce that are found wholly within that State, but recognizing, as has been demonstrated, the ineffectiveness of the miscellaneous sorts of legislation upon this subject by the various States, recognizing how inoperative have been statutes looking to the control of commerce passing out of one State into another, there has been, as I said in the beginning, a universal demand for the interposition of Congress, within the power which is vested in it by the Constitution, not only to regulate commerce between the States in the sense of controlling common carriers, but to go further and exercise such police power in connection with this commerce that nothing which is deleterious or deceptive or is a fraud or an imposition upon the people shall pass from one State to another.

Instead of being an interference with the administration of justice and the execution of the food laws of the various States, it is intended to be an auxiliary to those laws, and to help preserve to the people of the respective States pure food, pure drugs, saving them from fraud and deceit.

That there is an interest on the part of the people in this subject and that there is a demand on their part that Congress shall do something upon this important matter is evidenced by the fact that in nearly all the States of the Union pure-food laws are in existence and are being enforced with more or less success. I am informed that the legislature of the State from which my friend [William C. Adamson], who represents the minority in the discussion of this matter comes—the State of Georgia—I understand that within the last few weeks, by a unanimous vote of the Senate and House of Representatives of that State, a pure-food law has been enacted.

I do not understand that there is any organized opposition to this measure, except possibly as to the method of executing its provisions. Upon the sentiment that the people should be protected against fraud and deception, upon the proposition that health should be preserved by withholding from market impure food, there can be no dissension in the opinion of our people. Congress, by interfering so far as the scope of interstate commerce extends with the manufacture of impure drugs and adulterated food, seeks simply to throw around the purchaser and the consumer the protection of giving notice to him of what he is buying and what he is consuming.

Your committee, Mr. Chairman, are of the opinion that,

while a man has the right *per se* to manufacture a substance which looks like strawberry jam, he has no right to manufacture that substance and inject into it timothy seed and brand the vessel containing this fabrication with the name "strawberry jam." Your committee feel that the manufacturer or the dealer who sells this product should sell it for what it actually is, and should say: "While this looks like strawberry jam, while the timothy seed which it contains looks like strawberry seed, neither is genuine." And when a man puts an article upon the market which he calls coffee we want it to be coffee, not stuff compounded from tree bark and soil, which, by an ingenious process of compression and drying, is made to resemble the coffee berry, when there is no coffee at all in it.

Mr. Adamson, of the minority of the committee, opposed the bill.

Mr. Chairman, in the protracted hearings before the Committee on Interstate and Foreign Commerce I discovered to my own satisfaction that there was not only no necessity for the enactment of the bill, but that such legislation would be fraught with pernicious and dangerous consequences. I then gave my attention not so much to the details of the bill itself as to bringing out in the way of question and answer from those who appeared before the committee whether the States and local communities could not determine for themselves what their people should eat and drink and wear, and where they should buy such articles, instead of requiring that the burden should be put upon the Government of the United States of doing that in which it was never designed to have any concern.

I believe that the bill drawn and introduced by the distinguished chairman of the committee was the best of its kind if such legislation must be resorted to.

Mr. Chairman, I do not propose to discount the importance of purity and, above all, honesty in all sorts of commercial dealings. I have gone so far, after listening to the hearings of the committee, as to suggest to my conferees that the laboratory proposed could be a great and useful institution as a gatherer of information and a disseminator of education among the people of the country. I have gone even farther and proposed to agree that every man shipping from one State into another should be required, if the product be a compound, to label upon the package the exact ingredients which make the compound. Farther than those things, Mr. Chairman, I am not willing to go.

The bill proposes to extend its provisions to all our domain and govern all interstate business. I do not desire my friend from Ohio to understand, as he intimated, that I am stickling here about the question of State's rights. I believe if he would consider the question he would decide that he is as proud of his State as I am of mine and as jealous of her rights and sovereignty. I desire to say to him that all that subject was thrashed over by the ablest and greatest statesmen the world ever saw. I desire to state that long since that, and long since some people fondly imagined that States' rights had been stamped out and it was all right to invade local authorities and local communities, there have appeared in every State in this Union which ever seemingly denied it as lively a recognition of the doctrine and as keen a demand for it as rests in my breast whenever interest awakened their conscience on the subject.

The statesmen who prepared and builded the great edifice of this Government designed it to discuss and deal with great questions involving the liberties, the independence, and the welfare of this growing Republic, the greatest the world ever saw, and make its success and glory a shining light to all mankind. They never expected, when placing in the great bulwark of our liberties the commerce clause, thereby to monopolize all the functions and attention of the Federal Government and prostitute and use all the efforts and abilities of its statesmen in talking about matters of trade which were never intended to attract their attention except for one purpose. That purpose was solely and purely to prevent one State from discriminating against and injuring the interests of the people of another State in commerce—that, and no more.

Mr. Chairman, I think that my State can punish every solitary act, every fraud, every crime that has been described in any of these hearings, and any other State in this Union can do the same if it will. I contend that it is utterly unnecessary to burden this Government with little police matters that all the local communities can better attend to, and I know that after science has done its best or its worst, after all the laboratories have exhausted themselves, when all has been done and said that can be done and said, in the last analysis it will be proved that the old ladies in the home, the housewives, the old cook who used the elbow grease to mix the dough to make the bread —not last year's wasp nests which we have now and which are called bread—knew more about the subject than all science and all scientists.

Mr. Chairman, there are two or three insuperable objections

to the framework of this bill. One of them provides that a person pretending to represent the Government may force a dealer, under penalty of prosecution for refusal, to sell or deliver a sample for analysis, the result of which shall be submitted to a court on a prosecution, to the exclusion of all evidence about other goods, even those coming in the same case or package.

Now, it is quite as much as we can expect of human infirmity if, when you are really swindled, you take upon yourself the burden of your own grievance and place in operation the machinery for the obtaining of justice that the law furnishes and go ahead and punish the man who has already defrauded you. But to provide for the encouragement, not only of violations of the law, but to aid and extend the operation of a pestilential lot of spies, meddlers, and informers, who work for *per diem* and mileage, and sometimes other rewards incident to informing, would make a system a great deal more impure than any food or drink any people ever consumed and less to be desired.

Mr. Chairman, there is another objection to the bill, and not only that, but a thing that in my mind exhibits the great demand in some quarters for the bill. That is the provision that exempts a citizen from the expense of remedying his wrongs in the courts and puts upon the department first the duty of getting up the evidence and then calling upon the Federal officers whose duties would be to proceed with the prosecution. In the State courts where there is an act of cheating and swindling the injured man must simply, as the negro says, "tote his own skillet" and take up his own burden and attend to his own business.

Now, Mr. Chairman, I believe in pure food, pure coffee, pure everything that we eat and drink; but I believe in pure government. I believe in domestic and local government. I believe in the government of the home circle primarily and originally. I believe in the government furnished by the States and municipalities, which for domestic and police purposes were recognized by the founders of this great Government as the best and most perfect system of government. Not that anybody is jealous of local rights and afraid of the central authority; but the business can be better transacted, and crime can be more surely and speedily punished, and justice can be more certainly reached, and the central government will not be overloaded.

I believe in the Federal Government as firmly, as strongly, and as proudly as any man who ever lived. In its proper channels, devoted to its proper purposes, it may be the greatest, most powerful, most glorious government the world ever saw. Out of its channels, condescending to functions it has no business with, it becomes contemptible and ridiculous, frittering away its time and the interests of the people who made it and endowed it with its powers and constituted it for better purposes. Long may the emblem of our power and glory wave far and wide; and around the world may our Government's influence increase for our uplifting and the good of mankind. But, Mr. Chairman, when it leaves its glorious purposes and condescends to things too small and too unnecessary for its attention, it is not strengthened, but weakened.

Augustus P. Gardner [Mass.] also opposed the bill.

Mr. Chairman, you cannot go down into that restaurant below here and eat a piece of bread which does not contain a poison injurious to human health. Every piece of bread you eat there contains alum or a salt of potash. I will venture to say that such is the case if they are prepared with any baking powder that has anything except the most limited sale. But we do not want to know it; we do not want to have these foods labeled. When I go into a sleeping car, where I know the air is surcharged with the germs of consumption, or where I know that the curtains surrounding my berth conceal the tubercle bacillus, I do not want to see a large placard saying so, when I enter the car anticipating a pleasant night's sleep.

It is exercise and moderation that are the true preservatives of health. I believe we have gone altogether too far with our anti-spitting ordinances and our health ordinances, and the various other complicated methods by which we attempt to get the better of the germ that is universal. I believe that the germinal theory of disease is a perfectly sound one, but I do not believe that these finical, annoying, expensive restrictions abate by one jot or one tittle the danger incident to the ills to which human flesh is heir. [Applause.]

On December 19 Herman P. Dahle [Wis.] supported the bill.

As a dealer in food as defined by this act, I will very much appreciate its passage personally, and for the people I represent.

It will be a benefit first to the consumer, who comprises all our people to a larger or smaller degree, by prohibiting the sale of all articles of food products that are deleterious, and providing that all adulterated food and drugs shall be sold under their true names in such manner as to advise the purchaser of what he is getting. He will also be protected from purchasing that which is deleterious according to this bill when enacted.

And with such consumers whose taste or imagination can best be satisfied with such products as are manufactured abroad and imported the label or name will then be a security or guaranty.

The consumer who is poor, whose means are small, who must live as cheaply as possible and yet not sacrifice health, also the better to do of fair means, who wishes to live an economic life, will be benefited, because he may now subsist on that which is so poor as to be deleterious to health and life on account of the very inferior, decayed, mixed raw material used or poisonous ingredient added in such manufacture or preparation so that the product becomes deleterious.

He will also be benefited because food which is cheapened in such different ways as mixture and adulteration must then be marked as such and will be sold on its merits, except in cases where advertising may have some effect.

Those who will lose by the enactment of this bill are the following:

First. All manufacturers or dealers in all articles the sale of which will be prohibited by this law because such articles are deleterious.

Second. Manufacturers who have in many instances made undue profits by manufacturing, preparing, or canning what is now called pure food from animal, cereal, vegetable, or fruit raw product, which has been of such inferior quality or so decayed that the manufactured or prepared article is deleterious.

Third. Those who manufacture or prepare articles of food or drugs, included in this bill, marking, labeling, and offering such for sale as pure and of a high standard, while such may be adulterated, or imitations under the names of other articles, thereby taking advantage of the consumer, because such adulterated, mixed, or imitation article will yield the manufacturer a larger profit both to himself and dealer—because such manufacturer will also aim so to arrange his price to the dealer that he also may share in the larger profit to the loss of the consumer.

The one of the two dissenting members of the committee reporting this bill admits that legislation which will insure pure food and protection to the consumers is wise, but claims that such legislation should not embarrass the manufacturer of and dealer in pure food. If a part of the manufacturers of food did not resort to the use of improper raw material, and make the food of low strength, as stated, there might be no necessity of this requirement, but with conditions as they are it is necessary.

Opponents of this measure claim that all that can be regulated which is involved in this bill by State officials through State laws better than by government officials through the enactment of the act before us. I wish to call your attention to the very marked improvement in reaching the object sought by government law enforced by government officials over State officials in the oleomargarine manufacture and sale when the late government law regulating the manufacture and sale of that product went into effect.

Before that time the unscrupulous manufacturer and dealer in that product made undue profits, taking undue advantage of the consumer by manufacturing, placing on the market, an imitation much more cheaply produced than the article it was made to imitate, placing same on the market and disposing of same for another product.

I do not find that the Government has any trouble in enforcing this law. The consumer who now wishes the genuine article can get such by paying the price it is worth, and the consumer of small means gets what he has to get along with at a proper price.

We keep our army and navy not for war but for peace, and so with the enactment of this bill, it will not be for war but for peace in the sense of the national law being effective where State laws are not in very many instances carried out.

The bill was passed by a vote of 72 to 21. The Senate committed it, and it was later reported and debated, but no action was taken upon it during the session.

On December 6, 1905, Weldon B. Heyburn [Ida.] introduced in the Senate a bill for "preventing the manufacture, sale, or transportation of adulterated or misbranded or poisonous or deleterious foods, drugs, medicines, and liquors, and for regulating traffic therein." It was referred to the Committee on Manufactures, of which Senator Heyburn was chairman.

The bill was duly reported, and came up for discussion on January 10, 1906.

PURE FOOD

SENATE, JANUARY 10-JUNE 30, 1906

SENATOR HEYBURN.—I submit that this bill is one of very great interest to all the people of the country in their homes and home life. I think it is only a question in this body as to whether this bill accomplishes what this body desires to accomplish. It is merely a question as to whether its provisions are fair to all of the people, those who manufacture, those who sell, and those who use the ordinary commodities of life. Committees of this body have been endeavoring for many years to reach a conclusion and to formulate a bill that would accomplish this purpose, and we sincerely hope that we have reached that point.

The first section of the bill provides that it shall be unlawful to manufacture forbidden or proscribed articles. It prescribes a fine and imprisonment against the manufacturer of such articles.

Section 2 of the bill provides against the introduction of forbidden articles from one State or Territory or district or insular possession into another jurisdiction, and prescribes practically the same fine for the introduction of the articles as it does for the manufacture of them.

Then there is a new feature to this bill that has not been heretofore embodied in any bill that has been introduced. Section 2 provides that

the fines and penalties may be enforced against the officers of such corporation personally responsible for such violation, and any violation of any of the provisions of this act by any corporation shall be deemed to be the act of the officer of such corporation directly responsible therefor, and such officer may be punished for such violation as though such violation was the personal act of such officer.

That is a new feature in bills of this kind. It was intended to obviate the possibility of escape by the officers of a corporation under a plea, which has been more than once made, that they did not know that this was being done on the credit of or on the responsibility of the corporation.

There is another new feature.

Three departments—the Treasury, Agriculture, and Commerce and Labor—shall make rules jointly covering the manner of collecting specimens for determination.

Then it is provided that, after such specimens are collected, the determination shall be made by the Bureau of Chemistry of the Department of Agriculture.

Another new feature in this bill is that we have separated liquors from foods. Heretofore the proposed measures have denominated all liquors, wines, and so forth as food. It did not appear to the committee reporting this bill that they should be so classified. Liquor is not a food necessary for the maintenance or sustenance of the human frame. If anything, it is a luxury.

As to the necessity for this legislation, I think it would be a waste of time to do more than suggest it. Nearly every State in the Union, Mr. President, has a pure-food law. The States have undertaken to legislate upon this subject, with, I believe, but one or two exceptions. Some of the laws upon the subject are very meager; some of them are very local; some of them are adapted to the peculiar local interests of the people of the particular State, but, as a rule, the States have enacted intelligent and appropriate legislation upon this question. The difficulty, which has been made plain to the committee, is that they can enforce the law only to the extent of the impure and adulterated products that are sent in unbroken packages within their borders from other States. There are a number of fraudulent articles that are under the ban of this legislation, not a pound or ounce of which is offered for sale in the State in which they are manufactured, because they are provided against by the legislation of that State; but they are manufactured in one State and sent to another in unbroken packages under the rule of law that is now established, perhaps forever. So that the State into which they are sent is helpless against the flood of these impure articles sent in unbroken packages under the protection of that rule of law and then offered for sale upon the retail market.

It is impossible for a State effectively to enforce a pure-food law without the coöperation of the general Government. It is obvious that it is only the general Government that can protect us from the influx of deleterious and poisonous articles from foreign countries. That must be done at the port of entry. There we stop such importations. There has been a law for this purpose on the statute book since 1848. That law is enforced, I believe, fairly and, perhaps, as efficiently as it can be under existing statutes and rules, but the proposed legislation fortifies the law of 1848 in providing a better method and more efficient coöperation between the branches of the Government in carrying out the spirit and intent of that law.

There are ports of entry in the West in States that prohibit

the manufacture or sale or distribution of these impure articles
and do so efficiently, except as against outside interference.
There is the point of necessity for the coöperation of the general Government with the States in the enforcement of this
class of legislation.

I will not at this time undertake to enumerate the frauds
perpetrated upon the people further than to state that, according to a statement which I have before me, received this morning, which is from an official source, in some of the great neigh-
boring States more than 60 per cent. of all the drugs that are
offered on the market are fraudulent, and not only do they not
possess the qualities for which the drug is distinguished, or
should be, but they are actually adulterated to such an extent
that they are dangerous to be used.

On January 23 Senator Heyburn further supported
the bill.

It has been suggested that this proposed legislation partook
too much of the paternal in character and that it was not necessarily one of the functions of Congress to determine what may
be designated as the small details of the public interest as it
affects private individuals. I believe that one of the primary
and most sacred duties of a legislative body governing and making laws for a country such as ours is the consideration of private interests relating to the welfare of the individual. Of
course, it seems to be more of a legislative function upon casual
glance to deal with international affairs, with great financial
problems, with high-sounding legislative terms, but we are here
primarily, Mr. President, for the individual people, and, when
the voice of the people is raised in behalf of a measure of legislation, we cannot, as the authorized representatives of the people, ignore that voice.

Now, I appeal to Senators, has there ever been in the history of this country a more universal demand for action upon
the part of Congress than the demand that has gone up from
one end of the country to the other in regard to legislation upon
the pure-food question? It affects the people more than the
river and harbor bill; it affects the people more than the public-
land question; it affects the people more than the relations between this country and some foreign country, because, unless
the people are safeguarded in their individual rights, they care
but little for the questions which are sometimes considered to
be of larger importance.

I class the man who foists a bogus or an adulterated drug or medicine upon the market with the man who poisons the spring out of which the unknown public drinks. He does not know who his victim is going to be when he does it. He manufactures it for individual gain and selfishness; but when the physician, standing at the bedside of the sick, diagnosing the case, knowing from his education in the science of medicine that a certain drug will bring relief, writes a prescription, with instructions that that certain drug be procured, contemplating it in its purity, measuring its effect because of his knowledge of it in a pure state, and that prescription is taken to the drug store, and, instead of being compounded of the drugs that the physician had in mind when he wrote the prescription, it is compounded of a substitute, either an absolute fraud or a deleterious composition that will produce exactly the opposite result from that contemplated by the physician when he wrote the prescription, what is the effect? The medicine is taken to the bedside of the helpless sick. It is administered by the nurse in the hope that it may accomplish the result which the physician had in mind; but, on the contrary, because of the fact that it is a fraudulent substitute for the real panacea for the ill, the patient dies. Can you imagine a condition of affairs crying louder for a remedy than that?

Aside from the question of fraud from a financial standpoint, aside from the question of substituting a medicine that, perhaps, does not cost one-tenth what the real substance would cost, aside from the fraud that is based upon the gain in price between the real and the bogus article, the effect upon human life is as serious a question as could be presented in the consideration of a public measure asking for relief through legislation at the hands of Congress. Is that too small a question for Congress to deal with?

Only last Sunday I picked up one of the great journals of this country that ranks among the very best, and I found a very excellent little editorial commending pure-food legislation, commending the regulation and restraint of these bogus articles, and then in the same paper I counted sixty-two patent-medicine advertisements, and advertisements of the worst frauds that could be imagined. I appeal to the newspaper fraternity of the country to assist us in a real and substantial manner in settling this question.

The Post-Office Department could exclude from the mails those papers that carry upon their pages the tempting inducements to those who have real or imaginary ills to invest their money in these poisonous, deleterious, and fraudulent substances. That is one way to reach them.

Congress alone can make effective the laws of the several States prohibiting the manufacture or sale of this class of articles. The States are helpless under the law. Under the Constitution, as it has been construed by the Supreme Court of the United States, these goods may go from one State to another in unbroken packages, and it is not until the package is broken that the jurisdiction of the State attaches. The State laws are helpless. There is a cry from every State in the Union—I think I may say that I have within my possession a demand from nearly every State in the Union—that the Congress of the United States should supplement their legislation and afford relief against the impositions that come from one State to another.

Seldom are these forbidden articles sold in the State of their manufacture. Seldom do they bring themselves within the law of the State which would regulate them. What higher duty can Congress perform than that of assisting the State governments in their local self-government in a matter which affects the people so closely?

This principle of self-government to which I have referred begins in the home. It begins with the individual, and it rises through the home and the local community and the various political governments until it reaches here, and we are the last arbiter and should be the first to afford relief.

On February 19 Joseph B. Foraker [O.] offered two amendments, the first striking out the word "added" in the provision of the bill that, "in the case of liquors, an article shall be deemed adulterated if it contain any added ingredient of a poisonous or deleterious character," and the second modifying the provision that the process of manufacture be stated on the package in which the liquor is offered for sale, so as to read that the liquor is to be labeled either "blended" or "rectified," or "vatted."

These amendments, said SENATOR HEYBURN, are supported by what is known as the "liquor interest." It is an attempt to take out of the bill which your committee has reported every element of protection against the very evil, so far as that trade is concerned, to which the bill is directed. It represents a controversy between what is known as the "strict whisky men" and the blenders or rectifiers.

The word "added," after very mature consideration by your committee, was adopted because of the fact that there are to be found in nature's products, as she produces them, poisonous substances, to be determined by analysis. Nature has so combined them that they are not a danger or an evil—that is, so long as they are left in the chemical connection in which nature has organized them; but when they are extracted by the artificial processes of chemistry they become a poison. You can extract poison from grain or its products, and when it is extracted it is a deadly poison; but if you leave that poison as nature embodied it in the original substance it is not a dangerous poison or an active agency of poison at all.

So, in order to avoid the threat that those who produce a perfectly legitimate article from a natural product might be held liable because the product contained nature's poison it was thought sufficient to provide against the adding of any new substance that was in itself a poison, and thus emphasizing the evils of existing conditions in nature's product. Fusel oil is a poison. If you extract it, it becomes a single active agency of destruction, but allow it to remain in the combination where nature has placed it, and, while it is nominally a poison, it is a harmless one, or comparatively so.

As to the second amendment, it has been sent doubtless to every member of this body. I have hundreds of them that have been received, of course at the instigation of some common center of movement, but all emanating from what is known as the "distillers" or "liquor interest" of the country.

They were too wily to propose to strike those words out; but under the advice of shrewd counsel as to the interpretation the court would place upon certain words of limitation they have substituted words of limitation, so that under the well-established rule of interpretation of words and phrases it will be held to limit the scope and intent of the entire paragraph. So that unless liquor comes within one of those three classes it will not come under the purview or within the scope and intent of any part of the paragraph. They become words of limitation.

Every lawyer knows and must see the effect of the objection. It would be very easy for these rectifiers or blenders or contractors of bogus liquors to invent a new name for their process and leave all reference to it off of the bottle, and if they were before the court upon the charge of violating this law they would say, "We have not violated the law; these are not blended goods, these are not rectified goods, these are not vatted goods; these are goods under some other process that was not mentioned or forbidden by the provisions of the statute.'' That is what they are after. They want to leave the field open to themselves, so they may change the name of the process and yet perform the same act and work the same evil against this trade.

Now, I desire to place all Senators upon guard against that amendment—plausible on its face, insidious in its power for harm to this bill. We must not adopt those words of limitation. If we do, we might as well strike out that provision of the bill. If I am not right, why do they want it?

Senator Foraker.—I want to call the Senator's attention to the fact that I offered this amendment without pretending to know as much about it as I perhaps should know. I offer it because I am in receipt not of a few letters and telegrams, nor scores, but hundreds from constituents living in my State, engaged in the liquor business in one form or another, asking me to offer the amendment. I do not know who prepared it. I know some of the men who have written to me, but most of them I do not know. Those whom I do know I can vouch for, at least so far as I shall make any reference to them here this morning, as men of honorable and good standing in every way in the community where they live and where they do business. I do not think they are men who would engage in an effort to get into a bill in a sly way something that would give them an unjust advantage, something that Senators would not understand, something that would be an imposition in the results which would flow from it upon those who would be interested in this legislation.

Addressing me, H. F. Corbin & Co., of Cincinnati, Ohio, say:

H. F. Corbin & Co., Whiskies Distillers,
Cincinnati, Ohio, February 9, 1906.

Dear Sir: You will be receiving inclosures similar to the one we send herewith—

Which is this amendment—

as this idea embodies the sentiment and desire of every upright wholesale whisky and liquor merchant in the United States, as evidenced by resolutions of the National Wholesale Liquor Dealers' Association and also the various independent State organizations.

There is no objection on the part of the liquor trade to a pure-food bill; in fact, it is something which the better element of the trade has desired for years; but while that is a fact it does not seem just to impose such an unfair, unreasonable, and uncommercial requirement as is embodied in the original bill.

Here is another letter from the Star Distillery Company, of Cincinnati, Ohio, one of the most reputable of the business houses of that character in our city.

February 10, 1906.

In the labeling of a barrel or a package containing blended whiskey, we do not consider it objectionable to use the words ''blended'' or ''vatted,'' but it would be directly against the interest of our blended business to be compelled to brand or print the formula of such a blend on each package, as it would be publishing to our competitors the exact contents of such a blended article upon which we have used many years' knowledge and experience in successfully introducing such an article to the trade. You will no doubt agree with us that anything which would compel us or any other firm in the liquor business to publish the secret knowledge of our different formulas would be unfair.

In this connection we wish to say that we are heartily in favor of the provisions which prohibit the sale of any liquors adulterated, or which contain any ingredient of a poisonous or deleterious character, and we shall always be ready to assist the Department in prohibiting the sale of such liquors.

PORTER J. McCUMBER [N. D.].—What portion of the Heyburn bill requires that the formula for blended whisky should be published? There is not a single thing that requires it, but on the contrary the bill is so drawn that it prevents any attempt to compel a disclosure unless there are impure ingredients put into the liquors themselves in addition.

SENATOR FORAKER.—Mr. President, that may be true, but it is not clearly the proper construction of the language that has been employed.

The gentlemen who write me say they are afraid the construction of that language would be such as to require them to put their formula on the label, and they do not want to put their formula on. What they want is that the bill will tell them what ought to go there. They have no objection to putting on that their goods are blended, or that their goods are rectified, or that their goods are mixed goods; but there ought to be some general term, like the term ''blended,'' that would satisfy the law, substituted for the present uncertain statement which might be so construed as to require the whisky manufacturers to expose on the label the formula by which they mix their goods.

Now, I wish to speak of the first amendment.

Why should it be an ''added'' ingredient of a poisonous or

deleterious character before it is required to be published to the world as an adulterated mixture?

If the word "added" serves any good purpose there, I do not object to its remaining; but gentlemen who are entirely familiar with this business do not think that it does; and to the average layman it would seem that any kind of an ingredient ought to be stricken out, whether it might be added or not, that was poisonous or deleterious in the alcohol in its natural state before it was rectified, blended, or vatted.

Benjamin R. Tillman [S. C.].—Possibly I can explain to the Senator. I have studied this whisky question a little. I used to be head barkeeper, as they called me in South Carolina, when the dispensary was inaugurated there, and I know a good deal about it.

The added ingredient would be some adulterant for the purpose of coloring or to give it some flavor. There might be a more dangerous ingredient that would be in the spirits as they come from the still, and that is fusel oil, the most deadly of poisons. The mean liquor—what is known as the "meanest of mean liquor"—is due to the fusel oil that is in the crude alcohol instead of deodorized alcohol from which fusel oil has been extracted. That would not be added, because it comes from the corn.

Senator Foraker.—I do not think that ought to be used as a beverage under any circumstances.

Senator Tillman.—Neither do I.

Senator Foraker.—I would so amend the bill, if whisky in its natural state has a poisonous ingredient in it that is dangerous to life and health, as to prohibit the sale of it. I wish the Senator, from South Carolina, out of the abundant knowledge that he has of this trade, would frame an amendment prohibiting the sale of liquor that has any fusel oil in it. Such an amendment would not do anybody any harm and might do a great deal of good.

Senator Tillman.—There are two kinds of alcohol. One has fusel oil in it, which comes with the grain and gives the flavor; the other has the fusel oil taken out and is known as "deodorized alcohol," and is the basis of every fine blended whisky in the world. Fusel oil is that chemical property which rests mainly in the hull of the grain and in the peeling of the fruit. It gives flavor, and it is a deadly poison. Therefore, new liquors, fresh from the still, are very dangerous to health and very injurious. You have to wait and age them for a year or two or three or five years before the fusel oil that is left in the liquor changes to ether of one kind or another and gives the nutty flavor of which connoisseurs are so fond.

SENATOR FORAKER.—In this connection I offer the following letter:

CLEVELAND, OHIO, *February 3, 1906.*

Amendment 1 was suggested in the interests of the health of the whisky consumers, who ought to be protected against too large a percentage of fusel oil in their whisky. The amount of fusel oil which is contained in any straight distillate depends entirely upon the care of the distiller.

I wish to add in connection I learn that Mr. Wiley is working to have the name ''whisky'' apply only to goods at 100 per cent. [*i.e.*, ½ alcohol and ½ water]. If for no other reason than to form temperate habits this should be defeated, as it would have a tendency to prejudice people against lower-proof whisky, and to drink the goods at 100 per cent. and higher, which is too strong, in my opinion.

Senator Tillman described the ''blending'' process:

You take a fine alcohol and pour it into a vat and add some two-stamp whisky, as it is known, or straight whisky, that has come out of the Government warehouse and been aged by natural process, with its aroma and flavor increasing every year. You add a certain percentage of this two-stamp whisky to your pure alcohol, and by adding some coloring matter and some sugar in the way of burnt caramel, you get what are known as the fine blended whiskies of commerce, selling for five or six dollars a gallon. But they all have at the bottom the deodorized alcohol, which is worth $1.27 a gallon. To take out the word ''added'' would simply destroy the opportunity of punishing the adulterator for adding coloring matter and sweetening matter and bead oil to the product in order to bamboozle his customers.

On February 21 Senator Heyburn replied to Senator Tillman:

This is not a prohibitive section of this statute. It is merely a definition. It says that the mingling of an added poison with the thing itself would constitute an adulteration of it. Well, it probably would, in any event, and the courts probably would hold that to take an article that was, as whisky is when it is distilled, in its natural condition as it comes from the still and mix anything with it that was of a character that would degrade it or would lessen its value, that would be to adulterate it. But this bill, in order to make that certain in describing what shall constitute the adulteration of these articles, whether it be foods, drugs, or liquors, says that in the case of liquors the article shall be deemed adulterated if it contain any added ingredient of poison. In other words, if you add to the venom of the article itself for destructive purposes, or the capacity of it to injure those who use it. To strike out the word "added" here would be an admission that, if a thing contains 5 per cent. poison, it would be no offence to add another 5 per cent. to it and make it that much more dangerous.

I will instance a point. Cologne spirits contain no fusel oil. The high grade of blended spirits is made with cologne spirits as a base. The word "added" would, through its application, prohibit the adding of fusel oil to that whisky for any purpose whatever if it had been made upon the base of cologne spirits, which contains none.

BOIES PENROSE [Pa.].—But how would it reach the case of straight whisky in which the fusel oil was inherent and had not been eliminated by age, or the various processes by which it is eliminated, into a mere trace, which is the largest amount of fusel oil permitted in the Pharmacopœia? How would this amendment reach that case where fusel oil has not been added, but is inherent in the whisky?

SENATOR HEYBURN.—It does not reach it at all, but there is another provision in this bill that prohibits the sale of or commerce in any article that is deleterious to human health.

SENATOR PENROSE.—In other words, the straight-whisky people are taken in under the general dragnet clause—which I do not suppose can have any practical effect—whereas the blended whisky people are singled out to be punished and have their goods discriminated against and prejudiced in the public mind.

SENATOR HEYBURN.—Not unless the blended-whisky men desire to add fusel oil to their product, and that they should not be permitted to do.

SENATOR PENROSE.—I will ask the Senator whether he has any objection to specifically having a provision inserted here applicable to the straight-whisky product which has fusel oil in it?

SENATOR HEYBURN.—What kind of a provision, I would ask the Senator?

SENATOR PENROSE.—That all straight whisky shall be of the standard established in the American Pharmacopœia.

SENATOR HEYBURN.—That would be to enter upon the fixing of standards. The Pharmacopœia is made the standard for determining the purity of all drugs and of all whisky used in connection with drugs by an express provision of this bill. It would be utterly impracticable for us in legislating upon this subject to attempt to settle the controversy that has existed, and perhaps always will exist, between what is known as the "manufacturers of straight whisky" and the "concoctors of blended and rectified whiskies." The committee tried to avoid that controversy. It is no part of our duty in legislating upon this question to settle these controversies any more than it would be to settle the question as to the superiority of any other article of food or commerce.

These contending schools of distillers, or, rather, the distillers and those who take the product of the still and change it into something else, have always existed, and they probably always will, but I had hoped that their contentions would not be brought into the Senate in the discussion of this bill.

The word "added" has nothing to do with that question, unless the rectifiers or blenders confess that they desire to add fusel oil to their blended whiskies, because when whisky is blended it contains none, if it is a genuine blend based upon cologne spirits. If it is not, then it is a fraud, and this bill is directed against frauds. That is what it is for; and if anyone complains that it interferes with his fraudulent business he complains against the legislation and the purpose for which it is proposed generally. We have no reply to make to that, except to say that we are here to legislate against that class of business.

Senator Foraker's amendments were defeated: the first by a vote of 24 yeas to 46 nays; the second by a vote of 33 yeas to 35 nays. The bill was then passed by a vote of 63 to 4.

The House referred the bill to the Committee on Interstate and Foreign Commerce, which reported it with amendments on March 7. After considerable debate, chiefly on the extension of the Federal police power within the States, the bill was passed on June 23 by a vote of 241 to 17.

The first conference on the differing bills of the Senate and House was abortive, and a second conference was held, which made its report on June 28.

On June 29 James R. Mann [Ill.] spoke before the House on the reported bill. He said that it was in the main the House bill. The provision requiring a man to sell articles of food which might be used against him in evidence had been eliminated as a bad feature and likely to cause the bill to be declared unconstitutional.

We struck out the provision which affected the question of States' rights and the control of the Federal Government over original packages, leaving the law as it stands without regard to this bill.

We made a slight change in the amendment which affected the case of whisky, by specifically providing what we thought we had already covered—and still think we had covered—in the House bill—by specifically providing that in the case of compounded, imitation, and blended articles the package label shall bear the word "compound," "imitation," or "blend." And on the drug provision, while we accepted one definition of drugs that was in the Senate bill—which is not quite so strong as the House definition—we retained the important provision in regard to labeling on the package all the habit-forming drugs, as set forth in the House bill, and struck out the proviso excepting alcohol used as a solvent or preservative; so that as the bill is reported from the conferees it requires on all medicines the labeling of the quantity or proportion of alcohol, opium, morphine, and other habit-forming drugs which are named in the bill.

Mr. Speaker, I would think that I was somewhat derelict in my duty in reference to this bill if I did not say a word or two in regard to the services of the man in this House who is principally entitled to the credit for the enactment of a pure-food law at all. The chairman of the Committee on Interstate and Foreign Commerce—and these words will come as a surprise and embarrassment to him—the gentleman from Iowa, Colonel Hepburn, for eight years and more has been a determined, constant, steady advocate of pure-food legislation. Three times at least the House, under his lead, has passed a pure-food bill. And when it shall become enacted into law, as I believe this shortly will be when this conference report is agreed upon, to him the most credit for the law will be due. [Loud general applause.]

The conference report was agreed to in both Chambers, and President Roosevelt approved the bill on June 30, 1906.

Date Due
